INSIGHT ● GUIDES

SCOTLAN

PLAN & BOOK
YOUR TAILOR-MADE TRIP

TAILOR-MADE TRIPS & UNIQUE EXPERIENCES CREATED BY LOCAL TRAVEL EXPERTS AT INSIGHTGUIDES.COM/HOLIDAYS

Insight Guides has been inspiring travellers with high-quality travel content for over 45 years. As well as our popular guidebooks, we now offer the opportunity to book tailor-made private trips completely personalised to your needs and interests. By connecting with one of our local experts, you will directly benefit from their expertise and local know-how, helping you create memories that will last a lifetime.

HOW INSIGHTGUIDES.COM/HOLIDAYS WORKS

STEP 1

Pick your dream destination and submit an enquiry, or modify an existing itinerary if you prefer.

STEP 2

Fill in a short form, sharing details of your travel plans and preferences with a local expert.

STEP 3

Your local expert will create your personalised itinerary, which you can amend until you are completely satisfied.

STEP 4

Book securely online. Pack your bags and enjoy your holiday! Your local expert will be available to answer questions during your trip.

BENEFITS OF PLANNING & BOOKING AT INSIGHTGUIDES.COM/HOLIDAYS

PLANNED BY LOCAL EXPERTS

The Insight Guides local experts are hand-picked, based on their experience in the travel industry and their impeccable standards of customer service.

SAVE TIME & MONEY

When a local expert plans your trip, you save time and money when you book, even during high season. You won't be charged for using a credit card either.

TAILOR-MADE TRIPS

Book with Insight Guides, and you will be in complete control of the planning process, from the initial selections to amending your final itinerary.

BOOK & TRAVEL STRESS-FREE

Enjoy stress-free travel when you use the Insight Guides secure online booking platform. All bookings come with a money-back guarantee.

WHAT OTHER TRAVELLERS THINK ABOUT TRIPS BOOKED AT INSIGHTGUIDES.COM/HOLIDAYS

Trip to Portugal

Every step of the planning process and the trip itself was effortless and exceptional. Our special interests, preferences and requests were accommodated resulting in a trip that exceeded our expectations.

Corinne, USA   ★★★★★

Trip to Vietnam

The organization was superb, the drivers professional, and accommodation quite comfortable. I was well taken care of! My thanks to your colleagues who helped make my trip to Vietnam such a great experience. My only regret is that I couldn't spend more time in the country.

Heather   ★★★★★

CONTENTS

Travel tips

Maps

LEGEND
○ Insight on
○ Photo story

THE BEST OF SCOTLAND: TOP ATTRACTIONS

△ **Glen Coe**. Full of drama for its bloody massacre of the MacDonalds in 1692, its powerful scenery and its challenging and notoriously dangerous mountain climbs. See page 208.

▽ **Edinburgh**. This elegant city is Scotland's capital and the site of the Scottish Parliament. The city is equally famous for its massive castle and its cultural festivals. See page 117.

△ **Robert Burns Birthplace Museum**. The birthplace of Scotland's most famous poet Rabbie Burns provides an insight into how much he has contributed to Scotland's life and culture. See page 166.

△ **Glasgow**. Scotland's second city has shaken off its grimy past and is now more noted for its lively nightlife, contemporary art scene, great shopping and lovely parks. See page 183.

△ **Loch Lomond and the Trossachs**. The bonnie banks of Loch Lomond enclose the largest body of water in Britain, which, along with the Trossach hills, form part of the magnificent national park. See page 248.

△ **Stirling**. A settlement since prehistoric times due to its strategic position, it gained city status in 2002. Stirling offers superb historic sites, including a magnificent castle, plus a national park on its doorstep. See page 173.

▷ **St Andrews**. A breezy seaside town acknowledged as the home of golf, and possessing Scotland's oldest university. See page 247.

◁ **Isle of Skye**. Romantically associated with Bonnie Prince Charlie and Flora MacDonald, it is the most scenically spectacular spot of the western seaboard, with superb mountain landscapes and dramatic sea lochs. See page 215.

▷ **Iona**. Known since the 6th century as the cradle of Christianity in Scotland. Beyond the abbey are beautiful beaches and an unspoilt landscape rich in birdlife. See page 227.

△ **The Cairngorms National Park**. These mountains are home to wildlife such as the capercaillie and the golden eagle, and are a magnet for walkers, climbers and skiers. See page 262.

THE BEST OF SCOTLAND: EDITOR'S CHOICE

The One O'Clock Gun on Edinburgh Castle's ramparts.

BEST CASTLES

Edinburgh Castle. High above the city stands Scotland's most popular tourist attraction. Listen out for the ritual firing of the One o'Clock Gun. See page 119.

Stirling Castle. Perched atop a craggy outcrop, a wealth of Scottish history is crammed into every corner of this ancient fortress. See page 174.

Dunvegan Castle. Northwest of Portree, Dunvegan Castle has been the stronghold of the chiefs of MacLeod for more than seven centuries. See page 218.

Glamis Castle. This beautiful, turreted castle in Angus has a rich and royal history, not least as former home of Queen Elizabeth, the Queen Mother. See page 259.

Dunnottar Castle. A ruined fortress in a striking setting that has been witness to Scotland's stormy and bloodstained past. See page 260.

Eilean Donan. This romantic castle stands before a backdrop of brooding mountains and a picturesque sea loch. See page 210.

Edinburgh Castle.

BEST GARDENS AND NATURE RESERVES

Inverewe Garden (Wester Ross). Created by Osgood Mackenzie in 1862, this subtropical oasis lies on the shores of Loch Ewe. The diverse plant collection includes specimens from the far ends of the earth. See page 211.

Royal Botanic Garden (Edinburgh). The garden was founded as early as 1670 as a resource for medical research. The Temperate Palmhouse, a huge Victorian glasshouse, is impressive and packed with ferns and palms. See page 129.

Arduaine Garden (Argyll). A 20-acre (8-hectare) woodland garden, with superb coastal views, specialising in magnolias, rhododendrons, ferns and azaleas. See page 206.

Sands of Forvie (Aberdeenshire). Part of the Forvie National Nature Reserve. The reserve has a large sand-dune system, and the biggest breeding colony of eider duck in Britain. See page 267.

Beinn Eighe National Nature Reserve (Wester Ross). Overlooking Loch Maree, parts of the reserve are home to the elusive pine marten, buzzards and golden eagles. See page 279.

Hermaness National Nature Reserve (Shetland). Overlooking Britain's most northerly tip, Hermaness is a haven for more than 100,000 nesting sea birds, including gannets, great skuas and puffins. See page 299.

ISLANDS OFF THE BEATEN TRACK

Gigha (Inner Hebrides). The term 'getting away from it all' is never truer than on this tiny island, where the few inhabitants share the environment with local seals. See page 231.

Rum (Inner Hebrides). Not only does Rum have some of the best scenery in this group of islands but the best hill walking, too. See page 230.

Barra (Outer Hebrides). A wild, stunning place, with empty white beaches and open roads. Don't miss a trip to Kisimul Castle. See page 238.

Taransay (Outer Hebrides). This idyllic island has many sandy beaches – access relies on the kindness of the Atlantic Ocean. See page 234.

Hoy (Orkney). In season, heather as far as the eye can see covers the island, and looking outwards views of the archipelago are unmatched. See page 292.

Rousay (Orkney). An archaeological delight, along with nearby Egilsay, and dubbed the 'Egypt of the North'. See page 292.

Foula (Shetland). Probably Britain's remotest inhabited island and a stronghold of true Shetland culture. See page 299.

Castlebay village and Kisimul Castle, Isle of Barra, Outer Hebrides.

ENTICING LOCAL DELICACIES

Loch Fyne kippers. These herrings are caught in Loch Fyne, a sea loch north of Arran. They are soaked in brine and slowly cured over smouldering oak fires.

Forfar Bridie. A delicious minced-meat pie that is said to have been made by Maggie Bridie of Glamis, when the county of Angus was called Forfarshire.

Arbroath smokie. Arbroath's speciality of lightly smoked haddock.

Highland malts. Among the famous Highland malts are Glenmorangie, Glenfiddich, Macallan and Laphroaig.

Selkirk bannock. This rich fruit bun was originally made by a baker in Selkirk, and eaten at Christmas.

Moffat toffees. A toffee-based sweet with a sherbet centre, traditionally made in Moffat in the southwest.

Scottish cheeses. Lanark blue, Seater's Orkney and Isle of Mull – just a few of the best.

Venison. Both wild and farmed, Scottish deer from the Highlands produce some of the finest venison in the world.

Stornoway black pudding. In 2013 this Hebridean island's famous blood sausage was given protected status, meaning no other producer outside the region can use the name for their produce.

TOP MUSEUMS AND ART GALLERIES

Kelvingrove Art Gallery and Museum (Glasgow). Scotland's most popular gallery is a treasure trove of cultural antiquities and modern idiosyncrasies. See page 187.

Shetland Museum and Archives (Lerwick). Housed in a striking timber-clad building, the museum charts Shetland's history and

Installation at Kelvingrove Art Gallery and Museum.

heritage with an amazing collection of artefacts and archives of written, photographic and musical records. See page 298.

National Museum of Scotland (Edinburgh). This remarkable museum charts the history of Scotland through its artefacts, from Neolithic standing stones to Viking treasures, to wonders of the industrial age. See page 125.

Aberdeen Art Gallery. The neoclassical building has a permanent collection of 18th- to 20th-century art by the likes of Raeburn and Toulouse-Lautrec. See page 270.

Traditional Selkirk bannock.

Dramatic Glen Docherty leading to Loch Maree in Wester Ross.

Massed Highland dancers perform at the Royal Edinburgh Military Tattoo.

Highland cows have long horns and shaggy coats.

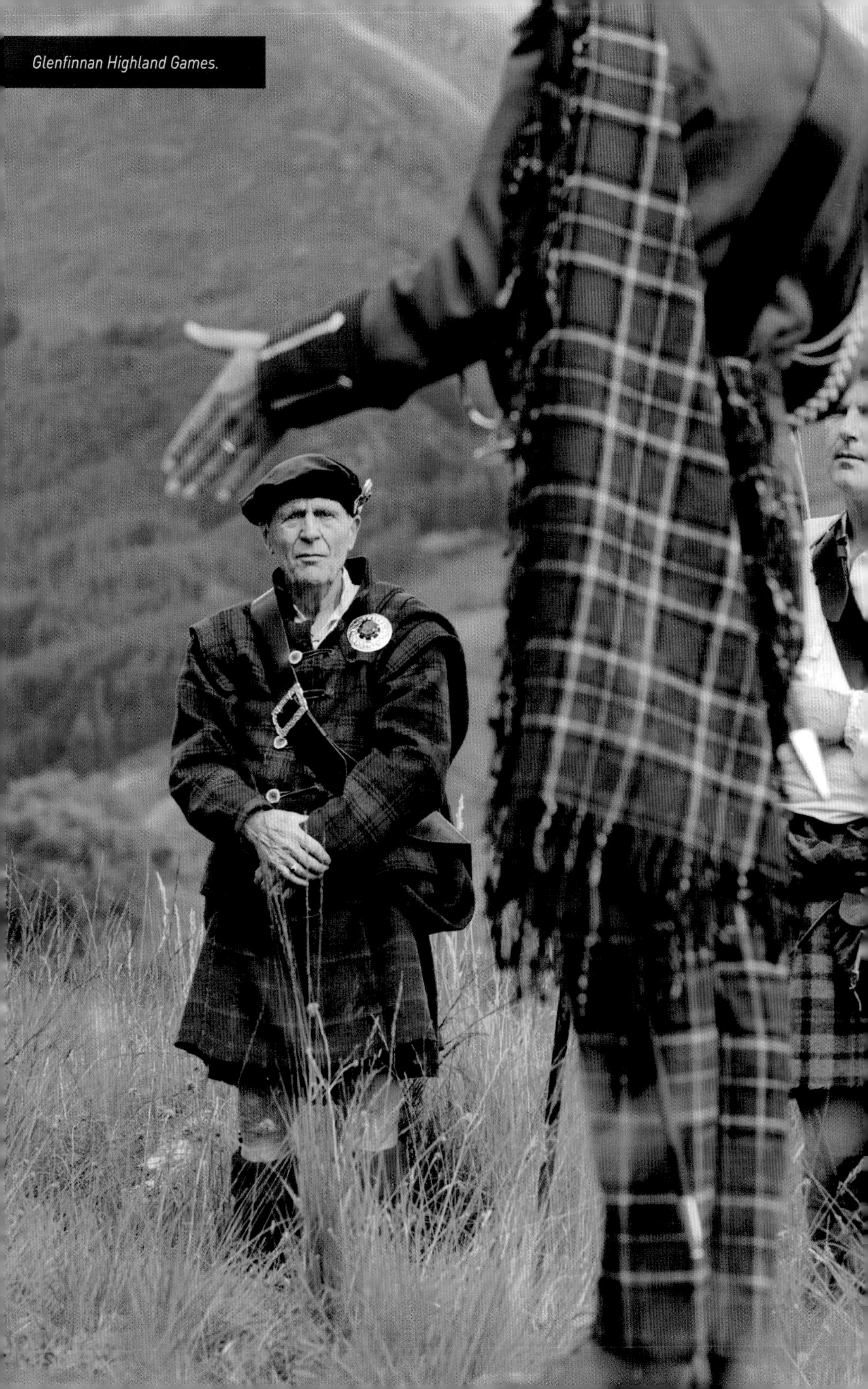

Glenfinnan Highland Games.

SCOTLAND THE BRAVE

From dramatically rugged landscapes to world-class cities, traditional foods and a rich history, Scotland has a strong sense of national identity of which it is fiercely proud.

Statue of King Robert the Bruce at Bannockburn.

A country of staggering natural beauty, Scotland is renowned for its atmospheric glens, arresting mountain ranges and swathes of isolated wilderness. With two national parks, Britain's highest peak (Ben Nevis) and some famous lochs, Scotland might be small but it certainly packs a punch. And it's not just the scenery that makes Scotland unique. Impressive castles evoke the country's rousing past, often marked by bloodshed, English invasion and divergent views on whether an independent or united Scotland was better – a debate that continues, albeit less savagely, today.

It is possible that the Scots' strong sense of national identity has to do with a desire to protect their culture from outside influence. Whatever the reason, from eccentric Highland Games to kilts, bagpipes, tartan and haggis, emblems of a bygone Scotland are very much alive. These national hallmarks might be exaggerated for the benefit of tourists, but you can still find authentic Scottish experiences – a local Highland Games or a village ceilidh – by venturing off the beaten track.

Smoking racks of haddock, known as Arbroath smokies.

A nation heralded for its inventiveness, Scotland has given the world penicillin and the telephone, as well as a disproportionate amount of intellectual thinkers. Perhaps most noteworthy are its native writers, who include Walter Scott, Robert Louis Stevenson and Robert Burns – for whom Burns Night is celebrated every year on 25th January. Robert (or 'Rabbie') Burns wrote poems and lyrics in the Scots language, English and also a Scottish dialect.

Today less than 2 percent of Scots 'speak the Gaelic', but the very fact it survives and flourishes is a sign that from Shetland to the Borders, the Scots are proud of their regional differences, and are staunchly protective of their national identity. Visitors may struggle to pronounce the name of a Scottish mountain, a Hebridean road sign, or toast friends with the words 'Slàinte mhath' over a fine malt, but you'll be admired for trying. Welcome to Scotland!

THE SCOTTISH CHARACTER

The Scots are a patriotic people – enduringly fond of their country, their history and their colourful national character.

The Scots take immense pride in who they are and where they come from. Even the most non-descript Scotsman is likely to be harbouring a strong sense of national identity beneath the surface.

From the Pictish leader Calgacus voicing his contempt for Rome to successive Scottish rebellions against the English, the Scots have always been protective of their heritage – a feeling that has continued into the 21st century. Whether or not the Scots remain suspi-

Dr Samuel Johnson, who delighted in goading his Scottish amanuensis James Boswell by slighting Scotland and the Scots, told him: 'The noblest prospect that a Scotchman ever sees is the high road that leads him to England.'

A skeleton models a joke Tam o'Shanter with red hair.

cious of the English because of their troubled history, recent years have marked a trend towards Scottish separatism. A successful referendum in 1997 led to the creation of the Scottish Parliament in 1999, which gave the country control over several significant political areas, including health, education, and housing. Although Scotland voted to remain part of the UK in the 2014 Scottish referendum, the recent successive gains of the SNP suggest a simmering of nationalist feeling, and for many the issue of Scottish independence is far from resolved. Whatever the future for Scotland, the devolution of political power to Edinburgh and the dominance of the SNP has showed Scotland to be increasingly in charge of its own destiny.

TRIBAL RIVALRIES

Scots may not warm to English patricians, but they often have little time for their own, Anglicised aristocracy – many of whom, apart from a propensity for tweed and tartan, are indistinguishable by accent or attitude from their English counterparts. It is not forgotten in the Highlands that it was Scottish lairds, not the English, who cleared their own clansfolk from their ancestral lands to make way for sheep. And if the average Rangers supporter looks with suspicion at the English, that dislike pales by comparison with the visceral tribal loathing that he feels for the green-and-white colours of Celtic.

And although it takes less than an hour to travel from Edinburgh to Glasgow, the psychological gap between the two cities can sometimes appear almost unbridgeable. Glaswegians tend to regard the natives of Edinburgh as cold and pretentious, while Edinburghers often look down on 'Weegies' as uncouth and overly familiar. All Central Belt Scots – the vast majority of the population – have a tendency to perceive their Highland neighbours as, at best, unsophisticated. And while the tight-fisted Scot is a favourite stereotype around the world, Aberdonians are singled out by their compatriots as the meanest of the mean. It is claimed, for example, that copper wire was invented by two Aberdonians fighting over a penny.

SCOTTISH WOMEN

The butt of most Scottish stereotypes is the Scots male, but female Scots have been tirelessly stereotyped as being bolshy and wilful – but perhaps these traits are no bad thing. From Jenny Geddes, who famously threw her stool at the minister who tried to read the Anglican Book of Common Prayer for the first time,

Optical illusions in Edinburgh's Camera Obscura.

⊘ SCOTTISH HOME RULE

The 2007 elections, bringing Scottish nationalists to power for the first time, caused Scots to think more seriously about their relationship with England. The SNP leader at the time, Alex Salmond, hoped to harness the romantic and patriotic side of the Scottish character when he set 2014 – the 700th anniversary of the Battle of Bannockburn – as the date for an independence referendum. Instead, the tried-and-tested side triumphed, with the majority of Scots preferring the security of the Union to the risk of going it alone. Current SNP leader Nicola Sturgeon is agitating for another referendum, citing differences over Brexit and future relationship with the European Union as a reason.

through to the bold Jacobite heroine Flora MacDonald, the 19th-century missionary Mary Slessor, and the SNP parliamentarian Winnie Ewing – whose by-election victory at Hamilton in 1967 started her party on the road to power – the history of Scotland is studded with strong and often inspirational women.

As Scotland prepared for its crucial referendum on independence in 2014, two of its three main political parties were led by women (both of whom were also gay); after the separatists failed, the SNP's deputy leader, Nicola Sturgeon, became the party's next leader and First Minister of Scotland. In contrast to the Church of England, which is still riven by the issue of women priests, the

Church of Scotland has elected three women Moderators of the General Assembly between 2004 and 2017.

SCOTTISH TRAITS

The democratic and egalitarian Calvinist tradition, allied with a taste for disputation born from theological hair-splitting, is often said to be central to the Scottish character. Or did the Scots choose Calvinism because it appealed to their natural ideals? Indeed, the strong socialist and trade-unionist movements that

stars to come out of Scotland include Frankie Boyle, Kevin Bridges and Susan Calman. Alcohol features prominently in Scottish jokes, but the image of grim old-style drinking dens is outdated. Scotland's 2006 smoking ban and the continued expansion of gastro pubs have helped to improve and freshen the reputation of the pub industry.

THE CULT OF THE KILT

Like the Irish, the Scots have realised that there's money to be made from conforming to

Prawn fishing in the west Highlands.

Glasgow's statue of the Duke of Wellington, with decorative headgear.

became so influential in 20th-century Scotland had at least as much support from Catholic workers as from Protestants.

The Scots character, if the mass of stereotypes are to be believed, is a confusing one. It combines dourness and humour, meanness and generosity, arrogance and tolerance, irritability and chivalry, sentimentality and hard-headedness. One aspect of these contradictions is caught by a *Punch* cartoon showing a hitchhiker with a sign reading 'Glasgow – or else!'

The situation is often resolved with laughter. Scottish humour is subtle and sardonic and, in the hands of someone as verbally inventive as the comedian Billy Connolly, can leave reality far behind. More recent comedy

a stereotyped image, however exaggerated it may be. If haggis isn't universally popular, it is offered to tourists as the national dish. Heads of ancient Scottish clans, living in castles or houses large enough to generate cash-flow problems, have opened their homes to tour groups of affluent overseas visitors. Others have opened 'clan shops' retailing an astonishing variety of tartan artefacts, such as tartan teddies, with clan heraldry stamped on everything from tea towels to key fobs.

But the image has the danger of obscuring the real Scotland. It's worth lingering long enough to draw back the tartan curtain and get to know one of Europe's most interesting peoples.

Mary of Scotland mourning the dying Douglas at the Battle of Langside, by F. Hartwich.

DECISIVE DATES

PREHISTORIC TIMES

c.6000 BC
First sign of human settlement on west coast and islands.

c.1000 BC
First invasion of Celtic tribes.

THE ROMANS

AD 82
Agricola's forces enter Scotland and reach Aberdeenshire.

142
Second Roman invasion reaches Firth of Forth.

185
Withdrawal of Roman forces behind Hadrian's Wall.

EARLY CHRISTIANS

397
First Christian church founded at Whithorn by St Ninian.

563
St Columba lands on Iona and founds monastery.

THE BIRTH OF SCOTLAND

843
Kenneth MacAlpin becomes first king of Scots.

973
Kenneth II defeats the Danish Luncarty, near Perth.

1018
Malcolm II defeats the Northumbrians at Battle of Carham.

THE EARLY YEARS

1040
Macbeth becomes king by murdering Duncan I.

Robert the Bruce.

1124–53
Reign of David I. Royal burghs founded, and Border abbeys established.

1249
Alexander III becomes king. Start of 'Golden Age'.

WARS OF SUCCESSION

1286
Death of Alexander III. Succeeded by infant granddaughter Margaret. Rival claimants to throne include John Balliol and Robert Bruce.

1290
Margaret dies en route to Scotland. Edward I of England declares himself feudal overlord of Scotland.

1291–6
Edward I (the Hammer of the Scots) invades Scotland; wins Battle of Dunbar.

1297
Rebellion led by William Wallace defeats English forces at Stirling Bridge.

1305
English put Wallace to death as a traitor.

1306
Robert the Bruce becomes King Robert I and is crowned at Scone. After a defeat he spends a year in exile.

1314
Scots forces under Robert the Bruce defeat English at Battle of Bannockburn.

1333
English defeat Scots at Halidon Hill.

THE EARLY STUARTS

1371
Robert II, first of the Stuarts, becomes king.

1406–1542
Reigns of James I–V.

1513
James IV killed in Battle of Flodden.

1542
James V dies after Battle of Solway Moss. Baby daughter, Mary, Queen of Scots, succeeds.

1547
Hertford wins Battle of Pinkie. Mary taken to France.

1561
Mary returns to Scotland to reclaim throne.

1566
Birth of James VI.

1587
Mary, Queen of Scots executed.

THE UNION OF CROWNS AND PARLIAMENTS

1603
Elizabeth I dies. James VI becomes James I of England.

1650
Cromwell seizes power in England. Scots proclaim Charles II as king in defiance. Lose to Cromwell at Dunbar.

1660
Charles II restored as king.

1689
James VII/II deposed by William and Mary. Scots supporters of James (Jacobites) win Battle of Killiecrankie.

1692
Massacre of Glencoe.

1707
Treaty of Union, abolition of separate Scottish parliament.

JACOBITE REBELLIONS AND THE CLEARANCES

1715
Rebellion led by Earl of Mar fails after battle at Sheriffmuir.

1745
Prince Charles Edward Stuart, Bonnie Prince Charlie's success at

The Battle of Culloden.

Prestonpans puts much of Scotland in Jacobite hands.

1746
Campaign ends in debacle at Culloden on 16 April.

1780s
Highland Clearances, people evicted to make room for sheep; 'Age of Enlightenment' in literature and the arts.

THE INDUSTRIAL AGE

1823
Caledonian Canal opened.

1836
Highland potato crop fails.

1850 onwards
Fast industrial expansion.

1852
Queen Victoria and Prince Albert buy Balmoral.

1882
The 'Crofters War', including Battle of the Braes on Skye.

THE MODERN AGE

1924
Ramsay Macdonald becomes first Labour prime minister.

1934
Scottish National Party (SNP) formed.

1964
Forth Road Bridge opened.

1975
Start of North Sea gas and oil exploitation.

1997
Referendum votes in favour of a 129-member Scottish Parliament with tax-varying powers.

1999
Scottish Parliament is elected.

2007
Alex Salmond (SNP) is elected First Minister of Scotland.

2013
Scottish Catholic Church in crisis as its cardinal, Keith O'Brien, is accused of inappropriate conduct with junior clergy.

2014
In the referendum on Scottish independence, slightly over 55 percent of voters elect to remain part of the United Kingdom. After the vote, Nicola Sturgeon (SNP) replaces Alex Salmond as the First Minister of Scotland.

2016
SNP maintains majority in Scottish Parliament for third term. The UK decides to leave the EU in a hotly contested referendum, with Scotland voting to remain by 62% to 38%.

2019
The UK fails to leave the EU on the planned withdrawal date of 31 March 2019, with an extension granted until 31 October 2019.

Romans building Hadrian's Wall.

BEGINNINGS

An endless battle for power, early Scottish history was dominated by the continual conflicts of ruthlessly ambitious families.

On a bleak, windswept moor three witches crouch round a bubbling cauldron, muttering oaths and prophesying doom. A king is brutally stabbed to death and his killer, consumed by vaulting ambition, takes the throne, only to be killed himself soon afterwards. 'Fair is foul, and foul is fair.'

To many people, these images from William Shakespeare's *Macbeth* are their first introduction to early Scottish history. But of course, the Scots will tell you, Shakespeare was English, and, as usual, the English got it wrong. There is perhaps some truth to the tale, they admit – Macbeth, who reckoned he had a better hereditary claim to the throne than its occupant, did kill Duncan in 1040 – but thereafter he ruled well for 17 years and kept the country relatively prosperous.

POWER GAMES

Where Shakespeare undeniably showed his genius, however, was in managing to heighten the narrative of a history that was already (and remained) melodramatic beyond belief. Scotland's story was for centuries little more than the biographies of ruthlessly ambitious families jostling for power, gaining it and losing it through accidents of royal marriages, unexpected deaths and lack of fertility.

A successful Scottish king needed cunning as well as determination, an ability to judge just how far he could push powerful barons without being toppled from his throne in the process. In a continuous effort to safeguard the future, marriage contracts were routinely made between royal infants and, when premature death brought a succession of kings to the throne as children, the land's leading families

A Pictish sculpted stone at St Vigeans.

fought for advancement by trying to gain control over the young rulers, occasionally by kidnapping them.

Summarise some of the stories and they seem more histrionic than historical. An attractive young widow returns from 13 years at the French court to occupy the throne of Scotland, lays claim to the throne of England, conducts a series of passionate affairs, marries her lover a few weeks after he has allegedly murdered her second husband, loses the throne, is incarcerated for 19 years by her cousin, the queen of England, and is then, on a pretext, beheaded. No scriptwriter today would dare to invent as outrageous a plot as the true-life story of Mary, Queen of Scots.

NAMELESS PEOPLE

Our earliest knowledge of Scotland dates back almost 8,000 years, when the cold, wet climate and the barren landscape would seem familiar enough to a time-traveller from the present day. Then the region was inhabited by nameless hunters and fishermen. Later, the mysterious Beaker People from Holland and the Rhineland settled here, as they did in Ireland, leaving as a memorial only a few tantalising pots. Were the eerie Standing Stones of Callanish, on the island of Lewis, built by

and mastered the use of iron implements. The blueprint for a tribal society was in place.

It was the Romans who gave it coherence. The desire of Emperor Vespasian in AD 80 to forge northwards from an already subjugated southern Britain towards the Grampian Mountains and the dense forests of central Scotland united the tribes in opposition. To their surprise, the Romans, who called the natives Picti, 'painted men', encountered fearsome opposition. An early Scots leader, called Calgacus by the Romans, rallied 30,000 men

Clava Cairns, the Bronze Age burial site.

> Feuds between clans were frequent and bloody, provoking one visiting scholar to state: 'The Scots are not industrious and the people are poor. They spend all their time in wars and, when there is no war, they fight one another.'

them as a primitive observatory? Nobody can be certain.

A TRIBAL SOCIETY

Celtic tribes, driven by their enemies to the outer fringes of Europe, settled in Scotland, as they did in Ireland, Cornwall, Wales and Brittany,

– a remarkable force but no match for the Roman war machine.

Soon, however, the 'barbarians' began to perfect guerrilla tactics. In the year 118, for instance, the Ninth Legion marched north to quell yet another rebellion and was never seen again. Was it really worth all this trouble, the Romans wondered, to subdue such barbarians?

Hadrian's answer, as emperor, was no. He built a fortified wall that stretched for 73 miles (117km) across the north of England, isolating the savages. A successor, Antoninus Pius, tried to push back the boundaries in 142 by erecting a fortified wall between the Rivers Forth and Clyde. But it was never an effective exercise. The Roman Empire fell without ever conquering these troublesome natives, and Scottish life carried on without the more lasting benefits of Roman civilisation, such as good roads. A complex clan system evolved, consisting of large families bound by blood ties.

BIRTH OF THE TRUE SCOTS

Europe's Dark Ages enveloped the region. What records remain portray raiders riding south to plunder and pillage. True Scots were born in the 6th century when Gaels migrated from the north of Ireland, inaugurating an epoch in which beau-

controlled the south of the country, were not subjugated until 1018. Feuding for power was continuous. It was in this period that Macbeth murdered his rival, Duncan, and was eventually killed in turn by Duncan's son.

THE NORMAN CONQUEST

The collapse of England to William the Conqueror in 1066 drove many of the English lords northwards, turning the Lowlands of Scotland into an aristocratic refugee camp. Scotland's king, Malcolm, married one of the

William Wallace rallies his Scottish forces against the English.

tifully drawn manuscripts and brilliant metalwork illuminated the cultural darkness.

Like much of Western Europe, Scotland's history at this time was a catalogue of invasions. The most relentless aggressors were the Vikings, who arrived in the 8th century in their Scandinavian longships to loot the monasteries that had been founded by early Christian missionaries such as St Ninian and St Columba.

Eventually, in 843, the warring Picts – a fierce Celtic race who dominated the southwest – united with the Scots under Kenneth MacAlpin, the astute ruler of the west coast kingdom of Dalriada. But Edinburgh was not brought under the king's influence until 962, and the Angles, a Teutonic people who

refugees, Margaret, a Hungarian-born Christian reformer and strong supporter of English standards. Partly to please her, Malcolm invaded England twice. During the second incursion, he lost his life. This gave William Rufus, the Conqueror's son and successor, an opportunity to involve himself in Scottish affairs by securing the northern throne for Malcolm's eldest son, Edgar, the first of a series of weak kings. A successor, David I, having been brought up in England, gave many estates to his Norman friends. Also, he did nothing to stop English replacing Gaelic and introduced feudalism into the Lowlands.

But true feudalism never really took root. French knights, accustomed to deference, were surprised to find that, when they rode through a field of crops, the impertinent Scottish peasants would demand compensation. Although the Normans greatly influenced architecture and language, they in no sense conquered the country. Instead, they helped create a social division that was to dominate Scotland's history: the Lowlands were controlled by noblemen who spoke the same Norman French and subscribed to the same values as England's ruling class, while the Highlands remained untamed, under the influence of independent-

Robert the Bruce.

minded Gaelic speakers, and the islands were loyal, more or less, to Norway. The Highland clans, indeed, were virtually independent kingdoms, whose chiefs, under the old patriarchal system, had the power of life and death over their people.

Over the next three centuries the border with England was to be constantly redefined. The seaport of Berwick-upon-Tweed, now the most northerly town in England, was to change hands 13 times. In the 1160s the Scots turned to French sympathisers for help, concluding what eventually came to be known as the Auld Alliance. In later years the pact would have a profound influence on Scottish life, but on this occasion it was no match for England's might.

After a comparatively peaceful interlude, England's insidious interference provoked a serious backlash in 1297. William Wallace, a violent youth from Elderslie, became an outlaw after a scuffle with English soldiers in which a girl (some think she was his wife), who helped him escape, was killed herself by the sheriff of Lanark. Wallace returned to kill the sheriff, and raised enough of an army to drive back the English forces, making him for some months master of southern Scotland.

But Wallace, immortalised in the film *Braveheart*, wasn't supported by the nobles, who considered him lowborn, and, after being defeated at Falkirk by England's Edward I (the 'Hammer of the Scots'), he was executed.

BRUCE'S VICTORY

The next challenger, Robert the Bruce, who was descended from the Norman de Brus family, got further as a freedom fighter – as far as the throne itself, in fact, in 1306. Things got off to a bad start however, and he spent a year's exile on Rathlin Island, off the coast of Ireland. This is where he is said to have been inspired by the persistence of a spider building its web in a cave, and he returned to Scotland full of determination and proceeded to win a series of victories. Soon the French recognised him as king of Scotland and the Roman Catholic Church gave him its backing.

England's new king, Edward II, although he had little stomach for Scottish affairs, could not ignore the challenge and, in 1314, the two forces collided at Bannockburn, south of Stirling. Bruce's chances looked slim: he was pitching only 6,000 men against a force of 20,000 English. But he was shrewd enough to hold the high ground, forcing the English into the wet marshes, and he won.

Because the Pope did not recognise the new monarch, Bruce's subjects successfully petitioned Rome, and the Declaration of Arbroath in 1320 confirmed him as king.

However, England's Edward III decided that Scotland was more trouble than it was worth and in 1328 granted it independence. He recognised Bruce as king and married his sister to Bruce's baby son. Peace had been achieved between two of the most rancorous of neighbours. It seemed too good to be true – and it was.

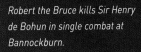
Robert the Bruce kills Sir Henry de Bohun in single combat at Bannockburn.

A messenger conveys Robert the Bruce's defiance to King Edward III, 1327.

BATTLE FOR THE THRONE

For centuries the throne of Scotland was a source of conflict, inextricably part of the turbulent relationship with England.

The outbreak in 1339 of the intermittent Hundred Years' War between England and France kept Edward III's mind off Scotland. He failed, therefore, to appreciate the significance of a pact concluded in 1326 between France and Scotland by Robert the Bruce. Yet the Auld Alliance, as the pact came to be known, was to keep English ambitions at bay for centuries and at one point almost resulted in Scotland becoming a province of France.

Principal beneficiaries of the deal were the kings of the Stuart (or Stewart) family. Taking their name from their function as High Stewards to the king, they were descended from the Fitzalans, Normans who came to England with William the Conqueror in 1066.

When the Bruce family failed to produce a male heir, the crown passed in 1371 to the Stuarts because Marjorie, Robert the Bruce's daughter, had married Walter Fitzalan. The first of the Stuarts, Robert II, faced a problem that was to plague his successors: he had constantly to look over his shoulder at England, yet he could never ignore another threat to his power – his own dissident barons and warring chieftains.

YOUTHFUL MONARCHS

His son, Robert III, trusted these ambitious men so little that he sent his eldest son, James, to France for safety. But the ship carrying him was waylaid and young James fell into the hands of England's Henry IV. He grew up in the English court and didn't return to Scotland (as James I) until 1422, at the age of 29. His friendliness with the English was soon strained to breaking point, however, and he renewed the Auld Alliance, siding with France's Charles VII and Joan of Arc against the English. But soon James was

Edward III takes Berwick in 1333.

murdered, stabbed to death in front of his wife by his uncle, a cousin and another noble.

His son, James II, succeeded at the age of six, setting another Stuart pattern: monarchs who came to the throne as minors, creating what has been called an infantile paralysis of the power structure. In 1460 James, fighting to recapture Roxburgh from the English, died when one of his own siege guns exploded. James III, another boy king, succeeded. He had time to marry a Danish princess (bringing the Norse islands of Orkney and Shetland into the realm) before he was locked in Edinburgh Castle by the scheming barons and replaced by his more malleable younger brother. The arrangement didn't last, and soon James's son, James IV, was crowned king, aged 15. He cemented relations with England in 1503 by marrying Margaret Tudor, the 12-year-old daughter of Henry VII, the Welsh warrior who had usurped the English throne 18 years before. The harmony was short-lived: the French talked James into attacking England, and he was killed at the battle of Flodden Hill. James's heir, predictably, was also called James and was just over a year old. The power brokers could continue plotting.

> *The Battle of Flodden Hill was Scotland's worst defeat to the English, wiping out the cream of a generation, and some argue that the country never recovered from the blow.*

MARY, QUEEN OF SCOTS

Torn between the French connection and the ambitions of England's Henry VIII, who tried to enrol him in his anti-Catholic campaign, the young James V declared his loyalties by marry-

Robert Herdman's depiction of the execution of Mary, Queen of Scots.

⊘ PREACHERS OF FIRE

The bid for power by a Catholic – Mary – in the mid-16th century set alarm bells ringing among Protestants. Their faith had been forged in fire, with early preachers such as George Wishart burned at the stake, and it contained little room for compromise. The Protestants' visionary was John Knox, a magnetic speaker and former priest whose aim, inspired by Calvinism, was to drive Catholicism out of Scotland. His followers had pledged themselves by signing the First Covenant to 'forsake and renounce the congregation of Satan', and carrying Calvin's doctrines to extremes by outlawing the Latin Mass throughout all of Scotland.

ing two Frenchwomen in succession. Life expectancy was short, however, for kings as well as for peasants, and James V died in 1542 just as his second queen, Marie de Guise, gave birth to a daughter. At less than a week old, the infant was proclaimed Mary, Queen of Scots.

Ever an opportunist, Henry VIII despatched an invasion force that reduced Edinburgh, apart from its castle, to rubble. It was known as the 'Rough Wooing' and left hatred that would last for centuries. The immediate question was: should Scotland ally itself with Catholic France or Protestant England? In the ensuing tug-of-war between the English and the French, the infant Mary was taken to France for safety and, at the age of 15, married the French dauphin. The Auld Alliance seemed to have taken on a new life, and Mary made a will bequeathing Scotland to France if she were to die childless.

When the king of France died in 1558, Mary, still aged only 16, ascended the throne with her husband. Her ambitions, though, didn't end there: she later declared herself queen of England as well, basing her claim on the Catholic assumption that England's new queen, Elizabeth I, was illegitimate because her father, the much-married Henry VIII, had been a heretic.

A Protestant, Bothwell divorced his wife and became Mary's third husband, three months after Darnley's death. Even Mary had gone too far this time. Protestant Scotland forced its Catholic queen, still only 24, to abdicate, locking her in an island castle on Loch Leven. Bothwell fled to Norway, where he died in exile. And so, in 1567, another infant king came to the throne: Mary's son, James VI.

Still fact rivalled fiction. Mary escaped from Loch Leven, tried unsuccessfully to reach France, then threw herself on the mercy of her

Scottish border raiders.

James I of England.

When Mary's husband died in 1560, she returned to Scotland, a vivacious, wilful and attractive woman. She married a Catholic, Henry Darnley, who was by contemporary accounts an arrogant, pompous and effeminate idler, and soon she began spending more and more time with her secretary, David Rizzio, an Italian. When Rizzio was stabbed to death in front of her, Darnley was presumed to be responsible, but who could prove it? Mary appeared to be reconciled with Darnley and, a few months later, gave birth to a son. Immediately afterwards, however, Darnley himself was murdered. Mary and her current favourite, James Hepburn, earl of Bothwell, were presumed responsible.

cousin, Elizabeth I. Her previous claim to the English throne, however, had not been forgotten. Elizabeth offered her the bleak hospitality of various mansions, in which she remained a prisoner for the next 19 years.

In 1587 she was convicted, on somewhat flimsy evidence, of plotting Elizabeth's death and was beheaded at Fotheringay Castle in Northamptonshire, England.

JAMES I OF ENGLAND

Mary's son, by this time secure on the Scottish throne, made little more than a token protest. Because Elizabeth, the Virgin Queen, had no heir, James had his sights set on a far greater prize than Scotland could offer: the throne of

England. On 27 March 1603 he learned that the prize was his. On hearing of Elizabeth's death, he departed for London, and was to set foot in Scotland only once more in his life.

Scots have speculated ever since about how differently history would have turned out had James VI of Scotland made Edinburgh rather than London his base when he became James I of England. But he was more in sympathy with the divine right of kings than with the notions of the ultra-democratic Presbyterians, who were demanding a strong say in spiritual matters of the powerful General Assembly of the Church of Scotland. Armed conflict soon followed: in 1639 the Scots invaded northern England, forcing Charles to negotiate.

Charles I's luck ran out in England, too. Needing money, he unwisely called together his parliament for the first time in 10 years. A power struggle ensued, leading swiftly to civil war. At first the Scottish Covenanters (so named because of their support for the National Covenant of 1638) backed parliament

Scottish Covenanters meet in Edinburgh.

civil affairs. And, as he wrote, ruling from a distance of 400 miles (644km) was so much easier.

His son Charles succeeded to the throne in 1625, not knowing Scotland at all. Without, therefore, realising the consequences, the absentee king tried to harmonise the forms of church service between the two countries.

CONFLICT AND CIVIL WAR

The Scots would have none of it: religious riots broke out, and one bishop is said to have conducted his service with two loaded pistols placed in front of him. A National Covenant was organised, pledging faith to 'the true religion' and affirming the unassailable authority

and the Roundhead forces of Oliver Cromwell; their hope was that a victorious parliament would introduce compulsory Presbyterianism in English and Irish churches as well as in Scotland. Soon the Roundheads began to outpace the Cavalier supporters of the king. Charles tried to gain the Scots' support by promising a three-year trial for Presbyterianism in England. But it was not to be: he was beheaded on 30 January 1649.

Charles's execution came as a terrible shock north of the border. How dare England kill the king of Scotland without consulting the Scots! Many turned to Charles's 18-year-old son, who had undertaken not to oppose Presbyterianism, and he was proclaimed

Charles II in Edinburgh. But Cromwell won a decisive victory at the Battle of Dunbar and turned Scotland into an occupied country, abolishing its separate parliament.

> 'We are bought and sold for English gold', the Scots sang following the Treaty of Union of 1707. Like so many Scottish songs, it was a lament.

By the time the monarchy was restored in 1660, Charles II had lost interest in Scotland's religious aspirations and removed much of the Presbyterian Church's power. Violent intolerance stalked the land and the 1680s became known as the Killing Time. The risk to Covenanters increased when, after Charles died of apoplexy in 1685, his brother James, a Catholic, became king. With the rotten judgement that dogged the Stuart line, James II imposed the death penalty for worshipping as a Covenanter. His power base in London soon crumbled, however, and in 1689 he was deposed in favour of his Protestant nephew and son-in-law, William of Orange.

HIGHLAND JACOBITES

Some Scots, mostly Highlanders, remained true to James. The Jacobites, as they were called, almost annihilated William's army in a fierce battle at Killiecrankie in 1689. But their leader Claverhouse was killed, and most of them lost heart and returned to the Highlands.

Determined to exert his authority over the Scots, William demanded that every clan leader swear an oath of loyalty to him. Partly due to a misunderstanding of where the swearing would take place, one chieftain, the head of the Clan MacDonald, took his oath after the deadline.

BLOODY MASSACRE

Here was a chance to make an example of a prominent leader. Members of the Campbell clan, old enemies of the MacDonalds, were ordered to lodge with the MacDonalds at their home in Glencoe, get to know them and

then, having won their confidence, put every MacDonald younger than 70 to the sword. The Campbells were thrilled to carry out their commission, and the Massacre of Glencoe in 1692 remains one of the bloodiest dates in Scotland's history. The barbarity of the massacre produced a public outcry, not so much because of the number killed but because of the abuse of hospitality.

Queen Anne, the second daughter of James II, succeeded William in 1702. None of her 17 children had survived, and the English were

Grief after the Massacre of Glencoe.

determined to keep both thrones out of Stuart hands. They turned to Sophie of Hanover, a granddaughter of James VI/James I. If the Scots would agree to accept a Hanoverian line of succession, much-needed trade concessions would be granted. There was one other condition: England and Scotland should unite under one parliament.

As so often before, riots broke out in Edinburgh and elsewhere. But the opposition was fragmented and, in 1707, a Treaty of Union incorporated the Scottish parliament into the Westminster parliament to create the United Kingdom. Unknown to the signatories, the foundation of the British Empire was being laid.

David Morier's portrayal of
Culloden, painted in 1746.

Oil painting of Prince Charles Edward Stuart in Edinburgh in 1745, by William Brassey Hole.

THE AGE OF REBELLION

The 18th and 19th centuries witnessed various rebellions in Scotland not only against the Union with England, but also in ideas, industry, agriculture and the Church, changing this small nation beyond recognition.

The ink was hardly dry on the Treaty of Union of 1707 when the Scots began to smart under the new constitutional arrangements. The idea of a union with England had never been popular with the working classes, most of whom saw it (rightly) as a sell-out by the aristocracy to the 'Auld Enemy'. Scotland's businessmen were outraged by the imposition of hefty, English-style excise duties on many goods and the high-handed government bureaucracy that went with them. The aristocracy who had supported the Union resented Westminster's peremptory abolition of Scotland's Privy Council. Even the hardline Cameronians – the fiercest of Protestants – roundly disliked the Union in the early years of the 18th century.

All of which was compounded by the Jacobitism (support for the Stuarts) that haunted many parts of Scotland, particularly among the Episcopalians of Aberdeenshire, Angus and Perthshire, and among the Catholic clans (such as the MacDonalds) of the Western Highlands.

Prince Charles in his finery as the Young Chevalier, c.1740.

JACOBITE INSURGENCY

Given that one of the main planks of Jacobitism was the repeal of the Union, it was hardly surprising that the Stuart kings cast a long shadow over Scotland in the first half of the 18th century. In fact, within a year of the Treaty of Union being signed, the first Jacobite insurgency was under way, helped by a French regime ever anxious to discomfit the power of the English.

In January 1708 a flotilla of French privateers commanded by Comte Claude de Forbin battered its way through the North Sea gales, carrying the 19-year-old James Stuart, the self-styled James VIII and III. After a brief sojourn in the Firth of Forth near the coast of Fife, the French privateers were chased round the top of Scotland and out into the Atlantic by English warships. Many of the French vessels foundered on their way back to France, although James survived to go on plotting.

On dry land, the uprising of 1708 was confined to a few East Stirlingshire lairds who marched around with a handful of men. They were quickly rounded up, and that November five of the ringleaders were tried in Edinburgh for treason. The verdict on all five was 'not proven' and they were freed. Shocked by this display of Scottish leniency, the British parliament passed the Treason Act of 1708, which brought Scotland into line with England, ensuring traitors a gruesome death.

BOBBING JOHN V. RED JOHN

The next Jacobite uprising, in 1715, was a serious affair. By then disaffection in Scotland with the Union was widespread, the Hanoverians had not secured their grip on Britain, there were loud pro-Stuart mutterings in England, and much of Britain had been stripped of its military.

But the insurrection was led by the Earl of Mar, a military incompetent known as 'Bobbing John', whose support came mainly from the clans of the Central and Eastern Highlands. When the two sides clashed at Sheriffmuir near Stirling on

lenient. Dozens of rebels – especially the English – were hanged, drawn and quartered, and hundreds were deported.

Not that the debacle of 1715 stopped the Stuarts trying again. In 1719 it was the Spaniards who decided to try to shake the Hanoverian pitch by backing the Jacobites. Again it was a fiasco. In March 1719 a little force of 307 Spanish soldiers sailed into Loch Alsh where they joined up with a few hundred Murrays, Mackenzies and Mackintoshes. This Spanish-Jacobite army was easily routed in the steep pass of Glenshiel by a

Culloden's victor, the Duke of Cumberland.

13 November, Mar's Jacobite army had a four-to-one advantage over the tiny Hanoverian force commanded by 'Red John of the Battles' (as the duke of Argyll was known). But, instead of pressing his huge advantage, Mar withdrew his Highland army after an inconclusive clash.

The insurrection of 1715 quickly ran out of steam. The Pretender himself (or the Old Pretender – James Stuart) did not arrive in Scotland until the end of December, and the forces he brought with him were too little and too late. He did his cause no good by stealing away at night (along with 'Bobbing John' and a few others), leaving his followers to the wrath of the Whigs. The duke of Argyll was sacked as commander of the government forces for fear he would be too

> Bealach-n-Spainnteach (the Pass of the Spaniards), a niche in the Kintail Mountains, recalls the defeat of the Spanish when they joined forces with the Jacobites in 1719 and were swiftly routed by the British.

British unit, which swooped down from Inverness to pound the Jacobite positions with their mortars. The Highlanders simply vanished into the mist and snow of Kintail, leaving the wretched Spaniards in their gold-on-white uniforms to wander about the subarctic landscape before surrendering.

THE YOUNG PRETENDER

But it was the insurrection of 1745, 'so glorious an enterprise', led by Charles Edward Stuart (Bonnie Prince Charlie or the Young Pretender), which shook Britain, despite the fact that the government's grip on the turbulent parts of Scotland had never seemed firmer. There were military depots at Fort William, Fort Augustus and Fort George, and an effective Highland militia (later known as the Black Watch) had been raised. General Wade had thrown a network of military roads and bridges across the Highlands. Logically, Charles,

Prince Charlie's much romanticised farewell to Flora MacDonald in 1746.

the Young Pretender, should never have been allowed to set foot out of the Highlands.

But having set up a military 'infrastructure' in the Highlands, the British Government had neglected it. The Independent Companies (the Black Watch) had been shunted out to the West Indies, there were fewer than 4,000 troops in the whole of Scotland, hardly any cavalry or artillery, and Clan Campbell was no longer an effective fighting force. The result was that Bonnie Prince Charlie and his rag-tag army of MacDonalds, Camerons, Mackintoshes, Robertsons, McGregors, Macphersons and Gordons, plus some Lowland cavalry and a stiffening of Franco-Irish mercenaries, was

able to walk into Edinburgh and set up a 'royal court' in Holyrood Palace.

In that September the Young Pretender sallied out of Edinburgh and wrecked General John Cope's panicky Hanoverian army near Prestonpans, and then marched across the border into England. But Stuart's success was an illusion. There was precious little support for his cause in the Lowlands of Scotland. Few Jacobite troops had been raised in Edinburgh, and Glasgow and the southwest were openly hostile. Some men had been drummed up in Manchester, but there

Culloden Cairn.

was no serious support from the Roman Catholic families of northern England. Charles got as far as Derby and then fled back to Scotland with two powerful Hanoverian armies hot on his heels.

BATTLE OF CULLODEN

After winning a rearguard action at Clifton, near Penrith, and what has been described as a 'lucky victory' at Falkirk in January 1746, the Jacobite army was cut to pieces by the duke of Cumberland's artillery on Drummossie Moor, Culloden, near Inverness on 16 April 1746. It was the last great pitched battle on the soil of mainland Britain.

It was also the end of the Gaelic clan system, which had survived in the mountains of Scotland long after it had disappeared from Ireland. The days when an upland chieftain could drum up a 'tail' of trained swordsmen for cattle raids into the Lowlands were over.

Following his post-Culloden 'flight across the heather', Charles, disguised as a woman servant, was given shelter on the Isle of Skye by Flora MacDonald, thus giving birth to one of Scotland's abiding romantic tales. He was then plucked off the Scottish coast by a French privateer and taken into exile, drunkenness and despair in France and Italy. A few dozen of the more prominent Jacobites were hauled off to Carlisle and Newcastle where they were tried, and some hanged. And for some time the Highlands were harried mercilessly by the duke of Cumberland's troopers.

In an effort to subdue the Highlands, the government in London passed the Disarming Act of 1746, which not only banned the carrying of claymores, targes, dirks and muskets, but also the wearing of tartans and the playing of bagpipes. It was a nasty piece of legislation, which impacted greatly on Gaelic culture. The British Government also took the opportunity to abolish

Glasgow in the 18th century.

⊘ INDUSTRIAL GLORY

The Enlightenment was not just confined to the salons of Edinburgh. Commerce and industry also thrived. 'The same age, which produces great philosophers and politicians, renowned generals and poets, usually abounds with skilled weavers and ship-carpenters,' the Scottish philosopher David Hume wrote in 1752.

By 1760 the famous Carron Ironworks in Falkirk was churning out high-grade ordnance for the British military and by 1780 hundreds of tons of goods on barges were being shuttled between Edinburgh and Glasgow along the Forth–Clyde Canal.

The Turnpike Act of 1751 improved the road system dramatically and created a brisk demand for carriages and stagecoaches. In 1738 Scotland's share of the tobacco trade (based in Glasgow) was 10 percent; by 1769 it was more than 52 percent.

There was also a huge upsurge of activity in many trades such as carpet-weaving, upholstery, glassmaking, china and pottery manufacture, linen, soap, distilling and brewing.

The 18th century changed Scotland from one of the poorest countries in Europe to a state of middling affluence. It has been calculated that between 1700 and 1800, the money generated within Scotland increased by a factor of more than 50, while the population stayed more or less static (at around 1.5 million).

Scotland's inefficient and often corrupt system of 'Courts of Regality' by which the aristocracy (and not just the Highland variety) dispensed justice, collected fines and wielded powers of life and wealth.

THE AGE OF ENLIGHTENMENT

It is one of the minor paradoxes of 18th-century European history that, while Scotland was being racked by dynastic convulsions, which were 17th-century in origin, the country was transforming itself into one of the most forward-

A Skye crofter prepares some winter comfort.

looking societies in the world. Scotland began to wake up in the first half of the 18th century. By about 1740 the intellectual, scientific and mercantile phenomenon that became known as the Scottish Enlightenment was well under way, although it didn't reach its peak until the end of the century.

Whatever created it, the Scottish Enlightenment was an extraordinary explosion of creativity and energy. And while, in retrospect at least, the period was dominated by David Hume, the philosopher, and Adam Smith, the economist, there were many others, such as William Robertson, Adam Ferguson, William Cullen and the Adam brothers. Through the multifaceted talents of its literati, Scotland in general and Edinburgh in particular became one of the intellectual powerhouses of Western Europe.

THE CLEARANCES

But the Enlightenment and all that went with it had some woeful side effects. The Highland 'Clearances' of the late 18th and early 19th centuries owed much to the 'improving' attitudes triggered by the Enlightenment, as well as the greed of the lairds. It was realised that, while the Highlands were capable of producing from £200,000 to £300,000 worth of black cattle every year, the land would produce double the amount of mutton, with the additional benefit of wool.

The argument proved irresistible. Sheep – particularly Cheviots – and their Lowland shepherds began to flood into the glens and straths of the Highlands, displacing the Highland 'tacksmen' and their families. Tens of thousands were forced to move to the Lowlands, coastal areas, or the colonies overseas, taking with them their culture of songs and traditions.

The worst of the Clearances – or at least the most notorious – took place on the huge estates of the countess of Sutherland and her rich, English-born husband, the marquis of Stafford. Although Stafford spent huge sums of money building roads, harbours and fish-curing sheds (for very little profit), his estate managers evicted tenants with real ruthlessness. It was a pattern that was repeated all over the Highlands at the beginning of the 19th century, and again later when people were displaced by the red deer of the 'sporting' estates. The overgrown remains of villages are a painful reminder of this sad chapter in Scottish history.

RADICALS AND REACTIONARIES

As the industrial economy of Lowland Scotland burgeoned at the end of the 18th century, it sucked in thousands of immigrant workers from all over Scotland and Ireland. The clamour for democracy grew. Some of it was fuelled by the ideas of the American and French revolutions, but much of the unrest was a reaction to Scotland's hopelessly inadequate electoral system. At the end of the 18th century, there were only 4,500 voters in the whole of Scotland and only 2,600 voters in the 33 rural counties.

And for almost 40 years Scotland was dominated by the powerful machine politician Henry Dundas, the first viscount Melville, universally known as 'King Harry the Ninth'.

As solicitor general for Scotland, lord advocate, home secretary, secretary for war and then first lord of the Admiralty, Dundas wielded awesome power.

But nothing could stop the spread of libertarian ideas in an increasingly industrialised workforce. The ideas contained in Tom Paine's *Rights of Man* spread like wildfire in the Scot-

Broomielaw Bridge, Carlton Place and Clyde Street in Glasgow, 1830.

land of the 1790s. The cobblers, weavers and spinners proved the most vociferous democrats, but there was also unrest among farmworkers, and among seamen and soldiers in the Highland regiments.

Throughout the 1790s a number of radical 'one man, one vote' organisations sprang up, such as the Scottish Friends of the People and the United Scotsmen (a quasi-nationalist group that modelled itself on the United Irishmen led by Wolfe Tone).

But the brooding figure of Dundas was more than a match for the radicals. Every organisation that raised its head was swiftly infiltrated by police spies and agent provocateurs.

Ringleaders (such as the advocate Thomas Muir) were framed, arrested, tried and deported. Some, such as Robert Watt, who led the 'Pike Plot' of 1794, were hanged. Meetings were broken up by dragoons, riots were put down by musket fire and the Scottish universities were racked by witch-hunts.

Although Dundas himself was discredited in 1806, after being impeached for embezzlement, and died in 1811, the anti-radical paranoia of the Scottish ruling class lingered on. Establishment panic peaked in 1820 when the so-called Scottish Insurrection was brought to an end in the legally corrupt trial of the weavers James Wilson, John Baird, Andrew Hardie and 21 other workmen. A special (English) Court of Oyer and Terminer was set up in Glasgow to hear the case, and Wilson, Baird and Hardie were sentenced to a gruesome execution, after making resounding speeches. The other radicals were sentenced to penal transportation.

REFORM AND DISRUPTION

By the 1820s most of Scotland (and indeed Britain) was weary of the political and constitutional corruption under which the country laboured. In 1823 Lord Archibald Hamilton pointed out the electoral absurdity of rural Scotland: 'I have the right to vote in five counties in Scotland, in not one of which do I possess an acre of land,' he said, 'and I have no doubt that if I took the trouble I might have a vote for every county in that kingdom.' Hamilton's motion calling for parliamentary reform was defeated by only 35 votes.

But nine years later, in 1832, the Reform Bill finally passed into law, giving Scotland 30 rural constituencies, 23 burgh constituencies and a voting population of 65,000 (compared to a previous 4,500). Even this limited extension of the franchise – to male householders whose property had a rentable value of £10 or more – generated much wailing and gnashing of teeth among Scottish Tories.

No sooner had the controversy over electoral reform subsided than it was replaced by the row between the 'moderates' and the 'evangelicals' within the Church of Scotland. 'Scotland,' Lord Palmerston noted at the time, 'is aflame about the Church question.' But this was no genteel falling-out among theologians. It was a brutal and bruising affair, which dominated political life in Scotland for 10 years and raised all kinds of constitutional questions.

At the heart of the argument was the Patronage Act of 1712, which gave Scots lairds the same right English squires had to appoint, or 'intrude' clergy on local congregations. Ever since it was passed, the Church of Scotland had justifiably argued that the Patronage Act was a flagrant and illegal violation of the Revolution Settlement of 1690 and the Treaty of Union of 1707, both of which guaranteed the independence of the Church of Scotland.

A FREE CHURCH

But the pleas fell on deaf ears. The English-dominated parliament could see no fault in a system that enabled Anglicised landowners to appoint like-minded clergymen. Patronage was seen by the Anglo-Scottish establishment as a useful instrument of political control and social progress. The issue came to a head in May 1843 when the evangelicals, led by Dr Thomas Chalmers, marched out of the annual General Assembly of the Church of Scotland in Edinburgh to form the Free Church of Scotland.

> Lord Cockburn summed up the relentless grip of the powerful Henry Dundas, also known as 'King Harry the Ninth', on Scotland: 'Who steered upon him was safe; who disregarded his light was wrecked.'

Chalmers, theologian, astronomer and brilliant organiser, defended the Free Church against bitter enemies. His final triumph, in 1847, was to persuade the London parliament that it was a folly to allow the aristocracy to refuse the Free Church land on which to build churches and schools. A few days after he had given evidence, Chalmers died in Edinburgh.

The rebellion of the evangelicals was brilliantly planned, well-funded and took the British establishment completely by surprise: 400 teachers left the kirk and, within 10 years of the Disruption, the Free Church had built more than 800 churches, 700 manses, three large theological colleges and 600 schools, and brought about a huge extension of education.

After 1847, state aid had to be given to the Free as well as to the established Church schools, and in 1861 the established Church lost its legal powers over Scotland's parish school system. This prepared the ground for the Education Act of 1872, which set up a national system under the Scottish Educa-

Scottish Presbyterians in the 17th century defying the law to worship.

tional Department. And, although it ran into some vicious opposition from landowners, especially in the Highlands, the Free Church prevailed.

In fact, it can be argued that the Disruption was the only rebellion in 18th- or 19th-century British history that succeeded. Chalmers and his supporters had challenged both the pervasive influence of the Anglo-Scottish aristocracy and the power of the British Parliament, and they had won. The Patronage Act of 1712 was finally repealed in 1874, and the Free Church merged back with the Church of Scotland in 1929, uniting the majority of Scottish Presbyterians in one Church.

Constructing the Cunard luxury liner 'Aquitania' in a Clydebank shipyard.

'First Steamboat on the Clyde'
by John Knox, c.1820.

INDUSTRIALISATION AND WAR

Like the rest of Great Britain, Scotland witnessed huge changes in the 19th and early 20th centuries, in particular a move to a more urban culture.

During the Victorian and Edwardian eras, Scotland, like most of Europe, became urbanised and industrialised. Steelworks, ironworks, shipyards, coal mines, shale-oil refineries, textile factories, engineering shops, canals and, of course, railways proliferated all over 19th-century Scotland. The process was concentrated in Scotland's 'central belt' (the stretch of low-lying land between Edinburgh and Glasgow), but there were important 'outliers' like Aberdeen, Dundee, Ayrshire and the mill towns of the Scottish borders. A few smaller industrial ventures found their way deep into the Highlands or onto a few small islands.

It was a process that dragged in its wake profound social, cultural and demographic change. The booming industries brought thousands of work-seeking immigrants flocking into Lowland Scotland. Most came from the Highlands and Ireland, and many nursed an ancient distaste for the British establishment that translated itself into left-wing radicalism – one reason why Scottish politics are still left of centre today. The immigrants were also largely Roman Catholic, which did something to loosen the grip of the Presbyterian churches on Scottish life.

GLASGOW – A HUGE METROPOLIS

The small Georgian city of Glasgow became a huge industrial metropolis built on the kind of rectangular grid common in the United States, with industrial princes living in splendour while Highland, Irish, Italian and Jewish immigrants swarmed in the noisome slums.

In many ways 19th-century Glasgow had more in common with Chicago or New York than with any other city in Britain. Working-class conditions were appalling. Rickets, cholera, smallpox,

Slum-dwellers in Glasgow's Gorbals.

tuberculosis, diphtheria and alcoholism were rampant. The streets were unclean and distinctly unsafe. Violence was endemic as Highlanders and Irishmen clashed in the stew and whisky dens, while Orangemen from Ulster were used as violent and murderous strikebreakers. The city hangman was never short of work.

But there was no denying Glasgow's enormous industrial vitality. By the middle of the century the city was peppered with more than 100 textile mills (an industry which by that time employed more than 400,000 Scots). There were ironworks at Tollcross, Coatbridge and Monklands, productive coal mines all over Lanarkshire, and the River Clyde was lined with boiler makers, marine-engineering shops, and world-class shipyards. For generations the label 'Clyde built' was synonymous with industrial quality.

Nor was industry confined to Glasgow and its environs. The Tayside city of Dundee forged close links with India and became the biggest jute-manufacturing centre in Britain. The Carron Ironworks at Falkirk was Europe's largest producer of artillery by the year 1800, while in West Lothian a thriving industry was built up to extract oil from shale. Scotland's east coast fisheries also flourished, and by the end of the century the town of Wick in Caithness had become Europe's biggest herring port.

As well as producing large quantities of books, biscuits and bureaucrats, Edinburgh was a centre of the British brewing industry; at one stage there were more than 40 breweries within the city boundaries. And, in the latter part of the 19th century, the Scotch whisky industry boomed, thanks to the devastation of the French vineyards in the 1880s by phylloxera, which almost wrecked the thriving cognac industry.

As a result, Scotland, with an educated workforce and proximity to European markets, was attracting inward investment. The American-

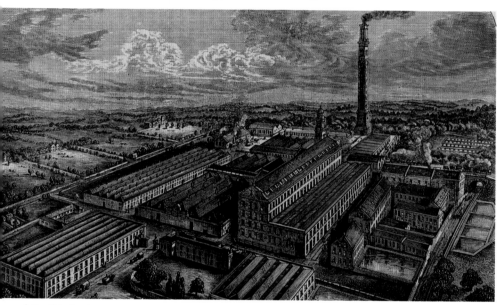

Jute mill in Dundee.

⊙ CASH INCENTIVES

The growth of industry in Scotland generated huge amounts of cash. Edinburgh and Dundee became centres for investment trusts, which sank cash into ventures all over the world, particularly in America. In 1873 the Dundee jute man Robert Fleming set up the Scottish American Investment Trust to channel money into American cattle ranches, fruit farms, mining companies and railways.

The biggest cattle ranch in the US – Matador Land & Cattle Company – was operated from Dundee until 1951. The outlaw Butch Cassidy once worked for a cattle company that was being run from the fastidious New Town of Edinburgh.

funded North British Rubber Company moved into Edinburgh in 1857. In 1884 the Singer Company built one of the biggest factories in the world at Clydebank to manufacture mass-produced sewing machines. It was the start of a 100-year trend, which did much to undermine the Scottish economy's independence.

HIGHLAND POVERTY

Despite the enthusiasm of Queen Victoria and the British gentry for the Highlands, dire poverty stalked upland Scotland. Land reform was desperately needed. Following riots in Skye in 1882 and the formation of the Highland Land League in 1884, Gladstone's Liberal government passed the Crofters (Scotland) Holdings Act of 1886, which gave crofters fair rents, security of tenure and the right to pass their crofts on to their families. But it was Lord Salisbury's Conservative government that put the Scottish Secretary in the British cabinet, and established the Scottish Office in Edinburgh and London in 1886.

By the end of the 19th century the huge majority of the Scottish population was urban, industrialised and concentrated in the towns and cities of the Lowlands. And urban Scotland proved a fertile breeding ground for the British Left. The Scottish Labour Party (SLP) was

With less than 10 percent of the British population, the Scots made up almost 15 percent of the British army. And when the butcher's bill was added up after the war it was found that more than 20 percent of all Britons killed were Scots.

In addition to which, the shipyards of the Clyde and the engineering shops of west central Scotland were producing more tanks, shells, warships, explosives and field guns than any comparable part of Britain. That explains why the British Government took such a dim view of the strikes and industrial disputes that hit the

Labour Party leader Ramsay MacDonald with his son and daughter in 1929.

founded in 1888, although it soon merged with the Independent Labour Party (ILP), which in turn played a big part in the formation of the (British) Labour Party. Britain's first Labour MP, Keir Hardie, was a Scot, as was Ramsay MacDonald, Britain's first Labour prime minister.

THE GREAT WAR

When World War I broke out in 1914, the Scots flocked to the British colours with an remarkable enthusiasm. Like Ireland, Scotland provided the British Army with a disproportionate number of soldiers. Like the Irish, the Scots suspended their radicalism and trooped into the forces to fight for king and empire, to the despair of left-wing leaders like Keir Hardie and John Maclean.

> *Industry transformed the city of Glasgow and the River Clyde. Between 1740 and 1840 Glasgow's population leapt from 17,000 to 200,000 and then doubled again to 400,000 by 1870.*

Clyde between 1915 and 1919 and led to the area being dubbed 'Red Clydeside'.

When Glasgow workers struck for a 40-hour week in January 1919, the Secretary of State for Scotland panicked and called in the military; Glaswegians watched open-mouthed as armed troops backed by tanks poured onto the Glasgow streets to nip the Red Revolution in the bud. At a huge rally in George Square on 31 January 1919, the police baton-charged the crowd.

THE HUNGRY YEARS

The 1920s and 1930s were sour years for Scotland. The 'traditional' industries of shipbuilding, steel-making, coal-mining and heavy engineering went into a decline from which they have never recovered, and the whisky industry reeled from the body blow of American Prohibition. The new light-engineering industries – cars, electrics and machine tools – stayed stubbornly

Glasgow children during the hungry Thirties.

south of the border. Unemployment soared to almost three in 10 of the workforce, and most urban areas were blighted by appalling housing conditions – an issue a new breed of Scottish women campaigned loudly about – and debilitating health issues. Scots boarded the emigrant ships in droves. An estimated 400,000 Scots (10 percent of the population) emigrated between 1921 and 1931, mostly to the US, Canada, Australia and New Zealand. Many of them, such as naturalist John Muir and Lachlan Macquarie, who served as Governor of New South Wales from 1810 to 1821, would go on to make lasting contributions to their newly adopted homes.

Most of urban Scotland saw its salvation in the newly formed Labour Party, which not only promised a better life but also a measure of Home Rule. Support for the Labour Party began early. At the general election of 1922 an electoral pattern was set which remained for many decades – England went Conservative even if Scotland voted Labour.

The 1920s and 1930s also saw the revival of a kind of left-wing cultural nationalism that owed a lot to the poetry of Hugh MacDiarmid, the writing of Lewis Grassic Gibbon and the enthusiasms of upper-crust nationalists like Ruaridh Erskine of Marr and R.B. Cunninghame-Graham. From the Scottish literary renaissance of the interwar years the nationalist movement grew increasingly more political. In 1934 the small (but right-wing) Scottish Party merged with the National Party of Scotland to form the Scottish National Party (SNP).

> *In 1937 Walter Elliot, Secretary of State for Scotland, described how in Scotland '23 percent of its population live in conditions of gross overcrowding, compared with 4 percent in England'.*

THE WORLD AT WAR

It wasn't until World War II loomed that the Scottish economy began to climb out of the doldrums. And when war broke out in September 1939 the Clydeside shipyards moved into high gear to build warships like the *Duke of York*, *Howe*, *Indefatigable* and *Vanguard*, while the engineering firms began pumping out small arms, bayonets, explosives and ammunition. The Rolls-Royce factory at Hillington near Glasgow produced Merlin engines for the RAF's Spitfires.

The Germans were well aware of this and on 13 and 14 March 1941, hundreds of German bombers, operating at the limit of their range, devastated Clydeside. More than 1,000 people were killed (528 in the town of Clydebank) and another 1,500 were injured.

War killed more than 58,000 Scots (compared with the 148,000 who had lost their lives in World War I) but had the effect of galvanising the Scottish economy for a couple of decades. And there's no doubt that the Labour Government that came to power in 1945 made major improvements to Scottish life.

LAYING DOWN THE LAW

Different in origin from that of England, the independent nature of Scottish law plays a vital part in cementing a sense of national identity and self-rule.

One curiosity of the Scottish legal system is Not Proven – 'that bastard verdict', as Sir Walter Scott called it. At the end of a criminal trial the verdict can be 'guilty' or 'not guilty', as in England, or the jury may find the charge 'not proven'. It's an option that reflects Scots logic and refusal to compromise by assuming a person innocent until proved guilty, but it does confer a stigma on the accused.

The jargon of Scots lawyers is distinctive, too. If you embark on litigation you are a 'pursuer'. You sue a 'defender'. If you disagree too outspokenly with a judge's decision, you may be accused of 'murmuring the judge'.

From the abolition of the Scottish Parliament with the 1707 Act of Union until its re-establishment in 1999, the UK Parliament in London made laws for the country. However, though few outsiders realise it, the Scots still managed to maintain their own distinctive legal system.

Scottish law is different in origin from that of England and those countries (such as the US and many Commonwealth nations) to which the English system has been exported. It was developed from Roman law and owes much more to Continental legal systems than England does – thanks partly to the fact that Scottish lawyers, during the 17th and 18th centuries, studied in Europe.

Solicitors, the general practitioners of the law, regard themselves as men of affairs, with a wider role than lawyers in some countries have adopted. Advocates, the equivalent of the English barrister, to whom a solicitor will turn for expert advice, are based in Parliament House in Edinburgh and also refuse to become too narrowly specialised. This is important if they wish to become sheriffs, as the judges of the local courts are called.

Some practitioners have demonstrated outstanding talents beyond the confines of the law. Sir Walter Scott was, for most of his life, a practising lawyer. In

Selkirk, you can still see the courtroom where he presided as sheriff. Robert Louis Stevenson qualified as an advocate, but he soon gave it up for literature.

Inevitably, English law has had its influence. Much modern legislation, especially commercial law, has tended to be copied from England. But it hasn't been all one way. In Scottish criminal trials, the jury of 15 is allowed to reach a majority verdict, a procedure recently adopted by England. The English have also introduced a prosecution service, independent of the police, similar to Scotland's. Some in England would also like to import the '110-day rule': this requires a prisoner on remand to be released if his trial doesn't take place within 110 days of his imprisonment. More controversially, Scottish judges have power in criminal cases to create new crimes – a power they use sparingly.

Parliament Hall in Edinburgh's Court of Session.

Many in England envy the Scottish system of house purchase. Most of the legal and estate-agency work is done by solicitors and seems to be completed far faster than in England. Scottish laws on Sunday trading are more liberal, and divorce was available in Scotland 500 years before it was in the south.

Along with the Kirk, the separateness of the Scottish legal system plays a vital part in establishing a sense of national identity. Many Scots lawyers resent the failure of Westminster to properly regard the fact that the law is different in Scotland. Whether it's better is another question; the best verdict in this case may be 'not proven'.

Oil rig moored off Cromarty Fife.

The Falkirk Wheel.

MODERN SCOTLAND

Despite the economic and social problems it encountered in the early 20th century, Scotland remains confident and proud, particularly in its moves towards political independence from Westminster.

The end of World War II saw Scotland, like the rest of Britain, having to tackle on-going problems back on their home turf. The emergence of the National Health Service proved an effective instrument against such plagues as infant mortality, tuberculosis, rickets and scarlet fever, while housing conditions improved in leaps and bounds as the worst of the city slums were pulled down and replaced by roomy (although often badly built) council houses. Semi-rural new towns like East Kilbride, Glenrothes, Cumbernauld, Irvine and Livingston were established throughout central Scotland.

What went largely unnoticed in the post-war euphoria was that the Labour Government's policy of nationalising the coal mines and the railways was stripping Scotland of many of its decision-making powers, and therefore management jobs. The process continued into the 1970s with the steel, shipbuilding and aerospace industries also being 'taken into public ownership'.

This haemorrhage of economic power and influence was compounded by Scottish companies being sold to English and foreign predators. In 1988 British Caledonian, originally a Scotland-based airline, was swallowed up by British Airways. To an alarming extent, Scotland's economy now assumed a 'branch factory' status.

A BID FOR HOME RULE

English enthusiasm for Labour's experiment flagged, and in 1951 Sir Winston Churchill was returned to power. Scotland, of course, continued to vote Labour (although in the general election of 1955 the Conservatives won 36 of Scotland's 71 seats, the only time they have had a majority north of the border). And, while Home

Home Rule for Scotland posters, 1951.

Rule for Scotland was off the political agenda, Scottish nationalism refused to go away.

In the late 1940s two-thirds of the Scottish electorate signed a 'national covenant' demanding Home Rule. In 1951 a squad of young nationalists outraged the British establishment by whisking the Stone of Destiny out of Westminster Abbey and hiding it in Scotland. And in 1953 the British establishment outraged Scottish sentiment by insisting on the title of Queen Elizabeth II for the new queen, despite the fact that the Scots had never had a Queen Elizabeth I.

INDUSTRIAL DECLINE

But while Scotland did reasonably well out of the Conservative-led 'New Elizabethan Age' of the

1950s and early 1960s, the old structural faults soon began to reappear. By the late 1950s the well-equipped Japanese and German shipyards were snatching orders from under the nose of the

---

In the 1970s the Royal High School in Edinburgh was purchased ready for the new Scottish Assembly to be installed. After years of indecision it was sold again in 1994.

---

and 1966, Labour's complacency was jolted in November 1967 when Mrs Winnie Ewing of the SNP snatched the Hamilton by-election. Despite losing the seat in 1970, her success marked the start of an upsurge in Scottish nationalism that preoccupied Scottish – and, to some extent, British – politics for the next decade.

STRIKING OIL

When Harold Wilson's Labour Government ran out of steam in 1970, it was replaced by the Conservative regime of Edward Heath – although,

Harvesting in Fife.

Clyde, the Scottish coalfields were proving woefully inefficient and Scotland's steelworks and heavy engineering firms were losing their grip on international markets.

And, although the Conservative Government did fund a new steel mill at Ravenscraig, near Motherwell, and enticed Rootes to set up a car plant at Linwood and the British Motor Corporation to start making trucks at Bathgate, it was all done under duress and they were abandoned. Scotland's distance from the marketplace continued to be a crippling disadvantage. The Midlands and south of England remained the engine-room of the British economy. The drift of Scots to the south continued.

Although the Scots voted heavily for the Labour Party in the general elections of 1964

once again, the Scots voted overwhelmingly Labour. But in the early 1970s, Scotland got lucky. The oil companies struck big quantities of oil. All round Scotland engineering firms and land speculators began snapping up sites on which to build platform yards, rig-repair bases, airports, oil refineries and petrochemical works.

The SNP was quick to take advantage of the new mood of optimism. Running on a campaign slogan of 'It's Scotland's Oil', the SNP won seven seats in the general election of February 1974 and took more than 20 percent of the Scottish vote. In October 1974 they did even better, cutting a swathe through both parties to take 11 seats and more than 30 percent of the Scottish vote. It looked as if one more push by the SNP would see the United Kingdom dissolved, and the hard-pressed British economy cut off from the oil revenues it so badly needed.

The Labour Government responded to the nationalists' political threat with a constitutional defence. It offered Scotland a directly elected assembly with substantial (although strictly limited) powers if the Scottish people voted 'yes' in a national referendum. At which point Westminster changed the rules. At the instigation of Labour MP George Cunningham, parliament decided that a simple majority was

classes. Support for the SNP slumped; the Alliance could do nothing. And the Labour Party, armed with the majority of the Scottish vote, could only watch helplessly as the aluminium smelter at Invergordon, the steel mill at Gartcosh, the car works at Linwood, the pulp mill at Fort William, the truck plant at Bathgate and much of the Scottish coalfields perished in the economic blizzard of the 1980s. Even the energetic Scottish Development Agency could do little to protect the Scottish economy and unemployment climbed to more than 300,000.

Pro-Independence march, Edinburgh, 2013.

not good enough, and that devolution would go ahead only if more than 40 percent of the Scottish electorate voted in favour. It was an impossible condition. Predictably the Scots failed to vote yes by a big majority in the referendum of March 1979 (although they *did* vote 'yes') and the Scotland Bill lapsed. Shortly afterwards, the 11 SNP members joined a vote of censure against the Labour Government – which fell by one vote.

Margaret Thatcher came into power and promptly made it plain that any form of Home Rule for Scotland was out of the question.

THE THATCHER YEARS

The devolution debacle produced a genuine crisis of confidence among Scotland's political

So the political triumph of Thatcherism in England found no echoes in Scotland. At the general election of June 1987 the pattern that first emerged in 1922 repeated itself: England voted Tory and Scotland voted Labour. Out of 72 Scottish MPs 50 were Labour and only 10 were Conservative. This raised the argument that the then Scottish Secretary, Malcolm Rifkind, was an English governor-general with 'no mandate' to govern Scotland. Rifkind's response was that the 85 percent of the Scottish electorate who voted for 'British' parties were voting for the sovereignty of Westminster and therefore had to accept Westminster's rules.

At the end of 1987, the Labour Party tabled yet another Devolution Bill, which was promptly thrown out by English MPs to the jeers of the SNP, who claimed that Labour's 'Feeble Fifty' could do nothing without Westminster's say so.

A NEW PARLIAMENT

The commitment to devolution remained, however, and following Labour's landslide victory in the general election of May 1997, which left Scotland with no Conservative MPs at all, the Scottish people were asked in a referendum whether they wanted their own parliament. The proposal received a ringing endorsement, a majority of two-to-one voting 'yes'. Proposals for the new parliament to have the power to vary taxes from UK standard rates were also approved.

In the first elections to the Edinburgh-based Scottish Parliament in 1999, only three out of five Scots bothered to vote. Labour won 53 of the 129 seats. This was not an overall majority, so Labour was forced to negotiate with the Liberal Democrats (17 seats) who became their coalition partners in a joint bid to keep at bay the pro-independence SNP (35 seats). The new parliament building finally opened at Holyrood in

Sunset over a wind farm in the Highlands.

☉ HEALTH AND HOME

Health and home-buying vary between England and Scotland. While healthcare in Scotland is under the umbrella of the National Health Service, since devolution services differ from their southern neighbour. Prescriptions and eye tests are free, and free dental care is also available. However, waiting times for appointments are higher than in England. Home-buying also differs. All negotiations are carried out by solicitors rather than estate agents, making for a quicker procedure. Scotland also employs an 'offers over' system whereby buyers bid for the property and the seller opts for the highest price.

2004, its construction costs having soared from an estimated £40 million to £431 million. Yet many voters regarded the assembly as a toothless beast, its energies sapped by the tendency of the more able politicians to direct their ambitions towards the London parliament rather than the Edinburgh one.

GROUND-BREAKING LEGISLATION

Land reform was one area where the Scottish Parliament did assert itself, notably by introducing the Land Reform (Scotland) Act to tackle the iniquity of most of the land of Scotland being owned by a few lairds, many absentee and many foreign. The new law brought much of that land into public ownership by establishing two national parks – the Loch Lomond and Trossachs, and the Cairngorms. Other ground-breaking legislation abolished upfront tuition fees at universities, provided better care for the old and disabled, and gave mothers the legal right to breastfeed in public.

THE FALKIRK WHEEL

In 2002 Scotland reasserted itself in the world of engineering by unveiling an iconic landmark, the Falkirk Wheel. This, the world's only rotating boat lift, replaced derelict locks and transfers boats by means of gondolas between two canals – the Union and the Forth & Clyde – that stand at different levels and link Edinburgh and Glasgow. While Edinburgh is Scotland's powerful 'financial hub', Glasgow's once-proud heavy industry has now been replaced by a thriving service sector. However, Glasgow and Edinburgh still both continue to have neighbourhoods plagued by poverty.

Scotland's economy is closely linked to the rest of Britain and the wider European community, and has also been badly affected by the recession of the early 21st century. Since the decline of industry and manufacturing, Scotland has been depending on the service and tourism industries, as well as the food and drink market and oil and gas. Figures reveal that the recession proved shorter in Scotland than in the rest of the UK but the future is still shaky and unsure, and the pace of recovery slow.

With its new legislative powers, Scotland led the way in banning smoking in all public places in 2006, encouraging England and Wales to follow suit.

THE STATE OF EDUCATION

Scotland has a long history of universal provision of public education. In comparison with the rest of the UK, at secondary level Scottish children learn a wider range of subjects: the English system is confined to a smaller number of subjects, each studied in more depth. The Scottish educators, believing their students are better equipped to face the modern world, have considered this a narrow approach. Universities in Scotland normally offer four-year courses, one year longer than the rest of the UK, with graduates achieving a Master's degree rather than a Bachelor's degree. With tuition fees abolished for Scottish students, the percentage of Scots studying close to home is high.

THE INDEPENDENCE DEBATE

The Scots have now been members of the United Kingdom for more than 300 years and Scottish history is deeply enmeshed with that of England and Wales, although separatist feeling continues to brew. When the SNP seized power at the 2007 elections, its then leader, Alex Salmond, once again took a decisive step to challenge the

Scottish Parliament, Edinburgh.

status quo and the 1707 Treaty of the Union. The resulting referendum on Scottish independence, held in September 2014, confirmed it to still be an integral issue – voting turnout was 84.6 per cent, the highest recorded figure for any election or referendum in the UK since the introduction of universal suffrage. Despite prompting wide-reaching political engagement, the majority of Scots voted to stay part of the United Kingdom.

However, with the UK voting to leave the European Union in the 2016 referendum – in which 62% of Scots opted to remain – the Brexit chapter opens up further questions about Scotland's future within the Union and relationship with the EU. Nicola Sturgeon, current leader of the SNP, is agitating for another referendum on these grounds.

Tug of war at the Scottish Game Fair.

Lonach Highlanders stop for refreshments.

HIGHLANDERS AND LOWLANDERS

Although the distinctions between Highlanders and Lowlanders that have been so much a part of Scottish history are disappearing, many of the original Gaelic traditions survive and are being preserved for future generations to enjoy.

The division between the Highlander and the Lowlander was one of the most ancient and fundamental in Scotland's history. Stereotypes – or at least Lowlander ones – dictated that while Lowlanders were civilised, urbane and peaceful, the Highlanders were uncivilised, independent and hostile to the English.

DIFFERENT LANGUAGES

One concrete way in which the Highlanders and Lowlanders differed was language: the Lowlanders spoke Scots, a version of Middle English, and the Highlanders spoke Gaelic. The line between the two languages broadly coincided with the line of the hills. North of the Highland fault running from just above Dumbarton to just above Stonehaven, and west of the plains of Aberdeenshire and the Moray Firth, Gaelic was spoken. Outside that area, Scots was spoken, except in the northern isles of Orkney and Shetland, where a kind of Norse was spoken, and perhaps in a few pockets of the southwest where a form of Gaelic lingered until late in the Middle Ages.

For hundreds of years, Lowlanders felt a sense of superiority over the Highlanders. When Patrick Sellar, a Lowland sheep farmer, wrote about the nature of the people over whom he was appointed as estate manager, he called them the 'aborigines of Britain'.

Then, in the 19th century, a startling turnabout occurred. Many Scots began to adopt as their national symbols the very trappings of the shunned Highland minority: the kilt and the tartan, the bagpipe and the bonnet, the eagle's feather and the dried sprig of heather – it blended into a kitsch everyone across the world can recognise. In the late 1980s, when

Sheep drovers in the 19th century.

the American broadcasting networks wished to devote a minute of their national news bulletins to the question of why Scotland felt unsympathetic to the policies of Britain's then prime minister, Margaret Thatcher, they set the scene with hairy-kneed men throwing pine trees at a Highland gathering.

The fact that many Scots only wear a kilt on formal occasions and have never attended a Highland Games is not very relevant. The adoption of these public symbols has something to do with the campaigns of Sir Walter Scott to romanticise the Highlanders; with the charismatic powers of the police pipe bands, which in Victorian days were largely recruited from Highlanders; and with a music hall that loved a stereotype.

At the same time, ironically, true Highland society was in a state of collapse. Ever since the 17th century its distinctive character and Gaelic culture had been eroded by the steady spread of hostile government power, the march of commercial forces tying Scotland together as one market, and the Lowlandisation of the clan chiefs as they sought wives with better dowries than the mountains could provide.

By the late 18th century, Highland landowners wanted their estates to produce

matters and strengthen its use within the education system. There are now Gaelic language centres on Islay and Skye, while the BBC airs news and cultural programmes in Gaelic.

BLURRED DISTINCTIONS

So the Highland–Lowland division today has a different meaning from what it had in the past. It is certainly not any longer the most obvious or important division, ethnically and culturally, among the Scottish people as a whole.

Road sign in Gaelic beside Skye bridge.

more cash more quickly, just as landowners did elsewhere in Scotland. Over the next 50 years they cleared most of the land of peasant farms, which paid little rent, in order to accommodate the Lowlander and his sheep, which paid a good deal more.

Simultaneously, Gaelic began a catastrophic decline, from being the language of the Highland area to being the language, as it is today, only of the Outer Hebrides and a few other communities, mainly on islands, in the extreme west. In the Scottish Parliament, however, members from those communities tried to reverse the trend by introducing the Gaelic Language Bill in 2005. The bill aimed to make more use of Gaelic in government

The Lowlanders themselves were never uniform: the folk of Aberdeenshire spoke 'Doric', a dialect of their own, very different in vocabulary and intonation from, say, those of Lothian or Galloway. In the 19th century, this sort of regionalism was greatly compounded and complicated by the immigration of the Irish, about two-thirds of them Catholic and one-third Protestant.

A CATHOLIC ELEMENT

The Catholic Irish crowded into distinct areas – Glasgow and Dundee among the cities, and the small mining or iron-working towns of Lanarkshire, Lothian and Fife. Today, especially in the west, it is the Catholic–Protestant division that continues to have most meaning in people's lives. The Catholics are, overall, still a minority in Scotland, but their Church now has more attenders on Sundays than any Protestant denomination – even the Church of Scotland itself. Intermarriage has dissolved animosities, but even today politicians deal cautiously with anything that touches, for example, on the right of Scottish Catholics to have their own state-aided schools.

Being a 'Lowlander' has less meaning than having a religious affiliation, or coming from

and doing Highland reels at party time – there is little that is distinctive about being a Highlander in most communities that lie beyond the geological Highland line.

In the west, however, in the Inner and Outer Hebrides and along the extremities of the mainland coast from Argyll to Sutherland, the ancient significance and meaning of being a Highlander is very much alive. Not all these communities necessarily speak Gaelic, but in the Western Isles the power of the language is still strong.

Dancers at the Perth Highland Games.

Edinburgh rather than Glasgow, or even than backing a particular football team.

WHAT IS A HIGHLANDER?

Being a 'Highlander' has an uncertain and ambiguous meaning over most of the area covered today by the Highland and Grampian region. The citizens of Pitlochry or Inverness don't, for the most part, speak Gaelic, are mostly ordinary lukewarm Protestants, and enjoy a lifestyle and a culture not obviously very different from that of the citizens of Perth or Aberdeen. They may have a name with the prefix 'Mac' or theoretically belong to some clan like Grant or Munro, but – apart perhaps from a greater fondness for dressing in tartan

All of them are, however, historically 'crofting communities': that is, they are the relics of a traditional peasantry who, thanks to a campaign of direct action in the 1880s, won from the British Parliament the right to live under the same kind of privileged land law as their brethren in Ireland. The Crofters Holding Act in 1886 conferred on them security of tenure, the right to hand on their holdings to heirs, and a rent fixed by the arbitration of a Land Court sitting in Edinburgh.

TODAY'S CROFTERS

Crofting is still largely the economic foundation of these communities. It can best be described as small-scale farming that involves individual use of arable land and some communal use of grazing on hills and moors. It rarely provides a viable way of making a living. Very often, crofting is (or was) combined with some other activity, such as fishing or weaving, especially on the islands of Harris and Lewis. Today crofters often run a bed and breakfast or an outdoor activity to supplement their income.

Inevitably, crofting involves regulation and subsidy, and the crofter can become quite an expert in tapping the various grants avail-

Crofters' house on North Uist, Outer Hebrides.

able. This can cause old animosities to rise in the Lowlander, but in return the Highlander resents the indifference of Edinburgh and London towards the real problems of remote living.

But the Highland way of life in these areas goes beyond the details of economic existence, and can best be understood in Scotland by a journey to the Outer Hebrides. In Lewis the visitor encounters the Protestant version of a Gaelic culture dominated, especially on Sundays, by grim Calvinist churches known to outsiders as the 'Wee Frees'. Jesus may have walked on water, but if he had dared walk on the glorious beaches of Harris or Lewis on a Sunday he would have been ostracised. In

Barra and South Uist is the Catholic version, implanted by the 17th-century Counter-Reformation and not involving such denial of life's pleasures.

Some people argue that the Highland way of life exists in a still purer form in the Canadian Maritimes, especially the Catholic Gaelic-speaking communities of Cape Breton Island, who trace their origins directly to the 1745 Rebellion and the Clearances of the early 19th century.

INTO THE FUTURE

Wherever it survives, irrespective of religious background, the Gaelic tradition often defies the dominant world outside. The Highlander is often stereotyped as unmodern in priorities, as materialistic yet with little sense of individual ambition, attaching little importance to clock-watching. Gaelic society is supportive of its members, has an abiding sense of kinship and an unembarrassed love of a song and story, and – it is said – a penchant for a drink.

> *Sports allegiances in Scotland are a blend of the regional and the religious. Celtic is Glasgow Catholic, Rangers is Glasgow Protestant.*

With every passing year it appears superficially less likely that the Highlands' distinctiveness can survive another generation, but its efforts to do so become more determined as the 21st century deepens. The creation of a unified local government authority, the Western Isles Council, which conducts its business in Gaelic, has given a remarkable new confidence and ability to deal with modern political society. The Highland way of life is far from finished on these islands.

On the other hand, elsewhere in Scotland, the bygone critics have really had the last word. It is their Anglicised Lowland Scotland that now runs from the Mull of Galloway to John o'Groats. The tartan and the bagpipe ought not to fool the visitor: the Scots are not fooled, though they enjoy the pretence of it all.

SCOTS IDIOMS

Whether it's an insult or an endearment, the Scots often have their own unique word for it that usually drives straight to the point.

There are moments in the lives of all Scots – however educated, however discouraged by school or station from expressing themselves in the vernacular – when they will reach into some deep-seated memory of language and produce the only word for the occasion.

The Scots idiom tends to operate at two ends of a spectrum: from abusive to affectionate. So the word for the occasion might well be 'nyaff'. There are few Scots alive who don't know the meaning of the insult nyaff – invariably 'wee nyaff' – and there are few Scots alive who don't have difficulty telling you. Like all the best words in the Scots tongue, there is no single English word that serves as a translation. The most that can be done for nyaff is to say it describes a person who is irritating rather than infuriating, whose capacity to inspire contempt is just about in scale with his diminutive size, and the cockiness that goes with it.

The long historical partnership between Scotland and France has certainly left its mark on the Scots tongue. Scottish cooks use 'ashets' as ovenware – a word which derives from *assiette,* meaning plate – while the adjective 'douce', meaning gentle and sweet-natured, is a direct import of the French *douce,* meaning the same. But the most satisfying Scots words – resounding epithets like 'bauchle' (a small, usually old and often misshapen person) and evocative adjectives like 'shilpit' (sickly looking) and 'wabbit' (weak and fatigued) – belong to the tongue that was threatened in 1603 when King James VI moved south to become James I of England.

Until then, the Lowland Scots (as opposed to Gaelic-speaking Highlanders), whose racial inheritance was part-Celtic and part-Teutonic, spoke their own version of a northern dialect of English, and 'Scots' was the language of the nobility, the bourgeoisie and the peasants. But when king and court departed south, educated and aristocratic Scots adopted the English of the 'elite', and the Scots tongue has never recovered. Yet what could be more expressive than a mother saying of her child, 'The bairn's a wee bit wabbit today'? Or more colourful than describing the newspaper vendor as 'a shilpit wee bauchle'? The words themselves almost speak their meaning and they are creeping back into the vocabulary of the middle classes.

The dialects of Glasgow and Scotland's urban west have been much influenced by the mass infusions of Gaelic and Irish from immigrants from the Highlands and Ireland, but Glasgow's legendary 'patter' has an idiom all its own, still evolving and still conscious of every subtle shift in the city's preoccupations. Glasgow slang specialises in abuse, which can be affectionate or aggressive. A 'bampot' is a harmless idiot; a 'hei-

A street entertainer takes inspiration from the film 'Braveheart'.

dbanger' is a dangerous idiot. Predictably, there is a rich seam of Glasgow vernacular connected with drink. If you are drunk you might be steamin', stotious, wellied, miraculous or paralytic. If you are drinking you might be consuming a wee goldie (whisky) or a nippy sweetie (any form of spirits).

If a Glaswegian calls you 'gallus', it is a compliment. The best translation today is probably streetwise, although it covers a range of values from cocky and flashy to bold and nonchalant. The word derives from gallows, indicating that you were the kind of person destined to end up on them. In Glasgow that wasn't necessarily a reason for disapproval.

Lorimer's 'Ordination of Elders in a Scottish Kirk'.

HOW THE KIRK MOULDS MINDS

The part played by the Church of Scotland in building a nation that believed in hard work and obedience is hard to overestimate.

The Church of Scotland (the Kirk) was formed as a result of the Reformation and the break with Rome in the 16th century, creating a radical Presbyterian Protestantism in its place. It was officially established as the national Kirk in 1690. Its Presbyterian ethic has been strict and challenging – well suited to promote survival in a poor country with a harsh climate. Until recent times the Sabbath was a day when profane activity ceased in some households. The intervals between services in the kirk were spent in prayer or with improving books. Whether the Kirk has shaped the Scots or the Scots their kirk, it is impossible to understand Scottish character and attitude without taking into account the austere religious background.

The reformer John Knox.

NO TRIMMINGS

Scots Protestants worship God, their Maker, in a plain dwelling dominated by a pulpit. There are no trimmings such as elaborate holy pictures, or altar hangings. The clergy are attired in sober black and a sparingly used Communion table replaces the altar. The appeal is to the conscience and to the intellect, with the minister's address based on a text from the Bible, the only source of truth. The one concession to the senses is the singing of hymns and a psalm.

The reason for this lack of 'outer show' is that ritual is thought irrelevant. What matters is the relation of the individual soul to his or her Maker; hence the emphasis on self-reliance and personal integrity. With honesty a prime virtue, Presbyterians bow their heads in prayer, but feel no need to grovel on their knees; they talk to God directly. This

directness characterises all other dealings, and strangers may be disconcerted by the forthright expression of opinion, prejudice, liking or disapproval.

The belief that all are equal in the eyes of the Lord has produced a people more obedient to the dictates of conscience than to rank or worldly status. A minister may have no qualms about berating sinners from the pulpit, but they in turn will take issue with him over errors in his sermon.

STRICT EDUCATION

Unlike the English, who generally tend to avoid confrontation, the average Scot has an aggressive zest for argument, preferably 'philosophical'. At its worst this fosters a contentious pedantry, at its best moral courage and the independence of mind which, from a tiny population, has engendered an astonishing number of innovative thinkers in many diverse fields.

The academic excellence of which the Scots are so proud owes its merit to John Knox, who insisted that every child, however poor, must attend a school supervised by the kirk. By the early 1700s Scotland was almost unique in having universal education. Knox's concern, however, was more spiritual than scholastic: the newborn babe is not innocent but 'ignorant of all godliness' and has to undergo an arduous pilgrimage towards knowledge of the Lord. With the help of the *tawse* (a strap), children were brought up as slaves to the 'work ethic': sober, frugal, and compulsively industrious.

Values are positive: duty, discipline, the serious pursuit of worthwhile achievement and a responsibility to the social good. Hardheaded and purposeful, Scots have no time

Attending Mass at St Patrick's Church in Glasgow.

⊘ AN INDEPENDENT CHURCH

Rigorously democratic, the Church of Scotland is without bishops or hierarchy. In most other churches, the attenders have no say in the appointment of clergy, who are imposed from above. The Scots minister, however, is chosen by the congregation, whose elders, having searched far and wide for a suitable incumbent, will invite the favourite candidate to test their worth by a trial sermon. Where other churches' cardinals and archbishops hold office for life, the kirk's leader, the Moderator, is elected for one year only.

The Kirk is also a symbol of national independence. At its General Assembly, the Sassenach (English) queen or her representative, the Lord High Commissioner, is invited as a courtesy but is not allowed to take part in any of the debates. These are much publicised by the media, since, as there has been no Scottish parliament until now, politics and economics have been discussed along with clerical matters, and a report submitted to the government of the day.

The General Assembly meets once a year in May for a week in Edinburgh (usually in the Assembly Hall on the Mound) and is chaired by the Moderator. It is attended by ministers and elders from almost every kirk in the country and its deliberations are keenly observed (sometimes critically) by the general public, who can attend in the public gallery.

to waste on frivolous poetics. Scotland has produced philosophers like David Hume; the economist Adam Smith; Watt, Telford and Macadam, whose roads revolutionised public transport; lawyers, doctors, scientists, engineers; and radical politicians in search of Utopia – Knox's Godly Commonwealth in secular translation. Yet Scotland would give the world, especially Africa, more Protestant missionaries – such as David Livingstone, John Phillip, Robert Moffat, Mary Slessor – than any other European country.

> More than 40 percent of Scots are still identified as members of the Church of Scotland, compared with the 16 percent who are Catholics. But church attendance for both faith communities has declined steeply in the past decades.

BALANCE SHEET

With the pressure to achieve so relentless, there's short shrift for the idle. Religious imagery is businesslike: at the Last Day people go to their *reckoning* to settle *accounts* with their Maker; it's not sins or trespasses for which pardon is implored but, 'Forgive us our *debts* as we forgive our *debtors*'. In a land where it's a struggle to survive, the weakest, who go to the wall, have *earned* their just deserts.

But with one slip from the 'strait and narrow' leading to instant perdition, it's said the Scots have a split personality: Jekyll and Hyde. God's Elect are teetotal, but alcoholism is 'the curse of Scotland'; while it's almost unheard of for a Kirk member to go to prison, Glaswegians proudly boast of having one of the busiest criminal courts in the UK. It would seem, therefore, that the unofficial influence of the Kirk is defiance of all it stands for.

Its ministers have, at all times, lashed 'the filthy sins of adultery and fornication', and the taboo on the flesh is so intense that some critics have accused mothers, fearing to 'spare the rod and spoil the child', of showing too little physical affection towards their babies. Yet the poet Robert Burns, a flamboyant boozer and wencher, is a national hero,

the toasting of whose 'immortal memory' provides an annual excuse for unseemly revels. Visitors to puritan Scotland may be puzzled by the enthusiasm for his blasphemous exaltation of sensual delights. But perhaps, if paradoxically, Burns's anarchic *joie de vivre* also stems from the teaching of the kirk, to whose first demand, 'What is the chief end of man?' the correct response is: 'To glorify God and *enjoy* Him for ever.'

Fire and brimstone sermons may be a thing of the past, and even in the devout Outer Heb-

Scott Rennie, Scotland's first openly gay minister.

rides the Sabbath is no longer totally sacrosanct. In 2016, the Church of Scotland voted to recognise Ministers and Deacons in same-sex marriages – although this does not mean that church ministers can register same-sex partnerships themselves. Although steps are being made in the right direction, sadly concerns surrounding gay marriage continue within the Church, with 25 ministers leaving over the issue of ministers in same-sex relationships since 2008.

As congregations have declined, the Kirk has been forced, reluctantly, to adopt a less strident approach to public affairs. The days when the Moderator could feel free to lecture Scotland's secular powers with impunity are over.

Eureka! A popular version of how James Watt discovered steam power.

SCOTS GENIUSES

For its size, Scotland has produced a disproportionate number of intellectual geniuses: great thinkers, inventors, scientists and writers who have helped changed the face of the modern world.

When the English social scientist Havelock Ellis produced his *Study of British Genius* (based on an analysis of the *Dictionary of National Biography*) he came up with the fact that there were far more Scots on his list than there should have been. With only 10 percent of the British population, the Scots had produced 15.4 percent of Britain's geniuses. And when he delved deeper into the 'men of Science' category he discovered that the Scots made up almost 20 percent of Britain's eminent scientists and engineers.

Not only that, but the Scots-born geniuses tended to be peculiarly influential. Many of them were great original scientists like Black, Hutton, Kelvin, Ramsay and Clerk Maxwell, whose work ramified in every direction. Others were important philosophers like the sceptic David Hume or the economist Adam Smith, whose words, according to one biographer, have been 'proclaimed by the agitator, conned by the statesmen and printed in a thousand statutes'.

Noted Scottish explorer David Livingstone.

GREAT SCOTS

Scotland, like Ireland, produced a long string of great military men such as Patrick Gordon (Tsar Peter the Great's right-hand man), James Keith, David Leslie and John Paul Jones. There are also great explorers such as David Livingstone, Mungo Park, David Bruce and John Muir, and accomplished financiers like John Law, who founded the National Bank of France, and William Paterson, who set up the Bank of England. Andrew Carnegie, also a Scot, ruthlessly put together one of the biggest industrial empires America has ever seen, sold it when it was at its peak, then gave much of his money away on the fine Presbyterian basis that 'the man who dies rich dies disgraced'.

Just why a small, obscure country on the edge of Europe should produce such a galaxy of talent is one of the conundrums of European history. As nothing in Scotland's brutal medieval history hints at the riches to come, most historians have concluded that Scotland was galvanised in the 16th and 17th centuries by the intellectual dynamics of the Protestant Reformation. This is a plausible theory. Not only did the Reformation produce powerful and challenging figures such as John Knox and his successor Andrew Melville, but it created a Church that reformed Scotland's existing universities (Glasgow and St Andrews), set up two new ones (Edinburgh and Aberdeen) and tried to make sure that every parish in Scotland had its own school.

RADICAL THINKERS

When Thomas Carlyle tried to explain the pro-liferation of genius in 18th- and 19th-century Scotland, he found 'Knox and the Reformation acting in the heart's core of every one of these persona and phenomena'. This is a large claim, and overlooks the well-run network of primary schools inherited from the Roman Catholics.

But, whatever the reason, 18th-century Scotland produced an astonishing number of talents. As well as David Hume and his friend Adam Smith, Scottish society was studded with able men like

clergy homes. This meant that, in 1816, when Anglo-Catholics were squabbling over the precise date of the Creation, the Presbyterian intellectual Thomas Chalmers could ask: 'Why suppose that this little spot (the planet earth) should be the exclusive abode of life and intelligence?'

And nothing thrived more than the science of medicine. In the late 18th and early 19th centuries Edinburgh and Glasgow became two of the most important medical centres in Europe and produced physicians such as William Cullen, John and William Hunter (who revolution-

An 1827 view of the engineer John Macadam.

Adam Ferguson, who fathered sociology; William Robertson, one of the finest historians of his age; and the teacher Dugald Stewart. There were also gifted eccentrics like the High Court judge Lord James Monboddo, who ran into a barrage of ridicule by daring to suggest (100 years before Darwin) that men and apes might, somehow, be related. It was a sceptical, questioning, intellectually charged atmosphere in which talent thrived.

INTELLECTUAL FREEDOM

Interestingly, that talent didn't fall foul of established religion: few Scots had a problem squaring their faith with their intellectual curiosity. An extraordinary number of Scotland's most radical thinkers were 'sons of the manse', born into

ised surgery and gynaecology in London), three generations of Munros, Andrew Duncan (who set up the first 'humane' lunatic asylums), Robert Liston and James Young Simpson (who discovered the blessings of chloroform). It was a Scot, Alexander Fleming, who, in 1929, discovered the bacteria-killing properties of penicillin, the most effective antibiotic ever devised.

While Scotland has never produced a classical composer of any note, or a painter to compare with Rembrandt or Michelangelo, the reputation of 19th-century portraitists like Raeburn, Wilkie and Ramsay are now being upgraded. And in the Adam family (father William and sons Robert, John and James), Scotland threw up a dynasty of architectural genius, which was highly influential. (One of the scandals of modern Scotland is the number of Adam-designed buildings that are collapsing into ruin.)

However, the number of technologists born in Scotland is truly remarkable: they include James Watt, who greatly improved the steam engine; the civil engineer Thomas Telford; R.W. Thomson, inventor of the fountain pen and the pneumatic tyre; John Macadam, the engineer who gave his name to the metalled road; Charles MacIntosh, who did the same to waterproofed fabric; James Nasmyth, who dreamed

Then there's the Scotsman who is said to have virtually invented the modern world: James Clerk Maxwell, the 19th-century physicist who uncovered the laws of electrodynamics. Albert Einstein described his work as a 'change in the conception of reality' which was the 'most fruitful that physics has experienced since the time of Newton'. And Max Planck, the German physicist, said he was among the small band who are 'divinely blessed, and radiate an influence far beyond the border of their land'.

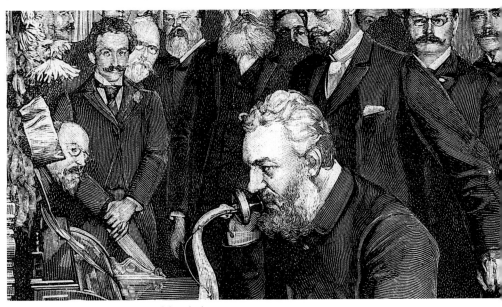

Alexander Graham Bell, the inventor of the telephone.

up the steam hammer; James 'Paraffin' Young, who first extracted oil from shale; Alexander Graham Bell, who is generally credited as the inventor of the telephone; and John Logie Baird, the father of television.

MAKERS OF THE MODERN WORLD

More important in world terms were Scotland's 'pure' scientists, such as John Napier, who invented logarithms; Joseph Black, who described the formation of carbon dioxide; James Hutton, Roderick Murchison and Charles Lyell, who developed modern geology; and Lord Kelvin, who devised the second law of thermodynamics and whose name is remembered (like Fahrenheit and Celsius) as a unit of temperature.

⊘ LITERARY GENIUSES

As celebrated by the Scottish Writers' Museum in Edinburgh, Scotland has three international-class writers in Robert Burns (1759–96), Walter Scott (1771–1832) and Robert Louis Stevenson (1850–94). Stevenson won acclaim with works such as *Treasure Island* and *Kidnapped*. To Scott, writing was as much a trade as an art, and he produced a long stream of work based on medieval and foreign themes. But it is Burns whose poetry and songs earned him pride of place in every Scottish heart, and whose birthday (25 January – Burns Night) is celebrated in rousing style around the world. Contemporary literary favourites include Irvine Welsh and crime writer Ian Rankin.

'Pitlessie Fair' by David Wilkie, 1804.

Raeburn's perennially popular Rev. Robert Walker Skating on Duddingston Loch.

SCOTTISH ART AND MUSIC

Scottish art is diverse, from flamboyant, sensuous paintings from the 18th and 19th centuries to innovative contemporary installations. Meanwhile the folk music revival has been hugely successful in nurturing home-grown talent.

In spite of its puritanism and thunderings from the Kirk against 'vain outer show', Scotland is unique among the British provinces in having a distinctive painterly tradition. The art of Protestant Northern Europe tends to be tormented and morbid and, given a Calvinist shadow of guilt and sin, one would expect Scottish painting to be gloomy and angst-ridden. Instead, as if in defiance of all that the Kirk represents, it is extroverted, joyful, flamboyant, robust – much more sensuous (even if less complex) than English art with its inhibiting deference to the rules of good taste.

It is significant that young Scottish artists have mostly bypassed the English capital to study abroad; those from Edinburgh in Rome, the Glaswegians a century later in pleasure-loving Paris. Growth of the arts in Scotland is linked to the relative importance of its two major cities, and the rivalry between them (culture versus commerce) has resulted in aesthetic dualism: where Edinburgh's painters are rational and decorous, raw but dynamic Glasgow has produced exuberant rebels.

Ramsay's portrait of David Hume.

THE ENLIGHTENMENT

Before the 18th century, Scottish art scarcely existed. There was no patronage from the Kirk, which forbade idolatrous images, or from the embattled aristocracy. In a country physically laid waste by the Covenanter Wars and mentally stifled by religious fanaticism, painters were despised as menial craftsmen.

The return of peace and prosperity, however, gave rise to a remarkable intellectual flowering, the Edinburgh Enlightenment, which lasted, roughly, from 1720 until 1830 and caused the city to be dubbed the 'Athens of the North'. The rejection of theology for secular thought was accompanied by a new enthusiasm for the world and its appearance, the brothers Adam evolving a style in architecture and design that was adopted all over Europe and remains to this day the classic model of elegance and grace.

A need arose, meanwhile, for portraits to commemorate the capital's celebrated sons. Though the earliest portrait painters, Smibert and Aikman, achieved modest recognition as artists not craftsmen, Allan Ramsay, son of a poet and friend of the philosopher David Hume, expected to be treated as an equal by the intellectual establishment, many of whose members he immortalised with his brush.

Considering he grew up with a background of visual austerity (Edinburgh had no galleries, no art school and only a few enlightened collectors), Ramsay's rise to fame is astonishing. Leaving home to study in Italy, he returned to

> *Raeburn's style is broader and more painterly than Ramsay's, the poses more dramatic: Judge Eldin looking fierce in his study, the Clerks of Penicuik romantically strolling, the Rev. Robert Walker taking a turn on the ice.*

in 1822 by George IV and made King's Limner (painter) for Scotland. Raeburn also studied in Italy, and his oeuvre, like Ramsay's, was confined to portraiture with an emphasis on individual character – the fiddler Neil Gow or an ordinary matron receiving the same attention as a scholar or fashionable beauty.

Raeburn was the first Scottish painter of national renown to have remained in his native Edinburgh and, in doing so, he established the arts in Scotland and their acceptance by the public. Interest and prestige led to ventures

'Porlock Weir' by Charles Rennie Mackintosh.

London in 1739 and was an instant success, finally ending up as court painter (in preference to Reynolds) to George III. Despite his classical training, Ramsay cast aside impersonal idealism for 'natural portraiture', concentrating on light, space and atmosphere, and the meticulous rendering of tactile detail: ribbons, cuffs, the curl of a wig, the bloom on a young girl's cheek. The refined distinction of his best work, such as the portraits of his two wives, has earned him an honourable position in the history not just of Scottish but also of British art.

SCOTTISH ARTS ESTABLISHED

Ramsay's achievement was rivalled in the next generation by Sir Henry Raeburn, knighted

in other genres, especially landscape. Though Alexander Nasmyth painted an Italianate Scotland, gilded and serene, the choice of local vistas – rather than a classical idyll in the manner of Claude – was startling in its novelty.

Equally novel was David Allan's transfer of the pastoral tradition of nymphs and shepherds into scenes from Scottish rural life. He was followed by David Wilkie, whose *Pitlessie Fair* (painted at 19) was the start of a career that earned him a knighthood and outstanding popularity; his 'low-life' comedies like *The Penny Wedding* created a taste for such subjects that persisted throughout the Victorian era.

Although no one equalled Raeburn or Wilkie, there was a new public interest in the arts, which flourished in Edinburgh during the 19th century. Notable in landscape are David Roberts with his views of the Holy Land and, later, William McTaggart, 'the Scottish Impressionist'.

THE GLASGOW BOYS

The academic mainstream, however, was confined to historical melodrama, sentimental cottagers and grandiose visions of the Highlands as inspired by Sir Walter Scott. The 1880s saw a new departure when a group of students, nicknamed the Glasgow Boys, united in pro-

devoted to gain, godliness and grand pianos (whose legs were prudishly veiled) was both affronted and bemused by Crawhall's lyrical cows, the voluptuous cabbages tended by James Guthrie's farm hands, the indecent brilliance of the rhubarb on Macgregor's *Vegetable Stall*.

Influenced by Whistler and the European Realists, most of the Glasgow Boys left Scotland in disgust to study in Paris – where they were subsequently acclaimed. This success abroad tickled civic pride (what Edinburgh

MacGregor's 'The Vegetable Stall'.

test against Edinburgh's stranglehold on the arts. Due to rapid industrial expansion, Glasgow had grown from a provincial town into 'the second city of the Empire' and, in contrast to 18th-century Edinburgh, there were galleries, an art school and lavish collectors among the new rich (one of whom was William Burrell), who were anxious to buy status through cultural patronage.

Initially, though, the Glasgow Boys scandalised their fellow citizens. Rejecting the turgid subjects and treacly varnish of the academic 'glue-pots', they abandoned their studios to paint in the open air, choosing earthy, peasant themes that lacked 'message' or moral and gave offence to the genteel. The public,

artist could compete?) and the canny burghers, who had once been so hostile, began to pay high prices for their pictures. Sadly, the Glasgow Boys then lost their freshness and became respectable: Lavery a fashionable portrait painter, Guthrie a conservative president of the Royal Scottish Academy, while Hornel retreated into orientalism. Today, there is a revival of interest – and investment.

EXPERIMENTAL COLOURISTS

The Glasgow Boys gave younger artists the courage to experiment through their flamboyant handling of paint and colour. Oppressed by the drab Calvinism of Scottish life, rebels of the next generation, led by Peploe, Cadell,

Hunter and Fergusson, again fled to Paris, where they were intoxicated by the decorative art of Matisse and the Fauves. Discarding conventional realism, they flattened form and perspective into dancing, linear rhythm, with colour an expression of a pagan *joie de vivre*. As with the Glasgow Boys, fame abroad brought the Scottish Colourists belated success at home. Peploe and Hunter returned to paint a Scotland brightened by Gallic sunshine and the witty Cadell to transform Glasgow housewives into flappers of the Jazz Age.

Douglas Gordon's 'Phantom' installation.

⊙ CHARLES RENNIE MACKINTOSH

An originator of Art Nouveau, the distinctive style of architect and designer Charles Rennie Mackintosh is typified by a simple geometrical manipulation of space based on combinations of straight line and gentle curves. Glasgow School of Art, his architectural masterpiece, is one of the city's most remarkable buildings. The Glasgow Style he initiated, with influences from Modernism and Japanese design, in furniture and the decorative arts, is now admired not only all over his native city but the world over. Yet in his day 'Toshie' was such a failure professionally that he abandoned architecture to paint watercolours in France.

MODERN TIMES

From the 1930s, landscape has tended to predominate in Scottish painting, but in the 1950s, Colquhoun and MacBryde adopted Cubism, not for formal reasons but as a means of conveying romantic melancholia.

Since World War II, while modern trends have been pursued with characteristic vigour, there's been a loss of optimism and sparkle. More poignant than the Modernists is Joan Eardley, who turned her back on artistic fashion to paint urchins in the Glasgow backstreets, then, after settling in a remote fishing village in the northeast, sombrely elemental landscapes.

John Bellany is unusual in that he had the tormented vision one might expect, but rarely finds, among artists brought up under Calvinism. Overwhelmed, after a visit to Buchenwald, by human wickedness, he gave up modish abstracts to return to figurative art of a tragic, often nightmarish monumentality. Later, towards the end of his life, he unleashed a prolific output of superb, lyrical autobiographical canvases.

GLASGOW GRADUATES

German Expressionism, with its energy and gloom, replaced the hedonistic influence of the French when Glasgow School of Art produced a new group of rebels. Known (unofficially) as the Glasgow Wild Boys, they have also rejected Modernism for gigantic narrative pictures with literary, political or symbolist undertones. The most successful, Adrian Wiszniewski and Stephen Campbell, have gone down well in New York.

Wiszniewski, a Pole born in Scotland, has adapted Slavic folk art to express nostalgia for the past, disenchantment with the present. Campbell, combining macho brutalism with whimsy, draws his inspiration from the contrasting writings of P.G. Wodehouse and Bram Stoker (author of *Dracula*).

Other brilliant Glasgow graduates include Stephen Conroy, Peter Howson, Martin Boyce, Mario Rossi, Craig Mulholland and Steven Campbell. And Allison Watt, Lesley Banks and Jenny Saville redress the balance for women. Watt earned notoriety for her painting of the Queen Mother with a teacup on her head.

Today – bolstered by the prestigious reputation of Glasgow School of Art – Scotland is a world-class centre for innovative contemporary art. Especially influential present-day Scottish artists include Susan Philipsz, a sculptor and producer of sound installations, and Douglas Gordon, another Glasgow graduate, who experiments with visuals and video. Both are winners of the Turner Prize.

PIPED MUSIC

The sound of Scottish music has changed dramatically in the past 25 years and nothing has been more dramatic than the forging of an alliance between two previously alien schools. On the one hand, the inheritor of the bagpipe tradition, regarded until then as a musical

---

Confidence in Scottish painting has been boosted by superb municipal collections, notably the Burrell in Glasgow – currently closed for renovation until 2020. Other highlights in the city include the Kelvingrove Art Gallery and Museum and the Gallery of Modern Art.

---

law unto themselves. On the other hand, the young adventurers of the folk music revival, ready to play and sing anything that had its roots embedded somewhere in Celtic culture.

Whether the piping establishment has benefited is debatable. They are a gritty, stubborn lot, much given to internecine warfare over the etiquette and mystique of piping disciplines that have been handed down like family heirlooms through the generations. Discipline still rules at the sponsored competitions, where pipers from all over the world challenge each other at what in Gaelic is called *pìobaireachd* (pibroch).

Just to confuse the uninitiated, *pìobaireachd* has another title, *ceòl mór* (Great Music). This is a truly classical music, built to complex, grandiloquent proportions and actually playable only after years of study and practice. Those who *can* play it do so by memory, in the manner of the great Indian raga players. The pipe music that most of us are familiar with – stretching from *Mull of Kintyre* to reels, marches, jigs and

strathspeys – is referred to by the classicists as *ceòl beag* (Small Music).

Great or small, much of it has survived thanks to patronage rather than household popularity. The earliest royal families in Scotland are credited with having a piper, or several, on their books, and no upwardly mobile landlord could afford to be without one. But it was in the warring Highland clan system that the pipes flourished. The blood-tingling quality of the Great Highland Bagpipe, with its three resonant drones, was quickly recognised by the early

Piper busking on Edinburgh's Royal Mile.

Scottish regiments, and the military connection remains to this day. Even now, the Scots use the pipes to soften up the English at football and rugby internationals.

Despite being bearers of the country's national music, the pipes can offer nothing to compare with the phenomenal resurgence of Scots fiddle music, which had thrived only in certain areas until the folk music revival got its full head of steam in the 1960s. Today, there are probably more fiddlers in Scotland than ever before. The best-known folk musicians are the Shetland fiddler Aly Bain and accordionist/songwriter Phil Cunningham, who perform widely at home and abroad. A few groups such as Blazin' Fiddles are also making their mark.

Another traditional instrument that has been revived is the *clarsach*, or Scots harp, which first appeared in 8th-century Pictish stone carvings. Some of the great *clarsach* music came from Ruaridh Dall Morrison (the Blind Harper) in the 17th century. Much smaller than the modern concert harp, the *clarsach* had become virtually extinct until its revival in the early 1970s.

But the fiddle and the *clarsach* were a long way behind folk song in returning to the mainstream of Scottish culture. The classic narrative ballads and *pawky bothy* (a Gaelic term meaning 'hut') ballads had survived largely in the hands of farm workers and the travelling folk (the tinkers) of Perthshire and the northeast until the tape recorder enabled collectors like the late Hamish Henderson to bring their songs to the young urban folk revivalists. Today's best-known singers are Fife-based Sheena Wellington (traditional) and Ishbel MacAskill from Lewis (Gaelic).

The folk clubs served, too, as spawning grounds for new songwriting, especially of

Live music in Tron Kirk, Edinburgh.

⊘ SCOTS FIDDLERS

The fiddle has been part of Scottish music for more than 500 years – King James IV had 'fithelaris' on his payroll in the 15th century. The fiddle reached its Golden Age in the 18th century, when Scots musicians sailed across to Italy to study the art of playing the instrument and brought back not only the tricks of the classical trade, but also a steady supply of exquisite violins, which were soon copied by enterprising local craftsmen. At the same time, the dancing craze had begun.

Country fiddlers found their robust jigs and reels much in demand at balls, parties and other social gatherings, and the first major collections of Scots fiddle tunes were published, making the music widely accessible.

By the early 19th century, though, high society had turned its fancy to the new polkas and waltzes that were flooding in from Europe. But the rural fiddlers played on regardless, and it was the Aberdeenshire village of Banchory that produced the most famous Scots fiddler of all – James Scott Skinner, who was born in 1843.

Classically trained, and technically virtuosic, Skinner – also known as the 'King of the Strathspey' – was internationally acclaimed, and with the arrival of recording in the later part of his career, the message of his music was spread even further – even as far as fiddle-packed Shetland, which had until then resolutely stuck to its own Norse-tinged style.

the polemical brand, producing some of the best songs since Robert Burns. The 18th-century poet is credited with more than 300 songs, many of them set to traditional fiddle tunes, and you can still hear them in all sorts of venues. You'll also hear Scotland's unofficial national anthem, the sentimental *Flower of Scotland*, written by the late Roy Williamson of folk duo The Corries. Recalling the Scots victory over the English at Bannockburn in 1314, it is sung at major sporting events in the hope of firing the national teams on to equal success.

CLUBS AND FESTIVALS

Many of the early folk clubs are still in existence – notably those in Edinburgh, Aberdeen, Kirkcaldy, Stirling and St Andrews. Sadly, the type of *ceilidh* laid on for tourists tends to be caught in a time warp of kilt, haggis and musical mediocrity. In Gaelic, *ceilidh* means a gathering. The Gaelic-speaking community, now mostly confined to the West Highlands and islands, holds its great gathering, the Royal National Mod, of beautiful competitive singing every October.

From Easter until autumn, there is hardly a weekend when there isn't a folk festival somewhere in Scotland. Glasgow's Celtic Connections is among the biggest festivals of its kind in the world and runs for two weeks in January, featuring around 1,500 artists performing in more than 300 events. But there is nothing to beat the smaller traditional folk festivals in rural areas, where the talent tends to be local rather than imported. Among the best events, the Hebridean Celtic Festival (July) in Stornoway on Lewis attracts a large crowd from as far away as the US. Kirriemuir (September), Shetland (May) and Orkney (May) are also famous for their annual celebrations of traditional music.

Most folk festivals have their unofficial 'fringe', and many pub sessions can match the finest organised *ceilidh*. Today, it's also fashionable to have a *ceilidh* at a wedding reception or a private party.

THE HIGHLAND FLING

The cunning Irish centuries ago devised a way of dancing in tight cottage corners. For the Scots, dancing is reserved for the village hall or the ballroom. Many of the traditional dances, including the famous Highland Fling, call for the raising of the arms to depict the antlers of the red deer. Popular formations like the *Eightsome Reel* and *The Dashing White Sergeant* also involve much whirling around in large groups.

Like the accordion-pumped music that fires these breath-sucking scenes, Scottish dancing has its more rarefied moments. There are country-dance societies where members dance with the kind of practised precision that

The annual Belladrum Festival.

must have been essential at the earliest Caledonian balls.

In the 1980s and 1990s, Scottish rock began to sit up and notice its Celtic heritage, with folk-rock bands such as Runrig and Wolfstone, all-electric but hitched to ancient Gaelic themes. In songwriting, too, folk music has made its mark in the rock venues. The leading singer-songwriters, such as Dougie MacLean, Rab Noakes and the brilliant Dick Gaughan, have found eager new audiences there, and their influence can be heard in the music of contemporary rock groups. One such group is Capercaillie, whose charismatic lead singer, Karen Matheson, comes from Oban and whose musical style is much closer to its Hebridean origins than most.

Perth Highland Games.

OUTDOOR PURSUITS

To play on the hallowed ground of Scotland's ancient golf courses, to catch your own trout or salmon, or take in the spectacle of a Highland Game, is to experience the essence of Scotland's outdoor life.

Visit the 19th hole at any of Scotland's 400 golf courses and you're likely to hear a heated argument as to where the game of golf originated. The discussion doesn't involve geography but rather topography: the 'where' refers to *which* part of Scotland. All involved will know that, in spite of the Dutch boasting about a few old paintings that depict the game, it began in Scotland centuries ago, when a shepherd swinging with his stick at round stones hit one into a rabbit hole.

SCOTTISH LINKS

Few courses have the characteristics of the quintessential Scottish course. Such a course, bordering the seashore, is called a links. The links of Muirfield, St Andrews, Troon and Turnberry are regular venues for the British Open championship.

The word links refers to that stretch of land that connects the beach with more stable inshore land, and a links course is a sandy, undulating terrain along the shore. One feature of such a course is its ridges and furrows, which result in the ball nestling in an infinite variety of lies. Another feature is the wind, which blows off the sea and which can suddenly whip up with enormous ferocity. A hole which, in the morning, was played with a driver and a nine-iron can, after lunch, demand a driver, a long three-wood and a six-iron.

Golfers who head to St Andrews for the first time may be surprised to find that the Old Course has two, rather than the customary four, short holes and only 11 greens. Yet it is categorically an 18-hole course: seven greens are shared. This explains the enormous size of the greens, on which you can find yourself facing a putt of almost 100yds (90 metres). Remember it

Teeing off at Castle Stuart Golf Links.

is the homeward-bound player who has the right of way on these giant double greens.

Ancient as the Royal and Ancient Golf Club of St Andrews is, it must bow to the Honourable Company of Edinburgh Golfers, which was formed in 1774 and is generally accepted as the oldest golf club in the world. Its present Muirfield course – which is at Gullane (pronounced *Gillun*), 13 miles (21km) east of Edinburgh – is considered to be the ultimate test of golf. The rough here is ferocious with nearly 200 deep pot-bunkers littering the course.

FIRST-CLASS COURSES

Back in Edinburgh are more than a score of courses, two of which are home to very ancient clubs. The Royal Burgess Golfing Society claims to be even older than the Honorable Company of Edinburgh Golfers, while the neighbouring Bruntsfield Links Golfing Society is only a few years younger.

On the road from Gullane to Edinburgh you pass through Musselburgh, where golf is known to have been played in 1672 and, most probably, even before that.

Glasgow, never to be outdone by Edinburgh, has nearly 30 courses. Outstanding among these are Killermont and Haggs Castle. The latter is less than 3 miles (5km) from the city centre. While golfers thrill over birdies and eagles at Haggs, their non-playing partners can enthuse over the renowned Burrell Collection, which is less than half a mile (1km) away. Even closer to the Burrell is the excellent Pollok course. Further afield at Luss, 23 miles (37km) northwest of the city is a course designed by Tom Weiskopf and Jay Morrish. Ranked in the top 20 courses in Britain, the Loch Lomond Golf Club is renowned worldwide.

Troon, 30 miles (48km) south of Glasgow and frequently the scene of the Open, is the kingpin

Alfred Dunhill Links Championships at St Andrews.

Colin Montgomery celebrates winning the Dunhill competition.

⊘ CLUB FORMALITIES

At the majority of Scottish golf courses no formal introduction is necessary: as a visitor, you just stroll up, pay your money and play. Some clubs do ask that you be a member of another club. Others require an introduction by a member, although if you are an overseas visitor this formality is usually waived. And the better courses demand a valid handicap certificate, which usually must be below 20 for men and 30 for women.

Access to the course doesn't mean you will gain entry to the clubhouse – that remains the private domain of a particular club whose members happen to make use of the adjacent course.

in a series of nearly 30 courses bordering the Atlantic rollers. Here, you can play for almost 30 miles (48km). Troon itself has five courses.

To the north is Barassie with one, and Gailes with two courses. South of Troon are three at Prestwick – scene of the first Open in 1860 – and Ayr, also with three courses. Fifteen minutes further down the 'course' are the exclusive Arran and Ailsa links of Turnberry. There's an excellent one at Brunston Castle, just to the southeast.

On the east coast is another remarkable conglomerate of courses, with St Andrews as its kingpin. About 30 miles (48km) to the north, across the Tay Bridge, are the three Carnoustie courses. The Medal course here has been called brutal, evil and monstrous.

Then, 20 miles (32km) south of St Andrews and strung along the north shore of the Firth of Forth, are the Elie, Leven, Lundin Links and Crail golf courses. The Crail course is claimed by golf-storians to be the seventh-oldest in the world.

Other glittering gems are found in the northeast. Here are Balgownie and Murcar, two of Aberdeen's half a dozen courses; nearby is Cruden Bay; Nairn, which is close to Inverness; and

INLAND COURSES

Scotland, home of golf, also has some superb inland courses. Many aficionados consider the King's at Gleneagles to be the best inland course in Britain. In 1993, it was joined by the PGA Centenary Course, which is from the drawing board of Jack Nicklaus and has the flavour of an American rather than a Scottish course. These are just two of the four courses, which make up the luxurious Gleneagles complex.

A mere 30 miles (48km) to the north is Blairgowrie with its fabled Rosemount course, and

Stalking in the Alladale Wilderness Reserve.

Dornoch, which stands in splendid isolation in the extreme northeast.

Dornoch is, even for a Scottish course, underplayed and may be Britain's most underrated course. Authorities believe that this course, all of whose holes have a view of the sea, would be on the Open rota if it were closer to a town.

Down at the extreme southwest of Kintyre is Machrihanish, whose turf is so naturally perfect that 'every ball is teed, wherever it is'. Its first hole, which cuts across the Atlantic, is considered one of the most spectacular in the world. And if the views from here, which include those to Ireland and the Inner Hebrides, seduce you, then you might wish to make your way over the seas to Islay, which is renowned for its Machrie course.

new courses are still being created: the 18-hole par 72 Spey Valley Championship Golf Course opened in 2006 in Aviemore and was designed by Ryder Cup player, Dave Thomas, and the American billionaire – and current US President – Donald Trump has created the Trump International Golf Links north of Aberdeen.

HUNTING, SHOOTING AND FISHING

While Scotland may have been blessed with more deer, grouse, salmon and trout than most small European countries, many of these assets are controlled by a few wealthy estates, whose owners may live a long way from Scotland. This means that 'field sports' such as deerstalking, salmon fishing and grouse shooting are touchy political issues, bound up with memories of the Highland Clearances and the ownership and use of the land.

Ownership of large Highland estates varies from local aristocrats who have been there for centuries to southern financiers, European entrepreneurs and oil-rich Arabs. While 'traditional' estate owners retain a paternalistic approach, some of the newer proprietors try to recoup their investment any way they can, often at the expense of local interests.

This happened when the then North of Scotland Hydroelectric Board (now Scottish

of walkers. Subsequently, the Land Reform (Scotland) Act 2004 now gives the public statutory rights to Scotland's mountains, moorlands, lochs and rivers. Based on the premise of 'responsible access', the act aims to balance the interests of land managers with conservationists and recreation. In sensitive areas, a 'Hillphone' system operates under which walkers can phone a recorded message, which tells them where stalking or grouse shooting is taking place.

The health of Scotland's field sports depends heavily on the state of the ecology, so environ-

Red deer in the Highlands.

Salmon leaping at the Falls of Shin.

Hydro-Electric) sold its fishing rights on the River Conon to a City of London financier for a reputed £1.5 million. He divided the river into weekly timeshare 'beats' which were sold at up to £15,000 per person per week. Locals who had long fished the river, but who could not afford such prices, were incensed.

There have also been problems in the past with estates covering large areas of hillwalking country trying to deny access to walkers and climbers during the shooting seasons.

However, the situation has eased considerably, thanks to greater cooperation between the various factions. In 1996, a national Access Forum was set up by Scottish Natural Heritage, recognising both the needs of the estates and the ambitions

mental groups and estate owners can have similar concerns. They are now working together on scientific studies into the reasons for the dramatic decline in grouse numbers in many areas. Other common concerns include acid rain and the damage caused by tributyltin, a marine pesticide, to salmon and sea trout.

DEERSTALKING

Stalking the magnificent red deer is one of Scotland's prime attractions for wealthy sportsmen. According to the Deer Commission for Scotland, there are 300,000 to 350,000 red deer in Scotland, most of them north of the 'highland line' between Helensburgh and Stonehaven. Since 1950, numbers have more than doubled, the increase in recent decades being partly due to more animals living in woodland – the cover is opening up as forests reach maturity. The annual cull, necessary to maintain a sustainable population level, is based on estimates of the numbers and density of deer herds.

The vast majority of the shooting is by professional stalkers, foresters or sporting parties under professional guidance who come from all over the world for the stag season (1 July to 20 October). When it ends, hind culling, though not for sport, continues until February.

of the season (July to September) on one of the classier rivers is likely to set the fisherman back between £1,500 and £2,000.

Yet demand is so high that a number of specialist firms, and even some estates, have taken to operating salmon beats on a 'time-share' basis. It works like this. The company buys a decent stretch of a good salmon river for a very large sum of money. The river is then divided into beats, and on each beat a week's fishing is sold 'in perpetuity' for up to £30,000 (depending on when the slot occurs in the season and the quality of the fishing).

Salmon fishing.

Stag hunting isn't cheap. A week's stalking (six days) can cost £2,000 to £3,000, and only the trophy (the head) belongs to the hunter; the venison will be sold by the estate.

There are between 200,000 and 400,000 roe deer in Scotland, and shooting roe deer bucks (males) is becoming more popular. It is less expensive, costs being roughly between half and two-thirds of those for a red deer stag shoot.

SEEKING THE SALMON

The up-market sport par excellence has to be salmon fishing in one of Scotland's great salmon rivers such as the Dee, the Spey, the Tay, the Tweed or the Conon. But a week's fishing on a good stretch (called a 'beat') at the height

⊘ EXPENSIVE PURSUITS

The 'Glorious Twelfth' is the popular name for 12 August, the day the red-grouse season opens. It has become less than glorious, with a sharp decline in grouse numbers due to predation and disease. There are about 500 grouse moors in Scotland and northern England, and they are carefully managed to provide the best heather conditions for the birds.

Like deerstalking, grouse shooting doesn't come cheap. Drive grouse (shot with the aid of teams of beaters) can cost around £140 a brace; even estate-reared pheasants can cost the shooter about £40 a brace.

All this is much against the wishes of those, like the Scottish Campaign for Public Angling (SCAPA), who believe that everyone should have the right to fish where they want and that no waters should be closed to the public.

With so much money at stake, it is little wonder that river proprietors have grown anxious as salmon stocks decline. Some commentators believe stocks of wild salmon could even be wiped out in a matter of decades; in 2018, 37,000 wild salmon were caught in the country, by far the lowest number since 1952. The

many Scottish lochs. Some remote lochs are still only visited by a few enthusiasts, and 100 fish in a day on two rods from a boat is not just a dream.

Tourist authorities promote this valuable resource through schemes whereby a single ticket will get the angler access to a variety of waters during a holiday. Who knows, you might get lucky and snag a ferocious ferox trout, found in the West Highlands. They can weigh up to 20lbs (9kg) and are cannibals, but as one angler said, 'a hell of an exciting fish to get on the end of your line'.

Pipers at a Highland Games gathering.

drop has been attributed to net fishing at river mouths, river and sea pollution, global warming, intensive salmon farming and declining fertility in the fish.

The net fishing has almost died out, thanks partly to the efforts of the Atlantic Salmon Conservation Trust. However, problems still exist. Drift netting continues in the far North Atlantic, off Greenland, Iceland and the Faroe Islands, and poachers are still busy on the rivers.

BROWN TROUT FISHING

While salmon fishing may be the glamour end of the sport, many anglers feel that too much is made of it. They argue that there is better sport in brown trout fishing, for far less outlay, on

HIGHLAND GATHERINGS

Highland gatherings, which are sometimes described as 'Oatmeal Olympics', are much more than three-ring circuses. As the gathering gets going, a trio of dancers are on one raised platform; a solitary piper is on another; a 40-piece pipe band has the attention, if not of all eyes, at least of all ears; the 'heavies' are tossing some unlikely object about; two men are engaged in some strange form of wrestling; a tug-of-war is being audibly contested and an 880yd (805-metre) race is in progress.

One of the original aims of the games was to select the ablest bodyguards for the king or chieftain, and this is reflected in today's heavy events. The objects used have evolved from what would be found in any rural community, such as a blacksmith's hammer or even a stone in the river bed.

Hurling the hammer and putting the shot are similar, yet different, to those events as practised at the Olympics. At the 'Oatmeal Olympics' the hammer has a wooden shaft rather than a chain; the 'shot', a 56lb (25kg) weight on the end of a short chain, is thrown with one hand; the length of weight and chain must not exceed 18ins (45cm). In this event it is not distance but height that counts. The competitor stands below and immediately in front of a bar with his back to it. Holding the weight in one hand, he swings it between his legs and throws it up and, with luck, over the bar. A correct throw will just miss the thrower on its way down, while a bad throw is liable to cause untold mischief.

Angling is worth millions of pounds a year to the Scottish economy, and this figure is bound to grow, as the hitherto secret delights of the upland rivers and lochs become better known.

The most spectacular event is tossing the caber, a straight, tapered pine-tree trunk shorn of its branches. It weighs about 125lbs (57kg) and is about 19ft (6 metres) long. The diameter at one end is about 9ins (23cm) and at the other about 5ins (13cm). Two men struggle to carry the caber to a squatting competitor. They place it vertically with the narrow end in his cupped hands. The competitor gingerly rises and, with the foot of the caber resting against his shoulder, and the remainder towering above, starts to run. Finally, at a suitably auspicious moment, the competitor stops, lets out an almighty roar, and thrusts his hands upwards. The wide end of the caber hits the ground; now is the moment of truth: will the quivering pole tumble backwards towards the hopeful competitor or will it stand up, turn over and fall away?

Caber tossing is believed to have evolved from throwing tree trunks into the river after they had been felled. They would then float to the sawmill. It was important to throw the trunks into the middle of the river or they would snag on the banks.

PIPERS AND DANCERS

Everywhere the sound of pipes can be heard. The solo pipers are undoubtedly the aristocrats of the games, and the biggest prize is awarded to the pibroch winner. There are three competitions for solo pipers: pibrochs (classical melodies composed in honour of birthdays, weddings and the like), marches (military music), and strathspeys and reels (dance music). While playing a pibroch the piper marches slowly to and fro, not so much in time to the music, but in sympathy with the melody. When playing dance

Hurling the hammer at the Perth Highland Games.

music, the pipers remain in one position tapping their foot, and, understandably, when playing a march, they stride up and down.

King Malcolm Canmore is credited with being responsible for one of the more famous dances seen at the games. In 1054 he slew one of King Macbeth's chieftains and, crossing his own sword and that of the vanquished chieftain, performed a *Gille Calum* (sword dance) before going into battle. The touching of either sword with the feet was an unfavourable omen.

The origin of the Highland Fling is curious. A grandfather was playing the pipes on the moors and his young grandson was dancing to them. Two courting stags were silhouetted against the horizon. The grandfather asked the lad: 'Can ye nae raise yer hands like the horns of yon stags?' And so originated the Highland Fling. The dance is performed on one spot, because the Scot, like the stag, does not run after his women, he expects them to come to him. Another explanation is that it was originally danced on a shield.

> *Most of the tartan-clad dancers who take part in Highland Gatherings are female, although a thorn may appear among the roses. Seldom are any girls older than 18, and competitions are even held for three- and four-year-olds.*

COLOUR CODES

Colour is the keynote of the games. All dancers and musicians are dressed in full Highland regalia, as are many of the judges and some spectators. Competitors in the heavy events all wear the kilt. The reds of the Stuarts, the greens of the Gordons and the blues

Highland dancing competition at the Isle of Skye Highland Games.

⊘ ROYAL CONNECTIONS

The Highlands of Scotland are famous for their games. Some claim that games were first held in 1314 at Ceres in Fife, when the Scottish bowmen returned victorious from Bannockburn. Others believe that it all began earlier when King Malcolm organised a race up a hill called Craig Choinnich. The winner received a *baldric* (warrior's belt) and became Malcolm's foot-messenger. A race up and down Craig Choinnich became a feature of the Braemar Gathering, which is the highlight of the circuit; this isn't so much because of the calibre of the competition but because, since Queen Victoria's time, it is often attended by the royal family.

of the Andersons all mingle with the green of the grass and the purple of the heather to produce a muted palette.

Highland Games are very much in vogue, and new venues are constantly announced. Currently, more than 90 gatherings are held during the season, which extends from May until mid-September. In spite of the spectacular appeal of the great gatherings (Braemar, Cowal, Oban), you might find the smaller meetings (Ceres, Uist in the Hebrides) more enjoyable. These have an authentic ambience, and competitors in the heavy events are certain to be good and true Scots and not professionals from foreign parts. And you may not even have to pay admission.

🔍 TARTAN

Tartanry is big business in Scotland, displaying its gaudy wares to willing tourists at every opportunity. But the pattern goes back a long way and links up with all things considered Scottish.

Tartanry is a subculture that, somehow, manages to lump together Bonnie Prince Charlie, John Knox, Queen Victoria, Rob Roy, Harry Lauder and Mary, Queen of Scots. Tartan tea towels and tea cosies, pencils and postcards, golf-club covers and a wide assortment of comestibles packaged in tartan – all are eagerly purchased.

Many resent the fact that this version of Gaeldom has come to represent the culture of Adam Smith, David Hume and Robert Burns. Others regard it as a harmless and feel that it keeps alive a sense of difference in the Scottish people. But it certainly demands expensive tribute. A set of Highland 'evening wear' consisting of kilt, Prince Charlie Coatee, sporran, jabots and cuffs, ghillie shoes, chequered hose and *sgian dubh (knife)* can cost up to £1,000. Even day wear – a kilt, Argyle Jacket, sporran and brogues – will set the wearer back £600. Of course, none of this applies to the actual Highlanders. The true day dress of a crofter or shepherd consists of boiler suit, Wellington boots and cloth cap. Tartanry could be regarded as Gaeldom's revenge on the country that once oppressed it. Right into the 19th century, the Highlanders' kilts, tartans and bagpipes were associated with the Jacobite uprising, and in 1746 the whole caboodle was banned by the British Government until 1782.

Not long after, Britain began instead to romanticise the Highland clans. Sir Walter Scott's novels became bestsellers and it was Scott who orchestrated the first outburst of tartan fervour: King George IV's state visit to Edinburgh in 1822. Scott wheeled into Edinburgh with tartan-clad Highland chieftains and gave them pride of place in the processions. The 20-stone (127kg) frame of George IV himself was draped in Royal Stewart tartan.

The tartan business got another boost when two English eccentrics known as the 'Sobieski Stuarts'

popped up, claiming to be the direct descendants of Bonnie Prince Charlie. They also claimed to have an 'ancient' (in other words fake) manuscript that described hundreds of hitherto unknown tartans. But the real clincher came in 1858 when Queen Victoria and Prince Albert bought Balmoral and furnished it almost entirely with specially designed 'Balmoral' tartan.

TARTAN ENTERTAINMENT

One arm of tartan imperialism is the Royal Scottish Country Dance Society (RSCDS; www.rscds.org), which, at last count, had more than 20,000 members and 160 branches all over the world. This may be understand-

Edinburgh taxi done up in tartan.

able in Scot-infested corners of the globe like the United States, Canada and New Zealand, but it isn't so explicable in France, Kenya or Japan. Just why they should want to dress in tartan to skip around to tunes like *'The Wee Cooper o'Fife'* is a mystery.

Yet another manifestation of tartanry is the Highland Games circuit. The Scottish Games Association represents more than 60 annually held Highland Games, most of which attract crowds of up to 5,000. But these cannot compete with the 40,000- or 50,000-strong crowds who flock to watch the big Highland Games in the US. Americans are very keen on 'clan gatherings', in which they get kitted out in Highland dress and march past their 'chief' brandishing their broadswords.

The perfect breakfast to start the day.

PORRIDGE, HAGGIS AND WHISKY

Cooked breakfasts, high teas and smoked salmon: traditional
Scottish food satisfies the heartiest of appetites, invariably
washed down with a drop of whisky.

Scots cuisine, uninspired and uninspiring for many years, has been largely transformed since the 1980s and 1990s. Some of Britain's top chefs now produce award-winning food in Scotland, relying on top-quality, locally produced fresh meat and fish prepared with an international twist – particularly Mediterranean flavours and the exotic tastes of Asian and Eastern cuisine.

The Scottish diet also has its hazards, however. Local tastes, especially the love of fried food, are held to be a major contributory factor to the Scots' high level of heart disease, although rates are improving. This is the home of the deep-fried Mars bar and the Scotch egg, a more traditional fast-food snack consisting of a hard-boiled egg wrapped in sausage meat, coated in breadcrumbs and then fried.

TRADITIONAL SCOTTISH FOOD

Despite the rise in international influences, Scottish cookery still has its roots in the soil, especially in some of those isolated hotels and restaurants far from the main cities. There, real Scottish cuisine is something the proprietors are genuinely proud of serving, notably the 'traditional full Scottish breakfast'. This generally starts with kippers (smoked herring) or porridge made from oats. Traditionalists take it with salt, but many prefer it with sugar. This is followed by bacon, egg, sausage, and black pudding (a variety of sausage made with blood). Expect also an array of breads, rolls, oatcakes and scones, topped off with an assortment of (often homemade) jams and conserves.

Scottish bakery ranges from the delectable to the stodgy and mass-produced. Not too long ago in Scotland there were fewer restaurants than tearooms. Here, people ate not only lunch

Traditional Scottish fare advertised in Edinburgh.

and afternoon tea but also 'high tea', which usually consisted of fish and chips and a generous selection of scones and cakes. High teas are still on offer in some hotels.

It is also significant that biscuit-making – the renowned shortbread – remains a thriving industry in both Edinburgh and Glasgow and as far north as Kirkwall in Orkney (where the oatcakes are arguably the best in the land). Dundee is renowned for its eponymous cake and for orange marmalade, its gift to the world's breakfast and tea tables – though the theory that the name 'marmalade' derives from the words *Marie est malade* (referring to the food given to Mary, Queen of Scots when she was ill) doesn't stand up to close scrutiny.

SCOTTISH FISH AND MEAT

Kippers are a treat. The best of them are from Loch Fyne, where their colour emerges properly golden, not dyed repellent red as they are in so many places. Arbroath smokies or finnanhaddies (types of smoked haddock) are a tasty alternative, simmered gently in milk and butter. Salmon and trout are just as likely to come from some west-coast or northern fish farm as fresh from the river, but the standard remains high.

The beef of the Aberdeen Angus cattle remains the most famous in the world. Good Scottish

A giant seafood platter at Ee-Usk restaurant, Oban.

When buying Scottish salmon, ask for 'wild'; it's more flavoursome than the farmed variety. However, farmed fish is generally preferred for the production of Scotland's renowned smoked salmon and trout, to ensure uniformity.

meat, the experts claim, should be hung for at least four weeks or even for eight and should never be sliced less than 1.25in (3cm) thick.

Venison, pheasant, hare and grouse are also established features of the Scottish pantry.

Admittedly, the romance of eating grouse after it has been ritually shot on or around the glorious 12 August is somewhat marred (if you are honest with yourself) by this bird's depressing fibrous toughness, which makes grouse shooting seem, at least to a gourmet, a complete waste of time.

THE NATIONAL DISH

As for haggis – though it, too, is hardly a gourmet delight – it does offer a fascinating experience for brave visitors. Scotland's great mystery dish is really only a sheep's stomach stuffed with minced heart, liver and lungs, along with onions, oatmeal and a blend of seasonings and spices. After being boiled, the stomach is sliced open, as spectacularly as possible, and the contents served piping hot.

Butchers today often use a plastic bag instead of a stomach; this has the advantage that it is less likely to burst during the boiling process, resulting in the meat being ruined. But no haggis devotee would contemplate such a substitute.

The tastiest haggis, by popular acclaim, comes from Macsween's of Edinburgh, who also make a vegetarian haggis – much maligned by traditionalists. Small portions of haggis are sometimes served as starter courses in fashionable Scottish restaurants, though the authentic way to eat it is as a main course with chappit tatties (potatoes), bashed neeps (mashed turnips) and a number of nips (Scotch whisky, preferably malt). This is especially so on Burns Night (25 January), when the haggis is ceremonially piped to the table, and supper is accompanied by poetry reading, music and Burns's own *Address to a Haggis*; or on St Andrew's Night (30 November).

COLOURFUL CUISINE

Many of Scotland's national dishes have names as rugged as Scottish speech. Soups such as Scotch broth (made with mutton stock, vegetables, barley, lentils and split peas), cock-a-leekie (made from chicken and leeks, but authentic only if it also contains prunes) and cullen skink (soup made from smoked haddock, cream and potatoes) are widely available, as are mutton pies (minced lamb in pastry) and the Forfar Bridie (a meat and onion pasty). But other dishes may be harder to track down: hugga-muggie (Shetland fish haggis, using the fish's stomach); crappit heids (haddock heads stuffed with lobster); partan bree (a soup made from giant crab claws, cooked with rice); stovies (potatoes cooked with onion); carageen mould (a Hebridean dessert); cranachan (a mixture of cream, oatmeal, sugar and rum), delicious with fresh Scottish raspberries; or hattit kit (an ancient Highland sweet made from buttermilk, milk, cream, sugar and nutmeg).

If you're in the southwest, Moffat toffees with a sherbet centre are a favourite, and, in Selkirk, the rich fruit bun eaten at Christmas, called a bannock. Plus there is an enormous variety of puddings and desserts, usually served with lashings of butterscotch sauce.

A RETURN TO REAL CHEESE

Real cheese, at last fighting back against anonymous mass production, has been making progress in Scotland. Lanark Blue, handmade from unpasteurised sheep's milk, has been a success and is worth looking out for in restaurants. Popular, too, is Cairnsmore, a hard ewe's-milk cheese from Wigtownshire, and Bonnett, made in Ayrshire from goat's cheese, while Island Cheese on Arran also finds favour with many a palate. Crowdie, Scotland's original creamed cottage cheese, has evolved into Caboc from the Highlands; with its original oatmeal coating, it is almost as creamy as France's crème fraîche. Pentland and Lothian cheeses are Scotland's answer to Camembert and Brie.

> The best places to eat in Scotland are members of 'A Taste of Scotland' with more than 500 establishments where you will be served good quality, fresh Scottish produce.

Cheese before pudding, as a running order, reflects Scotland's Auld Alliance with France, as does the large amount of fine claret to be found on the wine lists of good restaurants. But pudding before savoury is also an admirable tradition and is showing signs of a revival.

A WEE DRAM

At the end of sophisticated dinner parties in London, guests are invariably offered a choice of brandy or port but seldom a glass of Scotch. Familiarity, perhaps, has produced contempt for the native product – or, the Scots would argue, the English are showing their customary ignorance of all things Scottish.

The prejudice is an ill-founded one because good malt whiskies have a wider range of flavour and aroma than brandy and – an extra bonus – they are less likely to make the over-indulger's

Haggis and single malt whisky.

head throb the morning after. However, Scotland's unique drink has never quite managed to cultivate the exclusive image of cognac.

For one thing, there's a lot more of it on the international market. Scotch is one of Britain's principal export items, substantially contributing to the balance of trade: even the Vatican, on one annual reckoning, bought 18,000 bottles. More than 2,500 brands of Scotch whisky are sold around the world with the major export markets being the United States and Japan. And China and the Far East are catching up fast, showing a spectacular growth in sales.

In the 18th century, Scotch whisky was drunk as freely as the water from which it was made, by peasants and aristocrats alike. A spoonful was given to babies in the Highlands, and even respectable gentlewomen might start the day with 'a wee dram'. The poorest crofter could offer the visitor a drink, thanks to the home-made stills, which made millions of bottles of 'mountain dew' in the remote glens of the Highlands.

Yet something as easy to make cannot be made authentically outside Scotland. Many have tried, and the Japanese have thrown the most modern technology at the problem; but the combination of a damp climate and soft water flowing through the peat cannot be replicated elsewhere.

The earliest known reference to whisky occurred in 1494, when Scottish Exchequer Rolls record that Friar John Cor purchased a large quantity of malt 'to make aquavitae'. These days there are two kinds of Scotch whisky: *malt*, made from malted barley only; and *grain*, made from malted barley and unmalted barley, maize or other cereals. Most popular brands are blends of both types of whisky – typically 60 percent grain to 40 percent malt.

Copper vats in a Highland distillery.

⊘ TASTE THE DIFFERENCE

Despite the claims of distillers that each whisky blend has a unique taste, the truth is that most people, if taking part in a blind tasting, would be hard-pressed to say whether they were drinking Bell's, Teacher's, Dewar's, Johnnie Walker or J&B. Pure malt whiskies, on the other hand, are more readily identifiable.

The experienced Scotch drinker can differentiate between Highland malts, Lowland malts, Campbeltown malts and Islay malts, and there is certainly no mistaking the bouquet of a malt such as Laphroaig, which is usually described as tasting of iodine or seaweed.

So which is the best whisky, you may ask? Whole evenings can be whiled away in Scotland debating and researching the question with no firm conclusions being reached. It all comes down to individual taste – after all, in the words of Robert Burns: 'Freedom and Whisky gang thegither [together].'

However, the one point of agreement is that a good malt whisky should not be drunk with a mixer, which would destroy the subtle flavour; yet connoisseurs may be permitted to add a little water.

After dinner, malts are best drunk neat, as a liqueur. Blended whisky, in contrast, is refreshing in hot weather when mixed with soda and ice.

THE WHISKY-MAKING PROCESS

So automated are Scotland's 100-plus distilleries that visitors, sipping an end-of-tour glass of the product they have watched being manufactured, are left with an image of the beautifully proportioned onion-shaped copper stills and a lingering aroma of malted barley – but not with any clear idea of how water from a Highland stream turns into *uisgebeatha*, the water of life.

What happens is this: to make malt whisky, plump and dry barley sits in tanks of water for two or three days. It is then spread out on a concrete floor or placed in large cylindrical drums and allowed to germinate for between eight and 12 days. It is dried in a kiln, which ideally should be heated by a peat fire. The dried malt is ground and mixed with hot water in a huge circular vat called a mash tun. A sugary liquid, 'wort', is drawn off from the porridge-like result, leaving the remaining solids to be sold as cattle food. The wort is fed into massive vessels containing up to 9,900 gallons (45,000 litres) of liquid, where living yeast is stirred into the mix in order to convert the sugar in the wort into crude alcohol.

After about 48 hours, the 'wash' (a clear liquid containing weak alcohol) is transferred to the copper-pot stills and heated until the alcohol turns to vapour. This rises up the still to be condensed by a cooling plant into distilled alcohol, which is then passed through a second still.

The trick is to know exactly when the whisky has distilled sufficiently. Modern measuring devices offer scientific precision, but the individual judgement of an experienced distiller is hard to beat. Once distilled, the liquid is poured into oak casks which, being porous, allow air to enter. Evaporation takes place, removing the harsher constituents of the new spirit and enabling it to mellow. Legally it can't be sold as whisky until it has spent three years in the cask, and a good malt will stay casked for at least eight years.

It wasn't until the 1820s that distilling began to develop from small family-run concerns into large manufacturing businesses. What accelerated the change was the invention in 1830 by Aeneas Coffey of a patent still. This was faster and cheaper than traditional methods; more importantly, it did not need the perfect mix of peat and water, but could produce whisky from a mixture of malted and unmalted barley mashed with other cereals.

The industry's future, however, lay in the marriage between malt and grain whiskies. Blending tiny amounts of 30 or 40 malt whiskies with grain whisky, distillers found, could produce a palatable compromise between taste and strength. What's more, an almost infinite variety of combinations was possible.

FAVOURITE WHISKY BRANDS

In sales terms, the world's best-selling whisky brand is Johnnie Walker, selling almost 20 million cases in 2012. The Scots them-

A spirit safe at a Scotch whisky distillery.

selves tend to favour Glenmorangie, which is matured in old Bourbon casks, charred on the inside, for at least 10 years to produce a smooth spirit with hints of peat smoke and vanilla. The most popular malt in the United States is The Macallan, which is produced on Speyside and matured in 100 percent sherry casks seasoned for two years in Spain with dry oloroso sherry; connoisseurs argue that the 10-year-old is a better drink than the more impressive-sounding 18-year-old.

To decide on your own favourite, you need only take one of the many distillery tours on the Malt Whisky Trail or enjoy the Spirit of Speyside Whisky Festival held each spring and autumn.

Clyde Auditorium, Glasgow.

Rothiemurchus estate in the Cairngorms.

Edinburgh Castle's Esplanade hosts the Royal Edinburgh Military Tattoo.

Scotland

INTRODUCTION

A detailed guide to Scotland and its islands, with principal sites clearly cross-referenced by numbers to the maps.

Stained-glass window in Glasgow Cathedral.

Scotland has something to suit all tastes. Whether you want the peace of wide-open spaces or the excitement of dynamic cities, you can find it here. Even the unpredictable weather cannot dull Scotland's charm, as the wildest Highland storm only enhances the magnificence of the hills.

Edinburgh, a majestic capital city and home to the Scottish Parliament, enchants effortlessly, its castle towering over it on a rugged crag as a daily reminder of its turbulent history. Just 40 miles (64km) away, Glasgow, by contrast, is today one of Britain's most vibrant and cosmopolitan cities. Once suffering from an image of industrial grime and urban decay, it remodelled itself to become European City of Culture in 1990, and now has better shopping and nightlife than the capital.

Outside the two great cities lies an astonishingly varied landscape. To the southwest are the moorlands, lochs and hills of Dumfries and Galloway, haunt of Scotland's national poet Robert Burns; to the southeast, the castles, forests and glens of the Borders; to the west, the rugged splendour of the West Highlands, the jumping-off point for Skye and the Western Isles; to the northeast, the farms and fishing villages of Fife and on up along the North Sea coast through Dundee towards the granite city of Aberdeen, Scotland's oil capital. To the north are the elusive monster of Loch Ness, the splendour of the Highlands, and the islands of Orkney and Shetland – more Norse than Scottish.

Fairy Glen, Isle of Skye.

Scotland's greatest appeal is to people who appreciate the open air, from rambling across moors to arduous hill-walking and hair-raising rock climbs and mountain-bike trails. Or you can ski, canoe, surf, fish for salmon or play golf in the country that invented the game.

And the people? Their reputation for being reserved is unwarranted – you're unlikely to come across a taxi driver, shopkeeper or man in the pub who is unwilling to engage in lengthy and lively conversation, particularly on any matter of national debate.

Edinburgh

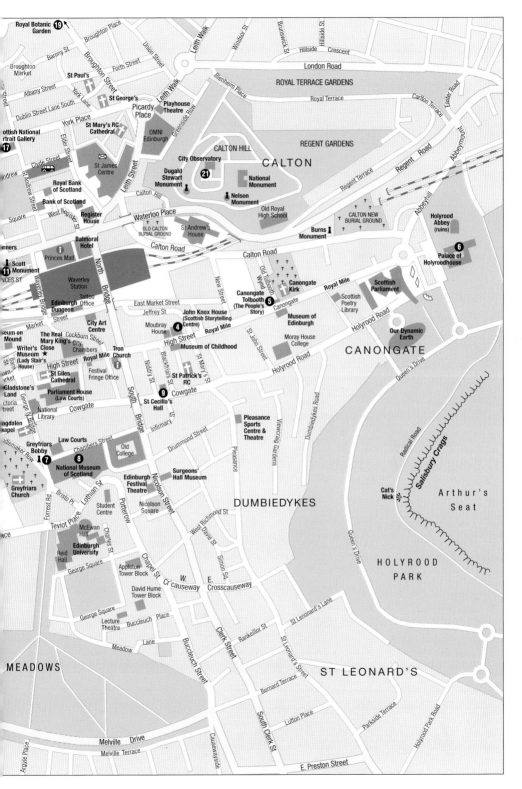

View of fireworks and the Balmoral Hotel's clock tower from Calton Hill.

EDINBURGH

Set among a series of volcanic hills, Edinburgh is a stunning mix of late medieval tenements and neoclassical terraces, with a history and charm that few other cities can rival.

Not for nothing was that great parable of the divided self, *Dr Jekyll and Mr Hyde*, written by an Edinburgh man, Robert Louis Stevenson. He may have set the story in London, but he conjured it out of the bizarre life of a respectable Edinburgh tradesman. More than one critic has taken the Jekyll and Hyde story as a handy metaphor for the city of Edinburgh itself: something at once universal yet characteristically Scottish. Where else does a semi-ramshackle late medieval town glower down on such Georgian elegance? What other urban centre contains such huge chunks of sheer wilderness within its boundaries? Does any other city in Europe have so many solid Victorian suburbs surrounded by such bleak housing estates? Stevenson himself was inclined to agree. 'Few places, if any,' he wrote, 'offer a more barbaric display of contrasts to the eye.' For all its duality, Edinburgh remains one of Europe's most beautiful and amenable cities.

LANDSCAPE AND PEOPLE

To the south, the city is hemmed in by the Pentland Hills – some of which are almost 2,000ft (600-metres) high – and to the north by the island-studded waters of the Firth of Forth.

At the last count, Edinburgh contained just under half a million people rattling around in 100 sq miles (40 sq km) on the Forth's south bank. While the city's traditional economy of 'books, beer and biscuits' has been whittled away by the ravages of recession and change, there is a powerful underpinning of banking, insurance, shipping, the professions (especially the law), universities, hospitals, and, of course, government bureaucracies (local and central). By and large, the North Sea oil boom passed Edinburgh by, although some of the city's financiers did well enough by shuffling investment funds around, and for a while

◉ Main attractions

Edinburgh Castle
Palace of Holyroodhouse
Kirk of St Giles
Museum of Childhood
Our Dynamic Earth
National Museum of Scotland
National Gallery of Scotland
Royal Botanic Garden
Scottish National Gallery of Modern Art
Royal Yacht Britannia

◉ Maps on pages 114, 134

Stained-glass window in St Margaret's Chapel, Edinburgh Castle.

Leith Docks was used as an onshore supply base, to coat pipes and to build steel deck modules.

And like every other decent-sized city in the western hemisphere, Edinburgh thrives on a rich cultural mix. The 'base' population is overwhelmingly Scots with a large Irish content (much of it from Northern Ireland), but there are also communities of Poles, Italians, Ukrainians, Jews, Pakistanis, Sikhs, Bengalis, Chinese and, of course, English.

In 2004, one aspect of Edinburgh's heritage was celebrated when it was named as Unesco's first City of Literature. Its current residents include Ian Rankin, creator of Inspector Rebus, J.K. Rowling, begetter of Harry Potter, Kate Atkinson, the award-winning inventor of detective Jackson Brodie, and Alexander McCall Smith, the prolific writer whose books include the successful *44 Scotland Street* series set in Edinburgh.

CAPITAL CITY

In 1999 Edinburgh once again became a capital city with a parliament (initially meeting at the Church of Scotland Assembly Hall, at Holyrood). Following a strong endorsement from the Scottish people in the referendum of September 1997, the devolved parliament signalled a significant start to the new millennium.

The new Scottish Parliament was elected by a form of proportional representation (unlike elections to Westminster, which use a traditional 'first-past-the-post' system) and it administers a wide range of local matters, although major areas such as defence and foreign policy are still dealt with by the United Kingdom Parliament in London. A Secretary of State for Scotland still represents Scotland's interests in the UK Parliament, but many regard this as an increasingly redundant post.

Even before the parliament was set up, Edinburgh wielded more power and influence than any British city outside of London. It has long been the centre of the Scots legal system, home to the Court of Session (the civil court) and the High Court of Justiciary (criminal

View from the Castle.

court), from which there is no appeal to the House of Lords: Edinburgh's decision is final.

Edinburgh is also the base of the Church of Scotland (the established church), whose General Assembly every May floods Edinburgh with sober-suited Presbyterian ministers. And anyone seeking to consult the records of Scotland (land titles, company registration, government archives, lists of bankrupts, births, marriages, deaths) must make a pilgrimage to the city.

THE EARLY DAYS

No one is quite sure just how old Edinburgh is, only that people have been living in the area for more than 5,000 years. But it seems certain that the city grew from a tiny community perched on the 'plug' of volcanic rock that now supports **Edinburgh Castle**. With steep, easily defended sides, natural springs of water and excellent vantage points, the Castle rock was squabbled over for hundreds of years by generations of Picts, Scots, British (Welsh) and Angles, with the

Scots (from Ireland) finally coming out on top. It was not until the 11th century that Edinburgh settled down to be the capital city of an independent Scotland, and a royal residence was built within the walls of Edinburgh Castle.

But Edinburgh proved to be a strategic liability in the medieval wars with the English. It was too close to England. Time after time, English armies crashed across the border laying waste to the farmlands of the southeast, and burning Edinburgh itself. It happened in 1174 (when the English held Edinburgh Castle for 12 years), in 1296, in 1313 (during the Wars of Independence), in 1357, in 1573, in 1650, and as late as 1689, when the duke of Gordon tried, and failed, to hold Edinburgh Castle against the Protestant army of William of Orange.

The hammering of Edinburgh by the English came to an end in 1707 when the Scottish Parliament, many of whose members had been bribed by English interests, voted to abandon the sovereignty of Scotland in favour of a union with England. 'Now there's

☉ Tip

For an introduction to Edinburgh's colourful past, you can join one of the excellent guided tours around the Castle or the Old Town. Alternatively, download a free Literary Trail from www.cityofliterature.com. Produced by Unesco City of Literature they cover the places in the books of Alexander McCall Smith, J.K. Rowling, Ian Rankin, Robert Louis Stevenson and many more.

The Castle's Great Hall.

Inside Edinburgh Castle.

Old Town architecture.

an end of an auld sang,' the old earl of Seafield was heard to mutter as he signed the act. But in fact, power and influence had been haemorrhaging out of Edinburgh ever since the Union of the Crowns in 1603 when the Scottish King James VI (son of Mary, Queen of Scots) became the first monarch of Great Britain and Ireland.

Stripped of its royal family, courtiers, parliament and civil service, 18th-century Edinburgh should have lapsed into a sleepy provincialism. But the Treaty of Union guaranteed the position of Scots law and the role of the Presbyterian Church of Scotland. With both these powerful institutions entrenched in Edinburgh, the city was still a place where the powerful and influential met to make important decisions.

THE SCOTTISH ENLIGHTENMENT

In fact, for reasons that are still not clear, 18th-century Scotland became one of Europe's intellectual powerhouses, producing scholars and philosophers like David Hume, Adam Smith and William Robertson, architect-builders like William Adam and his sons Robert and John, engineers like James Watt, Thomas Telford and John Rennie, surgeons like John and William Hunter, and painters like Henry Raeburn and Allan Ramsay.

That explosion of talent became known as the Scottish Enlightenment, and one of its greatest creations was the **New Town** of Edinburgh. Between 1767 and 1840 a whole impeccable new city – bright, spacious, elegant, rational and symmetrical – was created on the land to the north of the **Old Town**.

It was very quickly occupied by the aristocracy, gentry and 'middling' classes of Edinburgh, who left the Old Town to the poor and to the waves of Irish and Highland immigrants who flooded into Edinburgh from the 1840s onwards.

Like most British (and European) cities, Edinburgh's population burgeoned in the 19th century, from 90,786 in 1801 to just over 413,000 in 1901. There was no way that the Old Town and the New Town could house that kind of

population, and Victorian Edinburgh became ringed by a huge development of handsome stone-built tenements and villas in suburbs such as **Bruntsfield, Marchmont, The Grange** and **Morningside**, which in turn became ringed about by 20th-century bungalows and speculative housing.

Beginning in the 1930s, the Edinburgh Corporation (and later the Edinburgh District Council) outflanked the lot by throwing up an outer ring of huge council-housing estates.

Although the Old Town had been allowed to deteriorate in a way that is nothing short of disgraceful, it is steadily being revived. Serious efforts have been made to breathe new life into its labyrinth of medieval streets, wynds (alleys) and closes. As a way of rescuing Edinburgh's many architectural treasures, the city fathers have almost been giving away buildings (along with handsome grants) to private developers. Restored 17th-century tenements and converted 19th-century breweries now provide up-market city-centre living.

THE OLD TOWN

Even after two centuries of neglect, Edinburgh's Old Town packs more historic buildings into a square mile than just about anywhere in Britain. Stevenson, again, provides the reason. 'It [the Old Town] grew, under the law that regulates the growth of walled cities in precarious situation, not in extent, but in height and density. Public buildings were forced, whenever there was room for them, into the midst of thoroughfares; thoroughfares were diminished into lanes; houses sprang up storey after storey, neighbour mounting upon neighbour's shoulder, as in some Black Hole in Calcutta, until the population slept 14 to 15 deep in a vertical direction.'

In this late medieval version of Manhattan, the aristocracy, gentry, merchants and commoners of Edinburgh lived cheek by jowl. Often they shared the same 'lands' (tenements), the 'quality' at the bottom and hoi polloi at the top. They rubbed shoulders in dark stairways and closes, and knew one another in a way that was socially impossible in England. Any Lord of Session (High Court judge) whose verdict was unpopular could expect to be harangued or even pelted with mud and stones as he made his way home.

Not that life in the Old Town was entirely dominated by mob rule. Until the end of the 18th century the Old Town was the epicentre of fashionable society, a tight little metropolis of elegant drawing rooms, modish concert halls, dancing academies, and a bewildering variety of taverns, *howffs* (meeting places), coffee houses and social clubs. 'Nothing was so common in the morning as to meet men of high rank and official dignity reeling home from a close in the High Street where they had spent the night in drinking,' wrote Robert Chambers, a lively chronicler.

The heady social life of the Old Town came to an end at the turn of the 19th century, when it was progressively

Nave of St Giles Cathedral.

Busking on the Royal Mile.

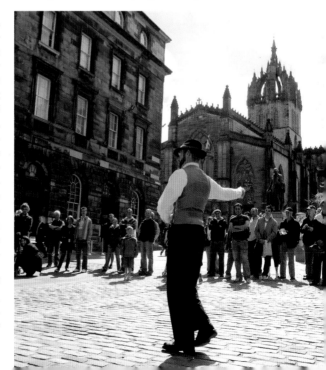

Statue of Greyfriars Bobby.

On the Royal Mile, looking towards Tron Kirk.

abandoned by the rich and the influential, whose houses were inherited by the poor and the feckless. 'The Great Flitting' it was called, and crowds used to gather to watch all the fine furniture, crockery and paintings being loaded into carts for the journey down the newly created 'earthen mound' (now called **The Mound**) to the New Town.

THE ROYAL MILE

The spine of the Old Town is the **Royal Mile**, a wide road that runs down from the Castle to the **Palace of Holyroodhouse**, and comprises (from top to bottom) Castlehill, Lawnmarket, the High Street and the Canongate.

The **Castle ❶** (tel: 0131-225 9846; www.edinburghcastle.scot; daily Apr–Sept 9.30am–6pm, Oct–Mar 9.30am–5pm) is well worth a visit, if only for the views over the city. Many of the buildings are 18th- and 19th-century, although the tiny Norman chapel dedicated to the saintly Queen Margaret dates to the 12th century. Go into the **National War Museum**, with its history of the Scottish military from medieval times to the present day, the **Great Hall** (which has a superb hammer-beam roof), and the **Crown Room**, which houses the Regalia (crown jewels) of Scotland; these were lost between 1707 and 1818, at which point a commission set up by Sir Walter Scott traced them to a locked chest in a locked room in the castle. Also here is Scotland's symbolic coronation seat, the Stone of Destiny, returned from London in 1996 after a 700-year absence. If you're there at lunch time you can see the master gunner fire the famous One o'Clock gun (not on Sundays).

Just below the Castle esplanade, on **Castlehill**, you will find an iron fountain marking the spot where, between 1479 and 1722, Edinburgh burned its witches; **Ramsay Garden**, the tenements designed by the 19th-century planning genius Patrick Geddes; and a **Camera Obscura ❷** (tel: 0131-226 3709; www.camera-obscura.co.uk; daily July–Aug 9am–10pm, Apr–June, Sept–Oct 9.30am–8pm, Nov–Mar 9.30am–7pm) built in the 1850s.

Across the road is **The Scotch Whisky Experience** (tel: 0131-220 0441; www.scotchwhiskyexperience.co.uk; daily 10am–6pm), where visitors can learn about the drink's origin from an audiovisual show and by travelling in a whisky barrel through 300 years of history. The shop sells a good selection of whiskies.

Next door, Tolbooth Kirk, where the city's Gaelic speakers used to worship, has reopened as **The Hub** (Edinburgh's Festival Centre; tel: 0131-473 2015; www.thehub-edinburgh.com), with a booking office, exhibition area, shop and café-bar.

On the north side of the Lawnmarket is **Gladstone's Land ❸** (tel: 0131 226 5856; daily 21 Mar–31 Oct 11am–5pm), a completely restored six-storey 17th-century tenement now owned by the National Trust for Scotland (NTS), which gives some insight into 17th-century Edinburgh life (dirty, difficult and malodorous). Next door is Lady Stair's

House, now the **Writers' Museum** (tel: 0131-529 4901; daily 10am–5pm; free), dedicated to Robert Burns, Sir Walter Scott and Robert Louis Stevenson; and **Deacon Brodie's Tavern**, named after William Brodie, a respectable cabinet-maker by day but ruthless burglar by night and generally thought to be the model for the Jekyll and Hyde story.

Further along, on what is now **High Street**, are **Parliament House** (now the Law Courts); the **High Kirk of St Giles** (tel: 0131-225 9442; www.stgilescathedral.org.uk; May–Sept Mon–Fri 9am–7pm, Sat 9am–5pm, Sun 1–5pm; Oct–April Mon–Sat 9am–5pm, Sun 1–5pm; donation); the **Mercat Cross**, from which kings and queens were proclaimed; and the **City Chambers**, which was one of the first buildings in the great drive to 'improve' Edinburgh in the late 18th century. Below, visitors can explore haunted **Real Mary King's Close** (tel: 0131 225 0672 for bookings; www.realmarykingsclose.com; Apr–Oct daily 9.30am–9.30pm, Nov–Mar Sun–Thu 10.15am–5.30pm, Fri–Sat 10.15am–9pm), a fascinating and atmospherically

preserved 17th-century tenement. Life during the period, from the upper classes to the lowly, is evocatively depicted through dioramas, recited tales and ghostly voices. The lower part of the High Street contains the 15th-century **Moubray House**, which is probably the oldest inhabited building in Edinburgh; the **John Knox House**  (tel: 0131-556 9579; www.scottishstorytellingcentre.com; Mon–Sat 10am–6pm, July–Aug also Sun noon–6pm), which is home to the **Scottish Storytelling Centre**; and the **Museum of Childhood** (tel: 0131-529 4142; daily 10am–5pm; free) with displays of historical toys, dolls and books. While principally geared towards children, it's regularly full of their accompanying adults in raptures of nostalgia over long-forgotten items.

Across the road is **Trinity Church** in **Chalmer's Court**, where enthusiasts can also make rubbings of rare Scottish brasses and stone crosses in the **Brass Rubbing Centre** (tel: 0131-556 4364; Apr–Sept Mon–Sat 10am–4.30pm, Aug also Sun noon–5pm; free, charge to make a rubbing).

The Writers' Museum contains artefacts belonging to Scotland's greatest authors.

The entrance to the Palace of Holyroodhouse.

Giant kaleidoscope in the Camera Obscura.

CANONGATE BUILDINGS

Further east, **Canongate** is particularly rich in 16th- and 17th-century buildings. These include the **Tolbooth** ❺ (see page 124); **Bakehouse Close**; the **Museum of Edinburgh** (tel: 0131-529 4143; daily 10am–5pm; free), the city's main museum of local history; **Moray House**, the most lavish of the aristocracy's town houses; the Dutch-style **Canongate Church**; **White Horse Close** (once a coaching inn); and the 17th-century **Acheson House**. Beyond Canongate Church is the '**mushroom garden**', a walled garden laid out in the 17th-century manner, and almost completely unknown.

The **Palace of Holyroodhouse** ❻ (tel: 0131-556 5100; www.rct.uk; daily Apr–Oct 9.30am–6pm, Nov–Mar 9.30am–4.30pm with exceptions) began as an abbey in the 12th century, grew into a royal palace in the early 16th century and was much extended in the late 17th century for Charles II, who never set foot in it. Mary, Queen of Scots witnessed the butchery of her Italian favourite, David Rizzio, here in 1566.

The **Scottish Parliament** building (tel: 0131-348 5200; www.parliament.scot; Mon–Sat 10am–5pm; free) opened its doors at Holyrood in 2004 at a final cost of £431 million. Barcelona architect Enric Miralles's innovative creation was described by one critic as being 'like a cluster of boats, a sweeping of leaves, a collection of seaside shells, a Pandora's box of architectural motifs laced together ingeniously, this side of pandemonium'. Opposite is a stunning, tented tourist attraction, **Our Dynamic Earth** (tel: 0131-550 7800; www.dynamicearth.co.uk; daily 10am–5.30pm, July–Aug until 6pm, closed Mon and Tues Nov–Mar), a family-oriented audio visual 'experience' documenting the formation and evolution of the planet.

SOUTH OF THE ROYAL MILE

Close to the Royal Mile, on George IV Bridge, are the **National Library of Scotland** (UK copyright library; tel: 0131-623 3700) and the little bronze statue of **Greyfriars Bobby** ❼, the devoted Skye terrier who, the story goes, was so bereaved by the passing of his owner that he spent the rest of his days sitting on his grave in nearby Greyfriars Kirk, soon to be taken into the hearts of local residents who fed and watered him until his own dying day. Later, he was, of course, immortalised by Walt Disney, to whom much of the schmaltz of the tale may be accredited. In Chambers Street is the **National Museum of Scotland** ❽ (tel: 0300-123 6789; www.nms.ac.uk; daily 10am–5pm; free), which houses a dazzling collection of 19th-century machinery, scientific instruments and natural history, plus the preserved remains of Dolly the sheep (1996–2003), the world's first cloned mammal. Since 2011 this has also incorporated the Royal Museum, whose spectacular glass-roofed Grand Gallery houses a whole host of eclectic exhibits from fossils to modern science.

On the corner of Chambers Street and the South Bridge lies Robert Adam's **The Old College**, the finest of Edinburgh University's buildings.

Running roughly parallel with the Royal Mile to the south are the **Grass-market** – lined by cosy pubs and once the site of riots and public executions – and a long and rather dingy street called the **Cowgate**, which in the 19th century was crammed with Irish immigrants fleeing the Great Famine. The Irish Catholic nature of the Cowgate is testified to by the huge but inelegant bulk of **St Patrick's Roman Catholic Church**. A more interesting building is **St Cecilia's Hall** ❾, which now belongs to Edinburgh University, but was built by the Edinburgh Musical Society as a concert hall in 1762, modelled on the opera house at Parma. Today the area throbs on Friday and Saturday nights as one of the city's nightclub heartlands.

PRINCES STREET

'A sort of schizophrenia in stone' is how the novelist Eric Linklater once described **Princes Street**, going on

to contrast the 'natural grandeur solemnised by memories of human pain and heroism' of the Castle rock with the tawdry commercialism of the north side of the street. Thanks to the developers and retailers of the 20th century it is no longer one of Europe's more elegant boulevards. Just about every decent building has been gouged out of the north side of the street and replaced by some undistinguished piece of modern architecture. Fortunately, on the south side, **Princes Street Gardens** ❿ remain as the 'broad and deep ravine planted with trees and shrubbery' that so impressed the American writer Nathaniel Willis in 1834. With Princes Street packed with visitors throughout the year, there had been talk of pedestrianising the whole length, but this went by the way with the building of the city's new tram network.

With the exception of the superb **Register House** by Robert Adam at the far northeast end of the street, and a few remaining 19th-century shops (such as Jenners, the venerable

A ledger containing Robert Burns' signature at the Writers' museum.

Canongate Tolbooth.

The Scott Monument.

National Museum of Scotland.

department store beloved by Edinburgh ladies of a certain age, which is now owned by House of Fraser), everything worthwhile is on the south side of the street. The most startling edifice, which may be ascended for splendid views, is the huge and intricate Gothic **monument to Sir Walter Scott** ⑪ (tel: 0131-529 4068; daily Oct–Mar 10am–4pm) erected in 1844 and designed by a self-taught architect called George Meikle Kemp. The unfortunate Kemp drowned in an Edinburgh canal shortly before the monument was completed, and was due to be buried in the vault under the memorial until some petty-minded member of Scott's entourage persuaded the Court of Session to divert the funeral. Britain's largest monument to a single literary figure is decorated with carvings of characters from Scott's novels, surrounding the marble statue of the writer himself.

CONNECTED ART GALLERIES

Much more typical of Edinburgh are the two neoclassical art galleries at the junction of Princes Street and The Mound. Since the completion of a multimillion pound project in 2003, both the **Royal Scottish Academy** ⑫ (tel: 0131-225 6671; www.royalscottishacademy.org; Mon–Sat 10am–5pm, Sun noon–5pm; free) and the **National Gallery of Scotland** ⑬ (tel: 0131-624 6200; www.nationalgalleries.org; daily 10am–5pm, Thu until 7pm; free) have been connected by an underground passageway (Weston Link), accessed off Princes Street Gardens East. Both buildings were designed by William Playfair between 1822 and 1845. The space surrounding the galleries has long been Edinburgh's version of London's Hyde Park Corner, and is heavily used by preachers, polemicists and bagpipers.

Exhibitions at the Royal Scottish Academy come and go, but the National Gallery of Scotland houses the biggest permanent collection of Old Masters outside London. There are paintings by Raphael, Rubens, El Greco, Titian, Goya, Vermeer and a clutch of superb Rembrandts. Gauguin, Cézanne, Renoir, Degas, Monet, Van

Gogh and Turner are well represented, and the gallery's Scottish collection is unrivalled. There are important paintings by Raeburn, Ramsay, Wilkie and the astonishing (and underrated) James Drummond.

At the southwest end of Princes Street is a brace of fine churches, **St John's** ⓮ (Episcopalian) and **St Cuthbert's** (Church of Scotland). St John's supports a lively congregation that is forever decking the building out with paintings in support of various global causes and animal rights. The church, a Gothic Revival building designed by William Burn in 1816, has a fine ceiling, which John Ruskin thought 'simply beautiful'.

THE NEW TOWN

What makes Edinburgh a truly world-class city, able to stand shoulder to shoulder with Prague, Amsterdam or Vienna, is the great neoclassical New Town, built in an explosion of creativity between 1767 and 1840. The New Town is the product of the Scottish Enlightenment. And no one has really been able to explain how, in the words of the historian Arthur Youngson, 'a small, crowded, almost medieval town, the capital of a comparatively poor country, expanded in a short space of time, without foreign advice or foreign assistance, so as to become one of the enduringly beautiful cities of Western Europe'.

It all began in 1752 with a pamphlet entitled *Proposals for carrying on certain Public Works in the City of Edinburgh*. It was published anonymously, but was engineered by Edinburgh's all-powerful Lord Provost (Lord Mayor), George Drummond. He was determined that Edinburgh should be a credit to the Hanoverian-ruled United Kingdom which he had helped create, and should seek to rid itself of its reputation for overcrowding, squalor, turbulence and Jacobitism.

To some extent the New Town is a political statement in stone. It is Scotland's tribute to the Hanoverian ascendancy, and many of the street names reflect the fact, as witnessed in their names: **Hanover Street,**

Princes Street Gardens.

Scottish National Gallery of Modern Art.

National Gallery of Scotland.

Cumberland Street, George Street, Queen Street, Frederick Street.

The speed with which the New Town was built is still astonishing, particularly given the sheer quality of the building. Built mainly in calciferous sandstone from Craigleith Quarry to a prize-winning layout by a 23-year-old architect/planner called James Craig, most of the more important New Town buildings were in place before the end of the century: **Register House** (1778), the north side of **Charlotte Square** (1791), the **Assembly Rooms and Music Hall** (1787), **St Andrew's Church** (1785), and most of **George Street**, **Castle Street**, **Frederick Street** and **Princes Street**.

The stinking Nor' Loch (North Loch) under the castle rock was speedily drained to make way for the 'pleasure gardens' of Princes Street. By the 1790s the New Town was the height of fashion, and the gentry of Edinburgh were abandoning their roots in the Old Town for the Georgian elegance on the other side of the newly built North Bridge.

INSIDE A NEW TOWN HOUSE

Some idea of how the gentry lived can be seen in the **Georgian House** 🄖 (tel: 0131-225 2160; daily Mar and Nov 11am–3.15pm, April–Oct 10am–4.15pm, 1–22 Dec Thu–Sun 11am–3.15pm, with exceptions) at 7 Charlotte Square (on the block designed by Robert Adam), which has been superbly restored by the National Trust for Scotland. It is crammed with the furniture, crockery, glassware, silver and paintings of the period, and even the floorboards have been dry-scrubbed in the original manner. The basement kitchen is a masterpiece of late 18th-century domestic technology.

Also in Charlotte Square is **West Register House** (part of the Scottish Record Office; tel: 0131-535 1400), which was built by Robert Reid in 1811 and began life as St George's Church. Just along George Street are the **Assembly Rooms and Music Hall** 🄖 (tel: 0131-220 4348; www.assemblyroomsedinburgh.co.uk), built in 1787 and once the focus of social life in the New Town, and still a top venue during the

festival. Across the road is the **Church of St Andrew and St George** (1785), whose oval-shaped interior witnessed the 'Great Disruption' of 1843. The Church of Scotland was split down the middle when the 'evangelicals', led by Thomas Chalmers, walked out in disgust at the complacency of the Church 'moderates' who were content to have their ministers foisted on them by the gentry (the custom in England). Chalmers went on to form the Free Church of Scotland, proclaiming a sterner but more democratic form of Presbyterianism.

Parallel to George Street lies **Queen Street**, whose only public building of interest is an eccentric Doge's Palace housing the **Scottish National Portrait Gallery** ⓱ (tel: 0131-624 6200; www.nationalgalleries.org; daily 10am–5pm; free), the world's first dedicated portrait gallery, which holds paintings of all the great Scots worthies including Mary Queen of Scots and Robert Burns..

Although **St Andrew Square** at the east end of George Street has been knocked about a bit, it is still recognisable, with the most noteworthy building in the square being the head office of the **Royal Bank of Scotland**. Originally built in 1774 as the town house of Sir Laurence Dundas, it was remodelled in the 1850s, when it acquired a quite astonishing domed ceiling with glazed star-shaped coffers. The 150ft (45-metre) -high monument in the centre of St Andrew Square is to Henry Dundas, first Viscount Melville, who was branded 'King Harry the Ninth' for his autocratic (and probably corrupt) way of running Scotland. On those rare sunny days of spring and summer it's a popular outdoor lunching spot for local office workers and often stages small outdoor exhibitions.

GEORGIAN ELEGANCE

To the north of the Charlotte Square/ St Andrew Square axis lies a huge acreage of Georgian elegance, which is probably unrivalled in Europe. Most of it is private housing and offices. Particularly worth seeing are **Heriot Row**, **Northumberland Street**, **Royal Circus**, **Ainslie Place**, **Moray Place** and **Drummond Place**. **Ann Street** ⓲ near the Water of Leith is beautiful but atypical, with its gardens and two- and three-storey buildings. Nearby **Danube Street** used to house Edinburgh's most notorious whorehouse, run by the flamboyant Dora Noyes (the house has since reverted to middle-class decency).

The **Stockbridge** area on the northern edge of the New Town is an engaging bazaar of antique shops, curiosity dealers, picture framers and second-hand bookstores, with a sprinkling of decent restaurants and pubs. The **Royal Botanic Garden** ⓳ (tel: 0131-552 7171; www.rbge.org.uk; daily Mar–Sept 10am–6pm, Nov–Jan 10am–4pm, Oct, Feb 10am–5pm; free, charge for glasshouse), half a mile (0.8km) north of Stockbridge, comprises 70 acres (28 hectares) of

The unfinished National Monument honours soldiers killed in the Napoleonic Wars.

Inside the Scottish National Portrait Gallery.

Royal Yacht Britannia.

Royal Bank of Scotland head office.

woodland, green sward, exotic trees, heather garden, rockeries, rhododendron walks, elegant zoned plant houses and a Victorian glasshouse.

Also in this area, on Belford Road, is the **Scottish National Gallery of Modern Art** ❷⓿ (tel: 0131-624 6200; www.nationalgalleries.org; daily 10am–5pm; free), with a fine permanent collection of 20th- and 21st-century art, including works by Matisse and Picasso, Magritte and Hockney. In front of the gallery is a lovely area of gardens, comprising ponds and shrubbery, as well as wonderful sculptures by the likes of Henry Moore and Barbara Hepworth. The **Dean Gallery** (daily 10am–5pm; free), in a lovely 19th-century building across the road features the Paolozzi Collection of modern art donated by the Edinburgh sculptor, major Dada and Surrealist works and temporary exhibitions.

Stevenson's Edward Hyde lurks in the New Town, too. The designers of the New Town provided it with a plethora of handsome 'pleasure gardens' which range in size from small patches of grass and shrubbery to the three Queen Street Gardens, which cover more than 11 acres (4.5 hectares). All three are closed to the public and accessible only to the 'key-holders' who live nearby. You may often see puzzled tourists shaking the gates, at a loss to understand why they are barred from ambling round the greenery.

CALTON HILL

Between 1815 and 1840 another version of the New Town grew beyond the east end of Princes Street and Waterloo Place. **Regent Terrace**, **Royal Terrace**, **Blenheim Terrace** and **Leopold Place** were its main thoroughfares.

This eastward expansion also littered the slopes of **Calton Hill** with impressive public buildings, which probably earned Edinburgh the title 'Athens of the North' (although a comparison between the two cities had been made in 1762 by the antiquarian James Stuart). On the hill are monuments to Dugald Stewart, the 18th/19th-century philosopher, and to Horatio Nelson, whose memorial in the

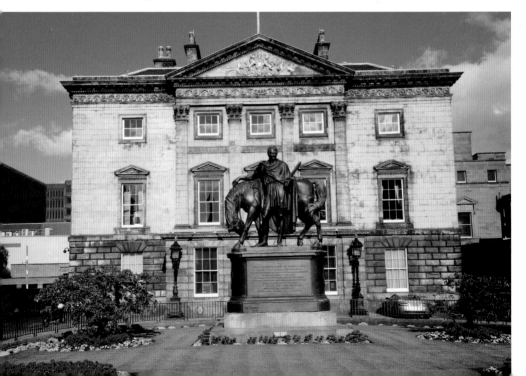

shape of a telescope may be climbed for great views; and the old **City Observatory** ㉑ where the city's Astronomical Society conducts public meetings most Friday evenings.

The oddest of the early 19th-century edifices on Calton Hill is known as 'Scotland's Disgrace'. It is a war memorial to the Scots killed in the Napoleonic Wars, which was modelled on the Parthenon in Athens. The foundation stone was laid with a great flourish during George IV's visit to Edinburgh in 1822, but the money ran out after 12 columns were erected and it remains incomplete to this day.

Beyond Calton Hill, on Regent Road, are the former **Royal High School** (called 'the noblest monument of the Scottish Greek Revival'), the **Robert Burns Monument**, modelled on the Choragic Monument of Lysicrates in Athens, and the **Old Calton Burial Ground**, with 18th- and 19th-century memorials (including one honouring the philosopher David Hume), in the lee of the empty, semi-derelict **Governor's House** of the Old Calton Jail.

MARITIME EDINBURGH

Although more ships now sail in and out of the Firth of Forth than use the Firth of Clyde, maritime Edinburgh has taken a terrible beating since the 1980s. Edinburgh's port of **Leith** ㉒ was, until recently, one of the hardest-working harbours on the east coast of Britain. The city's coastline on the Firth of Forth is studded with former fishing villages: **Granton**, **Newhaven**, **Portobello**, **Fisherrow**, and, further east, **Cockenzie**, **Port Seton** and **Prestonpans**. Ships from Leith exported coal, salt fish, paper, leather and good strong ale, and returned with (among much else) grain, timber, wine, foreign foods and Italian marble. The destinations were Hamburg, Bremen, Amsterdam, Antwerp, Copenhagen, and occasionally North America and Australia.

Right up to the mid-1960s at least four fleets of deep-sea trawlers plied out of Leith and the nearby harbour of **Granton**, and the half-Scottish, half-Norwegian firm of Christian Salvesen was still catching

On the decommissioned Royal Yacht Britannia.

Charlotte Square Gardens.

☉ EDINBURGH'S PUBS

Edinburgh's scores of 'watering holes' suggest its 478,000 residents are spoilt for choice. Yet it is an extraordinary fact of Edinburgh life that there is not one pub on the whole length of Princes Street. But affluent George Street and workaday Rose Street, a narrow and once infamous thoroughfare that runs just behind it, make up for it.

The more diverting Rose Street hostelries are the **Kenilworth** (which has a lovely ceramic-clad interior), **Dirty Dick's** and the **Abbotsford**. A favourite Edinburgh sport has been to try to get from one end of Rose Street to the other, downing half a pint of real ale or a dram in every pub, and still remain standing. On Rose Street you will also find a *howff* (meeting place) called **Milnes Bar**, which was once the haunt of 20th-century Edinburgh literati – writers like Hugh MacDiarmid and Norman MacCaig and jazz musicians such as Sandy Brown.

Live music is heard in many Edinburgh pubs today, particularly during the annual Edinburgh Jazz and Blues Festival. And the main August Festival transforms the city's pubs, which are granted extended licences to cope with the increased custom in these summer weeks. Not that drinkers here usually have a problem: ever since the relaxation of licensing regulations in 1976 genteel Edinburgh has been one of the easiest to buy a drink, with bars open well into the 'wee sma' hours'.

EDINBURGH'S MONEY MEN

Edinburgh's financial district is still going strong despite the blows of the last decade's recession, but winning back the trust of the Scottish people will take time.

Edinburgh is the second-biggest financial centre in the UK outside the City of London and one of the largest financial hubs in Europe. Until the world recession of 2008–9, Scottish investment houses managed over £500 billion in funds and one in 10 people in Scotland were employed in financial services. The huge bailout by the British taxpayer and the scandal surrounding the collapse of the Royal Bank of Scotland (resulting in the largest loss in corporate history) has given the industry a serious knock – one from which it is only slowly beginning to recover.

Just as 'the City' is shorthand for London's vast financial community, so Edinburgh's was known as 'Charlotte Square' until the 1990s, as the square and connecting George Street were the centre of the financial district. Many of the finance houses relocated to

Coins dating from the reign of Mary, Queen of Scots (1542–67), Museum on the Mound.

the Exchange Office district west of Lothian Road when they had difficulties upgrading the listed buildings, but George Street retains plush restaurants and shops, and Bute House in Charlotte Square is the official residence of Scotland's first minister. The result of the recession, however, has been unemployment and massive falls in profits, making the role of Edinburgh's moneymen decidedly shaky.

A RIGHT TO PRINT MONEY

Edinburgh's star role in the financial world can be traced back to the enthusiasm of the Scots for making and then keeping money. The Scots have always been among the modern world's best and canniest bankers. This is why the Scottish clearing banks, including Clydesdale Bank and the Royal Bank of Scotland, have a statutory right (dating from 1845) to print their own distinctive banknotes. This is a right the Scottish banks relish, particularly as the English banks were stripped of it following a string of bank failures in the 19th century; the Scots are remarkably attached to their Edinburgh-based banks.

Probably the biggest fish in Edinburgh's financial pond are the giant Scottish insurance companies, although they too saw profits reduced by the recession. The most important is the Standard Life Assurance Company, with its prominent position off Lothian Road and offices all over Britain, Ireland and Canada. Like most of the Edinburgh insurance companies, the Standard Life is a vintage operation (1825). Some are even older, with full names that have a satisfyingly old-fashioned ring, like the Scottish Widows Fund and Life Assurance Society or the Scottish Provident Institution for Mutual Life Assurance.

It was with money from Scottish investment trusts that much of the American West was built. In the 19th century, Charlotte Square was heavily into cattle ranching, fruit farming and railways in the United States. Nowadays, it prefers to sink its 'bawbees' into the high-tech industries. While Edinburgh as a whole benefited little from North Sea oil, parts of Charlotte Square did very nicely. It is time now, perhaps, for the Edinburgh financiers to exercise caution and to return to the days of thrift and Presbyterian principles in rebuilding the respect and trust of the Scottish people.

thousands of whales every year into the 1950s (which is why there is a Leith Harbour in South Georgia, which was then the world's largest whaling centre). The 2-mile (3km) stretch of shore between Leith and Granton was once littered with shipyards, ship-repair yards and dry docks. The streets of Leith itself were full of shipping agents, marine insurance firms, grain merchants, ships' chandlers, plus a burgeoning 'service sector' of dockside pubs, clubs, seedy boarding houses, bookies and brothels.

A REINVENTED LEITH

But most of this has gone. The trade has shifted to the container ports on the east coast of England, and Leith now has uneasy neighbours in the older, deprived residential areas and the increasingly up-market Shore, with 'yuppy' flats, offices and restaurants. The whole area continues to be under siege by private developers with old warehouses, office buildings, lodging houses and at least one veteran cooperage converted into high-priced flats and houses. Leith is also now home to the gigantic Scottish Executive building (with, opposite, a row of smart restaurants). In all, the port hosts a cluster of fashionable restaurants, an art gallery and, in a conversion of one of the dock-gate buildings, the successful Teuchters Landing Wine Bar.

Meanwhile, Scottish Enterprise and the local authorities have been spending millions restoring the exteriors of some of Leith's handsome commercial buildings, such as the old **Customs House**, the **Corn Exchange**, the **Assembly Building** and **Trinity House** in the Kirkgate. In Bangor Road is **Scotland's Clan Tartan Centre** (tel: 0131-553 5161; daily 9am–5.30pm; free) where, with the assistance of computers, you can learn that you, too, are a clan member.

Resident in Leith docks is the **Royal Yacht *Britannia*** (tel: 0131-555 5566; www.royalyachtbritannia.co.uk; visitor centre and yacht tours daily Apr–Oct 9.30am–4.30pm, Nov–Mar

Palm House, Royal Botanic Garden.

10am–3.30pm). Now decommissioned, it was used by the royal family for 44 years for state visits and royal holidays and was said to be the favourite 'home away from home' for the Queen. It is fascinating to see how simple and homey the private apartments are, the decor personally chosen and lined with family snapshots much as any cosy living room might be. The Grand Staircase, however, is something a little more out of the ordinary.

The old port is still worth a visit, too, if only for its powerful sense of what it used to be. And many of the buildings on **Bernard Street**, **Commercial Street**, **Constitution Street** and **The Shore** are handsome and interesting. Leith has an intriguing constitutional history, first part of Edinburgh, then a separate burgh, and then swallowed up by Edinburgh again (in 1920). Halfway up the street known as **Leith Walk** is a pub called the Bier Hoose (formerly the Boundary Bar), through which the municipal border between Edinburgh and Leith used to run.

NEWHAVEN

If ever a village has been killed by conservation it must be the little port of **Newhaven 23**, a mile west of Leith. Into the 1960s this was a brisk community, with a High Street and a Main Street lined with shops and other small businesses, through which trams, and later buses, used to trundle. But now that the picturesque houses have been 'restored' there is hardly a shop left in the place; the once-crowded Main Street is a ghostly dead end, and Newhaven harbour is occupied by a few pleasure yachts.

All of this is a great pity, because Newhaven is historically one of Edinburgh's more interesting corners. The village was founded in the late 15th century by James IV to build the *Great Michael*, then the biggest warship on earth and destined to be the flagship of a new Scottish navy. But like many such grandiose schemes – particularly those hatched in Scotland – the *Great Michael* was never a success. After the ruin of the Scots army (and the death of James IV)

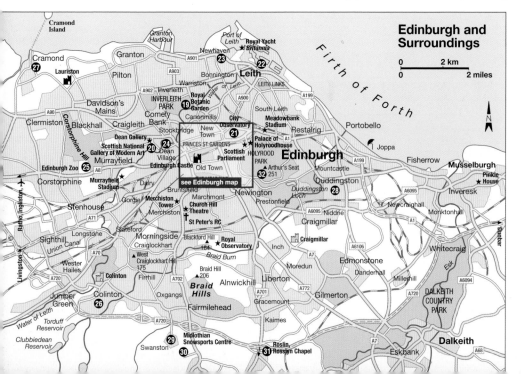

at Flodden in 1513, the great ship, which was the pride of Newhaven, was sold to the French, who left her to rot in Brest.

THE VILLAGES

Like most other cities sprawling outwards, Edinburgh has enveloped a number of villages. The most striking is probably **Dean Village** ㉔, a few minutes' walk from the West End of Princes Street. Now one of Edinburgh's more fashionable corners, Dean Village is at least 800 years old, and straddles the Water of Leith at a point that was once the main crossing on the way to Queensferry. The Incorporation of Baxters (bakers) of Edinburgh once operated 11 watermills and two flour granaries here. Its most striking building is **Well Court**, an unusual courtyard of flats built in the 1880s as housing for the poor by John Findlay, proprietor of *The Scotsman* newspaper.

Other villages that have been swallowed by the city include **Corstorphine** to the west, where the capital keeps its famous **Edinburgh Zoo** ㉕ (tel: 0131-334 9171; www.edinburghzoo.org.uk; daily Apr–Sept 10am–6pm, Oct, Mar 10am–5pm, Nov–Feb 10am–4pm), with a fine collection of penguins in the world's largest enclosure, as well as two very popular giant pandas, Tian Tian and Yang Guang, who were brought here from China in 2011 with hopes that they would breed in captivity. Ambitions were set back in 2013 when Tian Tian lost the cub she was carrying.

Colinton ㉖, in the south, features an 18th-century parish church and a wooded dell beside the Water of Leith. **Cramond** ㉗, on the Firth of Forth, used to sport an ironworks and was once the site of a Roman military camp.

Duddingston ㉘ is another interesting village, tucked under the eastern flank of Arthur's Seat, beside a small loch which is also a bird sanctuary. It has a fine Norman-style church, a 17th-century house that was used by Bonnie Prince Charlie in 1745 and Edinburgh's oldest pub, the Sheep Heid Inn. On the northern slopes of the Pentland Hills lies **Swanston** ㉙,

Leith's Shore area.

a small huddle of white-painted cottages, near where the Stevenson family used to rent Swanston Cottage as a summer residence for the sickly Robert Louis Stevenson. For some odd reason, the gardens of Swanston are adorned with statuary and ornamental stonework taken from the High Kirk of St Giles when it was being 'improved' in the 19th century.

THE HILLS OF EDINBURGH

If there is such a creature as the urban mountaineer, then Edinburgh must be his or her paradise. Like Rome, the city is built on and around seven hills, none of them very high, but all offering good stiff walks and spectacular views of the city. They are, in order of altitude, Arthur's Seat (823ft/251 metres), Braid Hill (675ft/205 metres), West Craiglockhart Hill (575ft/173 metres), Blackford Hill (539ft/162 metres), Corstorphine Hill (531ft/159 metres), Castle Hill (435ft/131 metres) and Calton Hill (328ft/98 metres).

Rosslyn Chapel, Roslin village.

In addition, Edinburgh is bounded to the south by the **Pentland Hills**, a range of amiable mini-mountains that almost (but not quite) climb to 2,000ft (600 metres). Here, too, is the **Snowsports Centre ㉚** (tel: 0131-445 4433; Mon–Sat 9.30am–9pm, Sun 9.30am–7pm), with the longest artificial ski and snowboarding slope in Britain. Non-skiers can take the lift and then a short walk to Caerketton Hill for magnificent panoramic views.

In the village of Roslin is **Rosslyn Chapel ㉛** (tel: 0131-440 2159; www.rosslynchapel.com; Mon–Sat 9.30am–5pm, Sun noon–4.45pm). It is claimed that the chapel contains the Holy Grail and other religious relics, a theory that appears in Dan Brown's best-selling book, *The Da Vinci Code*. The interior is decorated with remarkable carvings including the **Apprentice Pillar**, so called because it was carved by an apprentice stonemason while the master mason was absent. So jealous was the older mason that he killed the apprentice with a mallet.

Of the 'city-centre' hills, Calton Hill at the east end of Princes Street probably offers the best view of Edinburgh. But it is **Arthur's Seat ㉜**, that craggy old volcano in the Queen's Park, which must count as the most startling piece of urban mountainscape. It is one of the many places in Britain named after the shadowy (and possibly apocryphal) King Arthur. The area around the city was a British (Welsh) kingdom before it was overrun by the Angles and Scots.

THE OUTER CITY

Although Edinburgh may not have an inner city problem, it certainly has had its outer city difficulties. It is ringed with sprawling council estates, places like **Craigmillar** and **Niddrie**, **Alton**, **Muirhouse** and **Wester Hailes**. Some of the people who live here were decanted there from the High Street, Cowgate and Leith, and perhaps many would return if only they could find affordable housing.

THE WORLD'S BIGGEST ARTS FESTIVAL

For sheer atmosphere, bonhomie and the celebration of all things creative, from the worthy to the wacky, few things can beat the world's largest arts festival.

When the Edinburgh International Festival and Festival Fringe explode into life every August, the city, as the *Washington Post* once pointed out, becomes 'simply the best place on Earth'. Certainly the display of cultural pyrotechnics is awesome. Every concert hall, basement theatre and church hall in the centre of Edinburgh over-flows with dance groups, theatre companies, comedians, cabaret, string quartets, puppeteers, opera companies and orchestras. And for three weeks the streets of Edinburgh are awash with fire-eaters, jugglers, bagpipers, clowns, warblers, satirists and theatrical hopefuls of every shape, size and colour.

In 2018 the main Festival hosted more than 2,400 artists who performed to audiences from 84 different countries, generating £4.2 million in revenue. Edinburgh's 'alternative' festival, the Festival Fringe (both began in 1947), puts on around 3,000 events and is now the largest arts festival in the world. In 2018, the Fringe issued more than 2.8 million tickets.

Over the years the Fringe has been a nursery for new talent: Alan Bennett, Tom Stoppard, Rowan Atkinson, Billy Connolly and Emma Thompson all made their entrance into the business on the Festival Fringe. Every year the cream of artistic talent makes its way to Edinburgh, and the Fringe has grown into arguably the largest showcase for performers in the world. While the original premise of the festival might have been a promotion of straight drama, over the years stand-up comedy has become a mainstay of the event's success. The Edinburgh Comedy Award (formerly the Perrier Award) is bestowed each year on the best act, and past winners, such as Stephen Fry, Lee Evans and Alan Davies, were virtual unknowns before their festival triumphs. A major venue for stand-up comedy is the appropriately named The Stand, which expands from its flagship York Place location to a number of other venues in the immediate area to cope with the high demand.

Venues, big and small, are pressed into service – in 2012 even a public toilet area was used. There are, however, some that are stalwarts: the Assembly Rooms on George Street and Assembly Hall on the Mound are the most long-standing, while the Pleasance, just off the Royal Mile, turns into a complex of stages and beer gardens for the heady month of August. Bristo Square becomes Udderbelly, a vast tent in the shape of a reclining cow and one of the festival's largest spaces.

The large festival programme brochure and ticket sales usually start in June, with some of the famous name shows being booked up within hours through online bookings. The central place for in-person ticket sales is The Hub, on Castlehill, although of course tickets can be purchased on the day at each venue subject to availability.

A 'fringe' of the Fringe has evolved, which includes about 10 other festivals throughout the year, including the stunning Edinburgh Military Tattoo and the Edinburgh Book Fair. Just prior to the Fringe is Edinburgh's Jazz and Blues Festival, at the end of July.

Nobody should think about attending the festival, however, without a bit of forward planning, particularly with regards to accommodation. Even the humblest B&B can be booked up months in advance and prices are, inevitably, hiked up for the month. Restaurants fill up quickly too, but you'll never go hungry: the city is packed with street-food stands.

Motorcycle stunt riders at the Edinburgh Festival.

OLD AND NEW TOWN ARCHITECTURE

Declared a Unesco World Heritage Site in 1995, the centre of Edinburgh is a fascinating juxtaposition of medieval confusion and classical harmony, cobbled streets and grand Georgian charm.

Architecturally, Edinburgh's Old and New Towns are utterly disparate. In the Old, everything is higgledy-piggledy; in the New – now more than 200 years old – order and harmony prevail.

The Old Town lies to the south of Princes Street Gardens. Its backbone is the Royal Mile, described by the writer Daniel Defoe in the 1720s as 'perhaps the largest, longest and finest Street for Buildings, and Number of Inhabitants...in the world'. Then it was lined with tall, narrow tenements, some with as many as 14 storeys, where aristocracy, merchants and lowly clerks all rubbed shoulders in friendly familiarity in dark stairways, and through which ran a confusing maze of wynds (alleys), courts and closes.

The Georgian House on Charlotte Square.

A NEW ORDER

In 1766 James Craig, an unknown 23-year-old, won a competition for the design of the New Town. His submission was a 'gridiron' consisting of two elegant squares – Charlotte and St Andrew – linked by three wide, straight, parallel streets: Princes, George and Queen. Robert and John Adam, Sir William Chambers and John Henderson, premier architects of the day, all contributed plans for glorious Georgian buildings. During the first part of the 19th century, the New Town was extended by the addition of an extraordinary grouping of squares, circuses, terraces, crescents and parks, all maintaining the neoclassical idiom and permitting the New Town to boast the largest area of Georgian architecture in all Europe.

The Covenanters Memorial and Old Town houses at the top of the Grassmarket.

Cannongate Tolbooth.

A fan window, Georgian neoclassical detail in Charlotte Square.

Stepping inside the past

Two of the finest examples of Edinburgh's Old and New Town architecture have been restored to their former glory and are open to visitors, thanks to the National Trust for Scotland (NTS), a charity founded in 1931 to promote the conservation of landscape and of historic buildings.

The Georgian House in Charlotte Square evokes elegant living in the New Town: it has been beautifully furnished to show how a wealthy family lived in the 18th century. Gladstone's Land on the Old Town's Royal Mile is a skilful restoration of a merchant's house. The six floors behind its narrow frontage were once occupied by five families, an example of a 17th-century Edinburgh skyscraper. The arcaded ground floor has been restored to its original function as a shopping booth.

Gladstone's Land.

Old Tolbooth Wynd off the Royal Mile.

Ironwork in Charlotte Square.

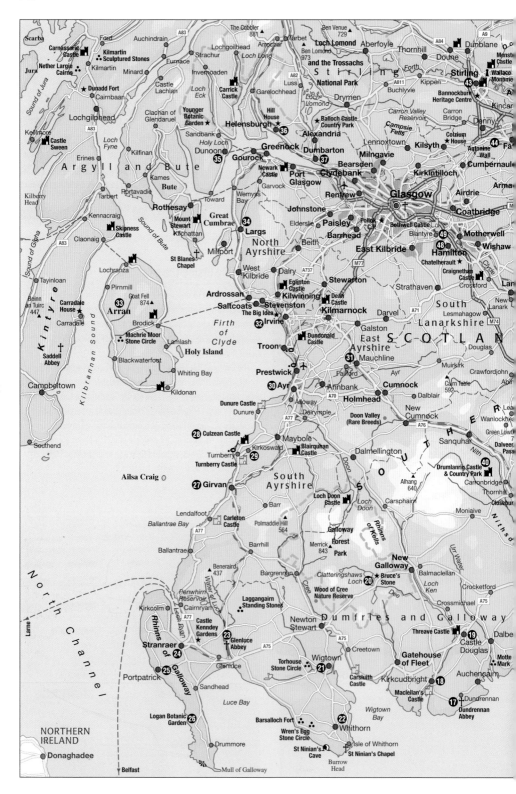

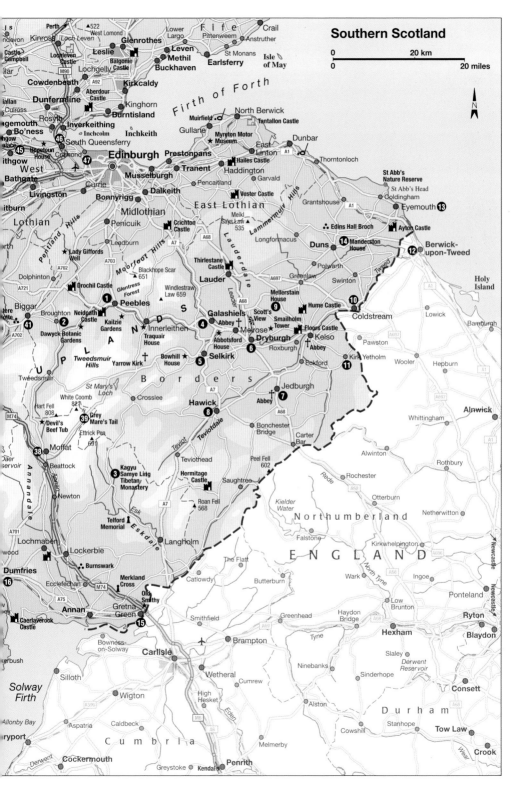

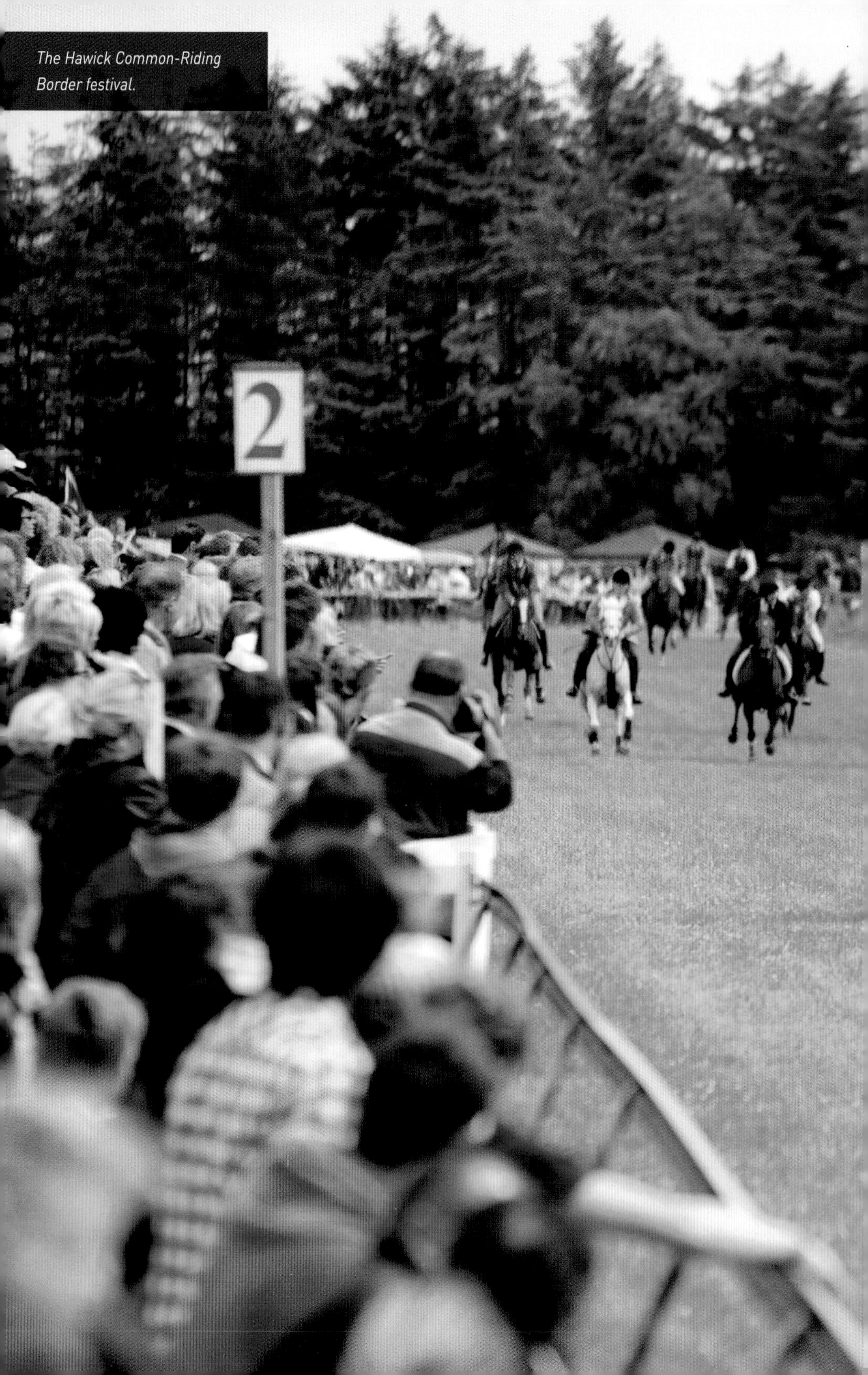

The Hawick Common-Riding Border festival.

The Eildon Hills.

THE BORDERS

Castles, ruined abbeys, baronial mansions and evidence of past turbulent struggles against the English give the green, rolling hills of the Borders a romance all of their own.

There's a mistaken assumption that, compared with all those northerly lochs and glens, rushing rivers and barren moors, the Borders have only marginal appeal. In reality this area of proud rugby-loving communities enjoys stunning scenery and a reputation for world-class mountain biking and fishing. Administratively, the Borders include the four 'shires' of Peebles and Berwick in the north (though Berwick-upon-Tweed is in England) and Selkirk and Roxburgh in the south.

PEEBLES

Directly south of Edinburgh, the town of **Peebles ❶** owes much of its charm to its Tweedside location. Here the river already runs wide and fast. Peebles' central thoroughfare is equally wide but much more sedate. Peebles was never renowned for its hustle and bustle; an 18th-century aristocrat coined an ungenerous simile: 'As quiet as the grave – or Peebles.' This is certainly not true in June when things liven up with the week-long 'Riding of the Marches' Beltane festival, a Celtic celebration of the sun marking the beginning of summer.

The **Cross Kirk** was erected in 1261 after the discovery of a large cross on this site. The remains include a 15th-century tower and foundations of a cloister and monastic buildings. St Andrew's

Neidpath Castle.

Collegiate Church, the forerunner of the Cross Kirk, sits in a cemetery on the Glasgow Road. Here, too, only a tower remains; the rest was burned by the English at the time of the sacking of the four great Border abbeys. At the bottom of Peebles High Street, the Gothic outline of Peebles Parish Church adds to the town's air of sobriety.

The **Chambers Institute**, Peebles' civic centre and home of the **Tweeddale Museum**, was a gift to the town from William Chambers, a native of the place and the founding publisher

⊙ Main attractions

Traquair House
Bowhill House & Country Park
Abbotsford House
Dryburgh Abbey
Melrose
Jedburgh
Kelso
Floors Castle
Mellerstain House
Berwick-upon-Tweed

Map on page 140

Robert Smail's Printing Works in Innerleithen (Apr–Oct tours Mon, Fri & Sat 11.30am, 2pm & 3.30pm; Sun 1.30pm & 3.30pm) is a working museum, on the A72, with early 20th-century machinery and equipment, including a restored waterwheel. Visitors can watch the printer at work and can try their hand at typesetting.

Rhododendron opening at Kailzie Gardens.

of Chambers's Encyclopaedia. It's also home to the **John Buchan Centre**, a museum dedicated to the author of the classic *The Thirty-Nine Steps* and who eventually became governor general of Canada (tel: 01721-723 525; www.johnbuchanstory.co.uk; Apr–Oct Mon–Sat 10am–4.30pm).

FOLLOWING THE TWEED

Just a few minutes out of Peebles (west on the A72), perched high on a rocky bluff overlooking the Tweed, **Neidpath Castle** (01721-720 333; open days only, check www.nedpethcastle.com) is a well-preserved example of the many medieval tower houses in the region. William Wordsworth visited in 1803 and wrote a famous poem lamenting the desolation caused in 1795 when the absentee landowner, the fourth duke of Queensberry, cut down all the trees for money to support his extravagant London lifestyle. Wordsworth would have been happier had he journeyed 8 miles (13km) southwest of Peebles on the B712 to the **Dawyck Botanic Garden** (tel: 01721-760 254; www.rbge.org.

uk; Feb–Nov daily from 10am, closure varies according to the season), an out station of Edinburgh's Royal Botanic Garden, containing some of the oldest and tallest trees in Europe.

Continue via the B712 to **Broughton ②**, the site of **Broughton Place**, an imposing 20th-century castellated house that looks much older. The writer John Buchan grew up in this village, and apparently frequented the **Crook Inn**, just outside **Tweedsmuir**, 15 miles (24km) south of Broughton. Now owned by the Tweedsmuir Community, whose plans to renovate it have stalled, the pub is one of the oldest Border coaching inns, and has strong literary associations. Robert Burns was inspired to write his poem '*Willie Wastle's Wife*' in the kitchen (now the bar). Sir Walter Scott also visited, as did James Hogg, the poet known locally as 'The Ettrick Shepherd'.

Step southwards outside the Borders towards Eskdalemuir, and you'll be greeted by a real surprise: the **Kagyu Samye Ling Tibetan Monastery ③** (tel: 01387-373 232; www.samyeling.org;

⊙ BORDER COUNTRY

The River Tweed has inspired romantic Borders ballads for hundreds of years and was considered by Sir Walter Scott to be the most precious river in the world. Its source is just a few miles south of the village of Tweedsmuir, and the river cuts through three of the most important Border towns: Peebles, Melrose and Kelso. Here, too, you will find rugged moorland and craggy terrain, reminiscent of the Scottish Highlands. The two highest points in the Borders, Broad Law and Dollar Law, rise to more than 2,750ft (840 metres) and 2,680ft (820 metres) respectively.

Draw a line between Hawick and Broughton and then stay south of it and you will see the best the Borders have to offer. A popular route is the side road out of Tweedsmuir up to the Talla and Megget Reservoirs. Steep slopes and rock-strewn hillsides provide a stunning panorama as you twist and turn down to the A708 where you come to St Mary's Loch, the only loch in the Borders, which is rich in pike for those who want a fishing challenge. If you love a good hike, follow the Southern Upland Way alongside the loch north across the moors to Traquair House. Alternatively, walk south to the valley of Ettrick Water, either way experiencing a wealth of local wildlife and, in spring, carpets of wildflowers.

temple daily 6am–9pm). Founded in 1967 for study, retreat and meditation, it's the first and largest Tibetan centre and Buddhist monastery in the West. Visitors, regardless of faith, can join free tours (booking in advance essential) around the centre's facilities.

East of Peebles on the road to Innerleithen, you will find **Kailzie Gardens** (tel: 01721-720 007; www.kailziegardens. com; Apr–Oct daily 10am–5pm, Nov–Mar wild garden and woodland walks only during daylight hours) adding to the beauty of the Tweed Valley with a formal walled garden, greenhouses and woodland walks. They've also got an Osprey viewing centre here too.

At Innerleithen on the A72 is **Traquair House** (tel: 01896-830 323; www. traquair.co.uk; daily Apr–June & Sept 11am–5pm, July & Aug 10am–5pm, Oct 11am–4pm, Nov Sat–Sun 11am–3pm), Scotland's oldest continually inhabited house (since 1107), where Mary, Queen of Scots stayed with her husband Lord Darnley in 1566. After Bonnie Prince Charlie visited in 1745, the fifth earl of Traquair closed the Bear Gates after

him and swore they would not open until a Stuart king had been restored to the throne; the wide avenue from the house to the gates has been disused ever since. As well as visiting the 19 rooms of the house, there are surrounding gardens that include a hedge maze, crafts shops and a tearoom.

HEART OF THE BORDERS

Though it has little to tempt today's visitor, **Galashiels ④**, on the A7 just over 30 miles (50 km) from Edinburgh, has played a pivotal role in the Borders' economy as a weaving town for more than 700 years. The School of Textiles and Design, founded in 1909, has helped to cement the reputation of the tartans, tweeds, woollens and other knitted materials sold in the mills here.

It is not only Galashiels that lets you sample the Borders' textiles. A further 7 miles (11km) south, **Selkirk ⑤** became a textile centre in the 19th century when the growing demand for tweed could no longer be met by the mills of Galashiels. Visit **Lochcarron**

Sir Walter Scott wrote all the Waverley novels at Abbotsford House, but only admitted to being the author late in life, feeling that it wasn't 'decorous' for a Clerk of Session to be seen writing novels.

Traquair House.

The heart of Robert the Bruce is said to be buried near the high altar in Melrose Abbey, but excavations have failed to locate any trace of it.

The ruins of Dryburgh Abbey.

of Scotland at the Waverley Mill in Dunsdale Road (tel: 01750-726 100; www.lochcarron.co.uk; Mon–Sat 9am–5pm; conducted mill tours Mon–Thu 10.30am, 11.30am, 1.30pm and 2.30pm). Other than shopping, there are several interesting places to visit, including the 18th-century **Halliwell's House Museum** (tel: 01750-20054; Easter–Oct Mon–Sat 11am–4pm, Sun noon–3pm; free), a former ironmongers which now tells the story of Selkirk in entertaining detail.

SIR WALTER SCOTT CONNECTIONS

Nearby is **Sir Walter Scott's Courtroom** (tel: 01750 726456; Apr & Sept Mon–Fri 10am–4pm, Sat 11am–3pm, May–Aug Mon–Fri 10am–4pm, Sat–Sun 11am–3pm, Oct Mon–Sat noon–3pm; free) where the great writer dispensed justice during his 35 years as sheriff here.

Don't leave the locality without visiting **Bowhill House and Country Park** (tel: 01750-22204; www.bowhill. org; house tour dates vary, check the website; country estate Apr–June, Sept Fri–Sun 10am–5pm, Jul–Aug daily 10am–5pm), west of Selkirk on the A708. Bowhill is the home of the Scotts of Buccleuch and Queensberry, once one of the largest landowners of all the Border clans. More than 300 years of discerning art collecting has amassed works by great painters such as Canaletto, Guardi, Raeburn, Reynolds and Gainsborough.

A few miles south of Galashiels off the A7 is **Abbotsford House** (tel: 01896-752 043; www.scottsabbotsford. co.uk; daily Apr–Oct 10am–5pm, Mar, Nov 10am–4pm). If the Borders have a sort of visitors' Mecca, then Abbotsford House undoubtedly lays claim to that title. Scott spent £50,000 and the rest of his life turning a small farm into an estate befitting his position as a Border laird.

Scott was buried at **Dryburgh ⑥**, one of the four great 12th-century abbeys in the Borders (tel: 01835-822 381; daily 9.30am–5.30pm, Oct–Mar 10am–4pm). While the ruins at Jedburgh, Kelso and Melrose lie near the

edge of their respective towns, Dryburgh, founded by Hugh de Morville for monks from Alnwick in Northumberland, is tucked away in an idyllic location among trees by the edge of the Tweed.

Dryburgh's setting is no match for **Scott's View** on the B6356, from where there is a magnificent sweeping view of the unmistakable triple peaks of the **Eildon Hills** (reputed to be the legendary sleeping place of King Arthur and his knights) and a wide stretch of the Tweed Valley. Scott came here many times to enjoy the panorama.

MELROSE ABBEY

The town of **Melrose,** between Dryburgh and Galashiels, escaped much of the industrialisation that affected Selkirk, Hawick and Galashiels. **Melrose Abbey** (tel: 01896-822 562; daily 9.30am–5.30pm, Oct–Mar 10am–4pm) seals the town's pedigree. The abbey was founded in 1136 by King David I, who helped to found all four of the great Border abbeys, and this was the first Cistercian monastery in Scotland.

Tragically, it lay in the path of repeated English invasions long before Henry VIII made his presence felt in the 16th century. An attack in 1322 by Edward II prompted Robert Bruce to fund its restoration, and it is believed that his heart is buried in the abbey.

Also in Melrose is **Priorwood Garden** (tel: 01896-209 504; Apr–Oct Mon–Sat 10am–5pm), a walled garden specialising in plants suitable for drying, and the **Trimontium Museum** (tel: 01896-822 561; www.trimontium.co.uk; Apr–Oct Mon–Sat 10.30am–4.30pm) outlining the Roman occupation of the area. Melrose is the starting point of the 60-mile (100km) **St Cuthbert's Way** walk to Lindisfarne (Holy Island) and, every April, hosts the Melrose (rugby) Sevens Tournament.

North of Melrose, on the outskirts of **Lauder**, is **Thirlestane Castle** (tel: 01578-722 430; www.thirlestanecastle.co.uk; May–Sept Sun–Thu 10am–4pm), once the seat of the Earls of Lauderdale and still owned by their descendants. It is one of Scotland's oldest castles and has renowned 17th-century plaster ceilings.

Collection of armoury at Abbotsford House.

JEDBURGH

Following the A68 south from Galashiels for 18 miles (29 km) brings you to **Jedburgh ❼** – historically the most important of the Border towns. It was also strategically important; as the first community across the border it often bore the full brunt of invading English armies. Earlier invaders came from even further afield: 2 miles (3km) north of Jedburgh one can follow the course of Dere Street, the road the Romans built in southern Scotland more than 1,900 years ago.

Elaborate stonework around the entrance of Jedburgh Abbey.

The oldest surviving building, **Jedburgh Abbey** (tel: 01835-863 925; daily 9.30am–5.30pm, Oct–Mar daily 10am–4pm), was founded in 1138 by Augustinian canons from northern France. Stonework in the abbey's museum dates from the first millennium AD and proves that the site had much older religious significance. Malcolm IV was crowned here, and Alexander III married his second wife in the abbey in 1285. Their wedding feast was held at nearby Jedburgh Castle, which occupied a site in Castlegate, though it was demolished

Floors Castle is the largest inhabited castle in Scotland.

in 1409 to keep it out of English hands. In 1823 the **Castle Gaol** (tel: 01835 864 750; Apr–Oct Mon–Sat 10am–4.30pm, Sun 1–4pm; free) was built on the castle's foundations; its museum of social history is well worth a visit.

MARY, QUEEN OF SCOTS

Near the High Street, displays in **Mary, Queen of Scots' House** (tel: 01835-863 331; Apr–Oct Mon–Sat 9.30am–5.30pm, Sun 10am–3pm, Mar & Nov Sun 10am–3pm; free) tell a short but crucial chapter in Scotland's history. It was in this house in late 1566 that Queen Mary spent several weeks recovering from a serious illness after her renowned dash on horseback to Hermitage Castle to see her injured lover James Hepburn, earl of Bothwell. Her ride resulted in a scandal that was made all the worse by the murder of her husband Darnley the following February. From then on, her downfall was steady. Years later, during her 19 years of imprisonment, Mary regretted that her life hadn't ended in the Borders: 'Would that I had died in Jedburgh.'

HAWICK TO KELSO

If you decide to retrace Mary's journey to **Hermitage Castle**, 23 miles (37 km) south of Jedburgh, you're likely to pass through **Hawick ❽** (pronounced *Hoik*). The Borders' textile industry is all around you here, not least at the **Hawico Factory Visitor Centre** (01450 371 221; Mon–Sat 9.30am–5pm; free). At the **Hawick Museum** in **Wilton Lodge Park** (tel: 01450 364 747; Apr–Sept Mon–Fri 10am–noon, 1–5pm, Sat–Sun 2–5pm, Oct–Mar Mon–Fri noon–3pm, Sun 1–3pm; free) a fascinating collection of exhibits picks up older sartorial threads.

Still retaining its cobbled streets leading into a spacious square, **Kelso**, 10 miles (16km) east of Dryburgh, is one of the most picturesque Border towns. Close to the town centre is **Kelso Abbey**, once the largest and richest of the Borders' abbeys, though it suffered the same fate as those at Melrose, Jedburgh and Dryburgh and is today the least complete of all of them.

It is ironic that, while the English destroyed Kelso's abbey, the Scottish were responsible for the much greater devastation of the nearby town of **Roxburgh** and its castle. Roxburgh had grown up on the south bank of the Tweed around the mighty fortress of Marchmount. An important link in the chain of border fortifications, Marchmount controlled the gateway to the north, but in the 14th century the English took Roxburgh and its castle and used it as a base for further incursions into Scottish territory. In 1460 James II of Scotland attacked Marchmount but was killed by a bursting cannon. His widow urged the Scottish troops forward.

On achieving victory they destroyed Roxburgh's castle (to make sure it stayed out of enemy hands for good) with a thoroughness that the English would have found hard to match. Today, on a mound between the Teviot and the Tweed just west of Kelso (the plain village of Roxburgh a few miles on is no direct relation of the ancient town) only fragments of Marchmount's walls survive.

FLOORS CASTLE

On the north bank of the Tweed, Kelso thrived, however. **Floors Castle** (tel: 01573-223 333; Apr–Sept daily 10.30am–5pm, Oct Sat & Sun 10.30am–5pm; www.floorscastle.com) was designed by Robert Adam and built between 1721 and 1726, though it owes its present flamboyant appearance to William Playfair, who remodelled and extended the castle between 1837 and 1845. An outstanding collection of German, Italian and French furniture, Chinese and Dresden porcelain, paintings by Picasso, Matisse and Augustus John, and a 15th-century Brussels tapestry are some of the many glittering prizes that give Floors an air of palatial elegance. There is also a licensed restaurant and coffee shop.

Interior of Floors Castle.

Jedburgh.

Berwick bridge spans the River Tweed.

Smailholm Tower (tel: 01573-460 365; Apr–Sept daily 9.30am–5.30pm) stands gaunt and foreboding 6 miles (10km) northwest of Kelso (B6404). Walter Scott made a deal with the owner of this superb 16th-century peel tower: in exchange for saving it, Scott would write a ballad, '*The Eve of St John*', about it. Today, the stern-faced fortress is a museum of costume figures and tapestries relating to Scott's *Minstrelsy of the Borders*.

MELLERSTAIN HOUSE

Northwest from Kelso on the A6089 is **Mellerstain House ➒** (tel: 01573-410 225; www.mellerstain.com; May–Sept Fri–Mon noon–5pm, last entry 4.15pm, grounds open at 11am), one of Scotland's finest Georgian mansions and the product of the combined genius of William Adam and his son Robert. Externally it has the dignity, symmetry and well-matched proportions characteristic of the period. Inside there is furniture by Chippendale, Sheraton and Hepplewhite; paintings by Gainsborough, Constable, Veronese and Van Dyck; and some exquisite moulded plaster ceilings, door heads and light fittings. As if all this weren't enough to impress, formal Italian gardens were laid out in 1909 to create a series of gently sloping terraces, and the house became a popular venue for fashionable dances.

NATIONAL BORDER

East of Kelso the Tweed marks the natural boundary between England and Scotland. **Coldstream ➓**, one of the last towns on this river before Berwick, has little to offer the visitor other than history. The town's name was taken by the famous regiment of Coldstream Guards that was formed by General Monck in 1659 before he marched south to support the restoration of the Stuart monarchy. The regiment today loans material to the **Coldstream Museum** (tel: 01890-882 630; Easter–Sept Mon–Sat 9.30am–12.30pm, 1–4pm, Sun 2–4pm, Oct Mon–Sat 1–4pm; free), set up in a house that was Monck's headquarters.

Nearly 150 years earlier, in 1513, James IV of Scotland crossed the Tweed at Coldstream to attack the English with a much larger force. Though Henry VIII was at that time fighting in France (James IV's invasion was a diversion intended to aid the French) an English army was sent north to meet the threat. The encounter, which took place near the English village of Branxton but was known as the Battle of Flodden, was a military disaster for Scotland: the king, his son, and as many as 46 nobles and 9,000 men were slain.

Happier endings are to be had at **Kirk Yetholm ⓫**, just 1 mile (1.6km) away from the English border. Overlooking the village green, the Border Hotel bills itself as the 'End of the Pennine Way'. A few miles outside, **Linton Kirk**, said to be the oldest building in continuous use for Christian worship in the area, sits proudly

on a hummock of sand in a picturesque valley.

BERWICK-UPON-TWEED

When it comes to identifying precise borderlines, **Berwick-upon-Tweed** ⑫ can be forgiven for feeling a little confused. Boundaries around here lack a sense of fair play: Berwick is not part of Berwickshire. And although the town takes its name from a river that has its source in the Scottish Borders, Berwick-upon-Tweed is not part of Scotland. It's in Northumberland, England, though it wasn't always like that. The town changed hands 13 times between 1147 and 1482 (when it was finally taken for England by Richard, duke of Gloucester – later Richard III).

Historically Berwick is very much a part of the Borders. The town's castle, built in the late 12th century by Henry II, once towered high above the Tweed. Much of it was demolished in 1847 to make space for the railway station, which bears an appropriate inscription by Robert Stevenson: 'The Final Act Of Union'. Berwick's town wall, built on the orders of Edward I, has fared better and is one of the most complete of its kind in Britain.

Situated in Scotland, along the coast just north of Berwick, **Eyemouth** ⑬ is a small working fishing town whose **museum** (tel: 01890-751 701; www.eyemouthmuseum.org; Apr–Oct Mon–Sat 11am–4pm) vividly outlines Eyemouth's long tradition as a fishing port. The museum's centrepiece is the Eyemouth Tapestry, made by local people in 1981 to commemorate the disaster of 1881 when 189 fishermen were drowned, all within sight of land, during a storm.

A few miles north, **Coldingham's Medieval Priory** and **St Abb's Head National Nature Reserve** (tel: 01890 771443; daily; free) are two further justifications for making this detour off the A1 to Edinburgh. An alternative route to Edinburgh is the A6105/A697. If you do go this way, stop at **Manderston House** ⑭ (tel: 01361 883 450; www.manderston.co.uk; May–Sept Thu and Sun, house 1.30–5pm, gardens 11.30am–dusk), just outside Duns, to enjoy 'the finest Edwardian country house in Scotland'.

Mellerstain House.

📷 HISTORIC CASTLES AND ABBEYS

It is often said that an Englishman's home is his castle, but with Scotland's impressive array of castles – some inhabited to this day – the saying might be better applied to the Scots.

Dotted throughout the Scottish landscape are more than 2,000 castles, many in ruins but others in splendid condition. The latter, still occupied, do not fulfil the primary definition of 'castle' – a fortified building – but rather meet the secondary definition: a magnificent house, such as Fyvie.

Either way, all are not merely part of Scottish history: they are its essence. Many carry grim and grisly tales. Thus, Hugh Macdonald was imprisoned in the bowels of Duntulm Castle and fed generous portions of salted beef, but he was denied anything – even whisky – to drink.

In 1746 Blair Castle was, on the occasion of the Jacobite uprising, the last castle in the British Isles to be fired upon in anger. Today, the Duke of Atholl, the owner of Blair Castle, is the only British subject permitted to maintain a private army, the Atholl Highlanders. Prior to the siege, Bonnie Prince Charlie slept here (visitors might be excused for believing there are few castles in Scotland where the Bonnie Prince and Mary, Queen of Scots did not sleep).

You, too, can sleep in Scottish castles. Culzean, Dalhousie (both Queen Victoria and Sir Walter Scott visited here) and Inverlochy all have rooms to let. And, for those eager to become a laird, don the kilt and own a castle, several are invariably on the market.

This tranquil view of 15th-century Blackness Castle belies its formidable past. Garrison fortress and former state prison, it served to protect the port and Royal Burgh of Linlithgow.

Completed in 1511, the Great Hall of Edinburgh Castle was designed for ceremonial use but was relegated to a barracks after Oliver Cromwell's invasion of 1650. It was finally restored in 1880.

Stained glass at Stirling Castle, once called "the key to Scotland" because of its strategic position between the Lowlands and Highlands. It became a favourite residence of Stuart monarchs. Nowadays it is also the home of the regimental museum of the Argyll and Sutherland Highlanders.

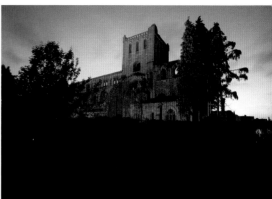

Jedburgh Abbey ruins.

Scottish Border abbeys

Scotland, especially the Borders, is full of abbeys that now lie ruined but were once powerful institutions with impressive buildings. During the reign of David I (1124–53), who revitalised and transformed the Scottish Church, more than 20 religious houses were founded. Outstanding among these is a quartet of Border abbeys – Dryburgh (Premonstratensian), Jedburgh (Augustinian), Kelso (Tironensian) and Melrose (Cistercian). All have evocative ruins, though perhaps it is Jedburgh, with its tower and remarkable rose window still intact, that is Scotland's classic abbey.

It was not the Reformation (1560) that caused damage to these abbeys but rather the selfishness of the pre-Reformation clergy, raids from the 14th through 16th centuries by both English and Scots, the ravages of weather, and activities of 19th-century restorers. The concern of the Reformation, spearheaded by firebrand John Knox, was to preserve, not to destroy, the churches they needed.

Monasteries continued to exist as landed corporations after the Reformation. Why upset a system that suited so many interests? After all, the Pope, at the king's request, had provided priories and abbeys for five of James V's bastards while they were still infants.

Nestling in the beautiful Perthshire countryside, Blair Castle is the ancient seat of the Dukes and Earls of Atholl. Now a top visitor attraction, its long history stretches back to the 13th century.

Once upheld as the finest example of French Renaissance architecture in Scotland, Earl Patrick's Palace in Kirkwall (Orkney) was built in 1600 by Patrick Stewart using slave labour. Along with his father, Robert Stewart, the pair are the most tyrannical earls in Scotland's history.

The four major Border abbeys are reduced to ruins.

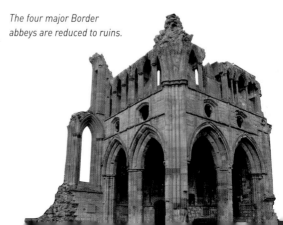

Lighthouse and harbour of Portpatrick.

SACRED
TO THE MEMORY OF
William Burns
FARMER in LOCHLIE,
who died on the 13th Feb' 1784,
in the 63d year of his age.
AND OF
Agnes Brown
HIS SPOUSE
who died on the 14th Jan' 1820,
in the 88th year of her age.
She was interred in Bolton Churchyard
East Loth.

THE SOUTHWEST

The Southwest is gentle country, with scattered farms and villages and a dense concentration of literary associations. Its colourful and sometimes brutal history belies the beauty of the land, which sweeps down to a beautiful coastline.

In the landscape and seascapes of Southwest Scotland, in the pretty villages of Dumfries and Galloway and the hill farms of South Lanarkshire, in the industrial townships of Ayrshire and the ports and holiday resorts of the Clyde coast, you will find something of the rest of Scotland. All that is missing, perhaps, is the inspiring grandeur of the West Highlands. The **Galloway Hills** are lonely, lovely places in their own right, but none rises to more than 2,800ft (850 metres).

Yet travellers from England often bypass the pastoral hinterland of the Solway in their scamper up the M74 to points north and the Highlands, hesitating only at a place that is legendary for just one reason. **Gretna Green** ⑮, just over the border (until the boundary between England and Scotland was agreed in 1552, this area was known simply as the Debatable Land), became celebrated for celebrating marriages. It was the first available community where eloping couples from England could take advantage of Scotland's different marriage laws.

Plenty of makeshift ceremonies have been performed at the **Old Black-smith's**, which is now a visitor centre (tel: 01461-338 441; www.gretnagreen.com; daily 9am–5pm; free), with exhibits telling the story of the town's claim to fame. You can still tie the knot here,

like many a romantic bride and Gretna FC football fan, who still choose to be married at Gretna Green today.

A few miles to the north is **Ecclefechan**, where the pretty white **Thomas Carlyle's Birthplace** (tel: 01556 502575; April–Oct daily 10am–5pm), in which the man of letters was born in 1795, is now a modest literary shrine. But the Southwest is more inescapably identified with the poet Robert Burns, whose short life and legend remains an integral part of the Scottish tourist scene.

Main attractions
Dumfries
Galloway Forest Park
Isle of Whithorn
Culzean Castle
Robert Burns Birthplace
  Museum
Scottish Maritime
  Museum
Arran
Island of Bute
Drumlanrig Castle
New Lanark

Map on page 140

Wedding at Gretna Green.

DUMFRIES

The urban centres of the Burns industry are Dumfries, 'the Queen of the South', and Ayr. Located 77 miles (124km) south of Glasgow on the A75, **Dumfries** ⓰ is an ancient and important Border town whose character survives the unsightly housing estates and factories on its periphery, and which is within easy reach of the haunting, history-rich Solway coast. Burns, the farmer-poet, took over Ellisland Farm some 6 miles (10km) outside the town in 1788, built the farmhouse and tried to introduce new farming methods. His venture collapsed and he moved to Dumfries to become an exciseman, but **Ellisland** (tel: 01387-740 426; www.ellislandfarm. co.uk; Apr–Sept Mon–Sat 10am–1pm, 2–5pm, Sun 2–5pm, Oct–Mar Tue–Sat 10am–1pm, 2–5pm), where he wrote 'Tam o'Shanter' and 'Auld Lang Syne', is now a museum. So is **Burns House** (tel: 01387-255 297; Apr–Sept Mon–Sat 10am–5pm, Sun 2–5pm; Oct–Mar Tue–Sat 10am–1pm, 2–5pm; free) in Mill Vennel (now Burns Street), Dumfries, where he died in 1796 at the age of 37.

There is more excellent Burns memorabilia at the **Robert Burns Centre** (tel: 01387-264 808; www.rbcft.co.uk; Apr–Sept Mon–Sat 10am–5pm, Sun 2–5pm; Oct–Mar Tue–Sat 10am–1pm, 2–5pm; free), located inside the old stone mill on the River Nith

AROUND DUMFRIES

The handsome waterfront of the **River Nith**, with its 15th-century bridge, and the red sandstone dignity of nearby **St Michael's Church**, in whose churchyard Burns is buried, give Dumfries its distinctive character. Its environs have just as much to offer. On opposing banks of the Nith estuary, where it debouches into the Solway, are **Caerlaverock Castle** (tel: 01387-770 244; daily Apr–Sept 9.30am–5.30pm, Oct–Mar 10am–4pm), the **Wildfowl and Wetlands Trust Reserve** (tel: 01387-770 200; daily 10am–5pm) – a winter haunt of wildfowl – and **Sweetheart Abbey** (tel: 01387-850 397; Apr–Sept daily 9.30am–5.30pm, Oct–Mar Sat–Wed, 10am–4pm).

The castle is strikingly well preserved, dates back to the 13th

Burns House.

century and was the seat of the Max-well family, later earls of Nithsdale – one of the most powerful local dynasties. It was besieged by Edward I during the Wars of Independence and in 1640 fell to a 13-week siege mounted by the Covenanters (see page 36).

The graceful ruin of Sweetheart Abbey, in the pretty village of New Abbey, is a monument to the marital devotion of the noble Devorgilla Balliol, who not only founded this Cistercian abbey in 1273 but also established Balliol College, Oxford, in memory of her husband. She also carried his heart around with her until her own death in 1290, when she and the heart were buried together in front of the high altar.

The shallow estuary of the Solway is noted for the speed of its tidal race and the treachery of its sands; but the hazardous areas are well signposted, and if you follow the coastal roads from River Nith to **Loch Ryan** you will find an amiable succession of villages, yachting harbours, attractive small towns and good beaches, not to mention many secret coves and snug, deserted little bays.

ANCIENT GALLOWAY

This is the ancient territory of Galloway, whose people once fraternised with Norse raiders and whose lords preserved a degree of independence from the Scottish crown until the 13th century. Many of Scotland's great names and great causes have seen action among these hills and bays. At **Dundrennan Abbey** ⑰ (tel: 01557 500 262; Apr–Sept daily 9.30am–5.30pm), 7 miles (11km) southeast of Kirkcudbright on the A711, Mary, Queen of Scots is believed to have spent her last night in Scotland, on 15 May 1568, sheltering in this 12th-century Cistercian house on her final, fatal flight from the Battle of Langside to her long imprisonment in England.

Kirkcudbright ⑱ (pronounced *Kir-koo-bree*), at the mouth of the River Dee, has the reputation of being the most attractive of the Solway towns, with a colourful waterfront (much appreciated and colonised by artists) and an elegant Georgian town centre. Little remains of the Kirkcudbright which took its name from the vanished Kirk of Cuthbert, but it has a **Market Cross** of 1610 and a **Tolbooth** from the same period.

Broughton House (tel: 01557-330 437; Easter–Oct daily 10–5pm) in Kirkcudbright was the home of E.A. Hornel, one of the Glasgow Boys (see page 85), and has a major gallery of his paintings. Don't miss the wonderful Japanese-style garden, inspired by his visit to Japan in 1893.

Ten miles (16km) northeast from Kirkcudbright is another dignified little town, **Castle Douglas** ⑲, on the small loch of Carlingwark, where you will find a formidable tower stronghold. **Threave Castle** (tel: 07711-223 101; daily Apr–Sept 10am–4.30pm, Oct 10am–3.30pm) was built towards

The ruins of Dundrennan Abbey.

The town of Castle Douglas serves as a market centre for a large tract of Galloway's rich hinterland, giving it some of the best food shops in the south of Scotland – particularly butchers.

Take the boat to Threave Castle.

the end of the 14th century by the wonderfully named Archibald the Grim, third earl of Douglas. These days, its star attraction is a pair of peregrine falcons who have taken up residence in the castle's upper floors. **Threave Garden** (tel: 01556-502 575; daily Mar–Oct 10am–5pm, Nov–Feb 11am–3pm) has superb flower, plant and tree displays all year. It is possible to visit the baronial Threave House by guided tour only (Easter–Oct Wed–Fri & Sun 11.30am–1.30pm).

VILLAGES OF GALLOWAY

In Galloway you will find pretty villages, whose characteristic whitewashed cottages with black-bordered doors and windows look as if they have taken their colour scheme from the black-and-white Belted Galloway cattle.

Many of the most pleasant villages – **New Galloway**, **Balmaclellan**, **Crossmichael** – are in the region of long, skinny **Loch Ken**, which feeds the River Dee. To the west, shrouding the hills to the very shoulders of the

isolated **Rhinns of Kells**, a tableland of hills around 2,600ft (800 metres), lies the massive **Galloway Forest Park** – 150,000 acres (60,000 hectares) crisscrossed by Forestry Commission walking and mountain-biking trails and the Southern Upland Way.

Among the trees you will find **Clatteringshaws Loch** ⓴, 12 miles (19km) northeast of Newton Stewart (a 'planned town' built in the late 17th century by a son of the earl of Galloway) on the A712. This is the site of the **Clatteringshaws Visitor Centre** (tel: 01644-420 221; Apr–Oct daily 10am–5pm, Sept–Oct 10am–4pm, Nov–Dec Sat–Sun 10am–4pm; free) and a fascinating introduction to the broad range of the area's natural history.

Nearby, **Bruce's Stone** represents the site of the Battle of Rapploch Moss, a minor affair of 1307 but one in which the energetic Robert the Bruce routed the English. There are, in fact, two Bruce's Stones in **Galloway Forest Park**, which creeps within reach of the coast at Turnberry, where Robert may have been born. The second stone – reached only if one backtracks from Newton Stewart and then travels northwest for 10 miles (16km) on the A714 before taking an unmarked road to the east – is poised on a bluff above Loch Trool and recalls the stones hefted down the hill by the hero in another successful wrangle with the English. About 4 miles (6km) away is a sombre landmark: the **Memorial Tomb** of six Covenanters murdered at prayer. It is a simple stone that records their names and the names of their killers.

COASTAL TOUR

Back on the coast, the A75 between benign **Gatehouse of Fleet**, and **Creetown**, which hugs the sea below the comely outriders of the distinctive hill, **Cairnsmore of Fleet**, was said by Thomas Carlyle to be the most beautiful road in Scotland. It has good views

across **Wigtown Bay** to the flat green shelf that was the cradle of Scottish Christianity. The **Creetown Gem Rock Museum** (tel: 01671-820 357; www. gemrock.net; Apr–Sept daily 10am–5pm, Oct daily 10am–4pm, Nov–Dec, Feb–Mar Wed–Sun 10am–4pm) has a wide range of precious stones on display.

On the other side of the bay is the pleasant town of **Wigtown ㉑**, whose **Martyrs' Monument** is one of the most eloquent testaments to the Covenanters, who were heroically supported in the Southwest – the site of the stake where in 1685 two women, one elderly and one young, were left to drown on the estuary flats.

On the promontory south of Wigtown, the coast becomes harsher and the villages bleaker, as if it required the gentling influence of Christianity. **Whithorn ㉒** is the birthplace of Christianity in Scotland, and the **Whithorn Story Visitor Centre** (tel: 01988-500 508; www.whithorn.com; Easter–Oct daily 10.30am–5pm), in the town centre, is on the site of the first-known Christian church in Britain, built by St Ninian around the year 400. Next to the centre is the **Priory** where Mary, Queen of Scots once stayed. Here you will find the Latinus Stone of 450, the earliest Christian memorial in Scotland, as well as a collection of early Christian crosses and stones.

Four miles (6km) away is the misnamed **Isle of Whithorn**, which is a delightful town built around a busy yachting harbour and with more St Ninian connections: the ruined **St Ninian's Chapel** dates from 1300 and may have been used by overseas pilgrims; and along the coast, **St Ninian's Cave** is believed to have been used by the saint as an oratory.

Just inland from the undistinguished shoreline of Luce Bay, the site of a Ministry of Defence bombing range, are some relics of the Iron Age and Bronze Age, including **Torhouse Stone Circle**, a ring of 19 boulders standing on a low mound. The most impressive sight in this corner, however, is **Glenluce Abbey ㉓** (tel: 01581-300 541; Apr–Sept daily 9.30am–5.30pm),

Bruce's stone at the entrance to Glen Trool.

THE PLOUGHMAN POET

Robert Burns is Scotland's national treasure, keeping the home fires burning across the world with his poems and ideals. He is remembered every New Year's Eve, when people join hands to sing 'Auld Lang Syne'.

Few poets could hope to have their birthday celebrated in the most unexpected parts of the world 200 years after their death. Yet the observance of Burns Night, on 25 January, goes from strength to strength. It marks the birth in 1759 of Scotland's national poet, Robert Burns, one of seven children born to a poor Ayrshire farmer. It was an unpromising beginning, yet today Burns's verses are familiar in every English-speaking country and are especially popular in Russia, where Burns Night is toasted with vodka. Millions who have never heard of Burns have joined hands and sung his words to the tune of that international anthem of good intentions, 'Auld Lang Syne' (dialect for 'old long ago'):
Should auld acquaintance be forgot,
And never brought to mind?
Should auld acquaintance be forgot,
And days o' auld lang syne?

Portrait of Burns by Alexander Nasmyth.

This was one of many traditional Scottish songs that he collected and rewrote, in addition to his original poetry. He could and did write easily in 18th-century English as well as in traditional Scots dialect (which, even in those days, had to be accompanied by a glossary). His subjects ranged from love songs ('*Oh, my luve's like a red, red rose*') and sympathy for a startled fieldmouse ('*Wee, sleekit, cowrin', tim'rous beastie*') to a stirring sense of Scottishness ('*Scots, wha hae wi' Wallace bled*') and a simple celebration of the common people ('*A man's a man for a' that*').

The key to Burns's high standing in Scotland is that, like Sir Walter Scott, he promoted the idea of Scottish nationhood at a time when it was in danger of being obliterated by the English. His acceptance abroad, especially in Russia, stems from his championing of the rights of ordinary people and his satirical attack on double standards in Church and State.

An attractive and gregarious youth, Burns had a long series of amorous entanglements and, once famous, took full advantage of his acceptance into Edinburgh's high society. Finally, he married Jean Armour, from his own village, and settled on a poor farm at Ellisland, near Dumfries. No more able than his father to make a decent living from farming, he moved to Dumfries in 1791 to work as an excise officer. It was a secure job, and riding 200 miles (320km) a week on horseback around the countryside on his duties gave him time and inspiration to compose prolifically. His affairs continued: the niece of a Dumfries innkeeper became pregnant, but died during childbirth. Four years later, in 1796, Burns too was dead, of rheumatic heart disease. He was 37.

The 612 copies of his first edition of 34 poems sold in Kilmarnock in 1786 for the sum of three shillings (15p); today each copy will fetch around £10,000. Almost 100,000 people in more than 20 countries belong to Burns clubs, and the poet's popularity embraces the unlikeliest locations. The story is told, for example, of a local man who rose to propose a toast at a Burns Night supper in Fiji. 'You may be surprised to learn that Scottish blood flows in my veins,' he declared. 'But it is true. One of my ancestors ate a Presbyterian missionary.'

a handsome vaulted ruin dating from the 12th century.

RHINNS OF GALLOWAY

From Glenluce the traveller crosses the 'handle' of that hammer of land called the **Rhinns of Galloway**, the southwest extremity of Scotland terminating in the 200ft (60-metre) high cliffs of the Mull of Galloway, from which Ireland seems within touching distance.

At the head of the deep cleft of **Loch Ryan** is the port of **Stranraer ㉔**, market centre for the rich agricultural area, modest holiday resort and Scotland's main seaway to Northern Ireland. The Rhinns' other main resort is **Portpatrick ㉕**, and among the somewhat limited attractions of this remote peninsula are two horticultural ones: the subtropical plants of **Logan Botanic Garden ㉖** (tel: 01776-860 231; Mar–Oct daily 10am–5pm) and the great monkey puzzle trees of **Castle Kennedy Gardens**, near Stranraer (tel: 01776-702 024;www.castlekennedygardens.com; Feb–Mar

Sat–Sun 10am–5pm, Easter–Oct daily 10am–5pm).

Stranraer has two trunk roads. The A75 – infamous for the volume of heavy traffic disembarking from the ferries from Ireland – strikes east to Dumfries and points south and blights Thomas Carlyle's 'loveliest stretch' between Creetown and Gatehouse of Fleet. The second road, the A77, takes you north past the cliffs of **Ballantrae** (*not* the Ballantrae of R.L. Stevenson's novel) to the mixed pleasures of Ayrshire and, ultimately, to the edge of the Glasgow conurbation.

En route is the pleasant resort of **Girvan ㉗**, first of a series of resorts interspersed with ports and industrial towns, stretching to the mouth of the Clyde. About 10 miles (16km) offshore is a chunky granite monolith over 1,000ft (300 metres) high – the uninhabited island of **Ailsa Craig**, sometimes called Paddy's Milestone for its central position between Belfast and Glasgow.

Here, too, you begin to see more clearly the mountains of Arran and

⊙ Tip

Portpatrick is the start of the Southern Upland Way, a coast-to-coast route across southern Scotland, which runs for 214 miles (344km) to Cockburnspath on the Berwickshire coast.

Culzean Castle.

Trysting Tree where visitors to the Robert Burns Birthplace Museum leave messages.

Souter Johnnie's Cottage, Kirkoswald.

the lower line of the Kintyre peninsula, while at **Turnberry**, a Mecca for golfers and site of some castle ruins – promoted as the birthplace of Robert the Bruce – there is a choice of roads to Ayr.

ROBERT BURNS COUNTRY

The coast road (A719) invites you to one of the non-Burnsian showpieces of Ayrshire – **Culzean Castle** ㉘ (tel: 01655-884 455; castle daily Apr–Oct 10.30am–5pm, country park 10am–dusk), magnificently designed by Robert Adam and built between 1772 and 1792 for the Kennedy family. Now owned by the National Trust for Scotland, it has a country park of 560 acres (226 hectares) – the first in Scotland. A few miles beyond Culzean, the road entertains drivers at the **Electric Brae**, where an optical illusion suggests you are going downhill rather than up.

The inland road (A77) takes you through **Kirkoswald** ㉙, where Burns went to school, and the first of the cluster of Burns shrines and museums: **Souter Johnnie's Cottage** (tel: 01655-760 603; Easter–Sept Fri–Tue 11.30am–5pm), once the home of the cobbler who was the original Souter Johnnie in *'Tam o'Shanter'*. The B7024 then leads to the Mecca of Burns pilgrims, the village of **Alloway**, where he was born.

Here, within the 10-acre (4-hectare) **Robert Burns Birthplace Museum** (tel: 01292-443 700; www.burnsmuseum. org.uk; daily 10am–5pm), you can visit **Burns Cottage** with recreated living spaces and farmyard of Burns and his family; **Alloway Kirk** (where his father is buried and which features in *'Tam o'Shanter'*); the pretentious **Burns Monument** (a neoclassical temple); and the 13th-century **Brig o'Doon**, whose single span permitted Tam o'Shanter to escape from the witches. Best of all is the modern **Burns Museum**, which includes some of the poet's original manuscripts and personal effects, and plays renditions of his many songs.

You are now on the doorstep of **Ayr** ㉚, a bustling resort associated not only with Burns but also with the warrior-patriot William Wallace, who is thought to have been born in **Elderslie**, near Paisley, and who was once imprisoned in Ayr.

Inland from Ayr, to the west and north, is another clutch of Burns associations: the village of **Mauchline** ㉛, where he married Jean Armour and where their cottage is now the **Burns House Museum** (tel: 01290-550 045; Tue–Wed 10.30am–6pm, Thu 1.30–8pm, Fri–Sat 10.30am–4pm); and **Poosie Nansie's Tavern** (still a pub), which inspired part of his cantata *The Jolly Beggars*. Nearby at **Failford** is Highland Mary's Monument, which allegedly marks the spot where Burns said farewell to his doomed fiancée Mary Campbell; and then there is the sprawling town of **Kilmarnock**, where the first edition of his poems was published in

1786. A hundred years afterwards the town built a monument in his honour.

COWAL PENINSULA

The A77 from Kilmarnock takes you straight into Glasgow. But if you are island or Highland bound, you should return to the coast for ferries to the Cowal peninsula and Clyde islands. Irvine ❷ is the home of the **Scottish Maritime Museum** (tel: 01294-278 283; www.scottishmaritimemuseum.org; daily 10am–5pm). Visitors can board various well-restored vessels, including *MV Kyles*, a coaster built in 1872, and the steam yacht *SY Carola*, tour a restored 1920s' shipyard worker's tenement flat and relax in Puffers Coffee Shop. South of Irvine are two of Scotland's most prestigious golfing resorts, **Troon** and **Prestwick**.

Ardrossan serves the island of **Arran** ❸, the ferries disembarking passengers and cars at **Brodick**, the capital. Arran is popular with walkers and climbers (the sharp profile of the Arran ridge, which reaches 2,866ft/874 metres at the rocky summit

of Goatfell, provides stunning views). Yet the 2-mile (3km) walk from Brodick's attractive harbour to **Brodick Castle** (tel: 01770-302 202; daily castle Apr–Oct 10am–5pm, country park all year 9.30am–sunset) is congenial and effortless. The castle, parts of which date from the 14th century, is the ancient seat of the dukes of Hamilton. It contains paintings and objets d'art from their collections, and has an excellent tearoom serving traditional food. The woodland garden of Brodick Castle is justly claimed to be one of the finest rhododendron gardens in Britain.

Other villages include **Lochranza, Blackwaterfoot**, **Whiting Bay** and **Lamlash**, where precipitous **Holy Island** spans the mouth of the bay. St Molaise once lived in a cave on its west coast. It is now a Buddhist retreat.

Bute (see box), another Clyde island, with the attractive, ancient capital of **Rothesay**, was a premier destination for day-trippers on the Clyde paddle steamers taking Glasgwegians 'doon the watter', as was the little island of **Great Cumbrae** with its family resort

The Burns Memorial at Kilmarnock.

Brig o'Doon.

☉ THE ISLAND OF BUTE

Bute is a comely island, especially at its northern end where the narrow Kyles of Bute almost close the gap with the Cowal peninsula (ferry). Rothesay, Bute's capital, is a royal burgh that gives the title of duke to the Prince of Wales. Its unusual moated ruined castle with four round towers dates back to the early 13th century, when it was stormed by Norsemen, soon to be routed at Largs. Its Winter Garden (with a Discovery Centre) and elegant promenade – now with its superb Art Deco Pavilion finally fully restored – are especially busy in summer. It's also worth spending a penny (literally) to see the restored Victorian toilets at the pierhead.

Mount Stuart (tel: 01700-503 877; www.mountstuart.com; Apr–Oct daily 11am–5pm, last entry 4pm), 3 miles (5km) south of Rothesay, is an astonishing Gothic Revival fantasy pile rebuilt following a fire in 1877. It reflects the third marquis of Bute's fascination with astrology, mythology and religion, particularly in the stained-glass windows of the Marble Hall, the all-white Carrara Marble Chapel, and the ceiling in the Horoscope Room. It was also, apparently, the first home in Scotland with a telephone installed, and the first in the world to house an indoor swimming pool.

Two sandy beaches at Ettrick Bay and Kilchattan Bay, on the east coast, are popular spots. However, it's easy to escape to the hills: the view from Canada Hill once won the award for the best view in Britain.

The Grey Mare's Tail waterfall near Moffat drops 200ft (60 metres) from a hanging valley.

Hillwalking amongst the bracken.

of **Millport**. This is reached from **Largs** , the most handsome of the Clyde resorts and the scene, in 1263, of a battle that conclusively repelled persistent Viking attempts to invade Scotland. The **Vikingar!** centre (tel: 01475-689 777; Mon–Fri 9am–9pm, Sat 10am–5pm) dramatically traces the history of the Vikings in Scotland through a number of multimedia exhibits. The ferry to Bute is from **Wemyss Bay**, between Largs and Gourock. From Gourock you can also board a ferry for Dunoon and the Cowal peninsula.

ESCAPING THE CITY

For many people in West Central Scotland, the Cowal peninsula represents Highland escapism. It now has a population of second-home owners from the Glasgow conurbation, which makes it busy during weekends and holidays, despite the time it takes to negotiate its long fissures of sea lochs (**Loch Fyne** to the west and **Loch Long** to the east, with several others in between).

Dunoon is its capital, another ancient township turned holiday resort,

with a 13th-century castle, of which only remnants remain on **Castle Hill**, where you will again meet Burns's fiancée, Highland Mary.

East of Gare Loch, the Clyde begins to be compressed between the once great shipbuilding banks of **Clydeside**, with its first resort town on the north bank at **Helensburgh** , now a stately dormitory for Glasgow. Those smitten with Charles Rennie Mackintosh will enjoy the recently renovated **Hill House** (tel: 01436-673 900; Easter–Oct daily 11.30am–5.30pm), his finest domestic commission.

Industrial **Dumbarton** is even closer to the city (approximately 20 miles/32km to the northwest) and its name confirms it has been there since the days of the Britons. Its spectacular lump of rock was their fort, and supports a 13th-century castle that has close connections with – inevitably – Mary, Queen of Scots.

MOFFAT TO LANARK

The eastern edge of Southwest Scotland is dominated by the M74, the frenzied highway that is Glasgow's access to the Borders and England. It carves through some of the shapeliest hills in Scotland, with some lovely, lonely places and unexpected treasures tucked away.

A detour south on the M74 brings you to **Moffat** , an elegant former spa town with the broadest main street in Scotland. Northwest of Moffat is the **Devil's Beef Tub**, a vast, steep, natural vat in the hills where Border raiders used to hide stolen cattle. Northeast of Moffat on the A708 is the spectacular **Grey Mare's Tail** waterfall. Further north is **Tibbie Sheil's Inn**, the meeting place of the circle of writer James Hogg (the 'Ettrick Shepherd').

On either side of the M74, a few miles driving will take you to the highest villages in Scotland: **Leadhills** and **Wanlockhead**. Once centres of mining, an idea of their past can be seen at the **Wanlockhead Museum of Lead**

Mining (tel: 01659-74387; www.leadmining museum.co.uk; Apr–Sept daily 11am–4.30pm). Here, too, are Drumlanrig Castle, the historic market town of Lanark and the lush orchards and dramatic falls of the River Clyde.

Drumlanrig Castle and Country Park ⓪ (tel: 01848-331 555; www.drumlanrigcastle.co.uk; Apr–Sept daily 10am–5pm) is at the bottom of the precipitous **Dalveen Pass**, a natural stairway between the uplands of South Lanarkshire and the rolling pastures and woodland of Dumfriesshire. It is built of pink sandstone and fashioned in late 17th-century Renaissance style on the site of an earlier Douglas stronghold and near a Roman fort. Its rich collection of French furniture and Dutch paintings (Holbein and Rembrandt) includes interesting relics of Bonnie Prince Charlie. The first duke of Queensberry, for whom Drumlanrig Castle was built, was so horrified by its cost that he spent only one night in it.

The A73 to **Lanark** skirts **Tinto Hill**, the highest peak in Lanarkshire and the site of Druidic festivals. Lanarkshire schoolchildren traditionally carry stones up to add to its enormous cairn.

LANARKSHIRE

Biggar ⓫ is a lively little town, with museums focusing on local history as if in defiance of the greater celebrity of its big neighbour, **Lanark**. The high, handsome old royal burgh was already important in the 10th century, when a parliament was held there, but is more closely identified with William Wallace. It is said that he hid in a cave in the Cartland Craigs, just below the town, after killing an English soldier in a brawl.

Lanark was also a Convenanting centre and is still a place of great character, much of it due to its weekly livestock market and the steep fall of the Clyde below the town at **New Lanark ⓬**, Scotland's most impressive memorial to the Industrial Revolution and a Unesco World Heritage

Site. Here, between 1821 and 1824, a cotton-spinning village became the scene of the pioneering social and educational experiment of Robert Owen. The handsome buildings have been regenerated and feature an imaginative Visitor Centre (tel: 01555-661 345; www.newlanark.org; daily Apr–Oct 10am–5pm, Nov–Mar 10am–4pm).

Nearby, the cataracts of the **Falls of Clyde Nature Reserve** are the preface to one of the river's prettiest passages, its last Arcadian fling among the orchards and market gardens of Kirkfieldbank, Hazlebank and Rosebank before it reaches industrial North Lanarkshire.

Near the pastoral village of **Crossford**, is one of Scotland's best-preserved medieval castles. **Craignethan Castle** (tel: 01555-860 364; Apr–Sept daily 9.30am–5.30pm) was built between the 15th and 16th centuries not far from the Clyde, and was a stronghold of the Hamiltons, friends of Mary, Queen of Scots. It claims to be the original Tillietudlem in Sir Walter Scott's *Old Mortality*.

Corra Linn waterfall on the River Clyde.

The Forth Rail Bridge.

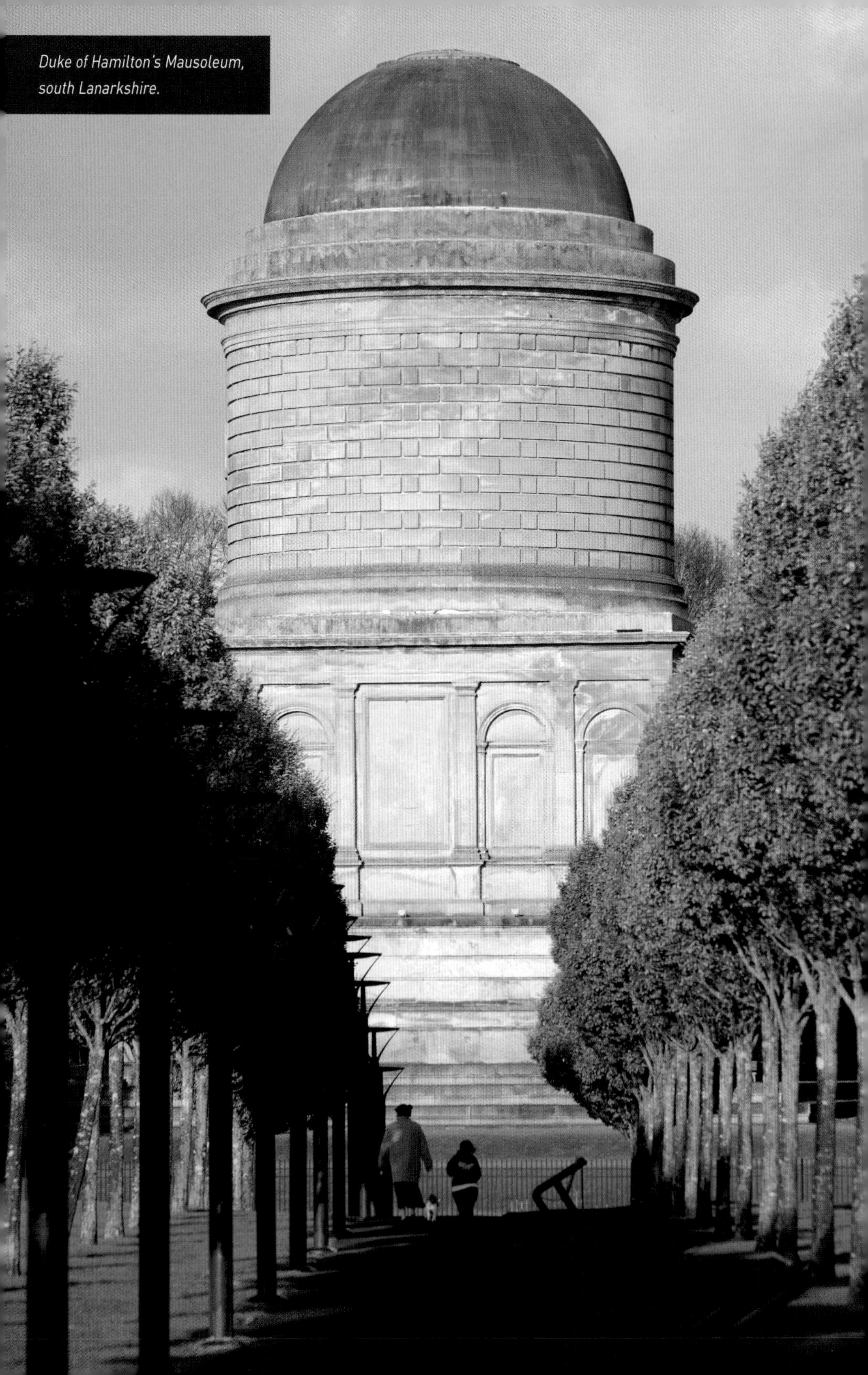

Duke of Hamilton's Mausoleum, south Lanarkshire.

FORTH AND CLYDE

Standing strategically as the gateway to the Highlands, the ancient town of Stirling is a focal point for any visit to Central Scotland and the waterways of the Forth and Clyde.

Map on page 140

For centuries, Stirling's Old Bridge has given access to the north across the lowest bridging point of the River Forth, while the 250ft (75-metre) volcanic plug, which supports the castle, was the natural fortress that made **Stirling ⓭** significant from the 12th century onwards.

The **Castle** (tel: 01786-450 000; www.stirlingcastle.scot; daily Apr–Sept 9.30am–6pm Oct–Mar 9.30am–5pm) – every bit as impressive as Edinburgh Castle – was the favourite residence of the Stuart monarchy and is one of Scotland's Renaissance glories (see page 174). Stirling Castle has been home to the Argyll and Sutherland Highlanders since 1881 and their illustrious history is recalled in the eponymous museum, through costumes, medals, weapons and paintings.

STIRLING ATTRACTIONS

One of Scotland's oldest and most atmospheric towns, Stirling became Scotland's newest city in 2002 to mark Queen Elizabeth II's Golden Jubilee. Its city status owes much to its excellent university, a national park on its doorstep, a huge regeneration project, a growing population and a good quality of life.

Stirling's historic past is well documented but it is its modern attitudes that make it a great destination in which to spend some time, owing to its cutting-edge culture and first-class art venues. You can take the historic Old Town Walk one day, then mingle with the locals in the excellent shopping areas, or take in an evening at the theatre, the next.

One of the top art venues of the city is the **Smith Art Gallery and Museum** (Dumbarton Road; tel: 01786-471 917; www.smithartgalleryandmuseum.co.uk; Tue–Sat 10.30am–5pm, Sun 2–5pm; free), which holds a superb collection of landscapes and portraits by Thomas

Main attractions

Stirling
Wallace Monument
Falkirk Wheel
Linlithgow Palace
South Queensferry
Inchcolm Abbey
Deep Sea World
Hopetoun House
Cramond
Chatelherault

Robert the Bruce statue with the Wallace Monument.

Pleasure boats by the loch.

Loch Katrine in the Trossachs.

Smith, as well as contributions from other artists, alongside a comprehensive overview of the city's history, covering everything from antiquity and archaeology, to trade and industry.

The medieval **Church of the Holy Rude** (St John's Street, Castle Wynd; www.holyrude.org; May–Sept 11am–4pm; admission by donation) is one of Scotland's finest churches with an original 15th-century hammer-beam roof. Directly opposite, **Cowane's Hospital** (St John Street; tel: 01786-472 247; www.cowanes.org.uk; daily Apr–Aug 10am–5pm, Sept–Mar 10am–4pm; free) is a popular destination for those seeking their Scottish heritage as it holds extensive family records.

The achievements of both Wallace and Bruce are recalled around Stirling. On the rock of **Abbey Craig**, above the site where Wallace camped, is the ostentatious **Wallace Monument** (tel: 01786-472 140; www.nationalwallace monument.com; daily July–Aug 9.30am–6pm, Jan–Feb, Nov–Dec 10am–4pm, Mar 10am–5pm, Apr–June, Sept–Oct 9.30am–5pm), home of the hero's two-handed sword. From its elevation at the top of 246 spiral steps you can see the leaping ramparts of the **Ochil Hills**, while to the southeast, the Forth spreads across its flat plain to the spectacular flare-stacks of **Grangemouth**.

THE OCHIL HILLS

The Ochil Hills are a range of hills extending from the Bridge of Allan, north of Stirling, tailing off eastwards to the south side of the Firth of Tay at Newburgh. These hills not only provide wonderful views of Stirling and its castle, they also offer great opportunities for walkers and some fine panoramas for motorists.

Taking the minor Sheriffmuir Road out of Stirling up from the university, after about a mile (1.5km) there are opportunities to pull off the road and look down on the city. Those wishing to walk can take the path up to Dumyat for an even better view. The starting point, on the right-hand side of the road opposite the sheep pens, is just north of the electricity cables, which

⊘ STIRLING CASTLE

The impressive bulk of Stirling Castle was a formidable challenge to any invaders. It had its most active moments during Scotland's Wars of Independence: surrendered to the English in 1296, it was recaptured by the warrior-patriot William Wallace after the Battle of Stirling Bridge (not today's stone bridge, built around 1400, but a wooden structure). It became the last stronghold in Scotland to hold out against Edward I, the 'Hammer of the Scots'. Eventually, it went back to the English for 10 years, until Robert the Bruce retook it in 1314 after the Battle of Bannockburn, which decisively secured Scotland's independence.

The Stuarts favoured Stirling Castle as a royal residence: James II and V were born in it, Mary, Queen of Scots was crowned there at the age of nine months, and its splendid collection of buildings reflects its history as palace and fortress. Perhaps the most striking feature is the exterior facade, with ornate stonework that was largely cut by French craftsmen. The Great Hall, or Parliament House (before 1707 this was a seat of the Scottish Parliament), also has exquisite carving and tracery, which has been carefully reconstructed. A programme of major restoration has also included the kitchens of the castle, which now recreate the preparations for a sumptuous Renaissance banquet given by Mary, Queen of Scots for the baptism of her son, the future James VI.

cross the road. The path to the beacon – keeping to the left – is around 2 miles (3km) long and, although it's only a climb of some 850ft (260 metres), the view is superb.

To the west, not far from Stirling, lies Scotland's first national park, the **Loch Lomond and the Trossachs National Park**, which was officially opened by the Princess Royal in 2002, and covers four distinct areas: the Argyll Forest in the west on the Cowal Peninsula, Loch Lomond, The Trossachs, east of Callander and Breadalbane in the northeast corner (see page 248).

THE BATTLE OF BANNOCKBURN

The site of the Battle of Bannockburn, a few miles south of Stirling, has been more or less consumed by a housing estate. No one is precisely sure where the battle was fought, but the rotunda beside the heroic bronze equestrian statue of Bruce is said to mark his command post. The **Bannockburn Heritage Centre** (tel: 01786-812 664; www.battleofbannockburn. com; daily Apr–Sept 9.30am–5.30pm,

Oct–Mar 10am–5pm) gives an audio-visual account of the matter. Also close to Stirling is the **Alloa Tower** (tel: 01259 211 701; mid-Apr–Sept Fri–Mon noon–5pm), the superbly restored former home of the earls of Mar, built in the late 15th century with a dungeon, medieval timber roof and an impressive rooftop parapet walk with fine views.

Stirling is almost equidistant from Edinburgh and Glasgow. If you take the M9 to Edinburgh, you stay roughly parallel to the broadening course of the Forth. There are rewarding diversions to be made on this route, the best of which is the **Falkirk Wheel** (tel: 08700-500 208; www.scottishcanals.co.uk/falkirk-wheel; daily 10am–5.30pm) just outside Falkirk. Opened in June 2002, this spectacular feat of engineering is a unique rotating boatlift that carries boats between the Forth & Clyde and Union canals. Fiftyminute boat rides lift you up 35-metres (115ft), before taking you along the canal for spectacular views.

Also near Falkirk are four good sections of the Roman **Antonine Wall** ⑭, which the Emperor Antoninus Pius had

The Falkirk Wheel.

Most of the original 18th-century furniture and wall coverings can still be seen at Hopetoun House.

The Shuttle Row tenement, David Livingstone Centre.

built between the Firths of Clyde and Forth around AD 140. The motorway itself has opened up a distracting view of the loch and the late 15th-century **Linlithgow Palace** ⓯ (tel: 01506-842 896; daily Apr–Sept 9.30am–5.30pm, Oct–Mar 10am–4pm), the well-preserved ruins of Scotland's most magnificent palace and birthplace of Mary, Queen of Scots.

From the M9, you can also visit the village of **South Queensferry** ⓰ on the southern bank of one of the Forth's oldest crossings, where river becomes estuary. Until the **Forth Road Bridge** was built, ferries had plied between South and North Queensferry for 900 years. Today, South Queensferry huddles between and beneath the giant bridges that provide such a spectacular contrast in engineering design – the massive humped girders of the 1890 rail bridge and the delicate, graceful span of the suspension bridge, which took six years to complete and was opened in 1964.

At South Queensferry, you can take a boat excursion to the island of **Inchcolm** in the Forth and visit the ruined abbey (tel: 01383-823 332; daily Apr–Sept

9.30am–5.30pm), monastic buildings and gardens. Be aware that adverse weather conditions could make the crossing impossible. Cross the Forth Road Bridge or take the train to North Queensferry to visit the huge aquarium at **Deep Sea World** (tel: 01383-411 880; www.deepseaworld.com; Mon–Fri 10am–5pm, Sat–Sun 10am–5.30pm).

Near South Queensferry are **Hopetoun House** (tel: 0131-331 2451; www. hopetoun.co.uk; Easter–Sept daily 10.30am–5pm), home of the earls of Hopetoun, situated in parkland beside the Forth and splendidly extended by William Adam and his son John between 1721 and 1754; and **Dalmeny House** (tel: 0131-331 1888; www.roseberyestates.co.uk; June–July Sun–Wed, guided tours at 2.15pm, 3.30pm), home of the earls of Rosebery, with a fine collection of paintings.

THE FORTH AND CLYDE

You can walk beside the Forth through the wooded Rosebery estate to the **River Almond**, where a little rowing-boat ferry transports you across this

minor tributary to the red pantiles and white crowstep gables of **Cramond** ㊼. Still very much its own 18th-century village, Cramond has a harbour that was used by the Romans. Its **Roman Fort**, whose foundations have been exposed, was built around AD 142, and may have been used by Septimius Severus.

Scotland's pre-eminent river, the **Clyde**, undergoes more personality changes than any other in its progress to the western seaboard. The limpid little stream, which has its source 80 miles (130km) southeast of Glasgow, moves prettily through the orchards and market gardens of Clydesdale before watering the industries of North Lanarkshire and welcoming the ships and shipyards of Glasgow.

STRATHCLYDE COUNTRY PARK

The lower reaches of the Clyde valley have been colonised by the city's satellites, and by a clutter of hill towns: Wishaw, Motherwell and Hamilton. Once drab coal and steel towns, they are attempting to recover their dignity and vitality: witness the creation of **Strathclyde Country Park**, a huge recreational area with a 200-acre (80-hectare) loch, formed by diverting the Clyde, and subsuming part of the old estate of the dukes of Hamilton.

Hamilton ㊽ has associations with Mary, Queen of Scots, Cromwell and the Covenanters, who were defeated by Monmouth at nearby Bothwell Bridge in 1679. Immediately south of Hamilton is **Chatelherault** (tel: 01698-426 213; visitor centre Mon–Sun 10am–5pm; house Sun–Thu 10am–4.30pm; free), a glorious restored hunting lodge and kennels built in 1732 for the duke of Hamilton by William Adam.

Bothwell Castle (tel: 01698-816 894; Apr–Sept daily 9.30am–5.30pm, Oct until 4.30pm, Nov–Mar Sat–Wed 10am–4pm), perhaps the finest 13th-century castle in Scotland, was fought over by the Scots and English.

Memories of more recent times can be found in adjacent **Blantyre** ㊾, birthplace of explorer David Livingstone, whose life is recalled at the **David Livingstone Centre** (tel: 01698 710 641; Apr–Dec Fri–Mon 11am–4pm).

The David Livingstone Centre.

Inner courtyard of Linlithgow Palace.

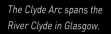
The Clyde Arc spans the River Clyde in Glasgow.

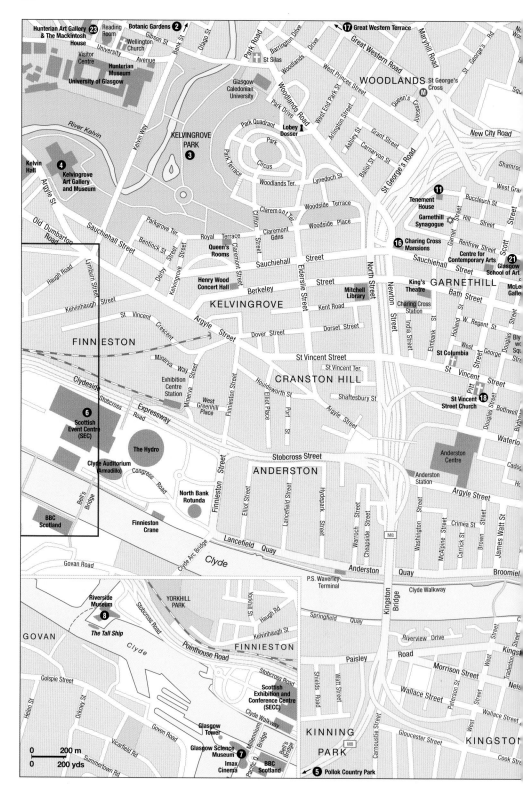

23 Hunterian Art Gallery & The Mackintosh House
Reading Room
2 Botanic Gardens
17 Great Western Terrace
Gibson St
Bank St
Otago St

University Avenue
Wellington Church
St Silas
Barrington Drive
West Princes Street
Woodlands
WOODLANDS
St George's Cross
Maryhill Road
St George's Rd
No Wo
Squ

Visitor Centre
Hunterian Museum
University of Glasgow
Glasgow Caledonian University
Woodlands Road
West End Park St
Arlington Street
Ashley St
Grant Street
Carnarvon St
Queen's Crescent
New City Road
Shamro

River Kelvin
Park Drive
Park Quadrant
Park Terrace
KELVINGROVE PARK
3
Park
Circus
Lobey Dosser
Woodlands Ter.
Lynedoch St
Baliol St
St George's Road
West Gran

4 Kelvin Hall
Kelvingrove Art Gallery and Museum
Kelvin Way
Claremont Ter.
Woodside Terrace
Woodside Place
11 Tenement House
Buccleuch St
West Grar

Argyle St
Old Dumbarton Road
Sauchiehall Street
Parkgrove Ter.
Royal Terrace
Queen's Rooms
Claremont Gdns
Claremont Street
Clifton Street
Garnethill Synagogue
16 Charing Cross Mansions
Garnet Hill Street
Renfrew Street
Scott Street
Centre for Contemporary Arts
21 Glasgow School of Art

Haugh Road
Lynburn Street
Bentinck St
Derby Street
Kelvingrove Street
Henry Wood Concert Hall
Berkeley
Street
Sauchiehall
Street
Street
Elderslie Street
Bath Street
GARNETHILL
McLe Galle

Kelvinhaugh Street
St Vincent Crescent
KELVINGROVE
Argyle Street
Kent Road
Dover Street
Dorset Street
Mitchell Library
North Street
Newton Street
King's Theatre
Charing Cross Station
W. Regent St
Holland St
Elmbank St
West George Street
Bly wo Squ

FINNIESTON
Minerva Way
Exhibition Centre Station
West Greenhill Place
Minerva Street
Finnieston Street
Houldsworth St
Elliot Place
Port St
St Vincent Street
St Vincent Ter.
Argyle Street
Shaftesbury St
CRANSTON HILL
St Columba
West George Street
18 St Vincent Street Church
Pitt St
Douglas Street
Bothwell
India Street
Stre

Clydeside Expressway
Stobcross
Expressway Road
6 Scottish Event Centre (SEC)
The Hydro
Clyde Auditorium (Armadillo)
Congress Road
Stobcross Street
ANDERSTON
Elliot Street
Lancefield Street
Hydepark Street
Anderston Centre
Anderston Station
Argyle Street
Waterlo
Cadoc
Birchv
Ho

North Bank Rotunda
Finnieston Street
Warroch Street
Cheapside Street
Washington Street
Crimea St
McAlpine Street
Carrick St
Brown Street
James Watt St

BBC Scotland
Bell's Bridge
Finnieston Crane
Lancefield Quay
Govan Road
Clyde Arc Bridge
Clyde
Anderston Quay
Kingston Bridge
Broomiel
Kings

GOVAN
Riverside Museum
8
The Tall Ship
Stobcross Road
YORKHILL PARK
Yorkhill St
Haugh Rd
Kelvinhaugh St
Pointhouse Road
FINNIESTON
Clyde
P.S. Waverley Terminal
Clyde Walkway
Springfield Quay
Riverview Drive
Road
West Street
Kings
Street

Golspie Street
Helen St
Orkney St
Stobcross Road
Scottish Exhibition and Conference Centre (SECC)
Clyde Walkway
Millennium Bridge
Bell's Bridge
Shields Road
Watt Street
Paisley
Road
Morrison Street
Paterson St
Wallace Street
Tradeston
West Street
Nelso
Street

Govan Road
Vicarfield Rd
Summertown Rd
Glasgow Tower
Glasgow Science Museum **7**
Imax Cinema
Pacific Drive
BBC Scotland
KINNING PARK
5 Pollok Country Park
Carnoustie Street
Gloucester Street
Cook Str
KINGSTON

0 200 m
0 200 yds

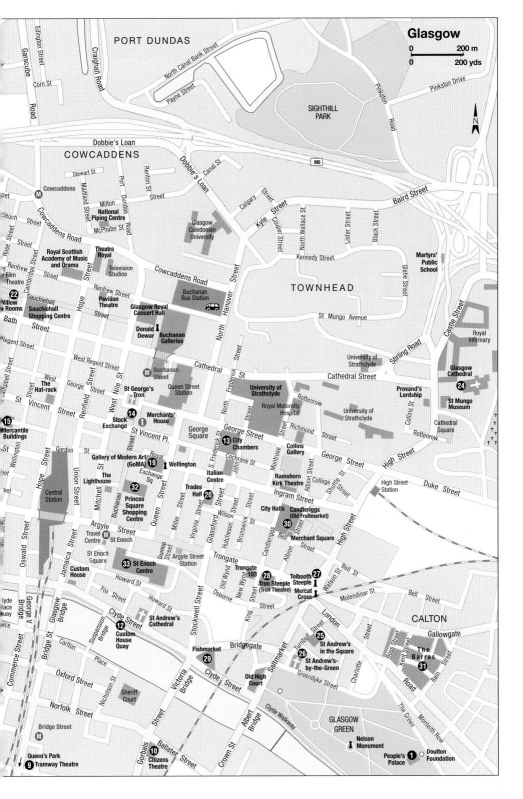

The Stock Exchange building.

GLASGOW

A city of noble character, handsome buildings and invincible spirit, Glasgow is attractive and down to earth.

Glasgow is a diverse and lively city. And yet there are few places in Europe that have been more publicly misunderstood and misrepresented. A city that has divided opinion, Glasgow exhibits the best and worst of commerce and capitalism, stunning architectural feats amid gritty urban scenery, and constant renewal and reinvention. Glasgow has – over the centuries – been a small fishing village, an industrial powerhouse, and a hotbed for severe social problems. Few cities can have changed so much, displayed so much character, or ignited so much controversy.

COSMOPOLITAN GLASGOW

Yet even in the darkest days of its reputation, when Glasgow's slums and violence were the touchstone for every sociologist's worst urban nightmare, it was still a city for connoisseurs. It appealed to those who were not insensitive to the desperate consequences of its 19th-century population explosion, when the combination of cotton, coal, steel and the River Clyde transformed Glasgow from elegant little merchant city to industrial behemoth; and who were not blind to the dire effect of 20th-century economics which, from World War I onwards, presided over the decline of its shipbuilding and heavy industries; but who were nevertheless able to uncover, behind its

grime and grisliness, a city of nobility and invincible spirit.

Its enthusiasts have always recognised Glasgow's qualities, and even at the height of its notoriety they have been able to give Glasgow its place in the pantheon of great Western cities. Today, it is fashionable to describe the city of Glasgow as European in character, for the remarkable diversity of its architecture and a certain levity of heart, or to compare it with North America for its gridiron street system and wisecracking street patter.

Main attractions
People's Palace
Botanic Gardens
Kelvingrove Park
Burrell Collection
Glasgow Science Centre
Clyde Walkway
Gallery of Modern Art
Glasgow School of Art
Glasgow Cathedral
Barras market

Map on page 180

Oversized seating outside the Riverside Museum.

Gates to the University of Glasgow.

The Glasgow City coat of arms in stained glass, Glasgow Cathedral.

But these resonances have long been appreciated by experienced travellers. In 1929, at a time when social conditions were at their worst, the romantic but perceptive travel writer H.V. Morton found 'a transatlantic alertness about Glasgow which no city in England possesses' and – the converse of orthodox opinion – was able to see that 'Edinburgh is Scottish and Glasgow is cosmopolitan'.

Modern Glaswegians have further reason to celebrate – Glasgow was voted the 'friendliest city in the world' by two separate polls in 2014.

CULTURE CITY

Glasgow today is visibly, spectacularly, a city in transformation. It hasn't allowed its 'hard, subversive, proletarian tradition' to lead it into brick walls of confrontation with central government. The result? A city which has massively rearranged its own environment; which sees its future in the service industries, in business conferences, exhibitions and indeed in tourism; which has already achieved some startling coups on its self-engineered road to becoming 'Europe's first post-industrial city'; and which has probably never been more exciting to visit since, at the apogee of its Victorian vigour, Glasgow held the International Exhibition of Science and Art more than 100 years ago.

Glaswegians allow themselves a sly smile over their elevation to the first rank of Europe's cultural centres. (It was European City of Culture in 1990, UK City of Architecture and Design in 1999 and hosted the Commonwealth Games in 2014.) But the smile becomes a little bitter for those who live in those dismal areas of the city as yet untouched by the magic of stone-cleaning, floodlighting or even modest rehabilitation.

Defenders of the new Glasgow argue that their turn will come; that you can't attract investment and employment to a city, with better conditions for everyone, unless first you shine up its confidence on the inside and polish up its image on the outside.

HILLS AND WATER

Like the other four main Scottish cities, Glasgow is defined by hills and water.

⊘ FISTS OF IRON

The Glaswegian comedian Billy Connolly said of Glasgow: 'There's a lightness about the town, without heavy industry. It's as if they've discovered how to work the sunroof, or something.' Yet Glaswegians themselves will admit that their positive qualities can have a negative side. Even today, mateyness can turn to menace, especially if there is alcohol involved. Religious bigotry – generally between Catholics and Protestants – simmers just below the surface, spilling out onto the streets and football terraces, although the city worthies are constantly trying to find ways to contain it. And Glasgow's legendary humour, made intelligible even to the English through the success of comedians like Billy Connolly, but available free on every street corner, is the humour of the ghetto. It is dry, sceptical, irreverent and often dark.

Its suburbs advance up the slopes of the vast bowl that contains it, and the pinnacles, towers and spires of its universities, colleges and cathedral occupy their own summits within it. It is, therefore, a place of sudden, sweeping vistas, with always a hint of ocean or mountain just around the corner.

Look north from the heights of Queen's Park and you will see the cloudy humps of the Campsie Fells and the precipitous banks of Loch Lomond. Look west from Gilmorehill to the great spangled mouth of the Clyde and you will sense the sea fretting at its fragmented littoral and the islands and resorts that used to bring thousands of Glaswegians 'doon the watter' for their annual Fair Fortnight.

The antiquity of this July holiday – Glasgow Fair became a fixture in the local calendar in 1190 – gives some idea of the long-term stability of the town on the Clyde. But for centuries Glasgow had little prominence or significance in the history of Scotland. Although by the 12th century it was both a market town and a cathedral city (with a patron saint, St Mungo) and flourished quietly throughout the Middle Ages, it was largely bypassed by the bitter internecine conflicts of pre-Reformation Scotland and the running battles with England.

Most of Scotland's trade, too, was conducted with the Low Countries from the east coast ports. But Glasgow had a university, now five centuries old, and a distinguished centre of medical and engineering studies, and it had the River Clyde. When trade opened up with the Americas across the Atlantic, Glasgow's fortune was made.

The tobacco trade with Virginia and Maryland brought the city new prosperity and prompted it to expand westwards from the medieval centre of the High Street. (Little of medieval Glasgow remains.) In the late 18th century the urbanisation of the city accelerated with an influx of immigrants, mainly from the West Highlands, to work in the cotton mills with the new machines that had been introduced by merchants who had been forced to desert the tobacco trade. The Industrial

View from Queen's Park.

Revolution had begun, and from then on Glasgow's destiny – grim and glorious – was fixed.

INSTANT CITY

The deepening of the Clyde up to the Broomielaw, near the heart of the city, in the 1780s and the coming of the steam engine in the 19th century consolidated a process of such rapid expansion that Glasgow has been called an 'instant city'. In the 50 years between 1781 and 1831 the population of the city quintupled, and was soon to be further swelled by thousands of Irish immigrants crossing the Irish Sea to escape famine and seek work. The Victorians completed Glasgow's industrial history and built most of its most self-important buildings, as well as the congested domestic fortifications that were to become infamous as slum tenements. Since World War II, its population has fallen below the million mark to fewer than 600,000, the result of policies designed to decant citizens into 'new towns' and the growing appeal of commuting from green-belt villages and towns.

*'Floating Heads'
installation in the
Kelvingrove Art Gallery
and Museum.*

GLASGOW GREEN

One translation of the original Celtic suggests that the city's name, Glasgow, means 'dear green place'. Other translations include 'dear stream' and 'greyhound' (which some say was the nickname of St Mungo), but the green reference is most apt, for Glasgow has, after all, more than 70 parks – 'more green space per head of population than any other city in Europe', as the tour bus drivers will proudly tell you.

The most unexpected, idiosyncratic and oldest of its parks – in fact, the oldest public park in Britain – is **Glasgow Green**, once the common grazing ground of the medieval town and acquired by the burgh in 1662. To this day Glaswegians have the right to dry their washing on Glasgow Green, and its Arcadian sward is still spiked with clothes poles for their use, although there are few takers. Municipal Clydesdale horses, used for carting duties in the park, still avail themselves of the grazing, and the eccentricity of the place is compounded by the proximity of Templeton's Carpet Factory, designed in 1889 by William Leiper, who aspired to replicate the Doge's Palace in Venice. It's now a mixed-use village incorporating office space, a brewery and a bar.

Here, too, you will find the **People's Palace ❶** (tel: 0141-276 0788; Mon–Thu, Sat 10am–5pm, Fri, Sun 11am–5pm; free), built in 1898 as a cultural centre for the East End community, for whom its red-sandstone munificence was indeed palatial. It's now a museum dedicated to the social and industrial life of the 20th-century city.

The most distinguished of the remaining 69-odd parks include the **Botanic Gardens ❷** (tel: 0141-276 1614; www.glasgowbotanicgardens.com; daily 7am–dusk, glasshouses 10am–6pm, winter until 4.15pm; free) in the heart of Glasgow's stately West End, with another palace – the **Kibble Palace** – the most enchanting of its two large hothouses. It was built as a conservatory for the Clyde-coast home of a Glasgow businessman, John Kibble, and shipped to its present site in 1873. The architect has never been identified, although legend promotes Sir Joseph Paxton, who designed the Crystal Palace in London.

Across from the gardens is one of Glasgow's most popular cultural centres, Òran Mór (tel: 0141-357 6200; www.oran-mor.co.uk) set in the converted Kelvinside Parish Church. All manner of theatre, live music and dance events are held here, including the ever-popular A Play, A Pie and A Pint series, and there's a range of bars, restaurants and cafés.

OTHER PARKS AND GARDENS

Kelvingrove Park ❸, in the city's West End, was laid out in the 1850s and was the venue of Glasgow's principal Victorian and Edwardian international exhibitions, although that function is now performed by the modern Scottish Event Campus (SEC) on the north bank of the Clyde (see page 188). It is a

spectacular park, traversed by the River Kelvin and dominated on one side by the Gothic pile of **Glasgow University** (this seat of learning was unseated from its original college in the High Street and rehoused on Gilmorehill in 1870) and by the elegant Victorian precipice of **Park Circus** on the other side.

The **Kelvingrove Art Gallery and Museum ❹** (tel: 0141-276 9599; Mon–Thu, Sat 10am–5pm, Fri, Sun 11am–5pm; free) includes a major collection of European paintings and extensive displays on the natural history, archaeology and ethnology of the area. Rembrandt, Matisse and Van Gogh are just three of the great artists on exhibit here, while there's also a superb focus on Scottish art, from the Colourists to the Glasgow Boys. It has a magnificent organ, which is regularly used for recitals, and in the main hall a World War II Spitfire hangs from the ceiling, above the vast stuffed elephant known as Sir Roger.

Victoria Park, near the north mouth of the Clyde Tunnel, has a glasshouse containing several large fossil trees some 350 million years old.

Strolling in the Botanic Garden.

Statue of Eve in the Kibble Palace, Botanic Gardens.

☉ Fact

Glasgow District Subway, opened in 1896, was one of the earliest underground train systems in Britain and the only one in the country that is called, American-style, 'the Subway'.

Pollok Country Park ❺ on the city's south side (those who live south of the Clyde consider themselves a separate race of Glaswegian) has a well-worn path beaten to the door of the **Burrell Collection** (tel: 0141-287 2550; free; closed for refurbishment until 2021), where there are more than 9,000 exhibits, from artefacts of ancient civilisations, to medieval treasures, to Impressionist paintings, including a wonderful Degas exhibition. It was all lovingly gathered together by the shipping tycoon Sir William Burrell, who donated the whole lot to the city in 1944, although a suitable exhibition space couldn't be found for almost 40 years, when the current site opened in 1983. Also in the park is the 18th-century **Pollok House** (tel: 0141 616 6410; daily house 10am–5pm, gardens until dusk), designed by William Adam and containing a remarkable collection of Spanish art, with pieces by El Greco, Murillo and Goya, among others. The windows look out on a prizewinning herd of Highland cattle and Pollok Golf Course.

Not far away, towards East Kilbride, is **Rouken Glen**, another lovely area of parkland with a walled garden and tumbling waterfall.

Also on the city's south side, south of Queen's Park in Cathcart, stands **Holmwood House** (tel: 0141 571 0184; Easter–Oct Fri–Mon noon–5pm, last entry 4pm), the best domestic example of the work of Alexander 'Greek' Thomson, Glasgow's most famous Victorian architect. It was built in 1857–8 for a paper manufacturer, James Couper.

RIVER CLYDE

Stobcross Quay on the north bank is the site of the ultramodern **Scottish Event Centre (SEC) ❻** (www.sec.co.uk) and the Clyde Auditorium, known as **The Armadillo**, a 3,000-seat concert venue designed by Lord Foster. Adjacent to these two vast buildings, and completing this trio of entertainment venues, is the 13,000-capacity **Hydro**, the city's main location for large music concerts and comedians' arena-style tours. Close by you can marvel at the industrial colossus of the **Finnieston**

'Le Château de Médan' by Cézanne, Burrell Collection.

Crane, now redundant from its original use for lifting heavy machinery but an admirable (and some might say beautiful, in its own way) testament to the importance of the Clyde in days gone by.

Across Bell's Bridge is the **Glasgow Science Centre** ❼ (tel: 0141-420 5000; www.glasgowsciencecentre.org; summer daily 10am–5pm, winter Wed–Fri 10am–3pm, Sat–Sun 10am–5pm), a collection of futuristic buildings that includes Glasgow's **IMAX Cinema**, with an 80ft (24-metre) -wide screen; the **Science Mall**, a hands-on extravaganza where visitors can explore, create and invent; a planetarium; and the **Glasgow Tower**, the tallest free-standing structure in Scotland and the only one in the world that will rotate through 360 degrees; the views are spectacular.

To the west, beyond Stobcross Quay and adjacent to Glasgow Harbour, the £74-million futuristic **Riverside Museum** ❽ (tel: 0141-287 2720; Mon–Thu, Sat 10am–5pm, Fri, Sun 11am–5pm; free) is now one of Britain's most popular attractions, even winning the European Museum of the Year award in 2013. Replacing the former Museum of Transport, this purpose-built glass-fronted space houses every manner of transport that has at one time or another graced Glasgow's streets, from horse-drawn omnibuses to old trams and vintage cars from the 1930s to the 1970s, many of which it's possible to clamber aboard The railway system is not forgotten either, with four locomotives from different time periods, while overhead a velodrome of bicycles displays life on two wheels over the ages; on the ground floor, look out for the bike which Graham Obree rode twice while breaking the one-hour world record. Two streetscapes have also been created, reimagining shops, pubs, sounds and aromas from the 1890s to the 1960s. The permission to 'climb aboard' many of the exhibits makes the museum particularly fun and exciting for children. In summer the forecourt in front of the museum is awash with food stalls, buskers and the occasional brass band.

Behind the museum is **The Tall Ship** (tel: 0141-357 3699; www.thetallship.com;

Kelvingrove Art Gallery and Museum.

🔍 A CULTURAL EXPLOSION

After the decline of the shipbuilding industry, Glasgow turned its mind to creating a more refined city of culture, winning loud applause for its combination of design, modern architecture and café lifestyle.

Glasgow's elevation to the position of European City of Culture in 1990 (a title bestowed by the European Community) was received with a mixture of astonishment and amusement in Edinburgh, which had long perceived itself as guardian of Scotland's most civilised values.

But, quietly, Glasgow had been stealing the initiative. Edinburgh had been trying to make up its mind for nearly 30 years about building an opera house, but Glasgow went ahead and converted one of its general-purpose theatres, the Theatre Royal, into a home for the Scottish Opera and venue for Scottish Ballet. The city is also home to two major orchestras and the Royal Scottish Academy of Music and Drama.

Besides its traditional theatres – the King's and the Pavilion – Glasgow has the **Tramway Theatre ❾** (www.tramway.org), the former home of the city's trams and

A recreated Glasgow street scene in the Riverside Museum.

now an internationally acclaimed contemporary visual and performing-arts theatre. Peter Brook inaugurated the theatre in 1988 when he staged his nine-hour epic *Mahabharata*, contributing to the cultural explosion that would lead to the city's prestigious title in 1990.

Studio theatres include the Tron, founded in 1979, the Mitchell Theatre, housed in an extension of the distinguished Mitchell Library, and two small theatres in the dynamic Centre for Contemporary Arts on Sauchiehall Street. However, Glasgow's most distinctive stage is the innovative **Citizens Theatre ❿** (www.citz.co.uk) started in 1943.

Each year, it seems, Glasgow adds a new festival to its calendar. The West End Festival, the city's biggest, has been followed by international jazz, cabaret and piping festivals, each held during successive summer months to keep visitors coming.

The turning point in Glasgow's progress towards cultural respectability came with the opening, in 1983, of the striking building in Pollok Country Park to house the Burrell Collection, bequeathed to the city in 1944 and now under major refurbishment. Until recently, the enormous popularity of the Burrell Collection has tended to overshadow Glasgow's other distinguished art galleries and museums: Kelvingrove, at the western end of Argyle Street, which has a strong representation of 17th-century Dutch paintings and 19th-century French paintings as well as many fine examples of the work of the late 19th-century Glasgow Boys; the Gallery of Modern Art (GoMA), opened in 1996; the university's Hunterian Museum and Art Gallery; and the St Mungo Museum of Religious Life and Art.

In 1999, The Lighthouse, designed by Charles Rennie Mackintosh and formerly the offices of *The Herald*, reopened as an architecture and design centre, with displays on the work of Mackintosh, and exhibition galleries. Other museums of note are Haggs Castle, a period museum, on the South Side and the miniature repository of social history, the red sandstone **Tenement House ⓫** (Mar––Oct daily 10am–5pm, Nov–Feb Sat–Mon 11am–4pm) a two-room-and-kitchen flat in an 1892 tenement in Garnethill, wonderfully preserved. The former Museum of Transport has now made way for the exciting Riverside Museum on the Clyde, which opened in 2011.

daily Mar–Oct 10am–5pm, Nov–Mar until 4pm), a restored 19th-century three-masted barque named *the Glenlee* that is now permanently moored so that visitors can explore what life was like on deck for crews who once sailed as far afield as Asia and Australia. As well as the crews' cabins there's an onboard hospital area and a galley kitchen.

THE CLYDE WALKWAY

Stobcross Quay is also a terminus of the **Clyde Walkway**, an area that has been part of a £1-billion 9-year-long 'Clyde Waterfront Regeneration' scheme introducing new residential and leisure developments to the once heavily industrialised banks of the Clyde. It is possible to walk from the quay through the centre of the city past Glasgow Green to the suburb of **Cambuslang**, but in its entirety it stretches 40 miles (64km) all the way to the Falls of Clyde at New Lanark (see page 169). It's particularly popular with cyclists, offering wonderful vistas without the pressures of motor traffic and links up with other cycle routes such as Glasgow to Inverness or Edinburgh.

Before you reach George V Bridge and Central Station's railway bridge, you come to the **Broomielaw**, an area rich in sailing history and being regenerated into the rapidly expanding financial services district with modern offices and hotels. It was once the departure point for regular services to Ireland, North America and the west coast towns and islands of Scotland. You can sail from here on the world's last seagoing paddle steamer, the *Waverley* (tel: 041 243 2224; www.waverleyexcursions.co.uk; July–Aug Mon–Fri, times vary), which cruises during the summer to the Firth of Clyde, the Ayrshire coast and the Isle of Bute.

Custom House Quay ⓬, which looks across to the delicately restored Georgian facades of Carlton Place on the south bank, is also the subject of a major regeneration project.

The central section of the walkway is the most interesting, taking in the city's more distinguished bridges and many of the buildings associated with its maritime life. The two most impressive bridges are the pedestrian **Suspension Bridge** and the **Victoria**

The Hydro arena on the Clyde.

◔ DEATH ON THE CLYDE

The old adage that 'the Clyde made Glasgow and Glasgow made the Clyde' cannot be taken as a true description of the relationship today. In his book In Search of Scotland, journalist and writer H.V. Morton describes the launching of a ship on the Clyde in a passage that brings tears to the eyes: 'Men may love her as men love ships … She will become wise with the experience of the sea. But no shareholder will ever share her intimacy as we who saw her so marvellously naked and so young slip smoothly from the hands that made her into the dark welcome of the Clyde'. That was written in 1929 – at a time when the Clyde's shipbuilding industry was on the precipice of the Great Depression from which it never recovered.

Soon, another writer, the novelist George Blake, was calling the empty yards and silent cranes 'the high, tragic pageant of the Clyde', and today that pageant is nothing more than a side-show. Not even the boost of demand during World War II, nor replacement orders in the 1950s, not even the work on supply vessels and oil platforms for the oil industry in the 1970s, could rebuild the vigour of the Clyde. Today Glasgow no longer depends on the river for its economic survival but developments like the Clyde Walkway, the Glasgow Science Centre and the Riverside Museum represent a new future for the river as part of the leisure industry.

The Gallery of Modern Art.

Interactive games in the Glasgow Science Centre.

Bridge. The Victoria Bridge was built in 1854 to replace the 14th-century Old Glasgow Bridge, and the graceful Suspension Bridge was completed in 1871, designed by Alexander Kirkland, who later became the Commissioner of Public Buildings in Chicago.

There is also new life on the inner-city banks of the Clyde, as cranes and wharves are replaced by modern residential apartments. On the south bank, near Govan, upmarket apartments have been built at the old **Prince's Dock**, the £20-million Clyde Arc links the Finnieston Quay with the BBC Scotland complex on the south bank at Pacific Quay, and the massive Rotunda at the north of the old Clyde Tunnel, designed for pedestrians and horses and carts, has been restored as a restaurant complex.

Other opportunities to get on the river are offered by **Seaforce** (tel: 0141-221 1070; www.seaforce.co.uk), which runs powerboat trips from beside The Tall Ship, and the Clyde Waterbus, a river taxi between the Broomielaw and Braehead.

GEORGE SQUARE AND MERCHANT CITY

George Square is the heart of modern Glasgow. Like most Scottish squares, it contains a motley collection of statues, commemorating 11 people who seem to have been chosen by lottery. The 80ft (24-metre) column in its centre is mounted by the writer Sir Walter Scott, gazing southwards, so they say, to the land where he made all his money. But the square is more effectively dominated by the grandiose **City Chambers** ⓭ (tel: 0141-287 4018; ground floor only Mon–Fri 8.30am–5pm, guided tours Mon–Fri at 10.30am and 2.30pm; free) designed by William Young and opened in 1888. The marble-clad interior is even more opulent and self-important than the exterior. The pièce de résistance is the huge banqueting hall, 110ft (33 metres) long, 48ft (14 metres) wide and 52ft (16 metres) high; it has a glorious arched ceiling, leaded glass windows and paintings depicting scenes from the city's history. The south wall is covered by three large murals, works of the Glasgow Boys (see page 85).

George Square's other monuments to Victorian prosperity are the former Head Post Office on the south side and the noble **Merchants' House** on the northwest corner (now home to the Glasgow Chamber of Commerce). Its crowning glory is the gold ship on its dome, drawing the eye ever upwards – a replica of the ship on the original Merchants' House.

Today the whole area south of George Square and down to Argyle Street is collectively known as Merchant City. The grandiose warehouses and mansions erected by the suddenly wealthy tobacco magnates of the late 18th and early 19th centuries have been preserved in all their exterior glory and converted into a bustling area of up-market shops, restaurants and cafés, many of which put out pavement tables on sunny days giving the whole area a decidedly European feel.

It's one of the most influential and successful aspects of Glasgow's 1980s regeneration projects.

Just off Buchanan Street is **Nelson Mandela Place** (its name having been changed from St George's Place in tribute to the South African political leader, who was granted Freedom of the City in 1993). Here you will find the **Glasgow Stock Exchange ⓮**, designed in the 1870s by John Burnet, whose reputation was to be eclipsed by his celebrated son J.J. Burnet; and the **Royal Faculty of Procurators** (1854).

Nearby are examples of the work of another distinguished Glasgow architect, the younger James Salmon, who designed the **Mercantile Buildings ⓯** (1897–8) in Bothwell Street and the curious **Hat-rack** in St Vincent Street, named for the extreme narrowness and the projecting cornices of its tall facade. Further west, J.J. Burnet's extraordinary **Charing Cross Mansions ⓰** of 1891, with grandiloquent intimations of French Renaissance style, were spared the surgery of motorway development which destroyed many 19th-century buildings around Charing Cross.

MAGNIFICENT TERRACES

On the other side of one of these motorways are the first buildings of the **Park Conservation Area**. These edifices have given rise to the statement that Glasgow is the 'finest piece of architectural planning of the mid-19th century'. Take a stroll upwards through this area to a belvedere above Kelvingrove Park and marvel at the glorious vistas.

The belvedere is backed by **Park Quadrant** and **Park Terrace**, which are probably the most magnificent of all the terraces in the Park Conservation Area. Still in the West End, in Great Western Road, you will find **Great Western Terrace ⓱**, one of the best surviving examples of the work of Alexander 'Greek' Thomson, the architect who acquired his nickname as a result of his passion for classicism.

Back towards the city centre in St Vincent Street is Thomson's prominent **St Vincent Street Church ⓲**. It is

Window detail on the Merchants' House.

⊘ THE BUILT ENVIRONMENT

'Rough, careless, vulnerable and sentimental.' That's how the Scottish poet Edwin Morgan, who died in August 2010 aged 90, described Glaswegians, and they are certainly qualities that Glaswegians have brought to their environment. The city has been both brutal and nostalgic about its own fabric, destroying and lamenting with equal vigour. When the city fathers built an urban motorway in the 1960s they liberated Glasgow for the motorist but cut great swathes through its domestic and commercial heart, and were only just prevented from extending the Inner Ring Road, which would have demolished in the process much of the Merchant City. But the disappearance of the last trams in the 1960s has been regretted ever since, even though Glaswegians have grown to love the 'Clockwork Orange' – the violently coloured underground transport system.

But to Morgan's list of adjectives might have been added 'showy' and 'aspirational', two sides of the architectural coin that represents Glasgow's legacy of magnificent Victorian buildings. They aren't hard to find: the dense gridiron of streets around George Square and westwards invites the neck to crane at any number of soaring facades, many bearing the art of the sculptor and all signifying some chapter of the city's 19th-century history.

fronted by an Ionic portico, with sides more Egyptian than Greek and a tower that wouldn't have been out of place in India during the days of the Raj. Here the streets rise towards **Blythswood Square**, which was once a haunt of prostitutes but now, with its surroundings, provides a graceful mixture of late Georgian and early Victorian domestic architecture.

ART AND ARCHITECTURE

In Buchanan Street is the **Glasgow Royal Concert Hall** (tel: 0141-353 8000; www.glasgowconcerthalls.com), a purpose-built venue that regularly attracts top artists and orchestras. Behind **St Vincent Place** is **Royal Exchange Square**, which is pretty well consumed by the city's **Gallery of Modern Art (GoMA) ⑲ ◗** (tel: 0141-287 3050; Mon–Wed & Sat 10am–5pm, Thu 10am–8pm, Fri, Sun 11am–5pm; free). The glorious building in which it is housed began life as the 18th-century mansion of a tobacco lord, and has since been a bank, the Royal Exchange, and more recently a public library and extensive archive.

Today all aspects of modern art, from painting, sculpture, photography and video installations, by both Scottish and international artists, are housed on four floors.

Among the city centre's most distinguished Georgian buildings are **Hutcheson's Hall**, in Ingram Street (now a restaurant), designed by David Hamilton; and, in nearby Glassford Street, **Trades Hall ⑳**, which, despite alterations, has retained the facade designed by the great Robert Adam.

But any excursion around Glasgow's architectural treasures must include the work of the city's most innovative genius, Charles Rennie Mackintosh, who overturned the Victorians in a series of brilliant designs between 1893 and 1911. Mackintosh's influence on 20th-century architecture, along with his leading contribution to Art Nouveau in interiors, furniture and textile design, has long been acknowledged and celebrated throughout Europe, although all his finest work was done in and around Glasgow.

Charles Rennie Mackintosh design.

MACKINTOSH FAVOURITES

Mackintosh's sometimes austere, sometimes sensuous style, much influenced by natural forms and an inspired use of space and light, can be seen in several important buildings: his greatest achievement, designed in 1896, the **Glasgow School of Art ㉑** (tel: 0141-353 4526; www.gsa.ac.uk; guided tours Apr–Sept daily 11am–5pm on the hour, Oct–Mar Mon–Sat 11.30am and 2.30pm; advance booking advisable) in Renfrew Street is not only one of Britain's most esteemed art schools but is considered by many to be the designer's masterpiece. Tragically, however, the school suffered two catastrophic fires within the space of four years (2014 and 2018), so remains off limits for the foreseeable future. **Scotland Street School**, on the South Side, opened in 1904 and is now a Museum of Education (tel: 0141-287 0500; Mon–Thu, Sat 10am–5pm, Fri, Sun 11am–5pm free) detailing experiences of Glasgow schoolchildren throughout the 20th century, including re-created classrooms. The **Martyrs' Public School** (tel: 0141-946 6600; closed to the public), perched

above a slip road to the M8 motorway near Glasgow Cathedral houses Glasgow Museum's Conservation Department.

In Sauchiehall Street, the facade of the Mackintosh-designed **Willow Tea Rooms ㉒** (1903) remains, and a room on the first floor has been turned over to teatime again, with reproduction Mackintosh furniture. But more stunning examples of his interior designs can be seen at the **Mackintosh House** at the University of Glasgow's **Hunterian Art Gallery ㉓** (tel: 0141 330 4221; www.gla.ac.uk/hunterian; Tue–Sat 10am–5pm, Sun 11am–4pm; gallery free) on Gilmorehill. There, rooms from the architect's own house have been reconstructed and exquisitely furnished with original pieces of his furniture, watercolours and designs.

Also worth a visit are the **House for an Art Lover** (tel: 0141-483 1600; www.houseforanartlover.co.uk; times vary, check first) in Bellahouston Park, erected long after his death, but to his exact specifications; the **Queen's Cross Church** (tel: 0141-946 6600; www.mackintoshchurch.com; Apr–Oct Mon–Fri 11am–4pm, Feb–Mar

Shiva as Lord of the Dance, in the St Mungo Museum of Religious Life and Art.

Trades Hall.

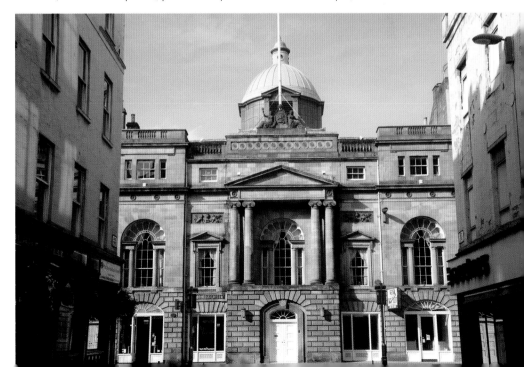

⊙ Fact

Scottish poet and author Tobias Smollett, writing in 1771, had no doubts about Glasgow's standing as a commercial centre: 'One of the most flourishing in Great Britain...it is a perfect bee-hive in point of industry.'

& Nov–Dec Mon, Wed, Fri 11am–4pm) – now often referred to simply as The Mackintosh Church and the only one he designed – in Garscube Road; and **The Lighthouse** (tel: 0141-276 5365; www.the-lighthouse.co.uk; Mon–Sat 10.30am–5pm, Sun noon–5pm; free) in Mitchell Lane near Central Station, now a Mackintosh study centre as well as a broad-based architecture and design centre.

GLASGOW CATHEDRAL

There's not much left in Glasgow that is old by British standards. The oldest building is **Glasgow Cathedral ㉔** (tel: 0141-552 8198; www.glasgowcathedral.org; Mon–Sat 9.30am–5.30pm, Sun 1–5pm, Oct–Mar until 4pm; free), most of which was completed in the 13th century, though parts were built a century earlier by Bishop Jocelyn. It was completed by the first bishop of Glasgow, Robert Blacader (1483–1508) and includes stunning stained-glass windows. The only pre-Reformation dwelling house is **Provand's Lordship** (tel: 0141 276 1625; Tue–Thu, Sat 10am–5pm, Fri, Sun 11am–5pm; free), built in 1471 as part of

Tomb of St Mungo in the crypt of Glasgow Cathedral.

a refuge for poor people and extended in 1670. It was preserved by William Burrell at the turn of the 20th century and now contains a museum of medieval material. Behind it is a Physic Garden, with a soothing array of herbs, and an orchard.

Both old buildings stand on **Cathedral Street**, at the top of the High Street – the cathedral on a site that has been a place of Christian worship since it was blessed for burial in AD 397 by St Ninian, the earliest missionary recorded in Scottish history. A severe but satisfying example of early Gothic, it contains the tomb of St Mungo.

Behind the cathedral, overseeing the city from the advantage of height, are more tombs – the intimidating Victorian sepulchres of the **Western Necropolis** (7am–dusk; free). This cemetery, modelled on Père Lachaise in Paris and intended to be a class-free interdenominational resting place, is a tribute to how important 19th-century society considered the rituals of burial. Many of the tombs, mausoleums and memorials are elaborately carved with statuary and symbolic motifs. It is all 'supervised' by

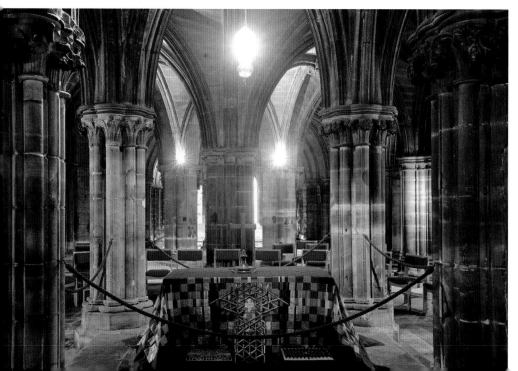

a statue of John Knox, the 16th-century reformer, and among the ranks of Glaswegian notables buried here is one William Miller, 'the laureate of the nursery', who wrote the popular bedtime jingle, 'Wee Willie Winkie'. In addition, on a clear day there are wonderful views of the city and surrounding countryside from here, including, in particularly fine weather, as far as Loch Lomond, so it's worth a visit even if roaming around headstones doesn't appeal.

A cream-coloured Scottish baronial building in front of the cathedral is home to the **St Mungo Museum of Religious Life and Art** (tel: 0141-276 1625; Tue–Thu, Sat 10am–5pm, Fri, Sun 11am–5pm; free), named after the city's patron saint and dedicated to the exploration of the six main world religions (Islam, Judaism, Hinduism, Christianity, Buddhism and Sikhism). There is also a Japanese Zen garden and some lovely stained-glass windows.

The two oldest churches in Glasgow, other than the cathedral, are **St Andrew's In the Square** 25, which contains some spectacular plasterwork, and the Episcopal **St Andrew's-by-the-Green** 26, once known as the Whistlin' Kirk because of its early organ. Both were built in the mid-18th century and both can be found to the northwest of Glasgow Green, in the Merchant City.

17TH-CENTURY STEEPLES

In the Merchant City you will also find two remnants of the 17th century, the **Tolbooth Steeple** 27 and the **Tron Steeple** 28. The Tolbooth Steeple at Glasgow Cross (where the Mercat Cross is a 20th-century replica of a vanished one) is a pretty substantial remnant of the old jail and courthouses, being seven storeys high with a crown tower. The Tron Steeple was once attached to the Tron Church, at the Trongate, and dates back to the late 16th and early 17th centuries. The original church was burned down in the 18th century and the replacement now

accommodates the lively Tron Theatre. Just to the west is Trongate 103, an art resource venue and centre of artistic creativity housed over six storeys.

MARKETS

Heavy industry has come and gone, but Glasgow still flourishes as a city of independent enterprise – of hawkers, stallholders, street traders and marketeers. Even the dignified buildings of its old, more respectable markets – fish, fruit and cheese – have survived in a city that has often been careless with its past, and have now become part of the rediscovery of the Merchant City area, which stretches from the **High Street** and the **Saltmarket** in the east to **Union Street** and **Jamaica Street** in the west. It contains most of the city's remaining pre-Victorian buildings.

The old **Fishmarket** 29 in Clyde Street is in fact Victorian, but it accommodates a perpendicular remnant of the 17th-century Merchants' House that was demolished in 1817. Known as the Briggait, a corruption of Bridgegate, it is now home to the Wasps Artists' Studios. (The

Dining room in the House for an Art Lover.

genuine fish market is now out of town off the M8 motorway.)

In **Candleriggs** , slightly to the north and so-named because at one time candlemakers traded here, the old fruitmarket now houses a variety of cafés, restaurants and shops, while Glasgow's market celebrity still belongs to the **Barras** ❸ (Sat & Sun 9.30am–4.30pm), a thriving flea market in the Gallowgate to the east, where both repartee and bargains were once reputed to rival those of Paris's flea market and London's Petticoat Lane. Founding queen of the Barras was Mrs McIver, who started her career with one barrow, bought several more to hire out on the piece of ground she rented in the Gallowgate, and was claimed to have retired a millionaire. A mixture of genuine vintage and genuine junk, it's heaven for any bargain hunter who enjoys a good rummage. Nearby is the **Glasgow Antiques Market** (tel: 0141-552 6989; Sat–Sun 9am–5pm), which is the place to go for more serious and more moneyed collectors. Also nearby is **Barrowland Ballroom**, one of the city's most thriving live-music venues for the past few decades. Its fame briefly turned to infamy, however, in the 1960s when a serial killer known as Bible John murdered three women whilst quoting passages from the Good Book.

SHOPPING DISTRICTS

Argyle Street, traversed by the railway bridge to Central Station, **Sauchiehall Street** and the more up-market **Buchanan Street**, with the Buchanan Galleries complex, are Glasgow's great shopping thoroughfares, while the cosmopolitan café culture area round **Great Western Road** and **Byres Road**, in the West End, is a centre for interesting bric-a-brac and boutiques. Ruthven Lane is the place to go for vintage finds. **West Regent Street** has a Victorian Village (small antique shops in old business premises) and the area around the **Italian Centre** in the Merchant City is alive with stylish café-bars.

Glaswegians have always spent freely, belying the slur on the open-handedness of Scots, and the city's commercial interests seem to believe that the appetite for shopping is insatiable. Just off Buchanan Street, up-market **Princes Square Shopping Centre** ❸ (www.princessquare.co.uk), with a range of high-end high street outlets and a number of cafés and bars, is worth visiting even for those who don't wish to shop or eat. It's also a welcome respite from the rain, which is no rare occurrence in Glasgow.

The site of the demolished St Enoch Railway Station and hotel (one of Glasgow's major acts of vandalism) is now occupied by the **St Enoch Centre** ❸ (www.st-enoch.com) a spectacular glass-covered complex of shops, a fast-food court, ice rink and car park. A popular leisure and retail development is the huge waterside **Braehead Centre** (www.intu.co.uk/braehead), at Renfrew on the western edge of the city.

'Edinburgh is the capital,' as the old joke goes, 'but Glasgow *has* the capital.' And it flaunts it.

East entrance to Barras weekend market.

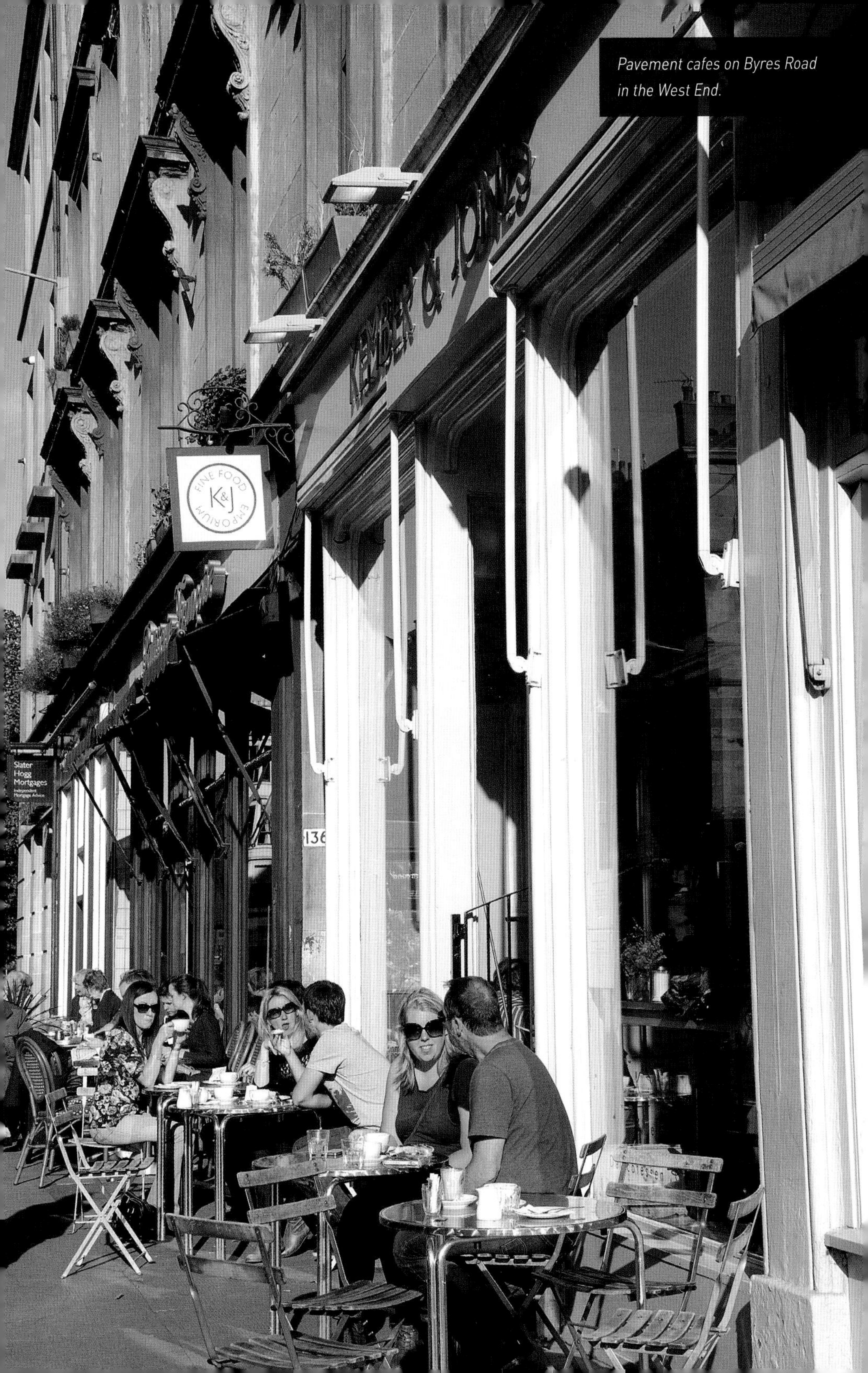

Pavement cafes on Byres Road in the West End.

Moody and magnificent Glen Coe.

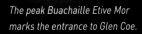
The peak Buachaille Etive Mor marks the entrance to Glen Coe.

THE WEST COAST

Mountain and moor, heather and stag, castle and loch – and a magical seaboard of isolated villages and small ports – are all to be found on the glorious west coast of Scotland.

From the long finger of Kintyre to the deep fissure of Loch Broom, the west coast is the part of Scotland that most perfectly conforms to its romantic image. Nowhere else in Scotland (outside Caithness and Sutherland) is a physical sense of travelling more thrillingly experienced; and few other areas provide such opportunities for solitude and repose, as well as the slightly awesome impression that this dramatic landscape is not to be trifled with.

KINTYRE

It all begins gently enough at the Clyde estuary, where the deep penetration of the sea at **Loch Fyne** has created Scotland's longest peninsula, which is 54 miles (87km) from Crinan to the Mull of Kintyre and never wider than 10 miles (16km). This mighty arm is neatly bisected by West Loch Tarbert into the two regions of Knapdale and Kintyre, and its isolated character makes it almost as remote as any of the islands.

Here there are rolling hills rather than mountains, rough moors and forests in Knapdale, grassy tops in Kintyre and a coast that is most interesting on its west side, with a close view of the island of Jura from **Kilberry Head ❶** (where you can also view a fine collection of medieval sculptured stones). **Tarbert ❷** is a port popular with yachties. Once a

Sheep graze on Beinn Eighe.

thriving herring-fishing base, it's now the annual host of the Scottish Series Sailing Festival. There's plenty of accommodation and several cosy pubs clustered around the pretty harbour.

Further south is **Tayinloan ❸**, from where you can take the 20-minute ferry ride across to the tiny island of Gigha, noted for the fine **Achamore Gardens** (www.gigha.org.uk). South again is the vast beach of **Machrihanish ❹**, but best known for its two fabulous golf courses. Beyond here, **Campbeltown** may not be the most

⊘ Main attractions
Loch Fyne
Tarbert
Mull of Kintyre
Inveraray
Arduaine Garden
Scottish Slate Islands
 Heritage Trust Centre
Oban
Glen Coe
Eilean Donan Castle
Inverewe Garden

Map on page 204

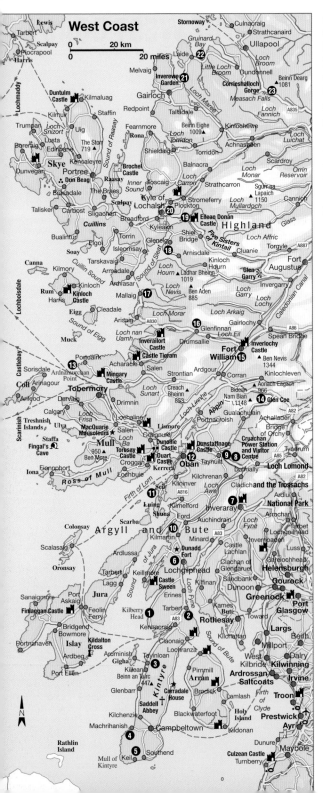

attractive of places but it does have the **Springbank Distillery** (tel: 01586 551710; www.sprinbank.scot; tours Mon–Sat 10 & 11am, 1,30 and 3pm), one of very few distilleries left that still does its own malting. From here it is only a short drive to the tip of the peninsula, the **Mull of Kintyre** itself (now an RSPB bird reserve), with the Northern Ireland coast just 12 miles (19km) away.Legend has it that St Columba first set foot in Scotland at **Keil** ❺, near the holiday village of Southend; you can see his 'footprints' imprinted on a flat rock near a ruined chapel.

KINTYRE'S EAST COAST

From the great lighthouse on the Mull, first built in 1788 and remodelled by Robert Stevenson, grandfather of Robert Louis, there is nowhere else to go. You can retreat back up the secondary road (B842) of Kintyre's east coast, which has its own scenic drama in the sandy sweep of **Carradale Bay** and the view across the water to the mountains of Arran, reached by car ferry from Claonaig. The hump behind Carradale is **Beinn an Tuirc**, Kintyre's highest hill (1,490ft/447 metres). The name means Mountain of the Boar, from a fearsome specimen said to have been killed by an ancestor of the Campbells. You can take in the ruined walls and sculptured tombstones of **Saddell Abbey**, a 12th-century Cistercian house, and **Skipness Castle and Chapel**.

From **Lochgilphead** ❻ – close to where, at Ardrishaig, the 9-mile (15km) Crinan Canal crosses the neck of the peninsula and connects Loch Fyne to the Atlantic Ocean – you have a choice of two main routes to the port and resort of Oban. The longer route, up Loch Fyne by Inveraray to Loch Awe (A83 and then A819) is the more dramatic, although the shorter route (A816) keeps you close to the coast and its vistas of those low-lying islands, which are the floating outriders of the mountains of Jura and Mull.

INVERARAY CASTLE

Both routes are punctuated by places of interest. The most celebrated castle in the area is **Inveraray** ❼ (tel: 01499-302 203; www.inveraray-castle. com; Apr–Oct daily 10am–5.45pm), the seat of the chiefs of Clan Campbell, the dukes of Argyll, for centuries and the venue for the **Inveraray Highland Games** held annually in July. The present building – Gothic Revival, famous for its magnificent interiors and art collection – was started in 1743, when the third duke also decided to rebuild the village of Inveraray. The result is a dignified community with much of the orderly elegance of the 18th century. By means of wax figures, commentary and imaginative displays, **Inveraray Jail** (tel: 01499-302 381; www.inveraray jail.co.uk; daily Apr–Oct 9.30am–6pm, Nov–Mar 10am–5pm) brings to life a courtroom trial and what it was like in the cells in the 19th century. You can interact with costumed characters, meet the warder, experience courtroom trials and even sample the punishments.

Some 5 miles (8km) south of town is **Auchindrain Township Museum** (tel: 01499-500 325; www.auchindrain.org. uk; Apr–Oct daily 10am–5pm), whose dwellings and barns of the 18th and 19th centuries were once a communal-tenancy Highland farm, paying rent to the duke.

LOCH AWE AND BEN CRUACHAN

Loch Awe, where the road takes you past the fallen house of the Breadal-bane dynasty – the romantic ruin of **Kilchurn Castle** on a promontory on the water – is the longest freshwater loch in Scotland. At its northwest extremity, where it squeezes past the mighty mountain of Ben Cruachan and drains into Loch Etive through the dark slit of the Pass of Brander, it's as awesome as its name promises.

Almost a mile inside Ben Cruachan is the **Cruachan Power Station and Visitor Centre** ❽ (tel: 0141 6149105; www.visitcruachan.co.uk; Apr–Oct Mon–Fri 9.15am–4.45pm, Nov–Mar Mon–Fri 9.45am–3.45pm), a

Inveraray Castle.

The Commando Monument near Spean Bridge commemorates Allied troops during World War II.

pumped-storage hydroelectric power station located in an artificial cavern, which you can view on an electric bus. The 30-minute guided tour takes you deep inside the mountain and gives you a chance to view the huge generators.

The road continues through **Taynuilt** ⊙, a village of more than passing interest. One of the earliest monuments to Nelson was erected here when locals dragged an ancient standing stone into the village and carved an inscription on it. It can still be seen, near the church. The main attraction, however, is the **Bonawe Iron Furnace** (tel: 01866-822 432; Apr–Sept Wed–Fri 9.30am–5.30pm), founded in 1753 by a North of England partnership and the most complete charcoal-fuelled ironworks in Britain. A little nearer to Oban, the road passes by the Connel Bridge, under which are the foaming **Falls of Lora**, a remarkable waterfall that appears in a series of dramatic cataracts as Loch Etive drains into the sea at ebb tide.

FORT AND PREHISTORIC SITES

If you take the A816 from Lochgilphead to Oban by the coast, you will pass one of the ancient capitals of Dalriada, the kingdom of the early Scots. The striking eminence of **Dunadd Fort** (c.AD 500–800) sets the mood for a spectacular group of prehistoric sites around the village of **Kilmartin** ⓾: standing stones, burial cairns and cists are all accessible. Start with the collection of sculptured stones in the churchyard then proceed to the excellent **Kilmartin Museum** (tel: 01546-510278; www.kilmartin.org; daily March–Oct 10am–5.30pm, Nov–Christmas 11am–4pm) nearby, which vividly documents the area's extraordinarily rich archaeological heritage.

As you drive north, the coast becomes more riven, while the natural harbours of the sea lochs and the protective islands of **Shuna, Luing** (noted for its slate) and **Seil** ⑪ attract the yachting fraternity. Here, too, is **Arduaine Garden** (tel: 01852-200 366; daily Apr–Sept 9.30am–5.30pm, Oct–March 9.30am–4pm), a 20-acre (8-hectare)

⊘ OBAN: SEAWAY TO THE HEBRIDES

Ringed by wooded hills and clasped within the sheltered bay, Oban has the finest harbour on the Highland seaboard. Here even a landlocked traveller feels the pull of the islands: there are regular ferries to Mull, Barra, South Uist and Colonsay, as well as to the nearby islands of Kerrera and Lismore. Oban is the focal point for tourists throughout the whole of Argyll, but also serves as the shopping centre for the rural population of the region, so it's likely to be busy all year round. In August there is the added attraction of the Argyllshire Highland Gathering, with displays of traditional dancing and folk music. Moreover, the town is one of the best places in the whole of Scotland to eat seafood, be it in one of the many fine restaurants, or at one of the shacks down by the ferry terminal.

Hotels and boarding houses abound. However, modern tourism hasn't been kind to the dignity of its high street; it lost the delightful Victorian buildings of its railway station in an act of institutional vandalism. But the town still has atmosphere – mostly centred on the busy harbour. Pulpit Hill is Oban's best viewpoint, along with the extraordinary folly of McCaig's Tower. John Stuart McCaig was a banker who financed this strange enterprise on a hill above the town centre to give work to the unemployed. The tower was raised between 1890 and 1900, but McCaig's grand plan was never completed. What remains looks like an austere Scottish Colosseum.

promontory owned by the National Trust for Scotland and renowned for superb rhododendrons, azaleas and magnolias, as well as many Asian plants such as Himalayan lilies.

Seil and its neighbours were supported by a vigorous slate industry until a great storm in 1881 flooded the quarries deep below sea level and efforts to pump them out failed. You can see vivid evidence of those days on Seil at the **Scottish Slate Islands Heritage Trust Centre** (tel: 01852-300 449; www.slateislands.org.uk; Apr–Oct daily 10.30am–4.30pm). Seil itself is so close to the mainland that it's reached by the single stone arch of the 1791 Clachan Bridge, the 'bridge over the Atlantic'.

ISLAND-HOPPING FROM OBAN

Every facility for visitors can be found in **Oban** ⑫, whose only beach, **Ganavan Sands**, is 2 miles (3km) north of the town. Whisky-making is explained on the interesting tours of **Oban Distillery** (tel: 01631-572 004; www.malts.com; Jan–Feb & Dec daily noon–4.30pm, Mar–Apr, Oct–Nov daily 9.30am–5pm,

May–Sept daily 9.30am–7.30pm) and there are castles to be visited: the scant fragment of **Dunollie** on its precipitous rock and, at Connel, the fine 13th-century fortress of **Dunstaffnage** (tel: 01631-562 465; Apr–Sept daily 9.30am–5.30pm, Oct–Mar Sat–Wed 10am–4pm).

Oban is a great base from which to explore Scotland's west coast. The island of **Mull** (see page 225) is just a 40-minute ferry ride away, as is the long fertile island of **Lismore**, whose name means 'great garden'. In Oban Bay is pretty little **Kerrera**, reached by a small foot ferry. A walk round the island takes you past the dramatic ruin of **Gylen Castle** at its southern tip, commanding a spectacular view of sea, coastline and islands.

North from Oban, the A828 crosses the Connel Bridge to reach the lovely landscapes of Benderloch and Appin.

Appin is a name that evokes romantic tragedy. In a historical incident made famous by Robert Louis Stevenson in *Kidnapped*, James Stewart of the Glens was wrongly hanged for the murder of Colin Campbell, the 'Red Fox' and

Oban harbour.

Glenfinnan Monument commemorates the final Jacobite Rising of 1745.

Sample a wee dram at Oban Distillery.

government land agent, following the Jacobite Rising of 1745. Further north still, at **Corran**, you can cross **Loch Linnhe** on a five-minute ferry ride to **Ardgour** and the tortuous drive to isolated **Ardnamurchan Point** , the most westerly point of the Scottish mainland.

POWER OF GLEN COE

Once across the Ballachulish Bridge, the full grandeur of the West Highlands lies before you. To the east is the sublime mountain scenery of perhaps the most famous glen in Scotland, though for the wrong reason: **Glen Coe** , where in a savage winter dawn in February 1692, 38 members of the Clan Donald were slaughtered by government soldiers to whom they had given shelter and hospitality. The landscape here exerts a great deal of power and even the unimaginative must feel a shiver up their spine as they follow the A82 between the dark buttresses of **Buachaille Etive Mor**, **Bidean nam Bian** and the **Aonach Eagach**. These mountains are notorious: they are among Britain's supreme

mountaineering challenges, and nearly every winter they claim lives. The National Trust for Scotland owns most of Glen Coe and exhibitions at its **Glen Coe Visitor Centre** (tel: 0844-493 2222; www.nts.org.uk/visit/places/glencoe; Easter–Oct daily 9.30am–6pm, Nov–Feb daily 10am–4pm) near the foot of the glen tell its story.

Some 15 miles (24km) north of Ballachulish on the A82 is **Fort William** . The fort itself was demolished, not by the Jacobites but by the railway. Bonnie Prince Charlie's bed and a secret portrait are among the Jacobite relics in the **West Highland Museum** (tel: 01397-702 169; www.westhighlandmuseum.org.uk; Mon–Sat May–Sept 10am–5pm,Oct–Apr until 4pm).

BEN NEVIS

Despite its fine position between the mountains and Loch Linnhe and its proximity to world-class mountain biking at Nevis Range (www.nevisrange.co.uk), busy Fort William has little to commend it beyond its proximity to **Ben Nevis** and glorious Glen Nevis. Britain's highest

mountain (4,406ft/1,344 metres) looks a deceptively inoffensive lump from below, where you can't see its savage north face, but the volatile nature of the Scottish climate should never be underestimated when setting out on any hill walk: the 'Ben' is a long, tough day, and you should take advice from the visitor centre at its foot in Glen Nevis.

THE ROAD TO THE ISLES

From Fort William, turn west on the A830, taking the 'road to the Isles' to Mallaig, another ferry port for the Hebrides (particularly the 'Small Isles' of Canna, Rum, Eigg and Muck). At **Corpach** you will find **Treasures of the Earth** (tel: 01397-772 283; www.treasuresoftheearth.co.uk; Nov–Feb daily 10am–4pm; Mar–June, Sept–Oct until 5pm; July–Aug 9.30am–6pm), an intriguing geology-based exhibition of gemstones and rare minerals.

In summer the **Jacobite Steam Train** (tel: 0844 850 4685; www.westcoastrailways.co.uk) runs through the spectacular scenery from Fort William to Mallaig. One of the world's great train

journeys, this was of course the track that accommodated the Hogwart's Express in the film version of *Harry Potter and the Chamber of Secrets*.

The road continues past Loch Eil to **Glenfinnan ⑯**. In August 1745 Charles raised the white-and-crimson Stuart banner here to the cheers of 5,000 men who had rallied behind the charismatic young prince's impetuous adventure, which was to cost the Highlands dearly. A monument was raised on the spot in 1815; the National Trust for Scotland's **Glenfinnan Visitor Centre** (tel: 01397 722 250; daily Mar & Oct 9.30am–5pm, Apr–Sept 9am–7pm, Nov–Feb 10am–4pm) tells the story convincingly.

LOCH NAN UAMH

The prince had landed from his French brig at **Loch nan Uamh**, a few miles further west. Just over a year later, after the disaster of Culloden, he left from the same place, having fled pursuing government troops for months around the Highlands and islands: despite a price of £30,000 on his head – a fortune for the time – he was never

⊘ Tip

From Glenelg you can cross the water of Loch Duich to Kylerhea in Skye, although the little car ferry (www.skyeferry.co.uk) runs only from Easter to October. Alternatively, use the Skye Bridge at Kyle of Lochalsh.

Glenfinnan Viaduct is part of the West Highland Railway and overlooks Loch Shiel.

A short diversion from Kyle of Lochalsh takes you to the popular holiday village of Plockton where, because of its sheltered position, palm trees flourish.

Mallaig fishermen splicing their ropes.

once betrayed. A memorial cairn on the shore of Loch nan Uamh marks his final exit from Scotland.

From **Arisaig** the road passes between the silver sands of **Morar** and the deep **Loch Morar** (said to be the home of Morag, another water monster) and comes to an end at **Mallaig** ⓱, an important landing place for white fish and shellfish. You can take a car ferry across the Sound of Sleat to **Armadale** on Skye or enjoy a cruise to the great, roadless mountain wilderness of **Knoydart** with its two long sea lochs, **Hourn** and **Nevis** – said to be the lochs of heaven and hell. Land at Inverie for a whisky or pint at The Old Forge (tel: 01687-462 267; www.the oldforge.co.uk), Britain's remotest mainland pub.

The alternative from Fort William is to continue on the A82 and at **Invergarry** turn west on the A87 to climb past a spectacular roadside viewpoint looking down Glen Garry, and then drop to the head of Glen Shiel, with the famous peaks of the **Five Sisters of Kintail** soaring above on your right.

At Shiel Bridge, a minor road turns left over the Mam Ratagan pass to reach **Glenelg** ⓲, worth a visit not only for its beauty but also for **Dun Telve** and **Dun Troddan**, two superb brochs – circular Iron Age towers with double walls which still stand over 30ft (9 metres) high. Here, too, are the remains of **Bernera Barracks**, quartered by Hanoverian troops during the 18th century.

EILEAN DONAN CASTLE

Go back to Shiel Bridge and continue on the A87 along lovely Loch Duich to reach **Eilean Donan Castle** ⓳ (tel: 01599-555 202; www.eileandonancastle. com; daily Apr–May & Oct 10am–6pm, June–Sept 9.30am–6pm, Nov–Feb 10am–4pm), a restored Mackenzie stronghold on an islet reached by a causeway and probably the most photographed castle in Scotland. The road runs on to Kyle of Lochalsh and the bridge across to Skye.

From **Kyle of Lochalsh** ⓴, mainland travellers continue north, and you can take the coast road via Duirinish for 6 miles (10km) to **Plockton**, one of the

most picturesque loch-side villages in Scotland. Continue to the lovely **Loch Carron**, leaving Inverness-shire for the tremendous mountain massifs of **Wester Ross**. Here, on the isolated peninsula of **Applecross** and among the mighty peaks of **Torridon** with their views to the Cuillins of Skye and the distant, drifting shapes of the Outer Hebrides, is some of Europe's most wild and spectacular scenery.

More gentle pursuits can be found in **Poolewe** village, where the road through Gairloch passes between Loch Ewe and **Loch Maree**, possibly the most sublime inland loch in Scotland. The loch's particular features are the old Scots pines along its shores and the impressive presence of **Slioch**, the 'mountain of the spear', on its eastern shore.

INVEREWE GARDEN

Just under two hours from Inverness on the A835/832, **Inverewe Garden ㉑** (tel: 01445 712 952; daily Jan–May & Sept 9.30am–5pm, June–Aug 9.30am–6pm,Oct until 4pm) provides a sumptuous collection of subtropical plants – growing thanks to the mild climate created by the North Atlantic Drift – on the same latitude as Siberia. The gardens were begun in 1862 by Osgood Mackenzie, further developed by his daughter Mrs Mairi Sawyer, and given to the National Trust for Scotland in 1952.

A few miles further north is the glittering 4-mile (6km) scoop of **Gruinard Bay ㉒**, with coves of pink sand from the red Torridon sandstone, nearly 800 million years old. The road then takes you round **Little Loch Broom**, below the powerful shoulders of **An Teallach** ('The Forge', 3,483ft/1,062 metres), the highest of these mighty peaks and a mountain which makes Scotland's Lowland hills seem almost insignificant. You are now within easy reach of **Loch Broom** and the substantial fishing port and tourist centre of Ullapool (see page 282). On your way, stop at the **Measach Falls ㉓**, 10 miles (16km) before Ullapool, to admire the 120ft (35-metre) drop into the spectacular **Corrieshalloch Gorge**, crossed by a swaying Victorian suspension bridge.

Rhododendrons in bloom in Inverewe Garden.

Eilean Donan Castle.

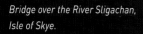
Bridge over the River Sligachan, Isle of Skye.

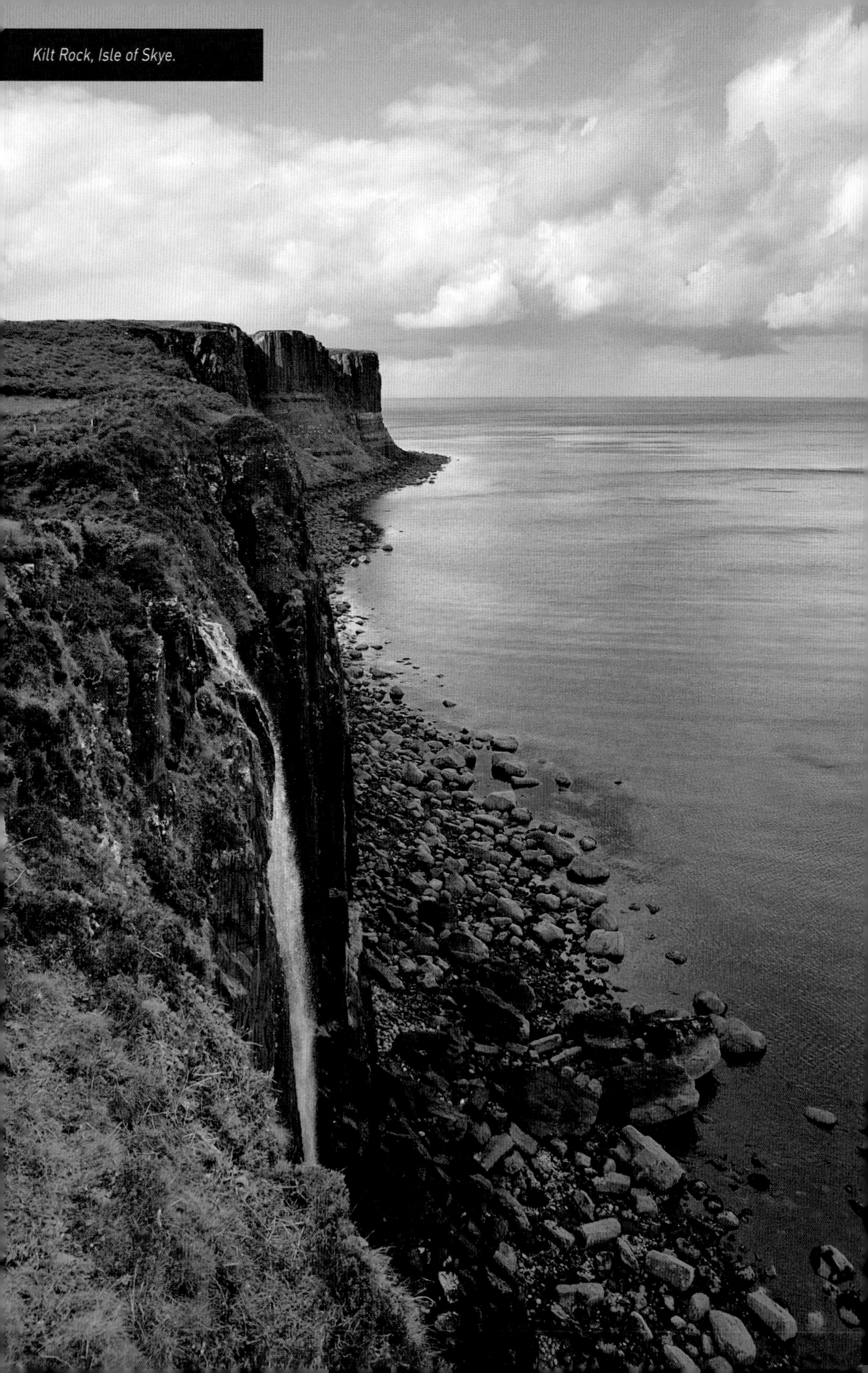

Kilt Rock, Isle of Skye.

SKYE

Arguably the most magnificent of the dozens of Scottish islands, Skye is a romantic, misty isle of dramatic sea lochs, rocky peaks and breathtaking views.

So deep are the incisions made by the sea lochs along the coast of Skye that, although the island is about 50 miles (80km) long and 30 miles (50km) wide, no part is more than 5 miles (8km) from the sea. The population, unlike that of most Scottish islands, is on the increase – mainly due to immigrants, many of whom are from south of the border.

Dominating the 'Misty Island' are the jagged **Cuillin Hills**, on a sharp winter's day providing as thrilling a landscape as any in Nepal or New Zealand. Strangely, these, the greatest concentration of peaks in Britain, are referred to as 'hills' rather than mountains; although they attain a height of not much more than 3,000ft (900 metres), they spring dramatically from sea level.

REACHING SKYE

Most visitors now reach Skye by driving over the road bridge that spans the **Kyleakin Narrows** between Kyle of Lochalsh and **Kyleakin ❶**. Alternative car-ferry routes are from Glenelg to Kylerhea and from Mallaig to Armadale. The former, a ferry (www.skyeferry.co.uk) accommodating a mere handful of cars, runs from Easter to October, while the latter becomes a passenger-only ferry in the winter.

The Storr escarpment.

Overlooking Kyleakin harbour are the scanty ruins of **Castle Moil**, once a stronghold of the Mackinnons and a lookout post and fortress against raids by Norsemen. Six miles (10km) out of Kyleakin, turn south on the A851 and, after 17 miles (27km), you will come to **Armadale ❷** and its ruined castle. **Armadale Castle Gardens and Museum of the Isles** (tel: 01471-844 305; www.armadalecastle.com; Mar & Nov Mon–Fri 10am–3pm, Apr–Oct daily 10am–5.30pm) was formerly the home of the

◎ Main attractions

Armadale Castle Gardens
Loch Scavaig
Portree
Aros Experience
Staffin
Skye Museum of Island
 Life
Dunvegan Castle
Colbost Folk Museum
Loch Bracadale
Talisker Distillery

Map on page 216

The natural harbour at Portree.

MacDonalds, who were once one of Scotland's most powerful clans and Lords of the Isles.

The **Clan Donald Trust**, which was formed in the 1970s and now has members throughout the world, has turned one wing of the ruined castle into a museum with audiovisual presentations. The old stables house an excellent restaurant, a good bookshop, gift shop and luxurious self-catering accommodation. There's a ranger service and guided walks through the grounds where there are many mature trees and rhododendrons. Further exploration of this area, called **Sleat** (pronounced *Slate*), reveals why it bears the sobriquet 'Garden of Skye'.

Return north to reach **Broadford**, from where a diversion southwest on the B8083 leads, after 14 miles (22km), to the scattered village of **Elgol ❸**. It was from here on 4 July 1746 that the Young Pretender, after being given a banquet by the Mackinnons in what is now called **Prince Charles's Cave**, finally bade farewell to the Hebrides. The view of the

Black Cuillins from here is one of the most splendid in all Britain.

In summer, motorboats go from Elgol across wide **Loch Scavaig**, past schools of seals, to land passengers on the rocks from where they can scramble upwards to **Loch Coruisk** in the very heart of the Cuillins. The scene was much painted by Turner and other Romantics and written about by Sir Walter Scott.

Backtrack once more to the A87 and, after 7 miles (11km) with the Red Cuillins to the left – they are much more rounded and much less dramatic than the Black Cuillins – you arrive at **Luib**, a crofting township once at the centre of the crofters' grievances (see page 220). Skye was the scene of some of the most intense fight-backs by crofters threatened with eviction during the Clearances. The Battle of the Braes (1882) was the last such 'battle' fought in Britain.

PORTREE – ISLAND CAPITAL

The road continues on through **Sligachan ❹**, a base for serious

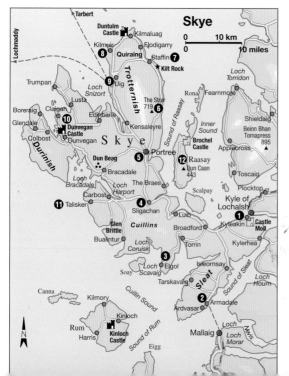

climbers of the Black Cuillins, and then descends into **Portree ❺**, the island's capital, an attractive town built around a natural harbour and with neat and brightly painted houses rising steeply from the water. In 1773, when they visited Portree, Dr Johnson and James Boswell dined in the Royal Hotel, then called McNab's Hostelry, believing it was 'the only inn on the island'. A quarter of a century before that, Prince Charlie had bade farewell to Flora MacDonald at McNab's. Just south of Portree is the **Aros Experience** (tel: 01478-613 649; www.aros.co.uk; daily 9am–5pm; charge for exhibition), where the story of the island is told from 1700 to the present day. There are also attractive woodland walks.

OLD MAN OF STORR

Magnificent rock scenery and breathtaking views can be enjoyed by driving north from Portree on the **Trotternish peninsula**. Seven miles (11km) out along the A855 is **The Storr ❻**, a 2,360ft (719-metre)

peak that is shaped like a crown and offers a stiff two-hour climb; to its east is the **Old Man of Storr**, an isolated 150ft (45-metre) pinnacle of rock. Further north is **Kilt Rock**, a sea cliff that owes its name to columnar basalt strata overlying horizontal ones beneath, the result bearing only the most fanciful relationship to a kilt.

A further 2 miles (4km) leads to **Staffin ❼**, immediately beyond which is **The Quiraing**, so broken up with massive rock faces that it looks like a range in miniature rather than a single mountain. The various rock features of the Quiraing – the castellated crags of **The Prison**, the slender, unclimbed 100ft (30-metre) **Needle** and **The Table**, a meadow as large as a football field – can be appreciated only on foot and can be reached readily by a path from a glorious minor road that cuts across the peninsula from Staffin to Uig.

However, to take this road rather than to loop around Trotternish peninsula is to forego some historic

Foxgloves bloom on Skye.

The Storr with the Black Cuillin mountains in the distance.

A moss-covered Celtic cross in a graveyard.

Wild Atlantic grey seal.

encounters. The annexe of the **Flodigarry Hotel** was Flora MacDonald's first home after her marriage in 1750 to Captain Allan MacDonald. Nearby is **Kilmuir churchyard** ❽, where Flora lies buried, wrapped in a sheet from the bed in which the fugitive prince had slept. On a clear day there are fine views from here of the Outer Hebrides, from where Charlie and Flora fled to Skye.

Then, at the northwest tip of the peninsula, is the ruined **Duntulm Castle**, an ancient MacDonald stronghold commanding the sea route to the Outer Hebrides. South of the castle is the **Skye Museum of Island Life** (tel: 01470-552 206; www.skyemuseum.co.uk; Apr–Oct Mon–Sat 9.30am–5pm), whose half a dozen thatched cottages show how the crofters lived. And so, after a few miles, to **Uig** ❾, from where the ferry departs for Lochmaddy on North Uist and Tarbert on Harris. The A87 south from Uig returns to Portree, but turn right at the junction with the A850 and travel westwards to Dunvegan 19 miles (30km) further on.

To the south you'll see **Macleod's Tables**, which dominate the **Duirinish peninsula**. Their flatness is attributed to the inhospitality shown to Columba when he preached to the local chief: in shame the mountains shed their caps so that the saint might have a flat bed on which to lie.

DUNVEGAN CASTLE

No other castle in Scotland can claim so long a record of continuous occupation by one family as **Dunvegan Castle** ❿ (tel: 01470-521 206; www.dunvegancastle.com; Apr–mid-Oct daily 10am–5.30pm), which has been home to the MacLeods for more than 700 years. Set on a rocky platform overlooking Loch Dunvegan, its stuccoed exterior lacks the splendour of at least a dozen other Scottish castles. Its interior, however, is another matter, with a wealth of paintings and memorabilia, including a painting of Dr Johnson by Sir Joshua Reynolds and a lock of Bonnie Prince Charlie's hair.

Best known, though, is the Fairy Flag, a torn and faded fragment of yellow silk spotted with red. Some say a fairy mother laid it over her half-mortal child when she had to return to her own people; others, more prosaic, that it was woven on the island of Rhodes in the 7th century and that a MacLeod captured it during the Crusades. Whatever its origins, the Fairy Flag is said to have three magic properties: when raised in battle it ensures a MacLeod victory; when spread over the MacLeod marriage bed it guarantees a child; and when unfurled at Dunvegan it charms the herring in the loch. The flag should be flown sparingly: its powerful properties will be exhausted when used three times. So far, it has twice been invoked.

Three miles (5km) before the town of Dunvegan, take the secondary B886 and travel northwards for 8 miles (13km) to **Trumpan** where, in

1597, the Fairy Flag was unfurled. A raiding party of MacDonalds from the island of Uist landed and set fire to a church packed with worshipping MacLeods. The alarm was raised and the MacDonalds were unable to escape as a falling tide had left their longboats high and dry and they were slain. The bodies were laid out on the sands below the sea wall, which was then toppled to cover them.

Primitive justice once practised on Skye is seen in the **Trumpan church-yard** in the shape of a standing stone pierced by a circular hole. The accused would be blindfolded and, if he could put his finger unerringly through the Trial Stone, was deemed innocent.

LOCAL CRAFTS

A few miles west of Dunvegan are Colbost, Glendale and Boreraig. The **Colbost Folk Museum** (tel: 01470-521 296; Easter–Oct daily 9.30am–5.30pm) is very atmospheric, with a peat fire on the floor of the blackhouse (a traditional dry-stone-wall thatched dwelling) waiting to cook a stew and a box bed uncomfortable enough to be genuine. Behind the house an illicit whisky still is no longer in use, but the restored 200-year-old watermill at **Glendale** is operating

Heading south from Dunvegan, the A863 follows the shores of **Loch Bracadale**, one of the most magnificent fjords of the west coast, with the black basalt wall of **Talisker Head** away to the south. At **Dun Beag**, near Bracadale, is a well-preserved broch (circular Iron Age fortified building). A left turn onto the B885 before reaching **Talisker** ⓫ leads back to **Portree**. Alternatively, remain on the A863 and at the head of **Loch Harport**, take the B8009, and cut back left into wooded **Glen Brittle** and more glorious views of the Black Cuillins. The B8009 continues to **Carbost** and the **Talisker Distillery** (tel: 01478-614 308; www.malts.com; Jan–Feb &

Nov–Dec Mon–Sat 10am–4.30pm, Sun 10.30am–4.30pm, Mar–Oct Mon–Sat 9.30am–5pm, Sun 10am–5pm,; tours throughout the day but booking advisable) where you can see how the 'water of life' is made at Skye's oldest working whisky distillery.

RAASAY – A PRINCE'S SHELTER

Some say that the sole purpose of Skye is to protect the small lush island of **Raasay** ⓬, just to the east. In the 18th century the English burned all Raasay's houses and boats because the laird had sheltered Bonnie Prince Charlie after the Battle of Culloden. Today the island has a population of about 200. **Dun Caan**, an extinct volcano, dominates the centre. Visitors can see the ruined **Brochel Castle**, home of the MacLeods of Skye and the grounds of Raasay House, now an outdoor pursuits centre. When Boswell stayed at the house with Dr Johnson he danced a jig on top of the 1,456ft (443-metre) -high Dun Caan ridge.

The coast around Neist Point, the most westerly point on Skye.

Dunvegan Castle.

📷 A CROFTER'S RUGGED LIFE

Almost 18,000 crofts in the Scottish Highlands keep people on the land, but they function more as a traditional way of living than as a source of income.

The word 'croft' derives from the Gaelic *croit*, meaning a small area of land. Often described as 'a piece of land fenced around with regulations', the croft is both much cherished and highly frustrating. Its emotive power comes from its origins. In the aftermath of the 19th-century Highland Clearances, groups of local men banded together to protect their families from being swept overseas to make way for sheep. At the time they were entirely at the whim of often absentee landowners.

By standing their ground despite all the odds – particularly at the so-called Battle of the Braes, in Skye – these men were rewarded in 1886 by an Act of Parliament which gave them security of tenure. It also regulated rents and entitled them to compensation for any improvements made to their properties. In May 2010, MPs at Holyrood backed a controversial Crofting Reform Bill to tackle the problems of absentee landlords and neglect of croft land.

CROFTING TOWNSHIPS TODAY

A croft is usually a combination of a house and a handful of barren, boggy acres for the crofter to cultivate or on which to graze livestock. The crofting community – commonly called a township – acts together in such activities as fencing, dipping or hiring a bull. Problems of isolation and remoteness are gradually being overcome as crofters become more connected through online organisations and communities.

Only around 5,300 crofts are owner-occupied. The rest are tenanted, although the rental they pay their landlord is minimal. In Scotland it's estimated there are around 20,000 crofts and 12,000 crofters, with around 30,000 people residing in crofting households.

Inhabited crofts on the Isle of Skye.

The interior of a traditional croft house, showing how people lived in the 19th century, at the Colbost Croft Museum, near Dunvegan on the Isle of Skye.

Sheep shearing on the island of South Uist in the Outer Hebrides.

Derelict croft near Ullapool in the Highlands.

A tradition that ties up the land

The most common criticisms of crofting are that it ties up land in segments too small ever to be economically viable, that most crofters are too old to cope, and that too many crofts are left to run down by absentee tenants – these are all problems faced by the government body known as the Crofters' Commission. Certainly, as far as agricultural production is concerned, crofting is a very small player, with estimates suggesting that some two-thirds of crofts are not actively farmed at all. But alternative agricultural projects have been shown to provide little employment, and would alter the landscape radically.

Crofting has lately been redefined to include any economic activity, so it can also cover such enterprises as running a B&B establishment. In Assynt and on the island of Eigg, crofters banded together to become landowners themselves, raising millions with internet appeals and the help of charities supporting traditional land use. There have been similar takeovers on Gigha and at Inverie, Knoydart Peninsula, where the Old Forge serves fresh seafood and venison from the local red deer, which wander freely in the single street.

Skye crofters drying seaweed.

The window of a traditional croft, also known as a blackhouse.

Portrait of an octogenarian Skye crofter.

Entrance to Fingal's Cave on the uninhabited island of Staffa.

Tobermory, Isle of Mull.

THE INNER HEBRIDES

The Inner Hebrides have a variety of pleasures to explore: the attractive landscape of Mull, the restored abbey on Iona and a host of smaller islands, some inhabited only by wildlife.

Visitors come to the volcanic island of **Mull ①** for the contrasting scenery – wooded and soft to bleak and bare; for fishing in the lochs; and for walking. Increasingly, it's an island renowned for exciting opportunities to see unusual birds and animals on land and at sea. Golden eagle and white-tailed sea eagle are among its rare bird species, while minke whale, killer whale, basking shark, dolphins and porpoises may be sighted close to Mull's shores. Visitors will find all types of terrain and weather; stroll on a wet day past Loch Scridain, through the boggy desolation of the **Ross of Mull**, or walk to the top of Mull's highest mountain, **Ben More**, a respectable 3,169ft (950 metres).

The island is not large, only 25 by 26 miles (40 by 41km), but don't be deceived: a drive on the mainly single-track roads, running mostly around the perimeter, is made even slower by Scotland's most feckless and fearless sheep, who regard roads as grassless fields.

AROUND MULL

Mull's trump card is **Tobermory**, the prettiest port in western Scotland, tucked in a sheltered natural harbour that has attracted mariners for more than 1000 years. The legend of the 'Tobermory Galleon' is cultivated by the island's tourism promoters. Local legend (they say) claims that a Spanish warship, fleeing

White-sand beach on the island of Iona.

the destruction of the Armada in 1588, sought a safe haven in Tobermory Bay only to be sabotaged by islanders, and sank to the bottom of the bay with its cargo of Spanish gold. Sadly, there's no more factual basis for this yarn than there is for the monster of Loch Ness – another highly profitable myth. Many have searched the bay, but not a scrap of treasure has ever been found.

The tall, brightly painted houses curving round the harbour go back to the late 18th century, when the British Fisheries Society planned a herring

Main attractions

Tobermory
Torosay Castle
Iona
Fingal's Cave
Coll
Tiree
Colonsay
Islands of Eigg, Rum, Muck and Canna
Jura
Gigha

Map on page 226

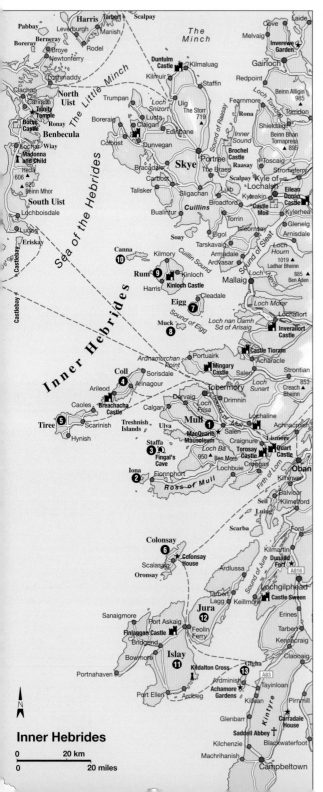

Inner Hebrides

```
0        20 km
0              20 miles
```

port. But the fish were fickle, and today Tobermory's sparkling harbour bobs with pretty pleasure yachts. Be sure to stop in at the small chocolate factory and shop, where the speciality is chocolate made with whisky.

The island's main villages – **Craignure** in the east where the Oban ferry docks, **Salen** at the narrow neck of the island, and **Dervaig** in the northwest – are neat, serviceable little places with useful amenities. Drive through Glen More, the ancient royal funeral route to Iona which bisects Mull from east to west, for some of the best scenery on the island. These 20 roads form part of the popular annual Tunnocks Mull Rally, held in October.

On the west, you will find **Calgary**, the silver-sand beach where, after the Clearances, despairing emigrant ships set sail for the New World. The beach held happy memories for one émigré: Colonel McLeod of the Northwest Mounted Police named a new fort in Alberta, Canada, after it.

Further proof of Scots influence overseas can be found south of Calgary at **Loch Ba** near Salen. The **MacQuarie Mausoleum** houses the remains of Major General Lachlan MacQuarie, the first governor general of New South Wales, who is sometimes called the 'Father of Australia'.

To understand what the 19th-century Clearances (see page 220) meant to all Hebrideans and to grasp the harshness of a crofting life visit the **Old Byre Heritage Centre** (tel: 01688-400 229; www.old-byre.co.uk; Easter–Oct Mon–Fri and bank holidays 10.30am–6.30pm) at Dervaig. This small private collection aims to enlighten the visitor with displays that cover 'everything from history to caterpillars': island geology, folkways, and the fauna and flora of Mull's six distinct wildlife habitats are all given due prominence. Models show how islanders would have lived from the distant past to the present day, and two 30-minute videos focus on Mull's history and its wildlife.

MULL'S CASTLES

Of Mull's two castles, both on the island's east coast, only one is open to visitors. Torosay Castle, yet another fake-baronial pile embellished by its owners with picturesque turrets and crenellations during the 19th century, was the ancestral home of the Guthrie James family for five generations. In 2012, Chris James, the fifth laird, reluctantly sold the castle to a 'mystery Swiss buyer' for a sum in excess of £1.65 million. Like many other Scots lairds, he could no longer pay for the castle's upkeep, and was facing a repair bill of £1.5 million.

Across the bay, the 13th-century **Duart Castle** (tel: 01680-812 309; www.duartcastle.com; May–mid-Oct daily 10.30am–5pm, Apr daily 11am–4pm), on a dramatic headland overlooking the Sound of Mull, was the MacLeans' stronghold. Mull belonged to the clan until it was forfeited when the MacLeans supported young Prince Charles Edward, who was defeated at Culloden in 1746. The castle was deserted for almost 200 years, and then restored by Sir Fitzroy MacLean early in the 20th century.

Mull is the jumping-off point for several islands: Iona, Staffa, the Treshnish Isles, Coll and Tiree.

PILGRIMAGE TO IONA

You feel like a pilgrim as you board the serviceable little 10-minute shuttle for a day trip to **Iona ❷**. Note that vehicles cannot be taken across to the Holy Island.

The main destination is the restored abbey (tel: 01681-700 512;; daily Apr–Sept 9.30am–5.30pm, Oct–Mar Mon–Sat 10am–4pm), which has been a place of Christian worship for more than 1400 years. The abbey aside, take time to view the adjoining museum, which possesses a superb assemblage of carved wood and stone crosses. 1From the abbey it is just 100yds/metres to the cemetery of **Reilig Oran** (see box).

Fingal's Cave on **Staffa ❸** is a big attraction; supposedly it inspired Mendelssohn to compose his overture. The experience of going into the cave, if the weather is good enough for landing, is

Local fisherman on Iona.

Torosay Castle and gardens, Isle of Mull.

⊘ HOLY PILGRIMAGE

Curiosity and a search for some intangible spiritual comfort draw well over half a million people from all over the world each year to the tiny 3-mile (5km) island of Iona. Here St Columba and 12 companions landed from Ireland in the 6th century to set up the mission that turned Iona into the Christian centre of Europe.

In 1773, Dr Samuel Johnson was impressed with the piety of Iona. The abbey, which had been suppressed at the Reformation, was still in ruins and there were not many visitors. In the 1930s, the low, sturdy building was restored by the Iona community, and the number of visitors has been growing ever since. Some of the best restoration is to be seen in the tiny cloister, especially the birds and plants on the slender replacement sandstone columns, which were meticulously copied from the one remaining medieval original.

Until the 11th century the Reilig Oran – or royal cemetery – was the burial place of Scots kings. Some 48 Scottish rulers are said to be buried here, including Kenneth MacAlpin, the first King of Scots, and Mac Bethad mac Findlaích, who was villainised by Shakespeare as 'Macbeth', but actually one of early medieval Scotland's better monarchs. Kings and princes from Norway, Ireland and France are also reportedly buried on this mystical islet.

⊙ **Fact**

Dr Johnson was well aware of the bleaker side of the Hebrides: 'Of these islands it must be confessed, that they have not many allurements, but to the mere lover of naked nature'.

well worth the 90-minute boat journey. The primeval crashing of the sea, the towering height of the cave and the complete lack of colour in the sombre rocks make a powerful impression. Even if the little 47ft (14-metre) partially covered passenger launch can't land, it's worth the journey just to see the curious hexagonal basalt rocks surrounding the gaping black hole of the cave. Birdwatchers, too, have plenty to enjoy.

Beyond Staffa are the uninhabited **Treshnish Islands** – a haven for puffins, kittiwakes, razorbills, shags, fulmars, gannets and guillemots.

COLL AND TIREE

From Mull's northern flank, the Caledonian MacBrayne ferry can be seen going from Oban to Coll and Tiree. There's the usual rivalry between these sister islands, most distant of the Inner Hebrides. People from Tiree can't understand why anyone would want to get off the ferry at Coll. The people of Coll maintain that the inhabitants of Tiree are permanently bent by the island's ceaseless wind.

With its gorgeous Atlantic beaches, turquoise bays and dunes and inland lochans, **Coll** ❹ draws those in search of peace and quiet. Part of Coll's allure is its windy isolation and lack of tourist infrastructure yet, ironically, it sometimes attracts more folk than it can easily cope with. With a population of around 220 people – almost all of whom live in Arinagour, the island's only village – Coll is very much for those seeking a spell of the simple life, shell-hunting on beaches or cycling on almost traffic-free roads.

Coll has no high-profile historic buildings. There are two castles, however, one of which sheltered Dr Samuel Johnson and his amanuensis James Boswell when they got stuck on Coll for 10 days during their tour of the Hebrides in 1773. Among Coll's more striking features are the 100ft (30-metre) -tall sand dunes, which divide the beaches of Feall Bay and Crossapool Bay.

The Gaelic name for **Tiree** ❺, *Tir fo Thuinn*, means 'land below the waves'. It's a good description of this flat, sunny island whose two hills are only 400ft (120 metres) high. One of the

View of Rum and Eigg from Morar village on Scotland's west coast.

island's most eccentric visitors was Ada Goodrich Freer, who claimed telepathic gifts and an ability to receive messages through seashells. She spent three weeks on Tiree in 1894 investigating Highland second sight. She spoke no Gaelic and was finally defeated, not by the language, but by the monotonous diet of tea, eggs, bread and jam provided by the Temperance Hotel.

Nowadays international windsurfers, who call Tiree the Hawaii of the North, are attracted to the island by the great Atlantic rollers that break on the long, curving silver beaches. The **Tiree Wave Classic** (www.tireewaveclassic.co.uk) in October is one of the world's great surf gatherings.

COLONSAY

Some people find **Colonsay ❻**, 40 miles (64km) southwest of Oban, too bland. But for others it is an antidote to the prettiness of Mull and the glowering Cuillins of Skye. It has its antiquities – seven standing stones and six forts – as well as excellent wildlife – birds, otters and seals. It also has good white beaches and isn't over-mountainous. Visitors are few as there are no organised day trips, and, even though the ferry calls six times a week (only three times in winter), accommodation has to be found either at the one hotel or with families providing bed and breakfast.

The island, 8 miles (13km) long and 3 miles (5km) wide, has a population of around 135 and is one of the largest British islands still in private hands. It is warmed by the North Atlantic Drift, and the gardens of **Colonsay House** (tel: 01951 200316; www.colonsayholidays.co.uk; Apr–Sept Wed & Fri noon–5pm, Sat 2–5pm) have a variety of exotic plants.

At low tide it's possible to walk across muddy sands to tiny **Oronsay**, off the southern tip of Colonsay; alternatively there are boat trips. Oronsay is about 2 miles (3km) square and has a population of six. Its fine 14th-century priory is the biggest medieval monastic ruin in the islands, after Iona.

TOURING THE SMALL ISLANDS

The small islands of Eigg, Muck, Rum and Canna can be reached from

Tractor disembarking from a ferry at St Ronan's Bay, Iona.

Loch Tarbert in front of the Paps of Jura.

Mallaig on the Sleat peninsula, at the end of the 'Road to the Isles'. There's not a great deal to do on the islands. Mostly people go for the wildlife, for a bit of esoteric island-hopping or for the superb walking, particularly on Rum.

The islands are all different, and, if you just want to see them without landing, take the little boat that makes the five- to seven-hour round trip six times a week in the summer, less often in winter. It's a service for islanders rather than a pleasure boat for visitors, and carries provisions, mail, newspapers and other essentials. Only those planning to stay are allowed to disembark. However, in summer, boarding the *MV Shearwater* at Arisaig, 8 miles (13km) before Mallaig, allows you to stop for several hours at either Eigg or Rum.

Eigg ❼ had a chequered history in the late 20th century. In 1975, the island was bought by millionaire Keith Schellenberg. Over the next 20 years, his relationship with his island tenants deteriorated. Schellenberg sold the island to an eccentric German artist, Maruma, who in 1996 was forced by debt to sell it to the Eigg Heritage Trust, a partnership formed by The Highland Council, Scottish Wildlife Trust, and the Eigg Residents Association. In a unique example of grassroots democracy in action, Eigg is now run almost entirely by and for its people. Among other achievements, the island now supplies all its own electricity needs from wind, water and solar power.

Muck ❽ is only 2 miles (3km) long and has neither transport nor shops. Visitors must bring provisions and be landed by tender. Eighty breeds of birds nest on Muck, whose name means 'pig' (local porpoises were called sea pigs).

An incongruous Greek temple stands on the rugged island of **Rum** ❾: the mausoleum of Sir George Bullough, the island's rich Edwardian proprietor. His castellated Kinloch Castle was used as a convalescent home during the Boer War just after it was built, and was for a time a hotel. The island is owned by Scottish

Natural Heritage, although in April 2010 a significant area of land and property was transferred to the Isle of Rum Community Trust. There is fine birdwatching and hill walking.

Graffiti adorns the rocks near the landing stage at **Canna** ⑩ ; they are at least 100 years old and record the names of visiting boats. The harbour's safe haven is one of the few deepwater harbours in the Hebrides. This sheltered island, the most westerly of the four, is owned by the National Trust for Scotland and is particularly interesting to botanists. There are just two holiday cottages, each with enough room for four people.

Islay ⑪ is the place to go if you enjoy malt whisky. Nine of Scotland's most renowned malt-whisky distilleries are to be found on this attractive little island, all offering tours and tastings. Islay, where Clan Donald started, was once the home of the Lord of the Isles. A fascinating insight into its medieval history is to be found at the archaeological site of **Finlaggan** (www.finlaggan. org; Apr–Sept Mon–Sat 10.30am–4.15pm). Islay also has some good beaches on the indented north coast, and for wildlife enthusiasts it offers the opportunity to get close to rutting red deer stags and to huge flocks of migrating wildfowl.

Also on this side of the island is one of the best Celtic crosses in Scotland: the 9th-century **Kildalton Cross** stands in the churchyard of a ruined, atmospheric little chapel. **Port Askaig**, where the ferry from the Kintyre peninsula docks, is a pretty little place with a hotel, once a 16th-century inn, on the old drovers' road a few steps away from the ferry.

WILD JURA

Jura ⑫, Islay's next-door neighbour, is so close you can nip over for a quick inspection after dinner. Three shapely mountains, the Paps of Jura, 2,500ft (750 metres) high, provide a striking skyline. Although palms and rhododendrons grow on the sheltered east side, warmed by the North Atlantic Drift, it's a wild island inhabited by sheep and red deer and is much favoured by sportsmen, birdwatchers and climbers. It was to the island of Jura that George Orwell came in 1947, seeking seclusion while working on his novel *1984*.

GIGHA

The tiny, community-owned island of **Gigha** ⑬ has one of the nicest hotels in the islands – bright, spacious and beautifully neat and simple. There is no need to take a car on the 3-mile (5km) crossing from **Tayinloan** to this small green island which is popular with the yachting fraternity: no walk is more than 3 miles (5km) from the attractive ferry terminal at **Ardminish**, which is lined with sparkling white cottages.

The formal attraction on Gigha is **Achamore Gardens** (tel: 01583 505 275; daily dawn to dusk). Seals, barking amiably, cruise in the waters off the little-used north pier.

European otter mother and cub, Islay.

Borve beach, Isle of Harris.

THE OUTER HEBRIDES

The dramatic islands of the Outer Hebrides are relentlessly pounded by the fierce Atlantic Ocean. Visitors are either thrilled by their wild bleakness or find their remoteness disconcerting.

The Outer Hebrides, 40 miles (64km) west of the mainland, are known locally as the Long Island. They stretch in a narrow 130-mile (208km) arc from the Butt of Lewis in the north to Barra Head in the south. Each island regards itself as the fairest in the chain. The people live mainly by crofting and fishing supplemented by tourism, with commercial fish farming – crabs and mussels as well as salmon and trout – and teleworking growing fast.

There are enormous flat peat bogs on Lewis and North Uist, and the islanders cut peat for domestic use rather than to export to the garden centres on the mainland. The peat is cut and dried on the spot in summer, then carted home to be painstakingly stacked against the house in a water-repellent herringbone pattern for use in fires and stoves throughout the next year.

These climatically extreme Western Isles of few trees and stark scenery are the Gaidhealtachd, the land of the Gael. When their Gaelic-speaking inhabitants change to English, as they politely do when visitors are present, they have a distinctively soft Hebridean accent that is much easier for visitors to understand than the broad accents found in the mainland cities. Since the dawn of Scotland's history, Hebridean islanders have maintained a distinctively

different culture, reinforced by their remote location, the Gaelic language, and a fierce adherence (on the Isle of Lewis and Harris) to a particularly austere Presbyterian version of Christianity and (on Barra and its neighbours) to the Catholic faith.

HARRIS AND LEWIS

Harris and the larger **Lewis** are really one island. Lewis is mostly flat moorland. Harris rises into high, rocky mountains, with the peak of Clisham at 2,622ft (799 metres).

⊙ Main attractions

Harris beaches
Taransay Island
Hushinish Point
Stornoway
Callanish
Berneray Island
Benbecula
South Uist
Eriskay Island
Barra Island

Map on page 234

A Broch house on the Isle of Lewis.

Outer Hebrides

```
0        20 km
0              20 miles
```

N

Flannan Islands

Butt of Lewis
Port of Ness

Lewis

Shawbost
Arnol
Barvas
North Tolsta

Carloway
Broch
Callanish
Stornoway
Portnaguran

Uig
Crulivig
Achmore
Col
Lewis Castle

Brenish
Loch Langavat
Balallan
Ranish

Scarp
Western
Kebock Head

Hushinish Point
Hushinish
Ardvourlie
Lemreway

Amhuinnsuidhe Castle
Clisham 799 ▲
Beinn Mhor 571 ▲

Taransay
Isles

Luskentyre
Tarbert ❶
Scalpay
Shiant Islands

Harris
Plocrapool

Pabbay
Manish
Leverburgh

Berneray
Boreray
Brove
Rodel ❷

Vallay
Newtonferry
Duntulm Castle
Kilmaluag

Balranald Nature Reserve
Blashaval
North List ❺
Lochmaddy
Kilmuir
Staffa

Clachan
Barna Lanyass
Trumpan
Loch Shizort
Uig

Baleshare
Carinish
Lusta
The Storr 719 ▲
Rona

Heisker or Monach Islands
Culla Beach
Trinity Temple
Ronay
Boreraig
Edinbane

Borve Castle
Benbecula
Kensaleyre
Brochel Castle

Eochar
Wiay
Dunvegan
Dun Beag
Raasay
Portree
Inner Sound

Loch Bee
Madonna and Child
Bracadale
Skye
The Braes
Scalpay

Loch Druidibeg Nature Reserve
Carbost
Lub
Broadford

Howmore
620 ▲
Hecla 606
Talisker
Sligachan
Cuillins
Torrin

Beinn Mhor
South Uist
Bualintur

Lochboisdale ❻
Soay
Elgol
Isleornsay

Pollachar
Ludag
Tarskavaig
Armadale

Barra
Eriskay
Canna
Kilmory
Cuillin Sound
Ardvasar

Kisimul Castle
❼
Castlebay
Rum
Kinloch
Mallaig

Vatersay
Sandray
Harris
Kinloch Castle
Cleadale

Rosinish
Sound of Rum
Arisaig

Mingulay
Sea of the Hebrides
Muck
Eigg
Loch nan Uamh

Castle Tioram

Ardnamurchan Point
Portuairk
Acharacle

Coll
Mingary Castle
Salen
Loch Sunart

Sorisdale
Tobermory

Arileod
Arinagour
Drimnin

Inner Hebrides
Caoles
Breachacha Castle
Dervaig
Lochaline

Barrapol
Scarinish
Treshnish Islands
Ulva
Mull
Salen
Oban

Tiree
MacQuarie
Maospleum
Loch Ba

Hynish
Staffa
Fingal's Cave
Ben More 950 ▲
Croggin

Iona
Lochbuie

Fionnphort
Ross of Mull
Firth of Lorn

Colonsay
Scarba

Scalasaig
Jura
Ardlussa

Oronsay
Port Askaig

Turn north from the ferry terminal at **Tarbert** ❶ for Lewis, south for Harris. Ferries from Lochmaddy on North Uist and Uig on Skye dock in this sheltered port tucked into the hillside. There are a few shops selling Harris Tweed, the Harris Hotel, a tourist office, a bank and some sheds.

A drive around South Harris (40 miles/64km) is rewarding. As you head south on the A859 along the west coast, you pass many glorious beaches – including **Luskentyre** and **Scarista** – before reaching **Leverburgh**, with the remains of the buildings erected by the industrialist Lord Leverhulme (who manufactured Sunlight soap) for a projected fishing port. The main road ends at **Rodel** ❷ with the 16th-century **St Clement's Church**, one of the best examples of ecclesiastical architecture in the Hebrides.

The single-track road up the east coast offers superb seascapes and views across the Minch to Skye and you will pass tiny crofts, from which you'll hear (as you will everywhere) the click-clack of crofters' looms producing tweed.

At Ardhasig, 2 miles (3km) north of Tarbert, you can take a boat (weather permitting) to the island of **Taransay** with some of the best beaches in the Hebrides and the location in 2000 for the BBC TV programme *Castaway*. Continuing north of Tarbert on the A859 after 4 miles (6km) turn onto the B887, which clings to the shore of **West Loch Tarbert**. The 16-mile (26km) drive from Tarbert to golden **Hushinish Point** is dramatic, particularly in the evening as the sun catches the peaks of Beinn Dhubh on Harris, across the water.

The road goes straight through the well-maintained grounds of **Amhuinnsuidhe Castle** (pronounced *Avin-suey*), so close to the house you can almost see inside. This pale turreted castle was built in 1868, and J.M. Barrie (best known as the author of *Peter*

Pan) began his play *Mary Rose* here. Close by, a salmon river runs into the sea, and Amhuinnsuidhe is now the hub of a sporting estate that offers fishing and deerstalking as well as very up-market accommodation and dining.

From Hushinish, about 5 miles (8km) away, ferries cross to the small island of **Scarp**, whose last inhabitants left for Harris more than 50 years ago. In the 1930s, German boffin Gerhard Zucker experimented with a rocket-mail service between Scarp and Harris. A special stamp was issued; the first rocket was fired, but it exploded, destroying both mail and project.

STORNOWAY

Return to the A859, which twists and turns past lochs and around mountains for 35 miles (56km) to **Stornoway ❸**, the capital of Lewis and the only town in the Western Isles. Most activity in this solid town of just over 6,000 inhabitants is at the harbour, where seals can often be seen.

Lews Castle (not Lewis castle, as one might think) is Stornoway's major landmark. It was built in 1847 for the opium millionaire Sir James Matheson, founder of the great Hong Kong trading firm Jardine and Matheson, who in the early 1840s bought the entire Isle of Lewis and financed a number of 'improving' projects. In 1918, the Castle was acquired by another millionaire, Lord Leverhulme, who gifted it to the community in 1923. Now owned by Comhairle nan Eilean Siar (Western Isles Council), it reopened in June 2016 as the **Museum nan Eilean** (tel: 01851 822 746; www.lews-castle.co.uk; Apr–Sept Mon–Wed & Fri–Sat 10am–5pm, Oct–Mar Mon–Wed & Fri–Sat 1–4pm ; free). The museum's collection features six of the famous 'Lewis Chessmen', on long-term loan from the British Museum. Discovered at Uig in 1821, these carved walrus ivory chess pieces are unique examples of 12th-century Norse-Celtic art.

To explore Lewis's many historic sites, leave Stornoway on the A859 and, after a couple of miles, bear right onto the A858. **Callanish ❹** and

The Callanish standing stones, Isle of Lewis.

⊙ FINDING YOUR WAY IN GAELIC

The official tourist map of the Outer Hebrides is essential for the Uists. Even though only one main road links the three islands of North Uist, Benbecula and South Uist, most signposts are in Gaelic; the map gives them in English, too. The Lochmaddy tourist office has a free sheet of English/Gaelic names put out by the Western Isles Council. To help preserve one of Europe's oldest languages, the council has put up dual-language Gaelic and English as well as Gaelic-only place names and signposts in the Outer Hebrides. To complicate matters still further, many place names were not originally Gaelic but Norse, dating from the Scandinavian settlement of the islands more than 1000 years ago; translating them into Gaelic arguably makes little sense.

Gaelic is a living language on these islands, with locals speaking it among themselves. Only a generation ago, the use of Gaelic outside the home or church was somewhat frowned on; today in the schools the children are taught in both English and Gaelic. Church services – on both the Protestant and the Catholic islands – are also usually held in Gaelic. Though it's not immediately obvious to non-Gaelic speakers, Lewis and Harris each have their own dialect, but as Lewis has the largest concentration of Gaelic speakers in Scotland, its version of the language has become the basis for 'broadcast' – or 'standard' – Gaelic nationwide.

its magnificent standing stones are 16 miles (26km) from Stornoway. The 13 ritual stones, some 12ft (3 metres) high, are set in a circle like Stonehenge. The **Callanish Visitor Centre** (tel: 01851-621 422; www.callanishvisitor centre.co.uk; Apr–May & Sept–Oct Mon–Sat 10am–6pm, June–Aug Mon–Sat 9.30am–8pm, Nov–March Tues–Sat 10am–4pm; free, charge for exhibition) is close by.

Keeping to the A858, you soon reach the upstanding remains of the 2,000-year old **Carloway Broch** and **Arnol** with its **Blackhouse Museum** (tel: 01851 710 395; Apr–Sept Mon–Sat 9.30am–5.30pm, Oct–Mar Mon–Tue, Thu–Sat 10am–4pm), which shows how the people of Lewis used to live. A different world unfolds if, just before Callanish, you take the B8011: it leads to **Uig** and its wondrous beaches.

THE UIST ARCHIPELAGO

Lochmaddy ❺, where the ferry from Uig in Skye docks, is the only village on **North Uist**, and is home to the **Taigh Chearsabhagh Museum and Arts Centre** (tel: 01870-603 970; www.taigh-chearsabhagh.org; Mon–Sat 10am–5pm, winter until 4pm), which is also the starting point for the **Uist Sculpture Trail** of seven specially commissioned works at outdoor sites on North and South Uist.

The Uist archipelago of low bright islands dominated by the glittering sea is 50 miles long and only 8 miles at its widest (80km by 13km), and is so peppered with lochs that on the map the east coast around Benbecula looks like a sieve.

Rather than going south on the A865, which runs for 45 miles (72km) and (because of the causeway and bridge) virtually makes North Uist, Benbecula and South Uist one island, travel around North Uist anticlockwise on the A867 and A865. On this 45-mile (72km) trip, you will pass superb beaches and ancient sites.

The standing stones of **Blashaval** are 3 miles (5km) north of Lochmaddy and 3 miles (5km) further on, a turn-off on the right (B893) leads to **Newtonferry** and the causeway to

Crofter's cottage on North Uist.

the island of **Berneray**, where Prince Charles occasionally recharged his batteries. Back on Uist, in the middle of the north shore, is the rocky islet of **Eilean-an-Tighe**, the oldest pottery 'factory' in Western Europe, where quality items were produced in Stone Age times.

Still on the north coast is the superb beach of **Vallay** (actually an island reached on foot: beware of the tides). Round on the west coast, which is greener than the east, is **Baleshare**, another island with a picturesque beach joined to Uist by a causeway. Before reaching here, you pass the **Balranald Nature Reserve** (tel: 01463-715 000; reserve open at all times, visitor centre daily Apr–Aug 9am–6pm), which was created to protect the breeding habitat of the red-necked phalarope, a small wader. Rare species to be spied at the sanctuary include the corncrake, lapwing and barnacle goose.

At **Clachan** the A865 turns south while the A867 runs northeast to return to Lochmaddy and the **Barpa Lanyass**, a 5,000-year-old squashed beehive tomb, 5 miles (8km) further along. Nearby is the **Pobull Fhinn** standing stone circle. Return to the A865; just before the causeway is **Carinish**, where Scotland's last battle with swords and bows and arrows took place. Not far away is the ruined 12th-century **Trinity Temple**.

Cross the North Ford by the 5-mile (8km) causeway to tiny **Benbecula**, whose eastern part is so pitted with lochs that most people live on the west coast. You can now go south for 5 miles (8km) to the southern tip of Benbecula or turn right onto the B892, which makes a 10-mile (16km) loop around the west of the island before rejoining the A865.

The loop road first passes the small airport and a military testing ground before reaching **Culla Beach** – the best of many excellent beaches – and the ruins of **Borve Castle** with 10ft (3-metre) thick walls. The castle, one of the most important medieval ruins in the Outer Hebrides, was built in the 14th century and was the home of the

Peat moors and mountains on South Uist.

Kisimul Castle, just off Castlebay, on the Isle of Barra.

The Isle of Harris has beautiful beaches.

MacDonalds of Clanranald, who once ruled Benbecula.

The South Ford, separating Benbecula and **South Uist**, is crossed by a 0.5-mile (800-metre) -long single-track bridge. On **Loch Bee** there are hundreds of mute swans.

SOUTH UIST TREASURES

The main road runs down the west of the island for 22 miles (35km). To the west are seascapes with yet more splendid beaches and, to the east, mountains and peat bogs are dominated by **Beinn Mhor** (2,034ft/620 metres) and **Hecla** (1,988ft/606 metres). After 4 miles (6km), atop **Rueval Hill**, 'hill of miracles', is the modern pencil-like statue of **Madonna and Child**, which was paid for by worldwide donations. Just beyond this, still to the east, is the **Loch Druidibeg Nature Reserve**, home to corncrakes and greylag geese.

Next, to the west, is **Howmore**. Once the ancient ecclesiastical centre of the island, it is now a cluster of protected whitewashed cottages, one a youth hostel. Continue beyond Howmore to reach another lovely beach. Further on is the renovated **Kildonan Museum** (tel: 01878-710 343; www.kildonanmuseum.co.uk; Apr–Oct daily 10am–5pm) with local-history displays, crafts shops and a tearoom. Nearby is a bronze cairn honouring the birthplace of Flora MacDonald. At the end of the main road lies tiny **Lochboisdale ❻**, the main village of the south and the terminal for the Oban ferry.

At **Pollachar**, at the southwest tip, is a 3,000-year-old standing stone surrounded by wild orchids and clover, from where you can gaze across to Eriskay and Barra. There is now a causeway from nearby Ludag to Eriskay.

Eriskay, the subject of the hauntingly beautiful song *Eriskay Love Lilt*, is tiny, but considering its size – only 2 by 3 miles (3 by 5km) with around 200 inhabitants – it has become very famous. Bonnie Prince Charlie landed on the long silver beach on the west side on 23 July 1745; 200 years later the *Politician*, a cargo ship laden with whisky, sank in the Eriskay Sound. Compton Mackenzie's *Whisky Galore* (known in America as *Tight Little Island*) was a hilarious retelling of the redistribution of the cargo.

Fishing has always dominated **Barra ❼**. In the 1920s, the Barra herring industry was so important that girls came from as far away as Great Yarmouth in southeast England to work 17 hours a day in **Castlebay**, the capital, to gut the silver fish. Today Barra still lives by crofting and fishing, but the Hebridean Toffee Company is a major local employer.

The Dualchas **Barra Heritage Centre** (tel: 01871-810 413; Apr–Sept Tue–Fri 11am–4pm, Sat 11am–2pm) tells the island's story. Also worth visiting is **Kisimul Castle**, the home of the Macneils of Barra (tel: 01871-810 313; Apr–Sept Tue–Sun 9.30am–5.30pm).

Migrating geese from Iceland and Greenland arrive in autumn at Loch Leven near Kinross.

Culross village.

CENTRAL SCOTLAND

Perth is a superb centre for exploring the Central Highlands – the lochs of the Trossachs and romantic castles in the hills – as well as the ancient city of St Andrews and picturesque harbours along the Fife coast.

Georgian terraces and imposing civic buildings line the riverside in the genteel city of **Perth** ❶ but principal streets are uncompromisingly Victorian. No dullness, though. 'All things bright and beautiful' as the 36 bells of the handsome 15th-century **St John's Kirk** strike, heralding the hour – a contrast to John Knox's iconoclastic preaching here in the mid-16th century.

Behind the imposing portico and dome of the **Museum and Art Gallery** (George Street; tel: 01738-632 488; Tue–Sun 10am–5pm; free) is drama in Sir David Young Cameron's landscape *Shadows of Glencoe*; in the stuffed but still snarling wildcat, its bushy tail black tipped; and in Perth's link with space, the Strathmore Meteorite of 1917.

PERTH CITY ATTRACTIONS

More art can be enjoyed in the roundhouse of the old waterworks, now the delightful **Fergusson Gallery** (Marshall Place; tel: 01738-783 425; Tue–Sun 10am–5pm; free) devoted to the life and works of the Perthshire painter J.D. Fergusson, one of the Scottish Colourists. Sir Walter Scott's virginal heroine in *The Fair Maid of Perth*, Catherine Glover, supposedly lived in **Fair Maid's House** (Curfew Row; tel: 01738-455 050; Apr–June & Sept–Oct

Thu–Sat 1–4.30pm, July & Aug Mon–Sat 1–4.30pm; free), the setting for his novel of the time of the Battle of the Clans on the meadow of the North Inch nearby. The city's oldest surviving house retains many original medieval features. Next door are lovely restored 18th-century stables.

For something more energetic pay a visit to **Bell's Sports Centre** (Hay Street; tel: 01738-454 647; www.liveac tive.co.uk), Scotland's largest sports facility. History and tradition take the stage in the **Perth Theatre** (High

⊘ Main attractions

Perth
Scone Palace
Loch Leven
Castle Campbell
Anstruther
St Andrews
Loch Lomond
Dunkeld
Pitlochry
Blair Atholl

Map on page 244

Sunset over Kinnoull Tower, near Perth.

Street; tel: 01738-621 031; www.horsecross.co.uk), the longest established theatre in Scotland.

Splendid views over the city and River Tay can be enjoyed from the top of **Kinnoull Hill** on the outskirts of the city, while **Branklyn Garden** (Barnhill, Tay Street; tel: 01738 625 535; Apr–Oct daily 10am–5pm) has been described as 'the finest two acres of private garden in the country'.

PERTH'S CASTLES

Perth is ringed with castles: some are family homes, others romantic ruins like **Huntingtower Castle** (tel: 01738-627 231; Apr–Sept daily 9.30am–5.30pm, Oct–Mar Sat–Wed 10am–4pm), 3 miles (5km) west. An intriguing rooftop walk gives glimpses of hidden stairs and dark voids. James I had a year's imprisonment here.

Scone Palace (tel: 01738-552 300; www.scone-palace.co.uk; daily Apr & Oct 10am–4pm, May–Sept 9.30am–5.45pm), 2 miles (3km) north of Perth, was Scotland's Camelot and home to the much-travelled Stone on which 40 kings of Scotland were crowned. Brought here in the 9th century and taken to London in 1296 by Edward I, it was stolen in 1950 from beneath the Coronation Chair in Westminster Abbey and recovered from Arbroath. (It is now in Edinburgh Castle.) The earl of Mansfield's home offers such diverse charms as six generations of family photographs, Highland cattle, ornamental fowls and giant trees, as well as period furniture and interiors.

A lake for all seasons, **Loch Leven ❷** is heaven for trout anglers and the chosen wintering ground for wild geese and other waterfowl. On an island and reached by ferry from the loch side is the ruined **Loch Leven Castle** (Castle Island; tel: 01577-862 670; daily Apr–Sept 10am–4.15pm, Oct 10am–3.15pm), where the notorious Wolf of Badenoch and Mary, Queen of Scots were once imprisoned.

Falkland Palace ❸ (tel: 01337 857 397; Mar–Oct Mon–Sat 11am–5pm, Sun noon–5pm), sitting cosily in the main street of its old Royal Burgh, was the favourite retreat of the Stuart kings.

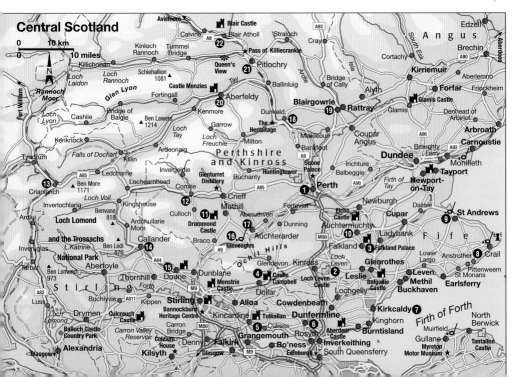

Stone lintels that top many doors carry the incised initials of the couples the houses were built for in the 1600s, the date and a heart. Loving care is evident everywhere in the many manicured green spaces and carefully conserved weavers' houses.

Castle Campbell ❹ (tel: 01259-742 408; Apr–Sept daily 9.30am–5.30pm, Oct–Mar Sat–Wed 10am–4pm) is rather impressively situated at the head of Dollar Glen, southwest of Perth. Near Stirling, Menstrie Castle (tel: 01259 211 701; Easter–Sept Wed, Sun 2–5pm; free) was the birthplace and home of Sir William Alexander, James VI's lieutenant and founder of Nova Scotia. The ground-floor exhibition is dedicated to this fascinating piece of Scottish-Canadian history.

THE KINGDOM OF FIFE

The M90 motorway that links Perth to Edinburgh does more than bypass Fife, thrust out into the North Sea between the Firth of Forth and the Tay. It bypasses an area rich in history, architecture and scenery. The kingdom's harbours nudge one another on a coast tilted towards Scandinavia, buildings reflecting the thriving trade it had in the 17th century with the Baltic and the Low Countries.

Culross ❺, where the Firth of Forth narrows, is a unique survival: a 17th- and 18th-century town that looks like a film set, and often is. Then it was a smoky, industrial town with coal mines and saltpans, manufacturing griddles and baking plates for oatcakes. Sir George Bruce, who took over where the mining monks left off in 1575, went on to such success that James VI made Culross a Royal Burgh. Today, the town's wealth of old buildings, with crow-stepped gables and red pantiled roofs, make it one of Scotland's finest historic towns.

Wynds, or pathways, lead past the 16th-century Culross Palace (tel: 01383 880 359; house Apr–Sept daily 10am–5pm, Oct–Mar Fri–Mon 10am–4pm) – probably the finest gentleman's house of its period in Scotland – the Study (access by guided tour only), with a 17th-century Norwegian painted ceiling, and Snuff Cottage (1673). Past The House with the Evil Eyes, so called because of its oval loft windows, are the church, the ruined abbey and the magnificent Abbey House. The clock tower of the Town House (access by guided tour only) dominates the waterfront and in the centre is the Mercat Cross, the tiny marketplace.

Thirty miles (48km) south of Perth is Dunfermline ❻. Although the city was for 600 years the capital of Scotland and burial place of kings, with a fine church and abbey (St Margaret Street; tel: 01383-724 586; www.dunfermlineabbey.com; Mon–Sat 10am–4.30pm, Sun 2–4.30pm), it owes its international fame to its humblest son, Andrew Carnegie. The great philanthropist opened the first of 3,000 free libraries here in 1881. The tiny cottage where he was born contrasts vividly with Pittencrieff House (tel:

Huntingtower Castle, Perth.

Crail harbour in the East Neuk of Fife.

01383-722 935; daily Apr–Sept 11am–5pm, Oct–Mar 11am–4pm; free), the mansion he left to the town on his death, which is now a museum with changing exhibitions on local history, costume and other period themes. The abbey is famed, above all, however, for being the burial place (in 1329) of Robert the Bruce (minus his heart and a few other bits).

KIRKCALDY'S FAMOUS SONS

Kirkcaldy ❼, or 'Lang Town' as it is often called, is 14 miles (22km) east of Dunfermline. The town's association with coal and floor coverings may not appeal, but it made important contributions to architecture, economics and literature. Robert Adam and Adam Smith were born here and the **Kirkcaldy Galleries** (tel: 01592 583 206; Mon–Wed & Fri 10am–5pm, Thu 10am–7pm, Sat 10am–4pm, Sun noon–4pm; free) has a superb collection of paintings by the Scottish Colourists, Sir Henry Raeburn and Sir David Wilkie, and the distinctive Wemyss Ware pottery can be viewed here as well.

The ruins of St Andrews Cathedral.

Further along the coast on the A915, behind the esplanade and the parked oil rigs at Leven, are marvellous **shell gardens**. Begun in 1914, the walls, menagerie and aviary are patterned with shells, broken china and Staffordshire figures.

Northwards along the coast there are some lovely fishing villages and sandy beaches. **Lower Largo**, its tiny harbour and inn stage-set beneath a viaduct, gave birth in 1676 to Alexander Selkirk, Daniel Defoe's 'Robinson Crusoe'. The original 'Fifie' fishing boats were built at **St Monans**, but the shipyard now builds only pleasure craft. A path leads from the harbour to the 14th-century church, its feet on the rocky shore.

Following the A917 from Upper Largo leads to **Pittenweem**, a village bustling with the business of fish. Nearby, **Anstruther ❽**, with the **Scottish Fisheries Museum** (tel: 01333-310 628; www.scotfishmuseum.org; Apr–Sept Mon–Sat 10am–5.30pm, Sun 11am–5pm, Oct–Mar Mon–Sat 10am–4.30pm, Sun noon–4.30pm), and **Crail**, which

⊙ ANCIENT AND ROYAL

The Scots are so obsessed with golf that it is said that Mary, Queen of Scots went off to play a round just days after her husband, Lord Darnley, had been assassinated. Wherever you are in Scotland there will always be a golf course nearby. There are more than 500 courses, from world-class to local ventures, and even tiny Highland villages have their own nine-hole courses. The game was developed as far back as the 15th century on the coastal courses known as 'links', and you can still play on some of the world's oldest courses along the east coast of Scotland (see page 91) – though for a cheaper round it's best to avoid the Championship courses.

At St Andrews, considered by many to be the birthplace of the game, golf qualifies as 'ancient' as well as 'royal': its Old Course was laid out in the 15th century and the Royal and Ancient Golf Club formed in 1754. There are no fewer than seven courses here. The Old Course is flanked by the New on the seaward and by the Eden on the inland side. Tucked between the New and the white caps of the North Sea is the shorter Jubilee Course. The Strathtyrum is an 18-hole course of modest length, while the Balgrove is a nine-hole beginners' layout. The newest of the seven is the 18-hole Castle Course (www.standrews.com).

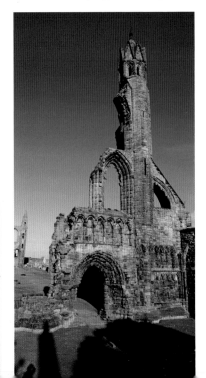

ends the run of picturesque harbours before Fife Ness is reached. The oldest Royal Burgh in East Neuk, Crail's crow-stepped gables and red roofs ensure that artists outnumber fishermen.

There is a nice contrast in leaving the simplicities of Crail for the concentration of learning, religious importance and historical significance that is **St Andrews** ❾. The city is best known as the home of golf, with seven courses and a collection of memorabilia on display at the **British Golf Museum** (Bruce Embankment; tel: 01334-460 046; www. britishgolfmuseum.co.uk; summer Mon–Sat 9.30–5pm, Sun 10am–5pm, winter daily 10am–4pm).

St Andrews Cathedral now lies in ruins, damaged in the 16th century and neglected ever since. **St Rule** nearby survives as a tower, and **St Andrews Castle** (The Scores; tel: 01334-477 196; daily Apr–Sept 9.30am–5.30pm, Oct–Mar 10am–4pm) fared little better, though it has a wonderful dungeon. Elsewhere, the **West Port** spans a main street and steeples abound, but not for climbing.

At the **Aquarium** (tel: 01334-474 786; www.standrewsaquarium.co.uk; daily 10am–6pm) all kinds of marine life can be seen in settings that resemble their natural surroundings. The **University**, whose buildings line North Street, is the oldest in Scotland.

Off the road back to Perth is **Hill of Tarvit** (tel: 01334 653 127; house Apr–Oct Sat–Tue 11am–4pm, grounds daily 9am–dusk), a superb mansion house remodelled by Sir Robert Lorimer with a magnificent garden and grounds. Further on, **Auchter-muchty** ❿ has surviving thatched cottages once used by weavers. The tea shop keeps the key to the Pictish, chimney-like church tower.

GLENTURRET AND DRUMMOND

Westward from Perth, roads follow rivers in the ascent to the lochs and watershed of the Grampians. At **Crieff** you can visit **Glenturret** (tel: 01764 656 565; www.thefamousgrouse. com; daily Mar–Oct 10am–6pm, Nov–Feb until 5pm), the oldest distillery

⊘ **Tip**

Near Crail you can visit Scotland's Nuclear Bunker (tel: 01333-310 301; www. secretbunker.co.uk; Mar–Oct daily 10am–5pm), which would have been the government headquarters for Scotland in the event of nuclear war.

Immaculate formal gardens at Drummond Castle.

The Black Watch memorial near Aberfeldy. The Black Watch is the oldest Highland regiment in the British Army.

The Queen's View vantage point overlooking Loch Tummel, near Pitlochry.

in Scotland, and glass, pottery and textile workshops. The romance of the **Drummond Arms** as the scene of Prince Charles Edward's council of war in 1746 endures, though it has been rebuilt. Five miles (8km) southeast of Crieff is the oldest public library in Scotland, the **Innerpeffray Library** (tel: 01764-652 819; www.innerpeffraylibrary.co.uk; Mar–Oct Wed–Sat 10am–5pm, Sun 2–5pm), founded in 1680. Also near Crieff, **Drummond Castle** ⓫ opens only its Italianate gardens (tel: 01764-681 433; www.drummondcastlegardens.co.uk; daily June–Aug 11am–6pm, Sept–Oct 1–6pm).

Situated on the River Earn where two glens meet, **Comrie** ⓬ is an attractive walking centre on the Highland Boundary Fault known as 'Scotland's Earthquake Centre'. The road then leads on past Loch Earn, with magnificent mountain scenery, to **Lochearnhead**. Beyond here the high peaks have it – **Ben More**, **Ben Lui** and **Ben Bhuidhe** – until the lochs reach in like fingers from the coast.

THE TROSSACHS

Crianlarich ⓭, about an hour and a half west of Perth on the A85, is a popular centre with climbers and walkers. For those on wheels, **Ardlui** is a beautiful introduction to **Loch Lomond**. The largest body of water in Britain, full of fish and islands, it is best known through the song that one of Prince Charlie's followers wrote before his execution. On the eastern shore, in Balmaha, is the **National Park Gateway Centre**, the visitor centre for the **Loch Lomond and the Trossachs National Park** – 720 sq miles (1,865 sq km) of wonderful scenery (see page 248).

The road back to **Aberfoyle** traverses the **Queen Elizabeth Forest Park** and leads to the splendid wooded scenery of the **Trossachs**, best viewed on foot or from the summer steamer on **Loch Katrine**. Scott's *Lady of the Lake* and *Rob Roy* attracted flocks of Victorian visitors. **Callander** ⓮ is an attractive and bustling town. Its **Toy Museum** (Main Street; tel: 01877-330 004; www.thehamiltontoycollection.co.uk; Easter–Oct Mon–Sat 10.30am–5pm, Sun noon–5pm) includes Victorian tin soldiers.

Follow the A84 southeast from Callander to visit **Doune** ⓯. Here you will find a remarkably complete 15th-century castle (tel: 01786-841 742; daily Apr–Sept 9.30am–5.30pm, Oct–Mar 10am–4pm) with two great towers and a hall in between. Close by is **Dunblane**; the west front of its 13th-century cathedral was described by the Victorian writer Ruskin as a perfect example of Scotland's church architecture. The famous moorland courses of **Gleneagles** ⓰, 11 miles (18km) east of Dunblane, are a golfer's paradise.

North of the Ochil Hills, **Auchterarder** ⓱ is a starting point for the **Mill Trail**. Thanks to good grazing and soft water, Scotland's world-famous tweeds, tartans and knitwear have been produced here in the Hillfoots Villages since the 16th century. The trail leads from the **Heritage**

Centre (tel: 01764-663 450; Mon–Sat 10am–5pm) in Auchterarder, with the only surviving steam textile engine and Tillicoultry's handsome Clock Mill powered by a water wheel, to the most modern mills in Alloa and Sauchie.

MOVING NORTH

From Perth, the road north bypasses the raspberry canes and motor museum of **Bankfoot**. At **Dunkeld** ⓲, cross Telford's fine bridge over the Tay's rocky bed for the charm and character of this old ecclesiastical capital of Scotland. A delightful museum in the cathedral's **Chapter House** (tel: 01738-710 654; daily Oct–Mar 10am–4pm, Apr–Sept 10am–5.30pm; free) introduces Niel Gow, the celebrated fiddler (1727–1807).

Romantics will feel at home at **The Hermitage**, west of the town. Built in 1758, this is the centrepiece of a woodland trail beside the River Braan, a folly poised over a waterfall. At the foot of the Highlands is **Blairgowrie** ⓳, which reserves its charm for anglers and lovers of raspberries and strawberries. At **Meikleour** the road to Perth is bordered by a remarkable beech hedge, over 120ft (36 metres) high and 1,804ft (550 metres) long, planted in 1746.

ALONG THE TAY

Aberfeldy ⓴, easily reached from Dunkeld, is noted for the fine Wade Bridge across the Tay, built in 1733. A beautiful walk is through the **Birks of Aberfeldy** to the **Moness Falls**. To the west of Aberfeldy is **Castle Menzies** (tel: 01887-820 982; www.castlemenzies. org; Apr–Oct Mon–Sat 10.30am–5pm, Sun 2–5pm), a good example of a 16th-century Z-plan tower house: a central tower with diagonally placed smaller towers surrounding it. Beyond is glorious **Glen Lyon**, the longest and one of the most beautiful glens in Scotland, with the village of **Fortingall**, where you can find Scotland's oldest tree, a yew over 3,000 years old. Nearby, **Loch**

Tay, a centre for salmon fisheries, has **Ben Lawers** 3,984ft (1,214 metres) towering above it.

Seek out **Pitlochry** ㉑, 15 miles (24km) northeast of Aberfeldy, for spectacle. The **Festival Theatre**, magnificently situated overlooking the River Tummel, has an excellent summer programme of drama and music. But it's upstaged by the dam at the hydroelectric power station where in spring and summer thousands of migrating salmon can be seen through windows in a **fish ladder** (tel: 01796-473 152; Apr–Oct Mon–Fri 8.30am–4pm; free, charge for exhibitions). The Queen's View, 8 miles (13km) northwest of Pitlochry, is a truly royal vista up Loch Tummel, dominated by the cone-shaped Schiehallion (3,547ft/1,081 metres).

Beyond the **Pass of Killiecrankie** where Soldier's Leap recalls the battle of 1689, is **Blair Atholl** ㉒, key to the Central Highlands, and 13th-century Blair Castle (see page 154; tel: 01796-481 207; www.blair-castle.co.uk; Apr–Oct daily 9.30am–5.30pm).

Loch Lomond and the Trossachs National Park includes the Lake of Menteith.

The summer steamer boat on Loch Katrine.

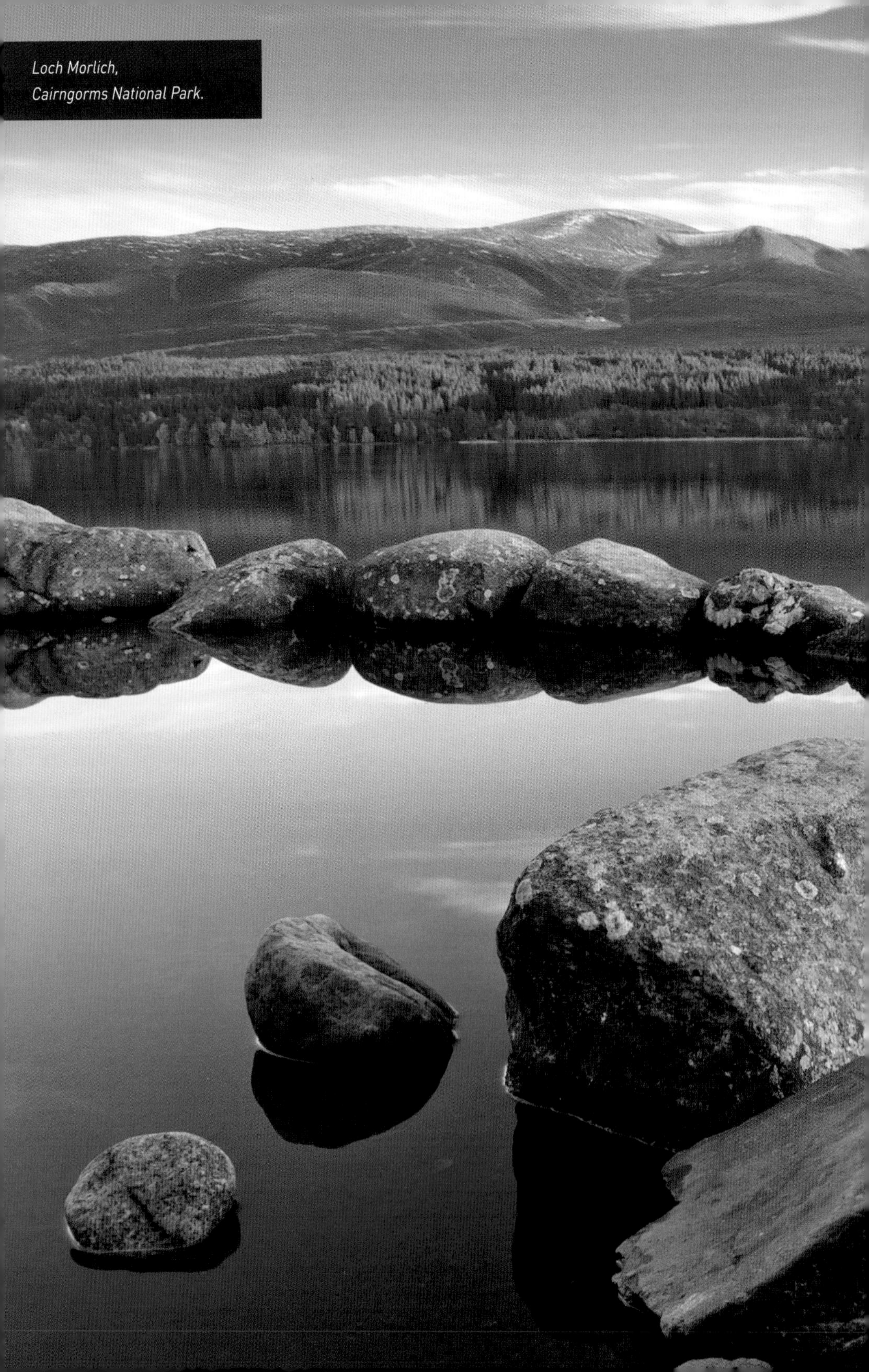
Loch Morlich, Cairngorms National Park.

Dunnottar Castle.

THE EAST COAST

The coast and countryside between the Firth of Tay and the sandy Moray Firth form a region of rare and subtle loveliness; the scale is human and the history dense.

Tourists often bypass Scotland's east coast and its hinterland, but the area has plenty of rewards that should not be missed. This is, after all, probably the most industrious (but not industrial) region of the country. Its ports and coastal villages have given Scotland its fishing industry. Its agriculture, from the rich croplands of Angus to the famous beef farms of Aberdeenshire – the largest stretch of uninterrupted farmland in Britain – has been hard won and hard worked. Toiling the land has often required endurance and imparted suffering.

THE SCOTS CHARACTER

It is, therefore, the east coast of Scotland that most physically and visibly exemplifies that which is most – stereotypically – dogged and determined (and perhaps dour) in the Scottish character, which in turn has learned how to exploit the region's assets.

The northeast port of Peterhead, for example, already Europe's busiest fishing harbour, turned itself into a major berth for North Sea oil-supply vessels; while the gentle, wooded valley of the River Spey is not only the centre of malt-whisky production but, with its own 'Malt Whisky Trail', has made tourist capital out of its celebrated local industry.

Along this coast you can learn to live without the majestic wilderness and

Gothic melodrama of the West Highlands and their archipelago – although you will find echoes of their atmosphere in the Grampian glens of Angus and the outriders of the Cairngorms, which stretch into Aberdeenshire – and here you can explore the versatility of man's dealings with the land and the sea.

EAST COAST CITIES

The east coast cities are **Dundee** and **Aberdeen**, of comparable size (populations about 200,000 each) and separated only by 70 miles (110km). Since

⊘ Main attractions

Dundee
Arbroath
Glamis Castle
Stonehaven
Ballater
Tomintoul
Grantown-on-Spey
Banff
Aberdeen

Map on page 254

Hay bales and wind turbines.

Northern Scotland

0   20 km
0   20 miles

N

NORTH

SEA

len
Macduff   Crovie   ⑰ Fraserburgh
rtsoy ⑯   Pennan   Inverallochy
   Banff   Gardenstown
                      A98   Rattray
erchirder   Strichen   Head
         Delgatie New   A90
         Castle Pitsligo   St Fergus
           New   Mintlaw   ⑱
           Deer   A952
         Fyvie   Peterhead
         Castle
luntly   Haddo   Slains
     Fyvie Ythan House Castle Bullers
                              O'Buchan
erdeenshire   Cruden
                          Bay
rdy Stone A96 Loanhead   Elion
         Stone Circle
Brandsbutt   Sands of
     Stone   Forvie
⑪   Alford Inverurie   A90
            Kintore   Balmedie
Craigievar Castle
 Castle   Fraser   Royal Aberdeen
⑩   Garlogie Westhill Denmore
phanan
  Banchory Drum Castle Aberdeen ⑲
yne   Crathes
   Dee ⑦   Castle
       Lochton   Cammachmore
                 A90
        Bridge
Cairn   of Dye   Stonehaven ⑥
1'Mount   Dunnottar Castle
454▲   A90
 Auchmull   Catterline
         A92
 Fettercairn   Inverbervie
⑤ Laurencekirk
zell
② ⑤   Lochside
hin   Montrose
erlerino
      Red Castle
ckheim Inverkeilor
A92
   Arbroath ③
Carnoustie
ifieth
ort

the late 1980s and continuing today, Dundee, which long had the feel of a city down on its luck, has capitalised on its vigorous industrial past – rooted in textiles, shipbuilding and jute – and has transformed itself into a popular destination and a vibrant centre for arts, culture and discovery.

On the other hand, Aberdeen, the 'Granite City', is as solid and unyielding as its nickname, a town of such accustomed prosperity and self-confidence that it assumed its new title of oil capital of Europe as though it were doing the multinationals a favour.

OLD AND NEW DUNDEE

Dundee ❶ is an oddity. It is Scotland's fourth-largest city (and was, until Aberdeen's oil-fuelled growth in the 1970s, the nation's third largest). In the 19th century, it was one of the wealthiest industrial centres in the British Empire. It has arguably the most spectacular location of any Scottish city, cradled among hills on a magnificent North Sea estuary, the Firth of Tay. In the last two decades, it has become a centre of excellence in fields as diverse as cancer research and game design. And yet its profile remains oddly low. If Dundee is known for anything, it is as the home of the 19th century's worst poet, William Topaz McGonagall.

Perhaps this is because Dundee – compared with colourful Glasgow, suave Edinburgh, and its self-assured East Coast rival Aberdeen – has never been good at blowing its own trumpet. And it has been spectacularly bad at preserving its past.

'Perhaps no town in Scotland has been oftener sacked, pillaged and destroyed than Dundee,' wrote an 18th-century historian, commenting on the fact that since the 11th century Dundee had the habit of picking the losing side in Scotland's many civil wars. Massive industrialisation in the mid-19th century erased much of Dundee's earlier architecture. The

Oil rig on Cromarty Firth.

graceful 18th-century Dundee Town House, designed by William Adam, was demolished in 1932 to provide a site for the grandiose **Caird Hall** (which is still a major concert venue). Town planners completed the job in the 1950s and '60s, when much of the historic centre was levelled to make way for redevelopment. But there are signs that things are changing for the better.

The purpose-built **Dundee Contemporary Arts centre** (Nethergate; tel: 01382-909 900; www.dca.org.uk; gallery: daily 10am–6pm, Thu until 8pm) has earned a worldwide reputation for fostering exciting work by adventurous, young artists. However, the new jewel of the £1-billion Dundee Waterfront regeneration project is without doubt the £45-million **V&A Dundee** (tel: 01382-411 611; www.vam.ac.uk; Sat–Thu 10am–5pm, Fri 10am–9pm; free), Scotland's first design museum with displays on everything from architecture and fashion to engineering and game design.

Completing this trio of galleries is **The McManus: Dundee's Art Gallery and Museum** (Albert Square; tel: 01382-307 200; www.mcmanus.co.uk; Mon–Sat 10am–5pm, Sun 12.30–4.30pm; free). Housed in a grand Victorian building, its galleries are state-of-the-art and display an important collection of paintings and ceramics, as well as Inuit, African, Asian, and ancient Egyptian artefacts. In pride of place is the skeleton of a Tay Whale, harpooned in 1883 after it made the fatal error of entering the Firth of Tay – then the base of the world's biggest whaling fleet.

BUILDING ON THE PAST

A few relics of medieval Dundee are scattered around the city. **The Old Steeple**, a square Gothic tower built in the 15th century, dominates the city centre and is Dundee's oldest building. You can spend a night in the second oldest – **Gardyne's House**, a five-storey tenement which was built around 1600 and is now a budget hostel (70–73 High Street; tel: 01382-224 646; www.hoppo. com). The spooky **Howff cemetery** on Meadowbank is full of medieval tombstones, many of them engraved with

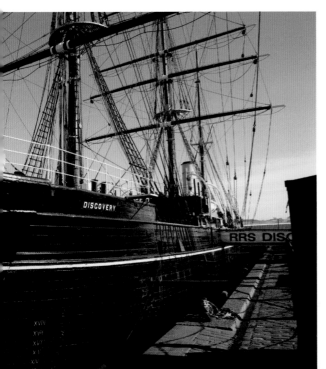
Climb on board Captain Scott's ship, RRS Discovery, at Discovery Quay.

skulls and other *memento mori*. The 16th century **Wishart Arch** or East Port is the only surviving part of the city walls. The Protestant martyr George Wishart is said to have preached here in 1544, two years before being burned as a heretic. Three small castles also survive. **Dudhope Castle**, a quaint tower house in a public park on the slopes of the Law, was built in the mid-15th century and now houses a business school.

Away from the centre, **Broughty Castle**, overlooking Broughty Ferry Harbour, dates from 1496. It is now the **Broughty Castle Museum and Art Gallery** (tel: 01382-436 916; Apr–Sept Mon–Sat 10am–4pm, Sun 12.30–4pm Oct–Mar Tue–Sat 10am–4pm, Sun 12.30–4pm; free), with a fine collection of paintings donated to the city by James Guthrie Orchar, as well as exhibits relating to the Dundee whaling industry. On the edge of the city at Claypotts Junction, **Claypotts Castle** (tel: 01786-450 000, call to arrange a viewing of the inside) has hardly changed since it was built in 1588.

Dundee's flagship attraction is **Discovery Point** (tel: 01382-309 060; www.rrsdiscovery.com; Apr–Oct Mon–Sat 10am–6pm, Sun 11am–6pm, Nov–Mar 10am–5pm, Sun 11am–5pm), which tells the story of Antarctic discovery and has displays on the 'last wilderness' of Antarctica. Captain Scott's ship *Discovery*, built in Dundee, is moored here and may be boarded. In Victoria Dock is the restored **HMS *Unicorn*** (tel: 01382-200 900; www.frigateunicorn.org; Apr–Oct daily 10am–5pm, Nov–Mar Wed–Sat 10am–4pm, Sun noon–4pm), the oldest British warship still afloat and one of only four frigates left in the world. Dundee had a high reputation for building clippers and whalers 100 years ago and its whalers sailed to both the Arctic and Antarctic.

Another reminder of past glories is to be found at the award-winning **Scotland's Jute Museum@Verdant Works** (West Henderson's Wynd; tel: 01382-309 060; www.verdantworks.com; Apr–Oct Mon–Sat 10am–6pm, Sun 11am–6pm, Nov–Mar Wed–Sat 10.30am–4.30pm, Sun 11am–4.30pm),

Below deck on RRS Discovery.

a former jute mill in which an imaginative range of displays now tells the history of Dundee's important jute and textiles industries.

Looking more to the future, the **Dundee Science Centre** (formerly Sensation Dundee; Greenmarket; tel: 01382-228 800; www.dundeesciencecentre.org.uk; daily 10am–5pm) is an innovative science centre that focuses on the five senses, with more than 80 hands-on interactive exhibits, and you can even have a go at keyhole surgery and meet some robots.

Science from an earlier era is celebrated at the **Mills Observatory** (Glamis Road; tel: 01382-435 967; Apr–Sept Wed, Sat 10am–4pm, Oct–Mar Mon–Fri 4–10pm, Sat–Sun 12.30pm–4pm; free), which stands atop Balgay Hill in Balgay Park, the city's biggest green space. Built in 1935, the observatory has a 19th-century refracting telescope as well as a modern computerised scope. A large plasma screen displays real-time images from Dundee University's satellite-tracking station.

Arbroath smokies are still produced in small family smokehouses in the fishing port of Arbroath.

ANGUS AND ARBROATH

To the northeast of Dundee, the county of Angus is an eloquent fusion of hill, glen, farmland, beach and cliff, and its towns and villages reach back into the dawn of Scottish history. **Brechin** ❷ has a 12th-century cathedral and one of the only two Celtic round towers remaining on the Scottish mainland.

The twin Caterthun Hills near Brechin are ringed with concentric Iron Age ramparts and there are Pictish sculptured stones in the churchyard of **Aberlemno**, off the A90, while the former Royal Burgh of **Arbroath** ❸, a fishing port and holiday resort now moving into light industry, was once a Pictish settlement.

Arbroath Abbey (tel: 01241-878 756; daily Apr–Sept 9.30am–5.30pm, Oct–Mar 10am–4pm), now a handsome ruin, dates back to 1178 and was the scene, in 1320, of a key event in the troubled history of Scotland: the signing of the Declaration of Arbroath. There, the Scottish nobles reaffirmed their determination to resist the persistent invasions of the English and to

⊘ WILLIAM MCGONAGALL

Even if you have no interest in outer space, it's worth visiting the Mills Observatory in Balgay Park for the spectacular views of the Firth of Tay. Widely accredited as the writer of some of the worst poetry in the English Language, William McGonagall's attempts to glamourise his adopted city by comparing it to the Bay of Naples – which at the time was one of the world's most admired tourist destinations – inspired a mocking piece of street-poetry:

'The Tay, the Tay, the silvery Tay
Seen fae the tap o' the Hill o' Balgay
Wonderful bay like the Bay o' Naples
Wonderful smell, like roaten aiples'

In a Dundonian accent, 'aiples' (apples) really does rhyme with 'Naples' and in terms of rhythm and scansion this vernacular verse is rather superior to any of McGonagall's own work.

preserve the liberty and independence of their country.

Arbroath's red cliffs and harbour at the Fit o' the Toon (foot of the town) remain atmospheric, and its local cottage industry of smoking haddock continues to produce the celebrated Arbroath smokies. The **Signal Tower** complex, built in 1813 to serve the families of the keepers of the lonely Bellrock Lighthouse, now houses a **museum** (tel: 01241-435 329; Tue–Sat 10am–5pm; free) telling the story of the lighthouse and its keepers, and the people of Arbroath. The flagstaff of the Signal Tower once signalled personal messages to the Bellrock Lighthouse. If a keeper's wife gave birth to a child, trousers or a petticoat would be hoisted to tell him whether the baby was a boy or girl.

GLAMIS CASTLE

Between Arbroath and Dundee is the resort of **Carnoustie**, which has a famous golf course and a lot of sand, while 13 miles (22km) to the north is the elegant town of **Montrose**, built at the mouth of a vast tidal basin, which is the winter home of pink-footed Arctic geese.

Inland, the country town of **Forfar** (where King Malcolm Canmore held his first parliament in 1057) is a striking point for the gloriously under-used and somehow secretive **glens of Angus**. It also lies close to what must be considered the county's star attraction, **Glamis Castle** ❹ (tel: 01307-840 393; www.glamis-castle.co.uk; daily Apr–Oct 10am–5.30pm, Nov–Dec until 4pm), the exquisite fairy-tale home of the earls of Strathmore and Kinghorne and the childhood home of the late Queen Elizabeth the Queen Mother. It was claimed by Shakespeare to be the setting for *Macbeth*. ('Hail Macbeth, Thane of Glamis!')

A visit to Glamis can be combined with a look at **Kirriemuir,** childhood home of *Peter Pan* author J.M. Barrie, and the fictional 'Thrums' of his novels. **J.M. Barrie's Birthplace** is now a museum (tel: 01575-572 646; Apr–Sept Fri–Mon 11am–4pm noon–5pm July–Aug Thu–Mon, Apr–June, Sept–Oct Sat–Mon) where you can see

Declaration Monument in Arbroath, celebrating the 1320 document signed by the earls and barons of Scotland who vowed to defend the nation's sovereignty.

⊙ Tip

The Scottish Wildlife Trust has an informative Visitor Centre (tel: daily 01674-676 336) on the south side of the east coast tidal basin at Montrose, from which many birds can be viewed.

Barrie's very first theatre. The author's gift to his native town was the **Kirriemuir Camera Obscura** atop Kirrie Hill (tel: 1575 575 885; www.kirriemuircameraobscura.com; Mar–mid-Oct Sat–Mon noon–4pm). It is one of three such attractions in Scotland.

WALKING IN THE GLENS

Kirriemuir is also the gateway to **Glen Prosen** and **Glen Clova**, from where the committed walker can penetrate deep into the heart of the Grampians to **Glen Doll** and pick up the old drover roads over to Deeside. These routes were once used by armies, rebels and whisky smugglers, as well as cattle drovers. They look easy walking on the Ordnance Survey map, but can be treacherous.

To the southwest is **Glen Isla** and to the north **Glen Lethnot** (route of a 'whisky road' formerly used by smugglers to outwit Revenue men). Here, too, is the graceful, meandering **Glen Esk**, which is reached through the pretty village of **Edzell** ❺, where **Edzell Castle** (tel: 01356-648 631; Apr–Sept daily 9.30am–5.30pm), the ancestral home of the Lindsay family, has a magnificent walled Renaissance garden.

HOWE OF THE MEARNS

Edzell lies on the Angus boundary with Aberdeenshire, and here the countryside begins to alter subtly. It lies, too, on the western edge of the **Howe of the Mearns**, which means something special to lovers of Scottish literature. This is the howe, or vale, which nurtured Lewis Grassic Gibbon, whose brilliant trilogy *A Scots Quair* gave the 20th-century Scottish novel and the Scots language its most distinctive voice: *Sunset Song, Cloud Howe, Grey Granite*. His lilting, limpid prose sings in your ears as you cross these rolling fields of rich red earth and granite boulders to a coast that becomes ever more riven and rugged as you near **Stonehaven** ❻ and the big skies, luminous light, spare landscape and chilly challenge of the northeast.

The A90 to Aberdeen bypasses Stonehaven, but this little fishing port-turned-seaside resort is worth a visit for the drama of its cliffs and **Dunnottar Castle** (tel: 01569-762 173; www.dunnottarcastle.co.uk; daily Apr–Sept 9am–5.30pm, Oct–Mar 9am–3/4pm), standing on its own giant rock south of the town. In the dungeons of these spectral ruins Covenanters were left to rot, and the Scottish Regalia – the 'Honours of Scotland' – were concealed in the 17th century from Cromwell's Roundheads. Today's brave souls may wish to take a dip in Stonehaven's Art Deco heated outdoor swimming pool, which is open throughout the summer.

From Stonehaven to Aberdeen is a clear, high, exhilarating run of 15 miles (24km) along the cliffs. But why not let the Granite City and the coast be the climax to your northeast tour and take, instead, the A957 to the lower Dee Valley? Called the Slug Road, from the Gaelic for a narrow passage, it takes you to **Crathes Castle** where you can visit the late 16th-century tower house and its renowned gardens (tel:

View down Glen Lethnot.

01330 844525; castle Jan–Mar, Nov–Dec Sat–Sun 11am–4pm, Apr–Oct daily 10.30am–5pm, gardens all year). Nearby is the little town of **Banchory ⑦**, where you can sometimes see salmon leaping at the **Bridge of Feugh**.

THE DEE VALLEY

The **Dee Valley** is justly celebrated for its expansive beauty and the pellucid, peat-brown grace of its salmon river. At the handsome village of **Aboyne**, between Banchory and Ballater, you begin to tread on the rougher hem of the Eastern Highlands. Deeside's royal associations make it the tourist honeypot of Aberdeenshire. **Ballater ⑧** is where the royal family pops down to the shops (look for the 'By Appointment' signs) while staying at **Balmoral** (tel: 013397-42534; www.balmoralcastle. com; grounds and exhibitions Apr–July daily 10am–5pm). Since 1852 Balmoral has been a private royal residence, and in midsummer the Queen shares her gardens with the public and her prayers with her subjects at nearby **Crathie** church.

On the A93, 8 miles (13km) west of Balmoral, is the village of **Braemar ⑨**, much loved by Queen Victoria, and best enjoyed in September when the Highland Gathering brings people from all over the world. The surprising charm and intimacy of fairy-tale **Braemar Castle** stem from it being lived in (tel: 013397-41219; www.braemarcastle.co.uk; 10am–5pm Apr–Oct Wed–Sun, July–Aug daily).

From Banchory you can strike over to Donside (the valley of Aberdeen's second, lesser-known river), taking the A980 through the village of **Lumphanan ⑩**, alleged to be the burial place of the doomed King Macbeth whose history has so often been confused with Shakespeare's fiction. But **Macbeth's Cairn** doesn't mark the grave of the king – it is a prehistoric cairn. (It has now been established that Macbeth, like so many of the early Scottish kings, was buried on Iona (see page 227). You can see at Lumphanan, however, one of Scotland's earliest medieval earthworks, the **Peel Ring of Lumphanan**.

Originally looking for an estate further west, Queen Victoria and Prince Albert were advised that the climate near the River Dee in the east would be better for Albert's delicate constitution.

Glamis Castle.

The CairnGorm Mountain Railway is a funicular railway that runs through the Cairngorm ski area.

Lairig Ghru mountain pass and the river Dee.

Near the village of Echt is the magnificent **Castle Fraser** (tel: 01330 833 463; Apr–Oct daily 10am–4pm, Mar & Nov to mid-Dec Sat & Sun 11am–2pm). Completed in 1636, it has been the home of the Fraser chiefs ever since. Extensive walks can be taken in the grounds (all year daily).

Donside's metropolis is the little country town of **Alford ⓫** where you can take a trip on one of the narrow-gauge **Alford Valley Railway** passenger trains (tel: 07879-293 934; 12.30pm–4pm May–Sept Sat–Sun, July–Aug daily), and visit the **Grampian Transport Museum** (tel: 01975-562 292; www.gtm.org.uk; daily Apr–Sept 10am–5pm, Oct until 4pm); and nearby **Kildrummy Castle** (tel: 01975-571 331; Apr–Sept daily 9.30am–5.30pm) a romantic and extensive 13th-century ruin which featured prominently in the 1715 Jacobite Rebellion.

AROUND THE CAIRNGORMS

The lonely, savage massif of the Cairngorms, which became Britain's biggest national park in 2003, dominates the Eastern Highlands. There is no direct route through its lofty bulk, but from Deeside and Donside you can pick up the road which circles around it for a thrilling journey.

At the hamlet of **Cock Bridge**, 32 miles (52km) west of Alford, beside the austere, curtain-walled **Corgarff Castle** (tel: 01975-651 460; Apr–Sept daily 9.30am–5.30pm), the A939 becomes the **Lecht Road**, which rises precipitously to some 2,000ft (600 metres) before careering giddily down into the village of Tomintoul. In winter, the Lecht is almost always the first main road in Scotland to be blocked with snow, encouraging an optimistic ski development at its summit. A mile or so to the north of that summit, look out for the **Well of the Lecht**. Above a small natural spring, a white stone plaque, dated 1745, records that five companies of the 33rd Regiment built the road from here to the Spey.

SPEYSIDE WHISKY TRAIL

Tomintoul ⓬, at 1,600ft (500 metres), is one of the highest villages in Scotland and a pick-up point for the 'Malt

Whisky Trail' which can take you mean-dering (or perhaps reeling) through seven famous malt whisky distilleries in and around the Spey Valley. The **Glenlivet Distillery** (tel: 01340-821 720; www.theglenlivet.com; mid-Mar–mid-Nov daily 9.30am–6pm; tours every 30min, last tour 4.30pm) was the first in Scotland to be licensed. From Glenlivet you can also enjoy the extensive walks and cycleway network on the Crown Estate.

Strathspey – *strath* means valley – is one of the loveliest valleys in Scotland, as much celebrated for the excellence of its angling as for its malt-whisky industry. When you descend from the dark uplands of the Lecht passage through Tomintoul to the handsome granite town of **Grantown-on-Spey** ⑬, you see a land gradually tamed and gentled by natural woodland, open pastures and the clear, comely waters of the River Spey itself. This pretty town is the focal point of the 935 sq mile (2,420 sq km) **Cairngorms National Park**, where you might see a golden eagle.

Grantown, like so many of the small towns and large villages in this area, was an 18th-century 'new town', planned and built by its local laird. It makes a good centre for exploring Strathspey and it's also within easy reach of the Moray Firth, and the leading resort and former spa town of Nairn. The route from Grantown (the A939) takes you past the island castle of **Lochindorb** – once the lair of the Wolf of Badenoch, Alexander Stuart, the notorious outlawed son of Robert II, who sacked the town of Forres and destroyed Elgin Cathedral.

Nairn ⑭, when the sun shines (and the Moray Firth claims to have the biggest share of sunshine on the Scottish mainland), is a splendid place, even elegant, with fine hotels and golf courses, glorious beaches and big blue vistas to the distant hills on the north side of the firth. Look out for the resident bottlenose dolphins; the best time to see them is between June and August.

On Nairn's doorstep is **Cawdor Castle** (tel: 01667-404 401; www.caw dorcastle.com; mid-Apr–mid-Oct daily

You can view the Cairngorm National Park in comfort and style from the Strathspey Railway: the heritage steam train runs through it, departing either from Aviemore, Boat of Garten or Broomhill, depending on the time of year.

Lily pads on Loch Garten, Cairngorms National Park.

10am–5.30pm), 14th-century home of the Thanes of Cawdor (more Macbeth associations). Eastwards up the coast are the ghostly **Culbin Sands**, and on the Ardersier peninsula to the west is the awesome and still garrisoned **Fort George** (tel: 01667-460 232; daily Apr–Sept 9.30am–5.30pm, Oct–Mar 10am–4pm), built to control and intimidate the Highlands after the 1745 Rebellion and regarded as the finest example of 18th-century military engineering in Britain.

BATTLE OF CULLODEN

The most poignant and atmospheric reminder of Charles Edward Stuart's costly adventure, however, is **Culloden Moor**, which lies between Nairn and Inverness. Culloden was the last battle fought on Britain's mainland, and here in April 1746 the Jacobite cause was finally lost to internal conflicts and the superior forces of the Hanoverian army. Now owned by the National Trust for Scotland, it is a melancholy, blasted place – in effect, a war graveyard where the Highlanders buried their dead in communal graves marked by rough stones bearing the names of each clan. The **Visitor Centre** (tel: 0844-493 2159; daily Mar–May & Sept–Oct 9am–6pm, June–Aug until 7pm, Nov––Mar 10am–4pm), complete with a 'Battle Immersion Theatre', tells the gruesome story of how in only 40 minutes the prince's army lost 1,200 men to the king's 310. 'Butcher' Cumberland's Redcoats even slaughtered some of the bystanders who had come out from Inverness to watch.

The coast and countryside to the east of Nairn is worth attention – a combination of fishing villages like **Burghead** and **Findhorn**, which is now famous for the Findhorn Foundation, an international 'alternative' community whose life and work, based on meditation and spiritual practice, have turned the sand dunes into flourishing vegetable gardens. And there are pleasing, dignified inland towns built of golden sandstone, such as **Forres**, **Elgin** ⑮ and **Fochabers**, the ancient capital of Moray. Elgin's graceful **cathedral**, now in ruins, dates back to 1224 (tel: 01343-547 171; daily Apr–Sept 9.30am–5.30pm, Oct–Mar

A headstone marks the area where several Jacobite clans died during the Battle of Culloden.

10am–5pm). With a medieval street plan still well preserved, Elgin is one of the loveliest towns in Scotland.

Monks clad in coarse white habits add a medieval touch to the giant **Pluscarden Abbey** (fax: 01343-890 258; www.pluscardenabbey.org; daily 4.30am–8.30pm; free), hidden in a sheltered valley 5 miles (8km) southwest of Elgin. The abbey, founded in 1230, fell into disrepair until, in 1948, an order of converted Benedictines started to rebuild it.

THE MOUTH OF THE SPEY

The **River Spey** debouches at wild and windy Spey Bay, which is the site of the **Scottish Dolphin Centre** (tel: 01343-820 339; www.dolphincentre.whales.org; Apr–Sept daily 10.30am–5pm, mid-Feb–Mar Thu–Sun 10.30am–3.30pm; free) run by the Whale and Dolphin Conservation Society, and housed in the former Tugnet Ice House, a thick-walled building with a turf roof, built in 1830 to store ice for packing salmon. The Spey marks something of a boundary between the fertile, wooded country and sandy coast of the Moray Firth and that plainer, harsher land which pushes out into the North Sea. Hikers can pick up the **Speyside Way** from here, a trail that follows the river all the way to Aviemore, large parts of it along disused railway track.

Now the motoring tourist, with Aberdeen just in sight, is faced with a choice. You can cut the coastal corner by driving straight through the prosperous agricultural heartland of Aberdeenshire by way of **Keith, Huntly**, **Inverurie** and yet more Aberdeenshire castles – Huntly, Fyvie and Castle Fraser (see page 262), to name but three.

BANFF TO PETERHEAD

Alternatively you can hug the forbidding littoral of Banffshire and Buchan and see atmospheric stony fields, the workmanlike ports of **Buckie**, **Fraser-burgh** and **Peterhead**, and that whole chain of rough-hewn fishing villages and harbours that has harnessed this truculent coast into something productive. Here you will find spectacular seascapes, rich birdlife and the enduring

Aberdeenshire is said to have more castles, both standing and ruined, than any other county in Britain.

Bottlenose dolphin in the Moray Firth.

BLACK GOLD IN THE NORTH SEA

The discovery of oil and natural gas in the North Sea has always been a controversial issue, but there is still more under the waves.

The Scottish National Party (SNP) would argue otherwise, but the days when it was assumed that the North Sea's 'black gold' would cure all Scotland's social and industrial ailments are long gone. The huge oil revenues have disappeared into the maw of the British Treasury, and little has returned. As one Scottish nationalist put it: 'Scotland must be the only country on Earth to discover oil and become worse off.'

Even after devolution, Scotland still has no access to the revenues, but it has acquired a technologically advanced industry that employs thousands of people and underwrites many other jobs all over the country. The birth of the offshore oil industry partly compensated for the jobs lost in traditional heavy industries.

Oil was discovered in the North Sea in the 1960s, and development proceeded rapidly. The early days between 1972 and 1979 were astonishing. Every week new schemes were announced for supply bases,

Drilling for oil.

refineries and petrochemical works. Scotland was galvanised. The SNP startled Britain by getting 11 members elected to parliament in 1974 on the crude but effective slogan 'It's Scotland's Oil'.

Heady days, but they didn't last. When the price of oil slumped in 1985–6 from $40 to less than $10 a barrel, recession struck the east coast. Nevertheless, recovery followed. Production peaked at almost 400 million barrels a year in 1999 but had fallen to 220 million by 2007, when the UK became a net importer of oil for the first time in almost 30 years. By 2010, it was estimated that around 76 percent of North Sea oil reserves had been extracted. 2016 witnessed a further plunge in Scotland's oil revenue due to another global price collapse – prices slumped to under $40 a barrel, down from more than $100 at the start of 2014.

MAJOR WORLD PLAYER

Minimal government regulation and free competition have made the area attractive to the oil companies. The high quality of the oil, political stability and proximity to large European markets have made the area a major world player despite relatively high production costs.

Oil and gas flow from more than 100 oilfields off the east coast of Scotland. Many oil platforms are in the deep, stormy waters of the East Shetland Basin, while others lie under the shallower seas east of Edinburgh.

The oil comes ashore in Scotland at three points: on the island of Flotta in Orkney, at St Fergus north of Aberdeen, and at Sullom Voe in Shetland. This last is Europe's largest oil and gas terminal. Its impact on the local environment is closely monitored by the Shetland Oil Terminal Environmental Advisory Group (SOTEAG) based at Aberdeen University. Aberdeen is the oil capital, where every oil company, exploration firm, oil-tool manufacturer and diving company has a foothold.

While the SNP continues to fight for Scotland's share of oil revenues, major oil companies are re-appraising their North Sea oil activity as older fields become less productive. But the days of North Sea oil production are far from over, with an estimated 920 million tonnes of recoverable crude still remaining. Exploration reveals that an area west of Shetland and the Outer Hebrides may well produce viable returns in the future.

fascination of working harbours, fish markets and museums dedicated to the maritime history.

Banff ⑯ is a town of some elegant substance with a Georgian centre, while the 16th-century merchants' houses around **Portsoy** harbour have been agreeably restored.

This village is also distinguished for the production and working of Portsoy marble, while there is beauty and drama to be found in **Cullen**, with its striking 19th-century railway viaducts and its sweeping stretch of sand.

Between Macduff and Fraserburgh, where the coast begins to take a right-angle bend, tortuous minor roads link the precipitous villages of **Gardenstown**, **Crovie** and **Pennan**, stuck like limpets to the bottom of cliffs. At **Fraserburgh** ⑰ is the **Museum of Scottish Lighthouses** (tel: 01346-511 022; www.lighthousemuseum.org.uk; Apr–Oct Mon–Sat 10am–5pm, Nov–Mar until 4.30pm), which tells the story of the lights and keepers who manned them.

South of **Peterhead** ⑱, around the corner, the sea boils into the **Bullers o'Buchan**, a high circular basin of rocky cliff which in spring and summer is home to hundreds of thousands of sea birds.

Close by are the gaunt clifftop ruins of **Slains Castle**, said to have ignited the imagination of Bram Stoker and inspired his novel *Dracula*. It is certainly true that Stoker spent holidays at the golfing resort of Cruden Bay, where the craggy shore begins to yield to sand until, at the village of Newburgh and the mouth of the River Ythan, you find the dramatic dune system of the **Sands of Forvie** nature reserve. South from here, an uninterrupted stretch of sand dune and marram grass reaches all the way to Aberdeen. Britain's largest breeding colony of eider ducks is established here with around 6,000 flying in each summer and 1,000 staying on for the winter.

ABERDEEN – A GRANITE CITY

Of all Britain's cities, **Aberdeen** ⑲ is the most self-contained. It comes as a shock to drive through miles of empty countryside from the south,

Ruin in Portsoy.

Marischal College, in Aberdeen, is the second largest granite building in the world – the largest is the Escorial near Madrid.

Robert Gordon University.

and, cresting a hill, find revealed below you the great grey settlement clasped between the arms of the Dee and the Don, as if it were the simple, organic extension of rock and heath and shore instead of a complex human artifice. On the sea's horizon you might glimpse a semi-submersible oil rig on the move; in the harbour, trawlers jostle with supply vessels; and there are raw ribbon developments of housing and warehousing to the north and south of the city. But otherwise Aberdeen, in its splendid self-sufficiency and glorious solitude, remains curiously untouched by the coming of the oil industry.

Aberdeen is largely indifferent to the mixed reception it receives from outsiders, and took the rejection of its bid to become the UK City of Culture 2017 with equanimity. Aberdonians are notoriously regarded by their compatriots as the thriftiest folk in Scotland, as numerous tasteless jokes testify. This appears to bother them not at all. This confidence has been Aberdeen's strength, but may not be its salvation when the North Sea oil wells run dry and the city

is confronted with the need to seek new sources of income and employment to replace revenues from oil and a fishing industry which has declined to a mere shadow of its former self.

Apart from its imposing cathedral and a few other historic buildings, surprisingly little of historic Aberdeen remains. Most of its imposing city centre dates only from the 19th century, with the building of **Union Street**, its main thoroughfare, in the early 1800s and the rebuilding of **Marischal College**, part of the ancient University of Aberdeen, in 1891. The facade of Marischal College, which stands just off Union Street in Broad Street, is an extraordinary fretwork of pinnacles and gilt flags in which the unyielding substance of white granite is made to seem delicate. Allowed to fall into disrepair for far too long, this grand landmark underwent an extensive repair and reconstruction before reopening in 2011 as the central headquarters of Aberdeen City Council.

Union Street's die-straight mile from Holborn Junction skirts the arboreal

⊘ STONY FACADE

There's no denying Aberdeen's visual impact. It looks distinctively different from Scotland's other cities. The mica-flecked granite of its dignified buildings glitters in sunlight, hence Aberdeen's 'silver city' soubriquet. Granite is the ideal building stone for a city on a coast that is exposed to wind and weather. Unlike the less erosion-resistant masonry of Scotland's other cities, Aberdeen's stony facades do not soften or acquire a mellow patina with age.

This gives the place a hard-edged beauty that some visitors find a little austere. The city can be surprisingly sunny, and its efforts to change its image from 'Granite City' to 'Rose City', lavishing attention on every flowerbed in town, have repeatedly won it 'Britain in Bloom' awards. In 2012, proposals to redevelop the city's Union Terrace Gardens, which were laid out in the 19th century, divided Aberdonians into two camps: those who favoured plans for a grandiose vision of city plazas and new arts and retail venues, and those who feared the destruction of a much-loved urban green space. In a narrow vote, the city council refused to give the £140-million project the green light, and the gardens returned to neglect. In 2016, the city council unveiled new plans for the site, which included a bridge across the gardens, along with shop and gallery units being fitted under the park's arches; work was finally due to commence in 2019.

churchyard of St Nicholas, Aberdeen's 'mither kirk', and terminates in the **Castlegate**, which remains almost unchanged since the 13th century. Its centrepiece is the 17th-century **Mercat Cross**, adorned with a sculptured portrait gallery of the Stuart monarchs. Castlegate has the best views of the city, looking over the square and down Union Street.

The cross is the focus of Aberdeen's long history as a major market town and import-export centre. For centuries fishwives from **Fittie**, the fishing village at the foot of the Dee, and farmers from the expansive hinterland brought their produce to sell round the cross, while more exotic products from Europe and the New World were hefted up the hill from the harbour by porters from the Shore Porters' Society, Britain's oldest company.

OLD ABERDEEN

Old Aberdeen, the city's oldest quarter and its historic heart lies to the northwest of the city centre on the banks of the River Don, whose narrow, sandy estuary was never developed as a harbour and port in the manner of its larger twin, the Dee. Although Aberdeen was already a busy port when it was granted a royal charter in the 12th century by King William the Lion, its earliest settlement was to be found clustered around **St Machar's Cathedral** in Old Aberdeen, once an independent burgh. The cathedral, founded in the 6th century, is one of the oldest granite buildings in the city (although it has a red sandstone arch which is a remnant of an earlier building) and has colourful, jewel-like stained-glass windows. The cobbled streets and lamp-lit academic houses surrounding it are atmospheric and peaceful. The medieval **King's College** is still the hub of the **University of Aberdeen**. Founded in 1495, the university is the third oldest in Scotland and the fifth oldest in the English-speaking world. Its campus is home to **King's Museum** (17 High Street; tel: 01224 274 330; www. abdn.ac.uk/museums; Tue–Sat 11.30am– 4.30pm; free) and the **Zoology Museum** (Tillydrone Avenue; tel and website as

Kinnaird Head lighthouse in Fraserburgh.

A commemorative plaque in the city centre marking the home of James Leatham, 'socialist, propagandist and journalist'.

The Mercat Cross in Aberdeen marks the location where a public market could be held in the city.

above; Mon–Fri 9am–5pm; free). The King's Museum has provided a home for the archaeology and history collections of the former Marischal Museum at Marischal College, with exhibitions changing every few months, while the Zoology Museum has wide-ranging displays from taxidermy to skeletons and great whales.

Provost Skene's House (Guestrow; tel: 01224-641 086; www.aagm.co.uk; temporarily closed to the public), dating from 1545, houses a series of period rooms furnished to show how people lived from the 17th to 19th centuries.

The **Tolbooth Museum** (Castle Street; tel: 01224-621 167; www.aagm.co.uk; Mon–Sat 10am–5pm, Sun noon–3pm) provides a unique experience in the form of its atmospheric 17th- and 18th-century cells, original doors and barred windows. Displays include the blade of Aberdeen's 17th-century guillotine.

Aberdeen's history has often been self-protective; the city gave the duke of Cumberland, later to become infamous as 'Butcher' Cumberland, a civic reception as he led his Hanoverian army north to confront Prince Charles Edward Stuart's Jacobites at Culloden. But it is to its credit that it offered protection to Robert the Bruce during Scotland's Wars of Independence in the 14th century. In return, Bruce gave the 'Freedom Lands' to the city (which still bring it an income) and ordered the completion of the **Brig o' Balgownie** (bridge), whose building had been interrupted by the wars.

ART GALLERY AND HIGHLAND HISTORY

The vigorous **Art Gallery** (tel: 03000 200 293; www.aagm.co.uk; closed for major refurbishment until 2020 at least) on Schoolhill, about 5 minutes north of the station, has an impressive collection of European paintings mainly from the 18th to the 20th centuries, with works by Toulouse-Lautrec and Raeburn, as well as by contemporary Scottish artists, and a sculpture court. For anyone with a military bent, the **Gordon Highlanders Museum** (St Luke's, Viewfield Road; tel: 01224-311 200; www.

gordonhighlanders.com; Feb–Nov Tue–Sat 10am–4.30pm), 2 miles (3km) west of the city centre, is a must. This unique collection tells the story of one of the most celebrated fighting units in the British Army. There is also an award-winning **Maritime Museum** (Shiprow; tel: 01224-337 700; www.aagm.co.uk; Mon–Sat 10am–5pm, Sun noon–3pm; free), just behind the Trinity Quay waterfront, that recalls Aberdeen's long and fascinating relationship with the sea. Children of all ages make a beeline for **Aberdeen Science Centre** (Constitution Street; tel: 01224-640 340; www.aberdeensciencecentre.org; Mon & Wed–Sun 10am–5pm, Tue until 3pm), a hands-on interactive science and technology centre, which is just a short walk northeast of the Maritime Museum.

Aberdeen offers excellent shopping with a good selection of individual shops, plus a thriving nightlife. A lively theatre and a succession of festivals provide entertainment to suit all tastes. Besides all of its more obvious attractions, the city confidently promotes itself as a holiday resort and is one of the few cities in Britain with a beach, giving it the nickname 'The Silver City by the Gold Sands'.

ON ABERDEEN'S BEACH

Between the mouths of the two rivers the sands are authentically golden; though don't expect to sunbathe often or comfortably on them: Aberdeen's beach is open-backed and exposed to the bitter North Sea breezes. Its parks, however, are glorious, wonderfully well kept and celebrated, like many of the other open spaces, for their roses.

Further afield, **Hazelhead** on the city's western edge, **Duthie Park**, with extensive winter gardens, and **Seaton Park** on the River Don are probably the best open spaces, and all have good play areas and special attractions for children in summer. At Maryculter, in the Dee Valley, is one of the country's most attractive small 'theme parks', **The Den & The Glen** (tel: 01224-732 941; www.denandtheglen.co.uk; daily 9.30am–5.30pm), with giant tableaux of childhood characters.

Oil supply ship off the coast of Aberdeen.

Quinag massif,
Northern Highlands.

THE NORTHERN HIGHLANDS

The remote landscape of the Northern Highlands has a wild and wonderful beauty, and the mountains, lochs, glens and rugged coastline tell their story in the museums of the towns and villages.

Map on page 254

Nowhere in Britain is the bloodied hand of the past so heavily laid as it is in the Highlands. The pages of its history read like a film script – and have often served as one. There are starring roles for Bonnie Prince Charlie, Flora Mac-Donald, Mary, Queen of Scots, Rob Roy, the Wolf of Badenoch and Macbeth, with a supporting cast of clansmen and crofters, miners and fisherfolk, businessmen and sportsmen.

Inverness ㉒ serves as a natural starting point, the 'capital' of the Highlands. It is assured of that title by its easily fortified situation on the River Ness where the roads through the glens converge. Shakespeare sadly maligned the man who was its king for 17 years, Macbeth. His castle has disappeared, but from **Castlehill** a successor dating from the 1830s dominates the city: a pink cardboard cut-out, like a Victorian doll's house, with an impressive bronze statue of Flora MacDonald and her dog. This is the backdrop for the Castle Garrison Encounter, a costume re-enactment of the life of an 18th-century soldier.

A CULTURAL TOUR OF INVERNESS

In the nearby **Inverness Museum and Art Gallery** (tel: 01463-237 114; Apr–Oct Tue–Sat 10am–5pm, Nov–Mar Tue–Thu noon–4pm, Fri–Sat 11am–4pm; free), the death mask of Flora's bonnie prince shares cases with Mr Punch in his 'red Garibaldi coat', renowned local puppeteer Duncan Morrison's puppet figure that once delighted local children. Traditions are strongly represented in silversmithing, taxidermy, bagpipes and fiddles, and even a 7th-century Pictish stone depicting a wolf.

Preserved in front of the **Town House**, on busy High Street, uphill from the river, is the **Clach-na-Cuddain**, a stone on which women rested

Inverness Castle.

their tubs of washing. **Abertarff House**, on Church Street, is the city's oldest secular building, dating from 1593. It has one of the few remaining examples of the old turnpike stair and is home these days to small art galleries.

Inverness today is modern and go-ahead, a small city with busy streets that conceal a fine selection of pubs, restaurants and late-night venues. An important cultural venue is the **Eden Court Theatre**, though this is just one among several venues that host a varied events programme. Boasting an attractive environment, and a former 'Britain in Bloom' award winner, the city is expected to become one of the fastest growing in the UK, with a 40 percent population growth estimated over the next two decades.

Dolphin-watching cruises run from Inverness harbour, out under the handsome Kessock Bridge, built to ease traffic from the North Sea oil firms in Easter Ross. The bridge replaced the ancient Kessock ferry between the city and the Black Isle.

LOCH NESS

From an area of Inverness rich in industrial archaeology the **Caledonian Canal** climbs through six locks like a flight of stairs to the 'Hill of Yew Trees', **Tomnahurich**. This highland waterway, which joins the North Sea and the Atlantic Ocean through the Great Glen, was predicted by a local seer a century before it was built: 'Full-rigged ships will be seen sailing at the back of Tomnahurich.' Now you can set sail here in summer for a trip on **Loch Ness**, and enjoy 'a wee dram in the lingering twilight'. The drink may assist you in spotting the monster, the lake's supposed ancient occupant. You can take a variety of combined bus and boat tours from Inverness all year.

Urquhart Castle ㉑ (tel: 01456-450 551; daily Apr–Sept 9.30am–6pm, July & Aug until 8pm, Oct until 5pm, Nov–Mar until 4.30pm) is a picturesque ruin on the loch's edge (15 miles/24km south of Inverness on the A82) which bears the scars of having been fought over for two centuries.

At **Fort Augustus ㉒** (29 miles/48km further south), the canal descends

⊙ **Tip**

If you fail to spot the real Loch Ness monster, you can always stop off at the two visitor centres at Drumnadrochit, where multimedia shows invite you to separate fact from fiction.

Ruins of Urquhart Castle overlooking Loch Ness.

down another flight of locks near the **Clansman Centre** (tel: 01320-366 444;www.clansmancentre.co.uk; Mar–Oct daily 10am–5pm), which illustrates the glen's history from Pictish to modern times. The garrison, set up after the 1715 Jacobite Rising, later became a Benedictine abbey.

Turn right at **Invergarry** onto the A87 for the beauty of glen and mountain on the road to Kyle of Lochalsh and Skye (see pages 210 and 215). Or, continuing south on the A82, stop at the 'Well of the Heads' monument, which records the murder of a 17th-century chieftain's two sons and, as reprisal, the deaths of seven brothers, whose heads were washed in the well, and then presented to the chief.

The A82 now crosses to the east bank of **Loch Lochy**. Six miles (10km) before Fort William is the **Nevis Range** (tel: 01397-705 825; www.nevisrange.co.uk), where Britain's only mountain gondola whisks you in 12 minutes up to 2,150ft (645 metres), giving stunning views of Scotland's highest mountains. On the outskirts of **Fort William ㉓** (see page 208), take the A830 and you will immediately reach 'Neptune's Staircase', eight locks taking the Caledonian Canal to the sea, from where there are grand views of Ben Nevis.

AVIEMORE'S ATTRACTIONS

From Inverness you can also head southeast towards **Aviemore ㉔** and the magnificent scenery and wildlife of the Cairngorms. Aviemore barely existed before the railway arrived on its way to Inverness in the 1880s, but today, it is a thriving hub for outdoor types with hiking in the summer and winter sports when the snows come. The town's centrepiece is the impressive **Macdonald Aviemore Highland Resort** complete with golf course and spa (tel: 0844-879 9152; www.macdonaldhotels.co.uk).

Nearby, at Carrbridge, is the **Landmark Centre** (tel: 01479-841 613; www. landmarkpark.co.uk; daily 10am–5pm with exceptions), whose attractions include a tree-top trail through the forest, horse-logging and a 'Runaway Timber Train' roller-coaster ride, among other things.

A lock on the Caledonian Canal at Fort Augustus.

⊘ AVIEMORE'S EXPANSION

It's doubtful if the Clan Grant, whose war cry was 'Stand Fast Craigellachie', could have resisted the forces at work in Aviemore, below their rallying place. The quiet Speyside halt has been transformed into a year-round resort by the opening of roads into the Cairngorms and chairlifts for the skiers. Brewers built the Aviemore Centre in the 1960s, and in 2004 it was extended to form the impressive Macdonald Aviemore Highland Resort at its centre. The resort – which includes four hotels, an activity centre, a 3D cinema and several restaurants – invested £550,000 in upgrading its golf courses in 2016.

The beginnings of Aviemore's expansion date back to the 1880s when the railway arrived here on its way to Inverness. Today, Aviemore is a central base from which to explore the spectacular mountains and moors and to enjoy the bounteous wildlife, and, when the snows melt, the pretty alpine flowers. A relaxing way to experience the scenery is on the Strathspey Steam Railway train (01479-810 725; www.strathspeyrailway. co.uk), which runs in the summer months en route from Aviemore to Boat of Garten. A year-round funicular railway carries skiers and sightseers to the summit of Cairn Gorm, which provides some breathtaking views of Rothiemurchus and Strathspey below (tel: 01479-861 261; www.cairngorm mountain.co.uk).

At Kincraig, 6 miles (10km) southwest of Aviemore, is the **Highland Wildlife Park** (tel: 01540-651 270; www.highlandwildlifepark.org; July–Aug 10am–6pm; Apr–June, Sept–Oct 10am–5pm; Nov–Mar 10am–4pm). Here once-indigenous animals, including wolves, boar and bison, run free. More recent arrivals include two Amur tigers, born in the park in April 2013, a pair of adult wolverines, and a trio of lynx cubs born here in 2016. Some parts of the park are drive-through, others walk-through.

Further south at **Kingussie** is the **Highland Folk Museum** (tel: 01540-673 551; www.highlifehighland.com; daily Apr–Aug 10.30am–5.30pm, Sept–Oct 11am–4.30pm; free). The museum has a whole replica 'township' of Highland blackhouses (thatched dry-stone wall dwellings) from about 1700, faithfully reproduced from excavations throughout the north. Craftsmen keeping alive the ancient skills in building, furnishing and various types of thatching are on hand to explain their secrets.

A HIGHLAND GATHERING

Back in Inverness, the A9 crosses the neck of the **Black Isle**, which is neither an island nor black but forest and fertile farmland, and is bisected by roads serving the oil centres on the north shore of the Cromarty Firth.

Just before you reach Fortrose, the one-time fishing village of **Avoch**, still with a pretty harbour, was a focal point during the Scottish Wars of Independence. Half a mile west along the coast stands the great mound of **Ormond Castle** with only the slightest remains of its one-time bastion still visible. This was the base of a largely unsung Highland hero, Andrew De Moray, who raised a Highland army that cleared the north of the English invaders in a brilliant guerrilla campaign that drove them back through the Southern Highlands. He then joined William Wallace to form a credible force for the notable

victory at the Battle of Stirling Bridge. In May each year there is a procession of villagers to the top of the castle hill to commemorate the Highland Gathering, as it is known.

On the golf links at **Fortrose** ㉕, on the east shore, a plaque marks the spot where – according to tradition – Coinneach Odhar the 'Brahan Seer' was burned as a witch on the orders of Lady Seaforth. The 17th-century seer is Scotland's answer to Nostradamus. Some claim that his gnomic pronouncements can be read to predict such events as the building of the Caledonian Canal, the Highland Clearances, and even the outbreak of World War II. Skeptics question whether he ever really existed. The annual St Boniface's Fair is held in the square adjacent to the magnificent ruins of a 14th-century cathedral; the fair's traders and entertainers wear medieval costume.

Nearby, at Rosemarkie, is **Groam House Museum** (tel: 01463-811 883; www.groamhouse.org.uk; Apr–Oct Mon–Fri 11am–4.30pm, Sat & Sun 2–4.30pm, Nov–Dec Fri–Sun 2–4pm,

An Amur tiger in the Highland Wildlife Park.

Hugh Miller's cottage.

Beinn Eighe is a fascinating geological "pudding" of old red sandstone topped with white quartzite.

Fyrish Monument near Alness.

Jan–Mar Sat–Sun 2–4pm; free), a Pictish interpretive centre with a superb collection of sculpted stones, audiovisual displays and rubbings.

Cromarty ㉖, at the extreme tip of the Isle, lost face as a Royal Burgh through declining fortunes as a seaport and trading community, but has earned rightful popularity as a place where visitors can step back in time in the unspoilt old town. Taped tours point out some of the most beautiful late-18th-century buildings in Britain, such as the **Courthouse** (tel: 01381-600 418; www.cromarty-courthouse.org.uk; Easter–mid-Oct daily noon–4pm; free), now a prize-winning museum with two exhibitions dedicated to the history of the building and to the journeys of local adventurer and Yukon gold prospector Sutherland Murray. Next to the museum are the thatched cottage where the 19th-century geologist Hugh Miller, Cromarty's most famous scholarly son, lived (tel: 01381-600 245; www.thefriendsofhughmiller.org.uk; Apr–Sept daily 1–5pm, Oct Tue, Thu & Fri 1–5pm) and the **East Kirk**, with three wooden lofts.

A road leads to **South Sutor**, one of two precipitous headlands guarding the narrow entrance to the Firth of Cromarty, where numerous oil rigs are moored. Around the rigs swim the North Sea's only resident group of bottlenose dolphins, plus innumerable grey and common seals.

STRATHPEFFER

Though Scots had long known the local sulphur and chalybeate springs at **Strathpeffer** ㉗, it took a doctor who had himself benefited to give substance to 'miracle' recoveries and, incidentally, recognise their profitable potential. Dr Morrison opened his pump room around 1820, and the new railway brought thousands to fill the hotels and, if they felt inclined, to enjoy a 'low-pressure subthermal reclining manipulation douche'. A couple of wars intervened and the spa declined, but, like all things Victorian, this elegant town is enjoying something of a revival as a resort of character. The old railway station is now a visitor centre..

On leaving Strathpeffer, join the A835, which, after **Garve**, winds through Strath Ben and **Achnasheen** ㉘. From here the southern leg (A890) through Glen Carron is the stuff of photo murals, with Kyle of Lochalsh at the end of the rainbow that leads across the sea to Skye. Achnasheen's northern leg (A832) leads to **Kinlochewe** ㉙ at the head of **Loch Maree** (see page 211) and close to the **Beinn Eighe National Nature Reserve**; buzzards fly above the pine forests, home to the elusive pine marten and rare and protected wildlife, and perhaps you might see a golden eagle; nature trails begin in the car park.

Alternatively, from **Dingwall** – was Macbeth really born here? – road (A9) and rail cling to the east coast. **Evanton** has an abundance of accommodation, and there's a good chance of seeing seals on the shore walk. Near **Alness** ㉚, on a hill, is a replica of the Gate of Negapatam in India, which General Sir Hector Munro (hero of its capture) had built by local men. Today Alness is dormitory to **Invergordon** on Cromarty Firth, which offered shelter to Britain's navy through two world wars and suffered the closure of its naval base in 1956. The area has also seen dramatic changes since the choice of Nigg Bay for the construction of oil-rig platforms.

COASTAL HIGHLANDS

Further along the A9, memories at **Tain** ㉛ are older, going back to 1066, when it became a Royal Burgh. Though St Duthac was born and buried here, it didn't save the two chapels dedicated to him from disastrous fires – or guarantee sanctuary. Today visitors can call in at the **Glenmorangie Distillery** (tel: 01862-892 477; www.glenmorangie.com; daily Apr–May, Sept–Oct 10am–3pm, June–Aug until 4pm, Jan–Mar, Nov–Dec by appointment) to see how the famous malt whisky is made and to sample some.

From Tain, the A836 leads to **Bonar Bridge**, and motorists have to adjust to negotiate single-track roads and the sheep that share them. **Carbisdale Castle**, at Invershin, is a splendidly overblown mock-baronial pile, built in 1914 for a duchess of Sutherland who

The Falls of Shin.

⊙ ENTER THE WOLVES

A rather inventive way of protecting the ecosystem in the Highlands has been the suggestion of reintroducing wild wolves (hunted to extinction in the 1700s) to control the number of red deer whose numbers pose a threat to plant and insect life. This project could lead to the regrowth of the forests of old, and winter nights reverberating with howling packs roaming the wilderness.

Public opinion in surrounding cities has been largely positive, with many wishing to see Scotland reverting to traditional landscapes. However, proposals have met with objections from farmers who fear for their livestock, and have little time for scientific claims that wolves will not hunt down entire herds of cows or flocks of sheep.

Spectacular cliffs carved out by the sea at Duncansby Head.

Dunrobin Castle.

was at the heart of a bitter family feud. Locally known as the 'Castle of Spite', it housed the exiled Norwegian Royal Family during World War II, and then became the world's grandest youth hostel. With the Scottish Youth Hostel Association unable to pay the repair bill of £2 million, it was put up for sale in 2014, and remains closed, though private investors have expressed interest as recently as 2019.

The nearby **Falls of Shin** offer glimpses of salmon ascending the cataracts as they migrate, while the visitor centre has educational wildlife events for children.

CROFTING COUNTRY

'All roads meet at Lairg,' so the saying goes. Sometimes in August it seems all the sheep in Scotland do as well. Located twenty-eight miles (45km) northwest of Tain, the village of **Lairg** ㉜ is in the heart of Sutherland crofting country, and the lamb sales identify it as a major marketplace. Mirrored in the quiet waters of Loch Shin is an Iron Age hut circle on the hill above the village.

The eastern spoke (A839) from Lairg's hub reaches the coast at Loch Fleet and **Dornoch** ㉝, where some regard Royal Dornoch (opened in 1616) as offering better golf than the Old Course at St Andrews. Dornoch Castle's surviving tower has been a garrison, courthouse, jail, school and private residence. Now it's a hotel. The lovely cathedral is also a survivor: badly damaged in a 17th-century fire, it was largely restored in the 1920s. The last witch to be burned in Scotland, Janet Horne, was condemned to death in Dornoch in 1727, though her commemoration stone reads 1722.

More happily, the Dunfermline-born industrialist and philanthropist Andrew Carnegie, who made his money in the United States, bought nearby Skibo Castle (now a country club) in the 1890s and lived there until he died in 1919; he funded the town's Carnegie Library.

THE SUTHERLAND CLAN

To the north is **Golspie**, which lives in the shadow of the Sutherlands. An oversized statue of the controversial

first duke looks down from the mountain; a stone in the old bridge is the clan's rallying point; and nearby is the duchess' **Dunrobin Castle** (tel: 01408-633 177; www.dunrobincastle.co.uk; Apr–May & Oct daily 10.30am–4.30pm, June–Sept until 5pm), an improbable collection of pinnacles and turrets which has been the seat of earls and dukes of Sutherland since the 13th century. Numerous additions have been made since then, but the original keep still stands within the walls, making it one of the longest-inhabited houses in Scotland. The formal gardens are a riot of colour in summer. The prehistoric fort at **Carn Liath** a little further along the coast is a simple antidote.

The gold rush that brought prospectors to the burns of **Helmsdale** ❸ in the 1860s was short lived. The town's main attraction today is the **Timespan Heritage Centre** (tel: 01431-821 327; www.timespan.org.uk; Mar–Oct daily 10am–5pm, Nov–Feb Sat–Sun 10am–3pm, Tue 10am–4pm), which brings the history of the Highlands to life; there is also a large garden with a unique collection of medicinal and herbal plants. Intrepid travellers keep going north to **Caithness**, for centuries so remote from the centres of Scottish power that it was ruled by the Vikings. Trade links were entirely by sea, and in the boom years of the fishing industry scores of harbours were built. The fleets have gone; the harbours remain.

The A9 to **Berriedale** twists spectacularly past the ravines of the Ord of Caithness and on to **Dunbeath**, where a few lobster boats are a reminder of past glories. Here, too, is the **Laidhay Croft Museum** (tel: 01593 731 270; www.laidhay.co.uk; Apr–Sept daily 9am–5pm), a restored longhouse with stable, house and byre all under one roof. **Lybster** ❸ offers more bustle, but at **Mid Clyth** leave the road at the sign 'Hill o'Many Stanes' for a mystery tour. On a hillside are 22 rows, each with an average of eight small stones, thought to be Bronze Age.

Herring were the backbone of **Wick**, and the town's prosperity comes to life again in the **Wick Heritage Centre** (tel: 01955-605 393; www.wickheritage.org; Easter–Oct Mon–Sat 10am–4pm). More than 1,000 boats used to set sail to catch the 'silver darlings'. Now the near-empty quays give the harbour a wistful charm.

NORTHERNMOST BRITAIN

For cross-country record-breakers, **John o'Groats** ❸, at the end of the A99, has a natural attraction – although, contrary to popular belief, it is not the northernmost point in Britain. A Dutchman, Jan de Groot, came here in 1500 under orders from James IV to set up a ferry service to Orkney to consolidate his domination over this former Scandinavian territory. A mound and a flagstaff commemorate the site of his house. In 2013, the shabby old John o'Groats Hotel, dating from 1875, reopened after being transformed into a luxury self-catering eco-resort (tel: 01625-416 430; www.togethertravel.co.uk). As well as apartments, the Inn at John o'Groats offers whale-watching trips, bike hire and guided walks.

⊘ Fact

Dutch founder of John o'Groats, Jan de Groot, responded to requests from his eight sons as to who should succeed him by building an octagonal house with eight doors and with an octagonal table in the middle so that each sat at the 'head'.

The coast at Thurso.

Catching brown crabs at Ullapool.

Sailing into Ullapool harbour.

Boat trips run from the harbour to Orkney and to **Duncansby Head**, 2 miles (3km) to the east, where many species of birds nest on the dramatic towering stacks. From here a road runs to the lighthouse. West of John o'Groats, on the A836, is the **Castle of Mey**, the late Queen Elizabeth the Queen Mother's home. **Dunnet Head** is the British mainland's most northerly point.

The approaches to **Thurso** ③ are heralded by the Caithness 'hedges' that line the fields, the flagstones that were once shipped from local quarries to every corner of the old empire. The streets of Calcutta were paved by Caithness. **Fisherbiggins**, the fishermen's old quarter, is a reproduction from 1940, but elsewhere there is pleasant Victorian town planning. **Scrabster** is Thurso's outport, with a ferry to Orkney. The site of Scotland's first nuclear power research station, now defunct, at **Dounreay** was partly chosen for its remoteness.

WILD CAPE WRATH

It's an odd feeling: nothing between you and the North Pole except magnificent cliff scenery. At **Tongue** ③ the sea loch pokes deep into the bleak moorland, and near **Durness** ③, which has some huge expanses of wonderful beach, the Alt Smoo River drops from the cliff into the Caves of Smoo. From Durness, a combined ferry and bus service travels to **Cape Wrath** from where you can see Orkney and the Outer Hebrides. Look out for cooties, sea cockies, tammies and tommienoories (puffins).

The return to Lairg can be made south from Tongue on the lovely A836 through **Altnaharra** ④, where crosses, hut circles and Pictish brochs (fortified towers) abound. From Durness the A838 joins the western coast at **Scourie** ④, where seals are mistaken for mermaids and palm trees grow.

Ullapool ④, 52 miles (83km) south of Scourie, is a resort for all seasons, beautifully situated on Loch Broom facing the sunset. The **Ullapool Museum and Visitor Centre** on West Argule Street (tel: 01854-612 987; www.ullapoolmuseum.co.uk; Apr–May, Sept–Oct Mon–Sat 11am–4pm,) has displays on the history and people of the area. Today, a car ferry serves Stornoway in Lewis and trippers leave for the almost deserted but delightfully named **Summer Isles**. Smoking is good for you at **Achiltibuie** ④, where fish and game have been traditionally smoked.

Another route south is through **Bettyhill**, where the 18th-century kirk is a museum of the Clan MacKay and the 19th-century Highland Clearances. Strathnaver, to the south, was the centre for this once-powerful clan, which raised thousands of mercenaries for campaigns in Europe. The most famous of these soldiers of fortune was Sir Hugh Mackay of Scourie (1640-92) who served the kings of France, the Netherlands and England before returning to his native land as King William III's commander in chief. Despite being defeated by Viscount Claverhouse (a.k.a. 'Bonnie Dundee') at Killiecrankie in 1689, he survived to crown his career by founding Fort William.

PEATLAND VERSUS PROFIT

The world's largest bogland in the far north of Scotland has suffered many threats to its survival in its long history, but now this important wildlife area is protected.

Travel throughout the far north of Scotland and you will be struck by the lack of people. It's hard to imagine that from Neolithic times until the controversial Highland Clearances of the 18th and 19th centuries, much of the wild landscape of Caithness and Sutherland was populated by crofters and scores of thriving coastal settlements.

Indeed, even the Flow Country, a rugged 'wilderness' that encompasses almost 1 million acres (400,000 hectares) of habitat-rich peatland, once supported settlers. Today, this fragile ecosystem and site of the world's largest bogland is owned or managed by an array of private shooting estates and national conservation and land-management agencies including the Royal Society for the Protection of Birds (RSPB), Forestry and Land Scotland, and Scottish Natural Heritage (SNH).

Incorporating more than 20 Sites of Special Scientific Interest, few doubt the ecological importance of the Flow Country, beloved by fishermen, walkers and twitchers alike. Indeed, ornithologists estimate more than 60 percent of Europe's greenshanks annually breed in the Flow Country, while the peatland's startling diversity of fauna and flora also supports rare mosses, short-eared owls, golden eagles, plovers and hen harriers.

However, until recently the Flow Country was a watchword for controversy. Until common sense prevailed (and generous tax concessions for wealthy investors were removed) conservation bodies struggled throughout the 1980s to counter the excesses of misguided commercial forestry projects designed to maximise revenue by planting and selling for timber huge swathes of (non-indigenous) conifer trees.

To the dismay of the 'green lobby', these ill-advised 'job and profit' motivated ventures threatened to unbalance a very fragile ecosystem that had existed on the peatland bogs for thousands of years.

Fortunately, today's forestry masters have ensured that a more enlightened approach has been adopted by formerly overzealous landowners. With more than 8 percent of Scotland's total land area under its control, the FCS is now actively involved in helping reverse some of the worst excesses of commercial land management that for decades blighted the Flow Country.

According to Tim Cockerill, Forest District Manager for Dornoch: 'We are now trying to find a balance [between sustainable forestry and conservation]. We accept that the process of afforestation in the past was a step too far and we are working with agencies such as the RSPB to identify forested areas where natural habitats can best be restored.'

The Royal Society for the Protection of Birds now owns more than 25,000 acres (10,000 hectares) of peatland, moor and former forest and aims to encourage the return of bird and plant species by restoring watercourses to more than 5,000 acres (2,000 hectares) of land that had been drained for forestry to recreate their natural habitat. The land is managed as the RSPB's Forsinard Flows Nature Reserve (tel: 01641-571 225; www.rspb.org.uk; visitor centre Apr–Oct daily 9am–5pm; reserve at all times) located 24 miles (39km) northwest of Helmsdale on the A897; three trains run daily from Inverness to Forsinard station.

Bog cotton, also known as common cottongrass, grows in peat soils.

📷 HIGHLAND FLORA AND FAUNA

The wilderness of northern Scotland may look timeless, but humans have had a major impact on its appearance.

The symbol of Scotland – the thistle – is not tough enough for the Highlands. Heather, bilberry, bog cotton, asphodel and sphagnum moss (a springy, water-retaining plant that eventually rots down into peat) are the plant survivors here.

But ranging across this unrelenting land are a couple of other particularly resilient symbols of Scotland – golden eagles and red deer. Red deer in the Highlands are thought to number 350,000, a population that is barely restrained by the huge deerstalking industry. In the summer the herds are almost invisible to all but the hardiest walkers, but in the winter they descend into river valleys in search of food. The golden eagle is elusive all year round, although the population is relatively stable in the mountains. Since 1985, moves have re-established pairs of white-tailed sea eagles on the island of Rum.

Causing concern is the capercaillie, a turkey-sized game bird with the mating call of a brass band. Although it is no longer hunted, it has never learned to cope with modern deer fences: flying low through woodland, it crashes straight into them at speed. Another distinctive Highland bird is also vanishing fast. The corncrake's unmistakable rasping call is only heard in remote corners of the outer Hebridean islands.

After years of lobbying by conservationists, controlled trials have been conducted to successfully reintroduce beavers into the wild in Scotland.

One thriving specimen of Highland natural history is often omitted from the brochures: the biting midge. Of Scotland's 34 species, only two or three attack humans, and *Culicoides impunctatus* (with distinctive speckled wings) does the lion's share. In the end, you have to laugh, or they'd drive you crazy. As they say, midges are compassionate creatures: kill one, and a couple of thousand arrive for the funeral.

A majestic red deer stag surveys Loch Torridon from Beinn Alligin. The idea that deer range for great distances in search of food is a romantic misconception: most animals remain "hefted" to the couple of square miles where they were born.

An adult male capercaillie in a forest in the Highlands. The birds favour native pine woods and are now at risk of extinction.

Scots pine trees by Loch Maree, near Kinlochewe village.

Return of the Lonesome Pine

Long ago, most of the now desolate areas of the Highlands were forested. Over the centuries the trees were felled for timber and to accommodate livestock. Deer and sheep are very effective grazers, and tree shoots don't stand a chance. Stop at a loch to compare the growth onshore with that of offshore islands and you will see how destructive grazing animals can be.

Several decades ago the Forestry Commission, a government body, set about fencing off areas of moorland for reforestation. To make the initiative economically viable they chose the fast-growing sitka spruce, which they planted in marching rows. The result is not particularly pleasing on the eye, and there has been controversy over the use of public money. There are also worries about the damage coniferisation causes to the unique habitats in many areas – like the areas of bogland in parts of Caithness.

Over the past 20 years, several initiatives to reforest large areas with native Scots pine and deciduous trees have been started on privately purchased land by charitable organisations such as the Royal Society for the Protection of Birds, John Muir Trust and Scottish Woodlands Trust. It will be many years before these large-scale plantings start to show themselves on the landscape.

A cabbage white butterfly. Females can be identified from males as they have two black spots and a dash on their wings.

Unspoilt landscape near Drumochter, a pass which divides the north and south central Highlands.

A male golden eagle. A young eagle will stay with its parents for up to a year before setting off in search of new territory and a mate of its own, with whom it will pair for life.

The Neolithic Ring of Brodgar on Mainland.

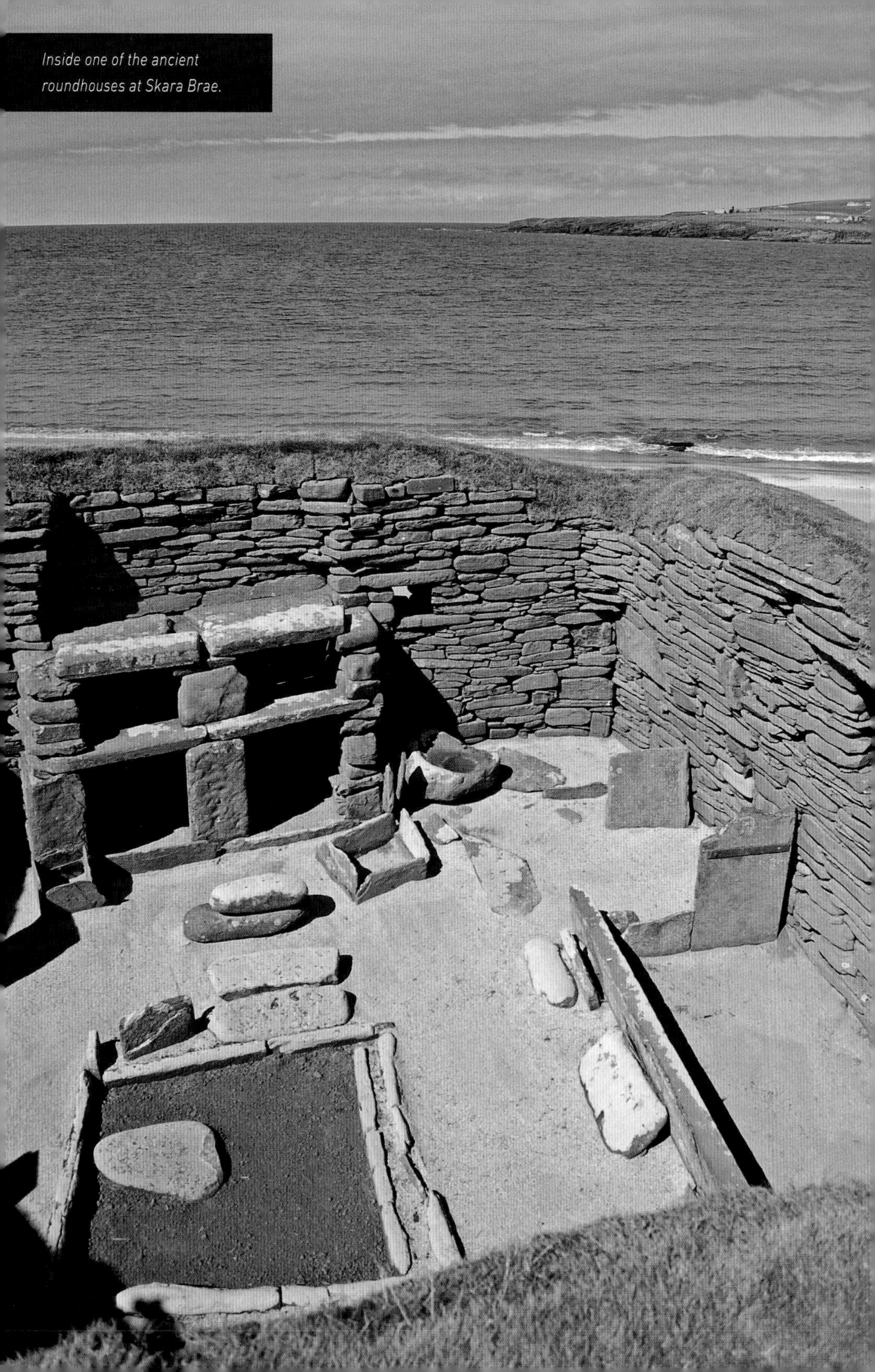

Inside one of the ancient roundhouses at Skara Brae.

ORKNEY

In few places in the world is the marriage of landscape and seascape so harmonious, or is there such a profusion of archaeological wonders and variety of wildlife.

Six miles (10km) of sea separate the northeast corner of Scotland from an archipelago of 70 islands, 20 of which are inhabited. This is Orkney (the word means 'seal islands' in old Icelandic), which extends over 1,200 sq miles (3,100 sq km).

NORWEGIAN LINKS

The 'ey' is Old Norse for islands, and so one should refer to Orkney and not 'the Orkneys' or 'the Orkney Islands'. It also announces an ancient affiliation with Norway, an affiliation historical rather than geographical, for Norway lies 300 miles (480km) to the east. Orkney was a Norwegian appendage until the end of the 15th century, and the true Orcadian is more Norse than Scot. With a rich tradition of sagas, it is no surprise that 20th-century Orkney produced such distinguished literati as Edwin Muir, Eric Linklater and George Mackay Brown.

To Orcadians, Scotland is the 'sooth' (south) and never the 'mainland', for that is the name of the group's principal island: when inhabitants of the smaller islands visit the largest, therefore, they journey to **Mainland**, and when they travel to the UK they are off 'sooth' to Scotland. Not that there are many of them to travel: the population is about 21,500, of whom one-quarter live in the capital, Kirkwall. Travel

within the archipelago is by ferry or more often by plane. The Loganair flight between Westray and Papa Westray is the shortest commercial flight in the world. In perfect weather conditions it takes only two minutes.

To wander these islands is, for the dedicated lover of archaeology, a taste of paradise. Orkney offers an uninterrupted continuum of mute stones from Neolithic times (about 4500 BC) through the Bronze and Iron ages to about AD 700, followed by remains from the days when the

Map on page 290

Main attractions
Kirkwall
Stromness
Maeshowe
Skara Brae
Hoy
Rousay
Stronsay
North Ronaldsay

Ruins of St Magnus Kirk, Egilsay.

The ruined Earl's Palace in Kirkwall.

St Magnus Cathedral, Kirkwall.

islands were occupied successively by the Celts and the Vikings.

KIRKWALL

Kirkwall ❶ is dominated by the 12th-century **St Magnus Cathedral** (tel: 01856-874 894; www.stmagnus.org; Mon–Sat 9am–6pm with exceptions; free). Construction began in the Norman style, but its many Gothic features attest to more than 300 years of building. Facing it is the ruined **Bishop's Palace** (tel: 01856-871 918; Apr–Sept daily 9.30am–5.30pm) a massive structure with a round tower reminiscent of a castle. In the 13th century the great Norwegian king, Haakon Haakonsson, lay dying here while Norse sagas were read aloud to him.

Nearby is a third historic building, the **Earl Patrick's Palace** (same times and joint ticket with Bishop's Palace), a romantic gem of Renaissance architecture. It is roofless because in the 17th century its slates were removed to build the town hall.

Other Kirkwall attractions are the **Orkney Museum** (tel: 01856-873 535; Mon–Sat 10.30am–5pm; free), which presents the complete story of Orkney from prehistory to the present; and the **Orkney Wireless Museum** (tel: 01856-871 400; Apr–Sept Mon–Sat 10am–4.30pm, Sun 2.30–4.30pm), which displays communications equipment from World War II. There is also a golf course and a sports and leisure centre.

SCAPA FLOW

South of Kirkwall is the great natural harbour of **Scapa Flow** where the captured German fleet was anchored after World War I and eventually scuttled. Only six of the 74 ships remain on the bed of this deep, spacious bay, which is bliss for the scuba diver and a peaceful cornucopia for the deep-sea angler.

The island of **Flotta**, at the south of Scapa Flow, is a North Sea oil terminal and the Orcadians' only concession to black gold.

Fifteen miles (24km) west of Kirkwall is picturesque **Stromness** ❷, Orkney's second town. A well on the main street testifies that, in the 17th century, Stromness was developed by

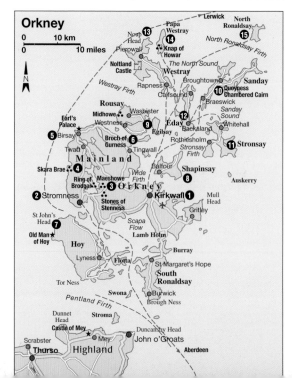

the Hudson Bay Company, whose ships made this their last port of call before crossing the Atlantic.

The **Pier Arts Centre** (tel: 01856-850 209; www.pierartscentre.com; Tue–Sat 10.30am–5pm; free) houses a good collection of 20th-century paintings and sculpture. Also of interest is the **Stromness Museum** (tel: 01856-850 025; www;stromnessmuseum.co.uk; daily 10am–5pm, Wed until 7pm), which has natural history exhibits, model ships and a display on the escaping of the German Fleet at Scapa Flow. There is a golf course and indoor pool here, too.

ARCHAEOLOGICAL SITES

Most of Mainland's major archaeological sites are to the north of Stromness. Crawl into awesome **Maeshowe ❸** (tel: 01856 841 815; guided tours from Skara Brae at 10am, noon, 2pm and 4pm), the most magnificent chambered tomb in Britain, which dates from 3500 BC. Within is a spacious burial chamber built with enormous megaliths; on some of these are incised the world's largest collection of 12th-century Viking runes.

Near Maeshowe are the **Ring of Brodgar** and the **Standing Stones of Stenness**, the remains of two of Britain's most spectacular stone circles. When the former (whose name means 'Circle of the Sun') was completed, in about 1200 BC, it consisted of 60 standing stones set along the circumference of a circle about 340ft (103 metres) in diameter. Today, 27 stones, the tallest at 14ft (4 metres), still stand. The four giant monoliths of Stenness are all that remain of that particular circle of 12 stones, erected about 2300 BC.

Skara Brae ❹ (visitor centre and replica house; tel: 01856-841 815; daily Apr–Sept 9.30am–5.30pm, Oct–Mar 10am–4pm), Britain's answer to Pompeii, sits on the Atlantic coast alongside a superb sandy beach. The settlement, remarkably well preserved, consists of several dwelling houses and connecting passages and was engulfed by sand 4,500 years ago after having been occupied for 500 years. Skara Brae is a quintessential

⊘ Tip

On average, every square mile (2.6 sq km) on Orkney has three recorded items of antiquarian interest. The key to these is often kept at the nearest farmhouse and payment is made by placing money in an honour box.

Layers of red sandstone can be seen in Orkney's cliffs.

Stone Age site; no metal of any kind has been found.

Five miles (8km) north is **Birsay** with its 16th-century **Earl's Palace**. Opposite is the **Brough of Birsay**, a tiny tidal island (avoid being stranded) covered with rich remains of Norse and Christian settlements. A further 8 miles (13km) east, and guarding Eynhallow Sound, is the **Broch of Gurness** ⊙ (tel: 01856-751 414; Apr–Sept daily 9.30am–5.30pm).

The principal southern islands are South Ronaldsay, Burray, Lamb Holm, Hoy and Flotta. Technically, the first three are no longer islands, being joined to Mainland by the **Churchill Barriers,** which were built by Italian prisoners during World War II after a German submarine penetrated Scapa Flow and sank the battleship *Royal Oak*. On **Lamb Holm** enter some Nissen huts and be astonished at the beautiful chapel built with scrap metal by these prisoners.

Hoy, the second largest island of the archipelago, is spectacularly different. The southern part is low-lying, but at the north stand the heather-covered Cuilags (1,420ft/426 metres), from where all Orkney, except Little Rysa, can be viewed. A stroll along the 1,140ft (367-metre) -high **St John's Head** ⊙, which teems with sea birds (beware the swooping great skuas) and boasts some rare plants, is sheer delight for the geologist, ornithologist and botanist, or for those who just like to ramble.

Immediately south of St John's Head is Orkney's most venerable inhabitant, the **Old Man of Hoy**, who, sad to say, appears to be cracking up. This 450ft (135-metre) perpendicular sandstone column continues to challenge the world's leading rock climbers.

THE NORTHERN ISLANDS

And so to the northern islands. Fertile **Shapinsay** ⊙ is so near Mainland that it is called suburbia. Also near Mainland, but further west and readily reached by local ferry, are **Rousay** ⊙ and **Egilsay**. Rich archaeological finds have earned the former the nickname 'Egypt of the North'. Visit

The ornate chapel, on Lamb Holm, built by Italian prisoners during World War II.

the remarkable 76ft (23-metre) -long Neolithic **Midhowe Chambered Cairn** (open access), aptly named the 'Great Ship of Death', which has 12 burial compartments each side of a passage. Nearby is the magnificent **Midhowe Broch,** Rousay's finest archaeological site. Ascend Mansemass Hill and stroll to Ward Hill for superb views of **Eynhallow**, medieval Orkney's Holy Island, between Rousay and Mainland.

On **Egilsay** an unusual round church, which has affinities with similar buildings in Ireland, marks the 12th-century site of the martyrdom of St Magnus.

WHITE SANDY BEACHES

Low-lying **Sanday**, with its white beaches, has room for a golf course but not to the exclusion of archaeological remains. Most important is the **Quoyness Chambered Cairn** ❿ (open access), standing 13ft (3 metres) high and dating from about 2900 BC. It is similar to, but even larger than, Maeshowe. **Stronsay** ⓫ , another low-lying island with sandy beaches, was formerly the hub of the prosperous Orkney herring industry. **Eday** ⓬ may be bleak and barren, yet it is paradise for birdwatchers and has the customary complement of archaeological edifices.

Westray, the largest northern island, is unique in that its population is increasing, largely because of a successful fishing fleet. **Noup Head** ⓭ is Westray's bird reserve and splendid viewpoint. The island also has a golf course and the ruined Renaissance **Notland Castle**. **North Hill Nature Reserve** on **Papa Westray** ⓮ is home to Arctic terns and skuas. At **Knap of Howar** (open access) there are considerable remains of the earliest standing dwelling houses in northwest Europe (approximately 3000 BC). Their occupants, archaeologists have found, had 'a strong preference for oysters'.

On the most northerly island, **North Ronaldsay** ⓯, a dyke around the island confines sheep to the shore, leaving better inland pastures for cattle. Seaweed, the sole diet of these sheep, results in a dark meat with an unusually rich flavour – an acquired taste.

Hoy Island.

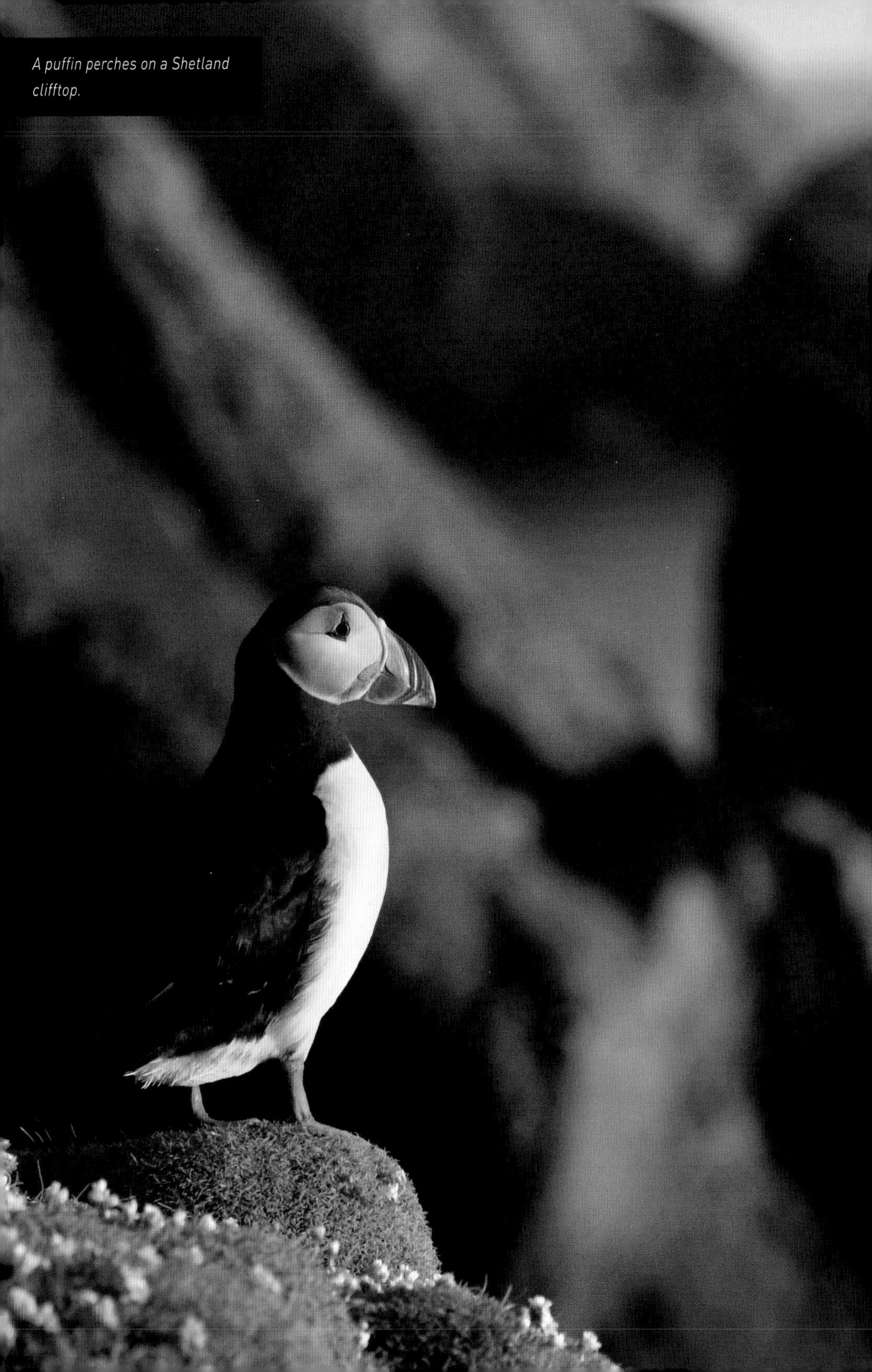

A puffin perches on a Shetland clifftop.

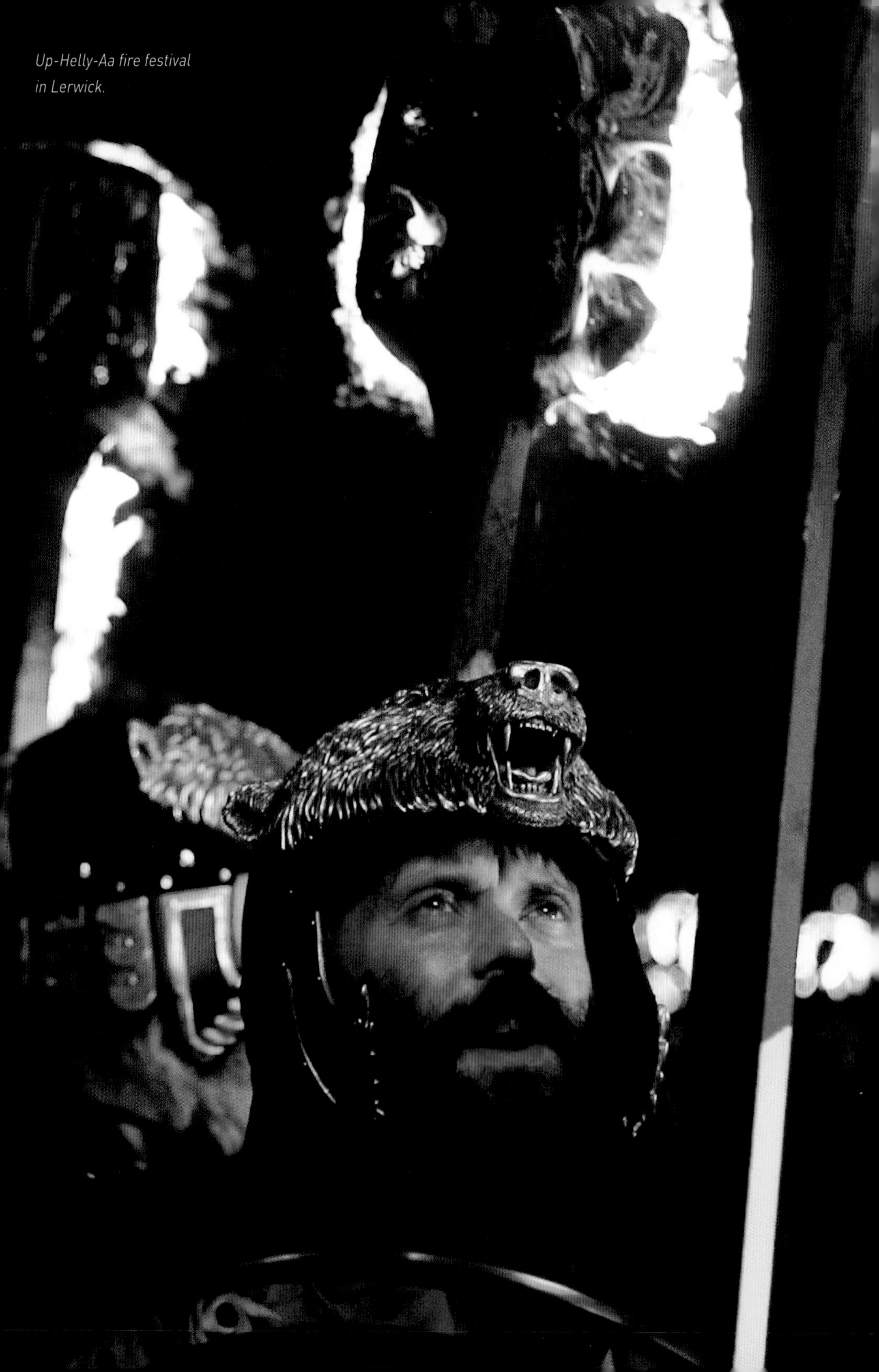

Up-Helly-Aa fire festival in Lerwick.

SHETLAND

Remote and mysterious, the Shetland Islands are a geologist's and birdwatcher's paradise, withstanding the pounding of the sea and – more recently – the invasion of oil companies.

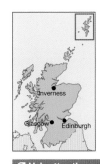

Main attractions
Jarlshof
Lerwick
Yell
Unst
Foula
Fair Isle

Map on page 298

The writer Jan Morris called them 'inset islands'. In those two words she succinctly defined the mystery of the **Shetland Islands**, whose remoteness (200 miles/320km to the north of Aberdeen) means that, in maps of Britain, they are usually relegated to a box in the corner of a page.

The 15 inhabited islands – 85 or so more are uninhabited – are dotted over 70 miles (112km) of swelling seas and scarcely seem part of Britain at all. The tiny population of 23,200 doesn't regard itself as British, or even as Scottish, but as Norse: one of the nearest mainland towns is Bergen in Norway, Norwegian is taught in the schools and the heroes of myths have names like Harald Hardrada.

SHETLAND ENVIRONMENT

Spring comes late, with plant growth speeding up only in June. Rainfall is heavy, mists are frequent and gales keep the islands virtually treeless. However, it's never very cold, even in mid-winter, thanks to the North Atlantic Drift; and in midsummer (the 'Simmer Dim') it never quite gets dark.

The late January festival of Up-Helly-Aa is loosely based on a pagan fire festival intended to herald the impending return of the sun. It is an authentic fiesta primarily for islanders,

who are exceptionally hospitable and talkative. When a Shetlander says, 'You'll have a dram,' it's an instruction, not an enquiry.

Two check-in counters confront passengers at **Sumburgh Airport** on the main island, **Mainland**. North Sea oil generates the traffic, and at one time threatened to overwhelm the islands. But the oil companies, pushed by a determined local council, made conspicuous efforts to lessen the impact on the environment and, although a large

View from Levenwick on the Mainland.

proportion of Britain's oil flows through the 1,000-acre (400-hectare) **Sullom Voe** terminal on a strip of land at the northern end of Mainland, they seem to have succeeded beyond most islanders' expectations. Since the 16 crude oil tanks were painted mistletoe-green, 124 species of birds have been logged within the terminal boundary, and outside the main gates a traffic sign gives priority to otters.

A concentrated anthropological history of the islands is located at **Jarlshof** ❶, a jumble of buildings near the airport. Settlers from the Stone, Bronze and Iron ages built dwellings here, each on the ruins of its predecessor. The Vikings built on top of that, and medieval farmsteads later buried the Viking traces. At the end of the 19th century the site was just a grassy mound, topped with a medieval ruin. Then a wild storm laid bare massive stones in a bank above the beach, and archaeologists moved in. Hearths were found where peat fires burned 3,000 years ago. Today old wheelhouses (so called because of their radial walls) have been revealed, and an **exhibition area** (tel: 01950-460 112; daily Apr–Sept 9.30am–5.30pm, Oct–Mar 9.30am–dusk) fleshes out Jarlshof's history.

En route to the capital, Lerwick, 27 miles (43km) to the north, the offshore island of **Mousa** is home to sheep and ponies, and also to a spectacularly well-preserved broch, a drystone tower more than 40ft (13 metres) high.

LERWICK – SHETLAND'S CAPITAL

Lerwick ❷ looks no more planned than Jarlshof. The old town has charm, with intimate stone-paved alleys leading off the main street of granite houses and dignified shops (no chain stores here). The windows of the baronial-looking **town hall** were presented by Norway, Holland and Germany as thanks for Shetland's kindness to seamen.

The sea and rural landscapes dominate the **Shetland Museum and Archives** (tel: 01595-695 057; www.shetland-museum.org.uk; May–Sept Mon–Sat

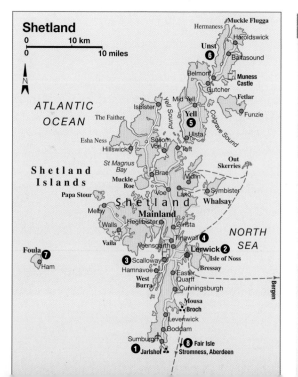

10am–5pm, Sun noon–5pm; Oct–Apr Tues–Sat 10am–4pm), sited above the library in Hillhead. Its theme is the history of life in Shetland from prehistory to the present. It has a collection of 5,000-year-old beads, pots and pumice stones found when excavating Sumburgh airport.

Scalloway ❸, the old fishing port 6 miles (10km) away, was once Shetland's capital. It features the charity-owned and volunteer-run **Scalloway Museum** (tel: 01595 880 734; www.scallowaymuseum.org; Mon–Sat 11am–4pm, Sun 2–4pm), with exhibits chosen by the local community to represent the area's history, there are also displays on the once-important whaling industry. Next door are the gaunt ruins of an early 17th-century castle built for Earl Patrick Stewart, a nephew of Mary, Queen of Scots (tel: 01856-841 815; hours as above; free; key available from the museum).

Deep voes (inlets) poke into the Shetland Islands like long fingers so that no part of the watery landscape is more than 3 miles (5km) from the sea. Arguably, Shetlanders were always more sailors than landlubbers, but clearly 'matters of state' were held on dry land. It is said that a Norse parliament once stood by the loch of **Tingwall** ❹.

REMOTE PLACES

Small ferries connect a handful of smaller islands to Mainland. **Yell** ❺, a peaty place, has the **Old Haa Visitor Centre** (tel: 01957-702 431; www.oldhaa.com; Apr–Sept Mon–Thu, Sat 10am–4pm, Sun 2–5pm; free) which includes a display of the story of the wrecking of the German sail ship, the *Bohus*, in 1924, and a craft centre selling genuine rather than generic Shetland garments.

Unst ❻, the UK's most northerly island, has an important nature reserve at **Hermaness** with a visitor centre (tel: 01595-693 345; Apr–mid-Sept daily 9am–6pm; free). Puffins breed on the cliffs and rare red-throated divers nest on the moor. From the cliffs at Hermaness gaze out on rocky **Muckle Flugga**, the last land before the Arctic Circle. **Fetlar's** name means 'fat island', a reference to its fertile soil.

Whalsay is prosperous, thanks to its notably energetic fishermen. The **Out Skerries**, a scattered archipelago, has a thriving fishing fleet. The peacefulness and abundant wild flowers of **Papa Stour**, a mile of turbulent sea west of Mainland, once attracted a transient hippy colony.

Foula ❼, 14 miles (22km) to the west of Scalloway, must be Britain's remotest inhabited island and, most winters, is cut off for several weeks by awesome seas. The spectacular 1,200ft (370-metre) cliffs are home to storm petrels, great skuas and a host of other sea birds. **Fair Isle** ❽, 20 miles (32km) to the southwest, is the home of Fair Isle sweaters, whose distinctive geometric patterns can be dated back 2,000 years to Balkan nomads.

Black guillemots prefer to breed on small rocky islands rather than in colonies on sea cliffs.

Remote and windswept Esha Ness.

SCOTLAND

TRAVEL TIPS

TRANSPORT

By air

There are excellent services from London (Heathrow, London City, Gatwick, Luton and Stansted airports) and several English regional airports to Edinburgh, Glasgow, Aberdeen and Inverness. You will get the cheapest fare by booking well in advance.

Flying time from London to Edinburgh or Glasgow is about 70 minutes, and under two hours from London to Aberdeen or Inverness.

EasyJet has very low-price, no-frills flights into Scotland, with routes from London (Gatwick, Luton and Stansted) to Edinburgh and Glasgow, and to Inverness and Aberdeen (from Gatwick and Luton). **Ryanair** flies from Dublin to Edinburgh and Glasgow. **Aer Lingus** flies from Dublin to Glasgow, Edinburgh and Aberdeen. **British Airways** has domestic routes from London (City, Gatwick and Heathrow) to Glasgow and Edinburgh and from London Heathrow to Aberdeen.

WizzAir operates flights from Central and Eastern Europe to Aberdeen and Glasgow.

Glasgow International Airport is Scotland's busiest airport with more than 40 airlines serving 100 worldwide destinations. Glasgow receives non-stop flights from New York (**United Airlines, Delta Airlines**), Orlando (**Virgin Atlantic**), Halifax (**Westjet**) and Toronto (**Air Transat, Westjet**). It also receives non-stop flights from Amsterdam (**KLM, easyJet**), Berlin (**easyJet, Ryanair**), Geneva (**Jet2.com, easyJet**), Dubai (**Emirates**), Malaga (**easyJet, Alba Star, British Airways, Ryanair, Jet2. com, Thomson**), Paris (**Air France**) and Reykjavik (**Icelandair**).

Direct Ryanair flights from Riga, Dublin, Brussels, Warsaw, Wroclaw, Berlin, Alicante, Malaga and Lisbon all land at Glasgow. Edinburgh airport handles non-stop flights from destinations including New York (**United Airlines, American Airlines, Delta, Flybe**), Dublin (**Aer Lingus** and **Ryanair**), Faro (**Jet2.com, Ryanair, Atlantic Airlines**), Shannon (**Aer Lingus**), Milan (**easyJet**), Amsterdam (**easyJet, KLM**), Barcelona (**Ryanair Norwegian, Vueling**), Brussels (**Ryanair, Brussels Airlines**), Chambery (**Jet2.com**), Copenhagen (**Norwegian, Ryanair, Scandinavian Airlines, easyJet**),Frankfurt (**Lufthansa**), Geneva (**easyJet, Jet2. com**), Oslo (**Norwegian, Ryanair, Scandinavian Airlines**), Paris (**Air France, easyJet, Vueling**), Alicante (**easyJet, Ryanair, Jet2.com, Vueling**), Madrid (**easyJet, Iberia**) and Zurich (**edelweiss**).

Direct flights into Aberdeen include from Amsterdam (**KLM**), Bergen (**Wideroe**), Copenhagen (**SAS**), Dublin (**Aer Lingus**) and Stavanger (**SAS, Wideroe**). Direct flights into Inverness include from Belfast (**Flybe**), Bristol (**bmi regional**) and Amsterdam (**KLM**).

By rail

There are frequent InterCity services to Scotland from many mainline stations in England. On most trains the journey time from London (Euston or King's Cross) to Edinburgh is just over four hours and to Glasgow about five and a half hours.

Sleeper services run between London (Euston) and Edinburgh, Glasgow, Aberdeen, Inverness and Fort William. Try to avoid travel on Sundays when services are often curtailed, and engineering works mean that journeys can take much longer. A limited number of cheap fares, known as Advance Ticket fares, are available for those booking at least seven days in advance. For current fares and timetables, call National Rail Enquiries on 08457-484 950; www.nationalrail.co.uk.

By road

There are good motorway connections from England and Wales. The M1/M6/

⊘ Airports

Edinburgh Airport (tel: 0844 448 8833; www.edinburghairport.com) is 8 miles (13km) west of the city centre with good road access and a useful Airlink bus service to the heart of town. A taxi will take approximately 20 minutes.

Glasgow International Airport (tel: 0844-481 5555; www.glasgowairport. com) is 8 miles (13km) west of the city centre alongside the M8 motorway at Junction 28. The Airport Express bus runs between the airport and Buchanan Street bus station and Queen Street Railway Station, in the city centre, and take about 25 minutes.

Glasgow Prestwick Airport

(tel: 0871-223 0700; www. glasgowprestwick.com) is 30 miles (48km) south of the city centre and easily reached by road, an express bus link to Buchanan Street or a 45-minute rail link to Central Station.

Aberdeen Airport (tel: 0844-481 6666; www.aberdeenairport.com) is 7 miles (11km) west of the city centre with excellent road access (A96). A coach service runs between the airport and city centre.

Inverness Airport (tel: 01667 464 000; www.invernessairport.co.uk) is about 10 miles (16km) east of the town. A bus link runs into the city centre.

A74 and M74 is the quickest route, though heavily congested at the southern end. The A1(M), a more easterly approach, is longer but may be a better bet if you plan to make one or two stopovers. Edinburgh and Glasgow are about 400 miles (650km) from London.

Bus services

National Express (tel: 0871-818 181; www.nationalexpress.com) and Stagecoach (www.stagecoachbus.com, visit website for local telephone number) operate daytime and overnight coaches from England to Scotland. The journey takes about nine hours from London to Edinburgh or to Glasgow. Coach travel may not be as comfortable or as fast as the trains, but it is a good deal cheaper, unless you can get an Advance Ticket rail fare.

By sea

Stena Line (0844-770 7070; www.stenaline.co.uk) operates ferry crossings from Cairnryan on the west coast to Belfast in Northern Ireland, while P&O Ferries (0800-130 0030; www.poferries.com) operate ferries from Cairnryan to Larne, north of Belfast. There are no ferry routes from Scotland to Europe – the closest crossing is from Newcastle to Amsterdam with DFDS ferries (www.dfdsseaways.co.uk). Newcastle is two hours by road or rail from Edinburgh.

GETTING AROUND

By air

There is a network of regular air services, which is especially valuable if going to the islands. Barra, Benbecula, Campbeltown, Islay, Kirkwall (Orkney), Stornoway (Lewis), Sumburgh (Shetland) and Tiree are all serviced by Glasgow International Airport. Some of these destinations can also be reached from Inverness, Aberdeen and Edinburgh airports. Flying there saves a lot of time and can also give a different perspective on the countryside. The major carrier is Loganair (0344-800 2855; www.loganair.co.uk).

By rail

ScotRail offers a wide variety of tickets that permit unlimited travel

Cutty Sark seaplane on Loch Lomond.

throughout Scotland. The Spirit of Scotland Travelpass permits unlimited travel on four out of eight or eight out of 15 consecutive days. Two other rover passes are available: a Central Scotland Rover ticket offers three days' unlimited travel out of seven, and the Highland Rover is valid for four out of eight consecutive days.

Rail and Sail Travelpasses permit unlimited travel for eight or 15 consecutive days on ScotRail and most of the Caledonian MacBrayne west coast ferries. Together with discounts on the P&O ferries and many buses and postbuses, these are truly comprehensive Scottish travel tickets. Details can be obtained from ScotRail, tel: 0344 811 0141; www.scotrail.co.uk.

A few routes to try are:
Glasgow to Fort William and Mallaig (164 miles/265km). Train enthusiasts head for the West Highland line, which operates regular trains from Fort William to the fishing port of Mallaig, from which a ferry departs for Skye. From Glasgow, the route passes alongside Loch Lomond, across the wild Rannoch Moor and over the majestic Glenfinnan Viaduct.
Glasgow to Oban (101 miles/163km). The train branches off the Fort William route at Crianlarich and heads past ruined Kilchurn Castle and the fjord-like scenery of the Pass of Brander to Oban, 'gateway to the Inner Hebrides'.
Perth to Inverness (118 miles/190km). The route, through forested glens and across the roof of Scotland, takes in Pitlochry, Blair Atholl and Aviemore. As well as being a ski centre, Aviemore is the departure point for steam trains on the 5-mile (8km) Strathspey Railway line.

Inverness to Kyle of Lochalsh (82 miles/132km). This twisting line with breathtaking scenery takes in lochs, glens and mountains from the North Sea to the Atlantic Ocean, and is especially dramatic towards Kyle of Lochalsh, from where the bridge leads over the water to Skye.
Inverness to Wick or Thurso (161 miles/260km). Passes by castles, across moorland and on to Britain's most northerly rail terminals.

Steam trains

Railway preservation societies are alive and thriving in Scotland. Over half a dozen other lines operate steam trains of one sort or another.

The **Northern Belle**, a luxury touring train, offers day excursions and short breaks in Scotland. These trips include all meals served at seats, accommodation in hotels and off-train visits; tel: 01270 899 666; www.northernbelle.co.uk/.

The **Caledonian Railway**, Brechin, Angus, runs steam-train rides at weekends from June to mid-September, from Brechin to Bridge of Don. Enquire at Brechin Station, 2 Park Road, Brechin, Angus DD9 7AF; tel: 01356-622 922; www.caledonianrailway.com.

The **Bo'ness & Kinneil Railway**, West Lothian, runs steam-hauled trains on Tuesdays and weekends between mid-March and October (daily in August), on a 3-mile (5km) branch line to Birkhill for a visit to the Avon Gorge and the Fireclay Mine. Historic Scottish locomotives, rolling stock and railway buildings. Contact Bo'ness Station, Union Street, Bo'ness EH51 9AQ; tel: 01506-822 298; www.srps.org.uk.

Strathspey Railway runs March to October and at Christmas for

⊘ Caledonian MacBrayne ferries

An essential item for any visitor who intends to explore the island-studded west coast – the Hebrides and the islands of the Clyde – is the Caledonian MacBrayne timetable, which can be obtained at www.calmac.co.uk. Reservations: 0800-066 5000

Faced with a myriad of island destinations, the uninitiated may find CalMac's timetable daunting, though locals whip through it with ease. Summer booking is vital to avoid the nerve-racking, time-consuming 'standby' queue.

Caledonian MacBrayne,

a fusion of two companies, grew out of the 19th-century passenger steamers and now has a near monopoly on west-coast routes. Calling in to more than 30 ports throughout the west coast, its 31 vessels service 24 routes, from the Isle of Arran in the south to Lewis in the Outer Hebrides.

The company sells various island-hopping ("Hopscotch") tickets and – best value for visitors with cars, bicycles and motor homes – and are valid for 31 days from the date of first travel.

5 miles (8km) from Aviemore (Speyside) through Boat of Garten to Grantown-on-Spey, providing good views of the Cairngorm Mountains. Enquiries to Aviemore Station, Dalfaber Road, Aviemore, Inverness-shire PH22 1PY; tel: 01479-810 725; www.strathspeyrailway.co.uk.

At the top end of the market is the **Royal Scotsman**, one of the world's most exclusive trains. This mobile hotel for just 32 passengers combines spectacular scenery with superb food and wine and impeccable service. A variety of tours are available, from two nights and up to seven nights; highlights include Glamis Castle and the islands of Bute and Skye. There's also a Grand Tour of Great Britain, a seven-night trip that takes in the Scottish Highlands as well as travelling as far south as Bath in England. Tours operate between April and October, departing from and returning to Edinburgh. Enquiries to Belmond, Shackleton House, 4 Battle Bridge Lane, London, SE1 2HP; tel: 0845 077 2222; www.belmond.com.

The **Jacobite Steam Train** chugs its way from Fort William to the fishing port of Mallaig; its picturesque route, including crossing the Glenfinnan Viaduct, appears in the Harry Potter films based on the novels of the celebrated Scottish writer, J.K. Rowling.

The train runs daily from the end of April to September, and Monday to Friday in October. Contact the West Coast Railway Company on tel: 0844-850 4685; www.westcoastrailways.co.uk.

Ferries

Scottish ferries are great. On long routes, like the five-hour

Oban-to-Barra ferry, there are car decks, cabins, comfortable chairs, a restaurant and self-service cafeteria. On others, such as the seven-hour round trip to the tiny islands of Eigg, Muck, Rum and Canna, ferries are basic with wooden seats and minimal refreshments. These working boats, carrying goods and mail as well as passengers, are mainly used by islanders, with some bird-watchers and occasional curious visitors. Take note that unless you specify beforehand, disembarking for sightseeing is not allowed.

There are plenty of small private businesses on the west coast providing cruises from Arisaig on the mainland to Skye and Mull as well as to Eigg, Muck, Rum and Canna. Day trips to the National Trust for Scotland's island of Staffa with Fingal's Cave, to the bird island of Lunga and the uninhabited Treshnish Islands start from Ulva Ferry, Dervaig and Fionnphort, all of which are on Mull, while Staffa can also be reached from Iona. There

Ferries are the ideal way to island-hop.

is a 10-minute shuttle service from Fionnphort on the southwest tip of Mull to Iona. These trips allow some time ashore, and there is no difficulty in finding out about such services when you arrive. Tourist information centres and many hotels have brochures.

If voyaging to the Outer Hebrides feels like sailing to the edge of the world, taking a ferry to the ancient isles of Orkney and Shetland (the Northern Isles) is equally exhilarating. Two major ferry companies ply these routes, and in summer it's essential to book ahead.

Orkney

Northlink Ferries Ltd run roll-on/roll-off car ferry services from Aberdeen (eight hours) or Scrabster (one hour 45 minutes) on the mainland to Stromness and Kirkwall in Orkney, and also services from Lerwick in Shetland (www.northlinkferries.co.uk).

A passenger ferry runs from May to September from John o'Groats to Burwick on South Ronaldsay (tel: 01955-611 353; www.jogferry.co.uk). The crossing takes around 40 minutes. Connecting buses can be boarded on Orkney, and there are cars for hire.

Once on Orkney, a dozen or so smaller islands can be visited by local ferries. The Kirkwall tourist office has more details.

Shetland

Northlink Ferries has six sailings weekly taking 12 hours 30 minutes between Aberdeen and Lerwick, Shetland's main port, on modern roll-on/roll-off vessels with cabins, shops, restaurants and cafeterias. Northlink Ferries Ltd: routes, timetables and fares may be obtained from Ferry Terminal, Stromness,

Take a leisurely cruise on the Waverley paddle-steamer.

Orkney KW16 3BH; tel: 0845-600 0449; www.northlinkferries.co.uk.

Once again, local ferries ply between the small islands.

Pleasure cruises

On Loch Katrine, which has supplied Glasgow with water since 1859, the **SS Sir Walter Scott**, Scotland's only screw steamer in regular passenger service, makes four daily return-trip voyages between the Trossachs and Stronachlachar piers from the end of March until early January. The two-hour morning trip permits a 10-minute landing at Stronachlachar, while the three one-hour afternoon trips are non-landing. Enquiries to Trossachs Pier Complex, Loch Katrine, Callander FK17 8HZ; tel: 01877-376 315; www.lochkatrine.com.

Clyde Cruises operates several different river cruises out of Glasgow including day and evening cruises along the Clyde in and around the city and a two-and-a-half-hour sightseeing cruise into the countryside. They also run the city RiverLink river bus, a novel way of seeing some of Glasgow's attractions, which departs from several points in the city centre. For further information contact Clyde Marine Cruises, Victoria Harbour, Greenock; tel: 01475-721 281; www.clydecruises.com.

Similar cruises from Wemyss Bay, with longer time ashore, can be enjoyed from the end of April to the end of September on **Caledonian MacBrayne** craft (see page 304).

Waverley, the world's last sea-going paddle steamer, sails on the Clyde (day trips) from Glasgow Science Centre, 50 Pacific Quay, Glasgow, from May until August. Tel: 0141-243 2224; www.waverleyexcursions.co.uk.

From April to October the **Maid of the Forth** sails from South Queensferry, just outside Edinburgh, to Inchcolm Island, which has a ruined medieval abbey; seals are often spotted during the voyage. Trips last about three hours with one and a half hours spent ashore. Contact Maid of the Forth, Hawes Pier, South Queensferry; tel: 0131-331 5000; www.maidoftheforth.co.uk.

From May to mid-September the 130-passenger **MV Sheerwater** sails each morning from Arisaig for a full day to the small islands (Rum, Eigg, Muck) of the Inner Hebrides. Several hours are spent ashore. Contact Arisaig Harbour, Inverness-shire PH39 4NH; tel: 01687-450 224; www.arisaig.co.uk.

From April to October the **MV Western Isles** makes half- and full-day cruises from Mallaig past dramatic scenery to surrounding lochs, or to the islands of Rum and Canna, or to Skye, with landings. Contact Western Isles Cruises, Mallaig; tel: 01687 462 233; www.westernislescruises.co.uk.

From April to September daily sailings (weather permitting) are made from Anstruther to the Isle of May aboard the **May Princess**. The trip lasts four to five hours, with two to three hours ashore to explore the island, whose cliffs, at least until July, are covered with breeding kittiwakes, razorbills, guillemots and shags. Scotland's oldest lighthouse and the ruins of a 12th-century chapel can also be visited. Contact Anstruther Pleasure Trips, 21 St Adrians Place, Anstruther, Fife KY10 3DX; tel: 07957-585 200; www.isleofmayferry.com.

Several companies run two- to four-hour cruises from Ullapool to the Summer Isles. Some are nature

⊘ The Hebridean Princess

The **Hebridean Princess**, more a stately country-house hotel on water than the usual run-of-the-mill luxury liner and accommodating only 49 passengers in elegant cabins, makes a series of cruises from Oban from March until early November. The region covered is the northwest coast of Scotland, Inner and Outer Hebrides, the Orkney and Shetland Islands and even St Kilda. The route varies from cruise to cruise, with voyages lasting four to seven nights, and the printed schedule may be altered to avoid bad weather. Cars can roll-on and roll-off the ship, thus enabling travellers to explore independently at the various ports of call.

Bookings can be made through Hebridean International Cruises, Kintail House, Carleton New Road, Skipton, North Yorkshire BD23 3AN; tel: 01756-704 704; www.hebridean.co.uk.

cruises, some are sunset cruises and some permit landing on the islands. Try Shearwater Cruises; tel: 01854-612 472; www.summerqueen.co.uk.

Summer Isles Cruises also depart from Achiltibuie aboard the **Isabella** from May to September. These last two-and-a-half hours and permit landing on the islands. Contact Ian Mcleod; tel: 01854-622 200; www.summer-isles.com.

Public transport

By bus

Major towns have their own bus services. For timetable information on all public transport services in Scotland contact **Traveline**, tel: 0871-200 2233; www.travelinescotland.com. In addition, there are bus services serving rural communities and linking the various towns. The national bus network is run by **Scottish Citylink**, tel: 0871 266 3333; www.citylink.co.uk. The visitor who intends to travel a lot on the buses should investigate the various tickets that allow unlimited use of buses for specific periods. Contact Scottish Citylink or the tourist board for more details.

⊘ Bikers welcome

Every summer, scores of motorcyclists don their leathers to tour Scotland's winding roads on two wheels. Glencoe, the Isle of Skye and the remote Applecross Peninsula are among the more popular routes. B&Bs and many pubs have positively responded to growing numbers of motorcyclists by displaying 'Bikers Welcome' signs on their premises.

Rentamotorcycle.co.uk offer guided and unguided tours of the Highlands and islands on two wheels, as well as top of the range bikes for hire. For more information, tel: 0131-603 4466; www.rentamotorcycle.co.uk.

By taxi

The major cities have plentiful taxi stands. Outside the cities, you will probably need to phone for a taxi.

Private transport

Scotland has an excellent network of roads that, away from the central belt, are usually not congested. Driving on the left is the rule and passengers must wear seat belts. In urban areas, the speed limit is 30 or 40mph (48 or 64kmh), the limit on country roads is 60mph (97kmh), and on motorways and dual carriageways 70mph (113kmh).

In some parts of the Highlands and on many of the islands, roads are single track with passing places. The behaviour of drivers on these roads tends to show that good old-fashioned courtesy is not dead. On these narrow roads, please use the 'passing places' to let oncoming vehicles pass, or to let others behind you overtake.

Traffic Scotland (www.trafficscotland.org) provides details of road conditions throughout the day, with details of particular problems, accidents or emergencies. If you prefer, the government-run body also hosts a radio station and a mobile App which provide the same information.

Even today you can travel many miles in the Highlands and on the islands without seeing a petrol station, so if you see one, fill up. If you are planning to drive on a Sunday in the Outer Hebrides, fill up your tank on the Saturday. This is because, in some places, strict Sunday observance means that filling stations will be closed.

Car rentals

Self-drive rental costs £30–70 a day, depending on the type of car and the duration of the rental. Watch out for hidden costs when booking, especially online. The rates are reduced in the October to April off-season. For more detailed information, apply directly to the car rental companies. All the major car hire companies (such as Alamo, Avis, Budget, Europcar, Hertz and National) are represented throughout Scotland and at the airports. Arnold Clark (tel: 0141 237 3484; www.arnoldclark.com) is Scotland's major car rental company.

Edinburgh
W.L. Sleigh Ltd (chauffeur-driven)
Turnhouse Road
Tel: 0131-339 9607
www.sleigh.co.uk

Glasgow
Little's Chauffeur Drive
1282 Paisley Road West
Tel: 0141-883 2111
www.littles.co.uk

The West Coast

Fort William
Easydrive
Lochybridge
Tel: 01397-701 616
www.easydrivescotland.co.uk
Slipway Autos
Annat Point
Corpach, Fort William
Tel: 01397-772 404
www.slipwayautos.co.uk

Oban
Flit
Glencruitten Road
Tel: 01631-566 553
www.flitselfdrive.co.uk

Inner Hebrides

Skye
Ewen MacRae
West End Garage, Portree
Tel: 01478-612 554

Outer Hebrides

Benbecula
Ask Car Hire
Linicleat
Tel: 01870-602 818
www.askcarhire.com

Lewis
Car Hire Hebrides
Ferry Terminal, Shell St, Stornoway
Tel: 01851-706 500
www.carhire-hebrides.co.uk

South Uist
Laing Motors
Lochboisdale
Tel: 01878-700 267
www.laingmotors.co.uk
Stornoway Car Hire (Airport)
Inaclete Road
Tel: 01851-702 658
www.stornowaycarhire.co.uk

Orkney

Kirkwall
W.R. Tullock & Sons Ltd
Castle Garage, Castle Street
Tel: 01856-876 262
www.wrtullock.com

Shetland

Lerwick
Bolts Car Hire
26 North Road
Tel: 01595-693 636
www.boltscarhire.co.uk

The empty road from Kinbrace to Altnaharra in the Highlands.

A

Accommodation

A wide range of accommodation is available in Scotland, from hotels of international standard and simple Bed & Breakfast (B&B) accommodation to campsites, bunkhouses and bothies Prices vary from under £25 per person a night for Bed & Breakfast to well over £200 at the most luxurious hotels.

VisitScotland (www.visitscotland. com) operates a system of grading accommodation concentrating on assessment of quality (although symbols still indicate services available). Star gradings range from one star (fair and acceptable) to five stars (exceptional/world-class), and these are applied to all types of accommodation, including hotels, Bed & Breakfasts and self-catering.

If you are planning a caravan or camping holiday, look out for the Thistle logo. The 'Thistle Award' is bestowed by the industry and VisitScotland to parks that meet standards of excellence in environment, facilities and caravans.

Staying in Bed & Breakfast accommodation is not only economical, it is also a flexible and potentially interesting way to see the country. Local tourist offices operate a convenient booking service (for which there is usually a small charge) and, except at the height of the tourist season in July and August, it is usually not necessary to reserve in advance. Bed & Breakfasts in VisitScotland's scheme will, at a minimum, be clean and comfortable. With luck you may find the proprietor friendly and a mine of local information on local routes and things to see and do. Most of the better Bed & Breakfast establishments serve dinner on request, which is usually excellent and modestly priced.

Particularly good value are Campus Hotels, the name given to Bed & Breakfasts and self-catering facilities offered by the Scottish universities in Aberdeen, St Andrews, Dundee, Edinburgh, Glasgow and Stirling, which are available during vacations. In addition, they offer the use of university facilities such as tennis courts and swimming pools. There is also a vast choice of self-catering accommodation in chalets, flats, cottages and castles.

Information on all types of accommodation is available from VisitScotland and local tourist information centres (see page 315), or visit their website, www.visitscotland. com, where you can find comprehensive listings, sorted by area, and refine your search to your specific requirements. Note that, for the hotel chains, room rates vary widely according to demand, and weekend rates in city business hotels are often much lower than weekdays. It's always worth enquiring about special offers: many hotels offer good-value short breaks outside the main holiday periods.

On occasions, the distinction between Bed & Breakfast establishments, guesthouses and private hotels becomes blurred, especially when the former have en suite facilities and serve dinner.

Admission fees

Many museums and galleries in Scotland are free to enter, including the Kelvingrove Museum and Art Gallery in Glasgow and the National Museums in Edinburgh. The National Trust for Scotland (NTS) and Historic Environment Scotland (HES; see page 311) do charge admission to many of their properties, though both offer substantial admission discounts to its members, so joining may be a worthwhile investment if you're planning to visit a number of places. The Historic Scotland Explorer Pass is also a cost-saving option. Some places, like Edinburgh Castle, can cost the best part of £20, so it's definitely worth asking about child and family discounts.

B

Budgeting for your trip

Despite Scotland's relatively small size, its rugged geography, narrow roads in remoter regions, and patchy public transport away from the central belt and major cities mean journeys by private or public transport can take longer than expected. For example, the 260-mile (420km) drive from Edinburgh to Thurso on the north coast takes almost as long as the 400-mile (650km) drive from Edinburgh to London. Fuel costs are similar to elsewhere in the UK – currently around £1.20 per litre, but expect to pay considerably more in remote regions and on islands. Bus travel is generally up to 50 percent cheaper than travelling by train on the same route, and for many journeys the bus is the only public transport option. There are accommodation and food options for every budget, from the almost five-figure cost of a five-star dining experience and a suite at the Gleneagles Hotel to camping free on beaches, moors and glens throughout the country.

However, as a rule of thumb, budget at least £40 per day for travel and food, and, depending on how you like to travel, £20–£200 per night for accommodation.

C

Children's activities

Scotland is a child-friendly nation, but attitudes definitely vary from place to place. For example, in cities and larger towns, some of the more established bistros and cafés generally welcome kids and are equipped with high chairs. However, many a parent has found their evening plans disrupted when their tiny offspring are deemed unwelcome at restaurants. In truth, access sometimes depends as much on the attitude of the owner of the establishment as the law, though Scottish pubs must obtain a special licence to permit under-16s into their bar. Invariably, parents will find the remoter parts of the Highlands and islands much more accommodating, though it's worthwhile considering self-catering as a cast-iron option for eating and accommodation.

That said, there are hundreds of child-friendly attractions across the country, from the child-oriented interpretive walks and interactive displays to be found at the Forestry and Land Scotland (formerly the Forestry Commission) centres (www.forestryandland.gov.scot) to the renowned Landmark Forest Adventure Park in Carrbridge (Speyside) that comes complete with tree-top and red-squirrel trail (tel: 0800-731 3446; www.landmarkpark.co.uk). Parents will find many tourist attractions, restaurants, hotels and bus/train routes offer substantially reduced rates for children.

Climate

No matter what you say about Scottish weather, you are bound to be wrong. There are those who rave about the cloudless two weeks they spent on Skye; others have made several visits and have yet to see the Cuillin Hills.

But it can be said that the west is generally wetter and warmer than the east. Summers are cool, with July temperatures averaging 13–15°C (55–59°F), though sometimes peaking above 20°C (68°F) in the afternoon. Winters are cold, with January temperatures averaging 3–5°C (37–41°F), frost at night, and the higher summits often remaining snow-covered from November until May.

Rainfall is heavy, except on the east coast, and exceeds 100ins (254cm) in the Western Highlands. January,

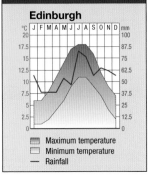

CLIMATE CHART

Edinburgh

- Maximum temperature
- Minimum temperature
- Rainfall

April, May and June are usually drier than July, August and September, but take waterproof clothing, footwear and headgear wherever you go.

What to wear

Given the climate, it follows that you should never be without a raincoat or a warm sweater. Neither should you be without light clothes in summer. For those attracted to the excellent opportunities for hill walking and rock climbing, it is essential to come properly prepared. In the mountains, the weather can change very quickly.

Each year people suffer serious and needless harm through setting out without adequate clothing and equipment; the Highlands are no place to go on a serious hill walk in a T-shirt and light trainers.

Crime and safety

Scotland is no more dangerous than any other part of the UK, and visitors are rarely affected. In truth, pickpockets and credit card fraud are two of the greatest risks a visitor must guard against. Tourists should avoid carrying large sums of cash on their person and keep a close eye on handbags or rucksacks.

Scotland's city-centre streets are generally safe to walk around in the evening, though do exercise common sense and avoid dimly lit streets. If eating or partying late into the night, it's advisable to call a taxi to get back to your hotel.

Should you be concerned for your safety, the emergency services (police, ambulance and fire) can be reached on tel: 999. Note that this is an emergency number only; in less urgent cases, for example to report a theft, dial 101.

Note, too, that airport terminals carry out stringent security checks on passengers. Ensure you allow yourself plenty of time to get through security for your flight. This includes domestic short-hop flights to the Highlands and islands.

D

Disabled travellers

All new buildings in Scotland must have appropriate facilities for disabled travellers, including wheelchair access. **Scotrail** (tel: 0800-912 2901 assisted travel helpline; www.scotrail.co.uk/plan-your-journey/accessible-travel) has ramps at station platforms for wheelchair-users to access trains, and such passengers also receive discounts on train travel.

Although buses don't offer such facilities, **Caledonian MacBrayne** (tel: 0800 066 5000 assisted travel helpline; www.calmac.co.uk) shore staff will assist wheelchair-users in negotiating the gangway on their ferries. There are also wheelchairs on many vessels.

Story wall at the Scottish Storytelling Centre, Edinburgh.

Disabled toilet facilities are now more commonplace in restaurants and cafés. However it remains difficult for some disabled visitors to access a number of the historic sites, though various (lower) parts of both Stirling and Edinburgh castles are accessible to wheelchair users.

While there remains much work to be done, many B&Bs and self-catering establishments, and most hotels, across the country provide some facilities for disabled travellers, including rooms with wheelchair-accessible bathrooms. **Association of Scotland's Self Caterers** (tel: 07379 257749; www.assc.co.uk) has a list of accessible self-catering properties, or check out the VisitScotland website (www.visitscotland.com) for information.

Further advice on travel and services that are available for disabled visitors can be acquired from Capability Scotland (tel: 0131-337 9876; www.capability-scotland.org.uk).

E

Eating out

Scotland is renowned for its produce from river and sea, from farm and moor. Fish is something of a speciality, with salmon being particularly good: kippers and Arbroath smokies (haddock smoked over wood) are delicious, too. Shellfish are excellent and exported all over the world, while Aberdeen Angus beef and Border lamb are both renowned. Various dishes are distinctly Scottish, such as haggis – which is probably more enjoyable if you don't know what should be in it (the heart, lungs and liver of a sheep, suet, oatmeal and onion).

Over the past decade culinary skills have come to match the quality of the produce, and today it is possible to enjoy superb meals in Scotland served in the most elegant of restaurants as well as in simple small spaces with scarcely more than half a dozen tables. The hours at which restaurants, especially smaller ones away from the main cities, serve meals tend to be less flexible than in many other countries. High tea, served from 5 to 7pm, usually consists of fish and chips or an egg dish followed by lashings of scones and pancakes, all accompanied by gallons of tea.

Breakfast is a hearty affair in Scotland. There is surely no better way to start the day than with a bowl of porridge followed by Loch Fyne kippers and Scottish oatcakes.

On a more mundane level, there is no shortage of fast-food outlets of one sort or another throughout Scotland. For a cheap and enjoyable takeaway meal, you could do a lot worse than try the humble 'chippie' (fish and chip shop). Fish and chips in Scotland is called a 'fish supper'.

Lunch is almost invariably considerably less expensive than dinner, and nearly all restaurants have set menus, which are about half the price of an à la carte dinner.

Taste of Scotland

The *Taste of Scotland* scheme invites eating places to apply for membership. Its original and continuing objective is to promote restaurants and producers that are believed to offer the very best of Scottish cuisine. All members are inspected before being admitted to the scheme; more than 400 restaurants, bistros and cafés are listed on its website where quality, service and in many cases considerable innovation can be guaranteed. Visit www.taste-of-scotland.com.

However, it's not only the above that offers an insight into the best of Scotland's culinary treats. VisitScotland runs a nationwide quality-assurance scheme called 'Taste Our Best', providing visitors with a handy reference for quality eateries. Visitors to Glasgow and Edinburgh can discover the latest gossip on cafés and restaurants in *The List's Eating and Drinking Guide* www.food.list.co.uk), while the wonderful Outer Hebrides have their very own 'Eat Drink Hebrides Trail' (www.visitouterhebrides.co.uk).

Electricity

220 volts is standard. Hotels usually have dual 220/110-volt sockets for razors. If you are visiting from abroad, you will probably need an adaptor to link other small electrical appliances to the three-pin sockets universal in Britain; it is usually easier to find these at home before leaving – or at the airport – than in Scotland.

Embassies and consulates

With the re-establishment of a Scottish Parliament in Edinburgh, many countries have opened consular offices in the capital *(if phoning from outside the area use code: 0131)*.

Canada Honorary Consulate
5 St Margaret's Road, EH9 1AZ
Tel: 07702-359 916
Ireland Consulate General
16 Randolph Crescent, EH3 7TT
Tel: 0131 226 7711
New Zealand Consulate
c/o Blackadders, 5 Rutland Square, EH1 2AX
Tel: 0131 222 8109
South Africa Honorary Consulate
10 Midlothian Drive
Waverley Park
Glasgow G41 3RA
Tel: 0141-649 3831
US Consulate General
3 Regent Terrace, EH7 5BW
Tel: 0131 556 8315

United Kingdom embassies and consulates

Australia
British Consul-General
17th Floor, 90 Collins Street
Melbourne 3000
Tel: 61 (2) 9652 1600
Canada
British High Commission
80 Elgin Street
Ottawa K1P 5K7
Tel: 1 (613) 237 1530
Ireland
British Embassy
29 Merrion Road
Dublin 4
Tel: 353 (1) 205 3700
New Zealand
British High Commission
44 Hill Street
Thorndon
Wellington 6011
Tel: 64 (4) 924 2888
South Africa
British Consulate General
15th Floor, Norton Rose House
8 Riebeeck Street
Foreshore
Cape Town 8000
Tel: 27 (21) 405 2400
US
British Embassy
3100 Massachusetts Avenue
Washington D.C. 20008
Tel: 1-202 588 6500

Emergencies

For emergency services such as police, ambulance, the fire service or lifeboat service dial 999. For non-urgent cases, for example to report a theft, dial 101.

Etiquette

There are no particular etiquette issues in Scotland and general manners, dress and attitudes do not differ a great deal from the rest of the United Kingdom.

Formal queuing is expected, as is respect for others and Scottish people, particularly in rural and remote areas, are extremely friendly and helpful.

Smoking is banned by law in all public places; special designated areas outside pubs are sometimes provided. It is customary to buy a round of drinks when out with a group.

If invited into a Scottish household it is appropriate to take a gift of, for example, good wine or chocolates. Avoid calling a Scottish person English.

F

Festivals and events

January

Burns Night. Haggis, neeps and tatties and an 'address tae the haggis' is accompanied by the skirl of bagpipes as families and dedicated Burns societies settle down across the land, and indeed across the world, to toast the birth of Rabbie Burns, the nation's most famous poet, on 25 January 1759; www.rabbie-burns.com or www.rbwf.org.uk. **Up-Helly-Aa**. On the last Tuesday of January, scores of Shetland Islanders dressed in Viking costume lead an atmospheric torchlit procession through the streets of Lerwick followed by the burning of a Viking longship; www.uphellyaa.org

February

Fort William Mountain Film Festival. From footage of sea kayaking adventures in the Outer Hebrides to climbing in Dumbarton, this action-packed festival attracts scores of outdoor enthusiasts and film buffs alike. Dates vary throughout February each year. See www.mountainfilmfestival.co.uk.

March

Spring into Easter at events organised by Scotland's five winter ski resorts; www.ski-scotland.com.

April

Sports fans can get their kicks at the **Scottish Grand National** at Ayr racecourse; www.ayr-racecourse.co.uk; and the famous **Melrose Sevens** rugby tournament taking place in the Borders; www.melrose7s.com. Both in mid-April.

May

Head for Loch Fyne where, on the last weekend in May, 200 yachts battle for supremacy in the **Scottish Series**, and for nightly festivities in the picturesque fishing port of Tarbert; www.clyde.org. Malt lovers should plan to be in the Highlands on the first weekend of May for the **Spirit of Speyside Whisky Festival**; www.spiritofspeyside.com. Alternatively, head to the Northern Isles for the **Shetland Folk Festival**, which is held on the first weekend of May; www.shetlandfolkfestival.com.

June

St Magnus Festival, Orkney. A spectacular, weeklong celebration of the arts in late June; www.stmagnusfestival.com. **Fort William Mountain Bike World Cup**. Almost 20,000 spectators converge on Lochaber on the first weekend of June to watch the thrills and spills of the world's best in action; www.fortwilliamworldcup.co.uk.

July

Hebridean Celtic Festival, Stornoway in the Outer Hebrides. High class festival of international Celtic music in mid-July; www.hebceltfest.com. **Kelburn Garden Party**, Largs. Intimate boutique festival of alternative and underground music in early July; www.kelburngardenparty.com

August

Piping Live! Glasgow. Dates vary. You'll hear many a skirl of the pipes at this extravaganza; www.pipinglive.co.uk. Equestrian-lovers will enjoy the spectacular Perthshire setting of the **Blair Castle International Horse Trials**; dates vary; www.blairhorsetrials.co.uk.

September

Join members of the Royal Family for bagpipes, caber-tossing and Highland dancing at the renowned **Braemar Highland Gathering**; dates vary, but usually first weekend in September; www.braemargathering.org. Alternatively, try to spot Nessie as you run all 26.2 miles (42km) of the annual **Loch Ness Marathon**; dates vary, but usually first Sunday of the month; www.lochnessmarathon.com.

October

First held in 1892, the **Am Mòd Nàiseanta Rìoghail** (Royal National Mod) is Scotland's main festival of the Gaelic language, arts and culture. This competition-based festival is held annually in October and always at a different Scottish location. Dates vary; www.ancomunn.co.uk.

However, if it's wet 'n' wild action you are after, then head for the Inner Hebridean Isle of Tiree to watch some of the world's best windsurfers defy gravity at the **Tiree Wave Classic**; dates vary; www.tireewaveclassic.co.uk. Of course, there's also the chance to understand why the population of Mull trebles for four days during the acclaimed **Tour of Mull Rally**; dates vary; http://mullrally.org.

November

St Andrew's Day. On 30 November, Scots celebrate their patron saint.

December

Join thousands of festive revellers to welcome in the **New Year** in Glasgow's George Square or Edinburgh's Princes Street. Note: it's strongly advised to purchase tickets in advance. www.hogmanay.net.

G

Gay and lesbian travellers

All of Scotland's cities have a gay and lesbian scene, though arguably it's in Glasgow and Edinburgh where the most nightclubs and bars targeting the gay community are to be found. Edinburgh's Broughton Street and Glasgow's Merchant City are the two main 'pink' areas of the respective cities.

The best sources of information on your travels are to be found in the pages of the weekly entertainment magazine The List (www.list.co.uk) and in the Scotsgay newspaper (www.scotsgay.co.uk).

H

Health and medical care

It is advisable to have medical insurance. Citizens of European

Capturing a jaguar at Edinburgh Zoo.

Union countries are entitled to medical treatment under reciprocal arrangements (EHIC card), and similar agreements exist with some other countries, including Australia and New Zealand. No matter which country you come from, you will receive immediate emergency treatment free at a hospital accident and emergency department. NHS 24 (tel: 111 free helpline) can provide advice on symptoms by phone.

Biting midges, which infest much of the west coast and islands in summer, do not carry disease but can be infuriating. An oil-based repellent such as Autan or Eureka!, can help keep them off, though even more effective is a beekeeper-style 'midge hat' with head net. Ticks, which carry a variety of diseases including Lyme disease, are increasingly prevalent in parts of the northwest.

Heritage organisations

The National Trust for Scotland (NTS) is Scotland's premier conservation body, caring for more than 100 buildings or areas of significant heritage interest. Its properties range from single boulders, such as the Bruce Stone in Galloway, through magnificent houses and castles including Culzean, Crathes and Fyvie, to large areas of outstanding countryside. These last include Glencoe, Mar Lodge in the Cairngorms, Kintail and Goat Fell on Arran. Some properties are available for holiday lets.

Membership allows free admission to all its properties and those owned by the English National Trust. Contact the NTS at: Hermiston Quay, 5 Cultins Road, EH11 4DF, tel: 0131-493 0200 or from outside the UK at: +44 (0)131 458 0303; www.nts.org.uk.

Historic Environment Scotland (HES) is a government body that looks after more than 300 sites of historical or archaeological interest. Its portfolio ranges from the magnificent Borders abbeys up to Stone Age sites in Orkney and Shetland.

Membership gains free admission to HS properties. Further information from: Longmore House, Salisbury Place, Edinburgh EH9 1SH; tel: 0131-668 8600; www.historicenvironment.scot.

Internet

Internet access is widely available, with wireless access available even in many remote locations, though it can be quite patchy in areas of the Highlands and Islands. There are free Wi-fi hotspots in all major cities and towns, as well as most cafés, bars, restaurants and public libraries.

Lost property

Left luggage facilities are available at most major railway stations and some bus stations. For lost-property and left-luggage facilities at stations visit www.networkrail.co.uk or www.scotrail.co.uk.

For lost property at Edinburgh Waverley Station or Glasgow Central, tel: 0330 024 0215. For luggage accidentally left on trains or buses, first contact the operating company.

The UK-wide site www.reportmyloss.com is a police-approved service that allows you to report lost or stolen property and receive a police report for insurance purposes.

Media

Newspapers
There are two quality dailies. *The Scotsman*, printed in Edinburgh, and *The Herald*, printed in Glasgow; both have good coverage of Scottish and other UK and foreign news, as well as material on the arts and business. Dundee prints the quirky *Courier*. Much of the Highlands is covered by the *Press and Journal*, published in Aberdeen.

The most popular is the tabloid *Daily Record*, a stable mate of England's *Daily Mirror*. English dailies circulate widely in Scotland.

The four main cities each have evening papers. The *Sunday Post*, from the same stable as Dundee's The *Courier, boasts 160,000 readers who are presumably drawn by its quirky mix of family values, pawky humour and local interest. Scotland on Sunday* and the *Sunday Herald* are the two quality home-grown Sunday newspapers.

Throughout Scotland, there are many local weekly papers, which you may find both entertaining and informative if you are drawn to a particular region or simply interested in newspapers. The community-run *West Highland Free Press* covers news, features, culture, sport and social issues across the Highlands and Islands.

Magazines
The *Scottish Field, Scots Magazine* and *Scotland Magazine* are good-quality monthly (or bi-monthly) magazines that deal with Scottish topics. The *Edinburgh Review* is a literary review of consistent quality. *The List*, an Edinburgh-based listings magazine, which appears every two weeks, provides lively and comprehensive coverage of events in both Edinburgh and Glasgow.

Radio and television
Radio and TV are excellent for the most part. Radio Scotland is the main BBC radio service, and national BBC radio stations also operate in Scotland.

Television services are provided by the BBC and commercial companies. BBC 1 is a general TV service, mirrored (with a more down-market emphasis) by the commercial networks on STV (previously Scottish Television), with channels varying according to region. A wide range of satellite channels are usually available, and can be found in most medium- and larger-sized hotels.

Television reception is poor in some of the remoter areas and islands of Scotland.

Money matters

Currency

The British pound is divided into 100 pence. The coins used are 1p, 2p, 5p, 10p, 20p, 50p, £1 and £2. Scottish banknotes issued by the Royal Bank of Scotland, Bank of Scotland and Clydesdale circulate along with Bank of England notes in denominations of £5, £10, £20, £50 and £100. It's best to keep notes to £20 and under, as some shops, especially the smaller ones, can be suspicious of the larger denominations. Although they are legal tender, Scottish banknotes are sometimes refused south of the border and are difficult to exchange outside the UK, so exchange any leftover notes for Bank of England tender before leaving Scotland.

Credit and debit cards

MasterCard and Visa are the most widely accepted credit cards, followed by American Express and Diners Club. Small guesthouses and Bed & Breakfast places may not take credit cards, preferring payment in cash. Debit cards using chip and Personal Identification Number (PIN) are accepted almost everywhere, even in small shops, bars and cafés – many also make use of contactless payments.

Banks

Scotland has its own banks: the Royal Bank of Scotland (RBS), the Bank of Scotland and the Clydesdale Bank. They still issue their own sterling notes, which circulate alongside Bank of England notes.

Don't expect consistent opening hours. As a rough guide, most banks open Monday to Friday from between 9 and 9.45am to between 4 and 4.45pm. Many are also open on Saturdays from 9am-12.30pm. In rural areas, banks may close between 12.30 and 1.30pm.

In these parts you may also find 'travelling banks' – large trucks which go round the smaller villages at set times each week and can provide most banking services. These times are advertised locally.

Automatic Teller Machines (ATMs) allow anyone with a debit or credit card using the chip and PIN system to withdraw cash, and can be found even in smaller communities, where they may be installed in post offices or shops. However, your bank or card company may charge a fee for such withdrawals.

Opening hours

Generally shops open 9am–5/5.30pm Monday to Saturday. In many cities, towns and villages Sunday opening is becoming increasingly popular. Late night opening is often on a Thursday in the larger shopping areas. Larger supermarkets open for longer hours – some even have 24-hour opening. Village stores and smaller towns often close one afternoon a week, generally a Wednesday or Thursday – though few towns are without a 'wee shoppie' that stays open at all hours and can provide food, drink and assorted necessities. The shops on the islands of Lewis, Harris and North Uist are all closed on Sundays.

Postal services

Main post offices are open 9am–5.30pm Monday–Friday, and 9am–12.30pm on Saturday. Sub-post offices (which often form part of another shop) keep similar hours, though they usually close for one half-day during the week.

Public holidays

Local, public and bank holidays can be frustrating for visitors, but generally there will be a supermarket open somewhere during the major public holidays, except for **25** and **26 December**, **1** and **2 January** and **Good Friday**. If you are having difficulty, try petrol stations, many of which have good small shops on the premises and are open until late, or even for 24 hours.

Other national holidays in Scotland are **May Day** (first Monday in May), **Spring Holiday** (Monday in late May), **Summer Holiday** (first Monday in August) and **St Andrew's Day** (30 November)

Religion

Scotland supports a diverse mix of communities from across the world. Most Scots pay at least lip service to mainstream Protestant or Catholic variants of the Christian faith, but Islamic, Sikh, Buddhist and Jewish services are among the others.

Sunday is the traditional 'day of rest' in Scotland, though the diminishing numbers who attend church (or kirk as it's called in Scotland) would suggest this rest isn't being taken in church. However, most churches will welcome visitors who simply turn up at the door on a Sunday morning. Further information can be found at: www.churchof scotland.org.uk.

The following religious contacts will be able to provide practical advice on their areas of worship.
Baptist Union of Scotland
48 Speirs Wharf
Glasgow G4 9TH
Tel: 0141-423 6169
www.scottishbaptist.com.
Catholic Church
5 St Vincent Place
Glasgow G1 2DH
Tel: 0141-221 1168
Church of Scotland
121 George Street
Edinburgh EH2 4YN
Tel: 0131-225 5722
www.churchofscotland.org.uk
Edinburgh Buddhist Centre
35–37 Bread Street
Edinburgh EH3 9AL
Tel: 07599 718556
www.edinburghbuddhistcentre.org.uk
Glasgow Buddhist Centre
329 Sauchiehall Street
Glasgow G2 3HW
Tel: 0141-333 0524
www.glasgowbuddhistcentre.com
Jewish Synagogue & Community Centre
4 Salisbury Road
Edinburgh EH16 5AB

Tel: 0131-667 3144
www.ehcong.com
Scottish Episcopal Church
21 Grosvenor Crescent
Edinburgh EH12 5EE
Tel: 0131-225 6357
www.scottish.anglican.org
Sikh Temple
1 Sheriff Brae
Edinburgh EH6 6ZZ
Tel: 0131-553 7207
UK Islamic Mission
19 Carrington Street
Glasgow G4 9AJ
Tel: 0141-331 1119

S

Senior travellers

If you are aged 60 or over, it's always worthwhile enquiring about discounts on buses, trains and at attractions. In Scotland, a Senior Railcard (www.senior-railcard.co.uk) costs £30 a year and offers discounts on standard fares, but is unlikely to pay for itself during an average holiday visit. Swimming pools, leisure centres and the National Trust for Scotland (www.nts.org.uk) are among locations where proving you're over 65 may prove beneficial to the wallet.

In addition to discounted fares, the most readily accessed seats on buses and trains are reserved for use by senior travellers. Unfortunately, that doesn't always mean that the younger person already sitting there will be willing to vacate their seat.

Shopping

What to buy

There is a wide range of 'typical' Scottish products, from tartan and heather-embellished souvenirs to cashmere and Highland crafts.

Textiles and knitwear

Although the industry is in decline, woollens production is still very much in evidence in the Borders region, where you can tour a number of mills and make reduced-price purchases at the factory shops.

Look out for cashmere and Harris tweeds as well as lamb's wool. Shetland knitwear, including Fair Isle jumpers, is also justly renowned. Sadly, the art of weaving Harris tweed is a dying tradition.

Glassware

There are a number of high-quality glass and crystal producers that have come out of Scotland, including Caithness Glass, Selkirk Glass, Edinburgh Crystal and Stuart Crystal.

Ceramics and crafts

Many regional potteries produce distinctive, high-quality lines. Look out for local outlets, especially in the Highlands and islands.

Celtic-style jewellery

Contemporary silver or gold jewellery with Celtic-influenced designs is very popular and widely available, with varying quality.

Scotch whisky

Malt whisky is a major Scottish export. Many of the whiskies you see will be Moray whiskies, produced in the Speyside region, where over half the country's distilleries are located; many of these offer 'malt whisky trails' and all have on-site shops. There you can go on a 'malt whisky trail' of more than seven distilleries and their on-site shops. Whiskies from the Northern Highlands and the west coast island of Islay are also renowned, the latter for their smoky flavour.

Speciality foods

Delicatessens abound to tempt you with haggis (if you don't read the list of ingredients), smoked salmon and other smoked produce, cheeses, marmalade, porridge and oatcakes, butter shortbread and a number of other Scottish-made delectables –see page 101. If you are self-catering, then fresh fish, often very fresh, can be an excellent buy. In the northwest, look out for fresh, hot-smoked salmon.

Outdoor equipment

With a burgeoning outdoor adventure sports market, it's little wonder that the country has several excellent specialist adventure sports stockists.

Sports

Thanks to the Land Reform (Scotland) Act 2003, visitors to Scotland can enjoy some of the most enlightened access laws in Europe. Add the fact that the nation possesses natural terrain of thousands of miles of rugged coastline, remote beaches, deep glens, rushing rivers and the highest mountains (Munros) in the UK, and it's

easy to understand why Scotland is one of the best destinations in Europe to enjoy a myriad of outdoor sports. Whatever the weather, fishing, mountain biking, walking, horse riding, winter sports, sailing and surfing are just some of the popular activities to be enjoyed in its great outdoors.

Wildlife enthusiasts, too, flock to these shores to enjoy wild sea and landscapes teeming with rare species. Indeed, within the boundaries of the Cairngorms National Park (www.cairngorms.co.uk) alone, over 25 percent of the UK's most threatened bird, animal and plant species can be found. Hikers and water sports enthusiasts also enjoy the forests, lochs and mountains of the Loch Lomond and Trossachs National Park. VisitScotland's website (www.visitscotland.com) provides a host of information about available activities across the country, key destinations and reputable tour operators.

Golf

Scotland is the home of golf, and, some would claim, it is the national sport. There are hundreds of courses, most of them open to the public. Even the most famous courses, such as St Andrews, Carnoustie and Turnberry, are public 'links' courses, and anyone prepared to pay the appropriate – though often expensive – fee and who can produce a handicap certificate (usually about 20 for men, 30 for women) is entitled to play on them.

It is advisable to book ahead at the 'name' courses. At **St Andrews** half of all start times on the Old Course (closed on Sunday) are allocated by ballot. To be included, contact the starter before 2pm two days before you wish to play. A handicap certificate (24 for men, 36 for women) or a letter of introduction is required. If the Old Course is fully booked, there are six other courses to choose from (tel: 01334-466 718; www.standrews.com).

Walking

Scotland is a paradise for walkers, and walking is a rapidly growing tourism sector. There are 284 mountains over 3,000ft (900 metres) – these are called Munros – and across the country you can find a wide range of climbs and walks suitable for the expert or the novice. The mountains, although not that high, should not be treated lightly. A peak which, when bathed in brilliant sunshine, looks an easy stroll can, a few minutes later, be covered by swirling mist, and become a death trap. The importance of proper equipment (compass and maps) and clothing cannot be over-emphasised.

VisitScotland has an excellent online walking guide (www.visitscotland.com) with routes, safety tips and lots more useful information.

Fishing

Some of Britain's best fishing is found in Scotland. Rivers and lochs of all shapes and sizes can be fished for salmon and trout. Salmon fishing need not be as expensive as most people believe, and trout fishing is available in far greater supply than is ever utilised. Local permits must be obtained; details are available from tourist offices.

The salmon fishing season varies from river to river, starting from January in some places and as late as March in others and running until October. The trout season is from mid-March to early October. Fishing for migratory fish (salmon and sea trout) is forbidden on Sunday.

Sea fishing is found around the entire coast, particularly Orkney and the Shetland Islands. Shark, halibut, cod, hake and turbot are just a few of the species that can be caught.

Surfing

The water may be colder than Brazil and Australia but with powerful Atlantic waves battering Scotland's coastline, and the north and eastern coastlines, dotted with reef breaks, also enjoying consistent sizeable swells, it's unsurprising that Scotland is one of the hottest emerging surf destinations in Europe.

The Isle of Lewis, Tiree and Machrahanish on the west coast are remote, popular destinations while the east coast beaches of Fraserburgh and Pease/Coldingham Bay (East Lothian) attract legions of hardy surfers. Yet it's the renowned Thurso East in the north of Scotland that is really making waves.

Sea kayaking

With miles of coastline, dozens of remote and uninhabited islands, countless sea lochs and a rich diversity of marine life including otters, whales and dolphins to observe, Scotland is paradise for paddlers who seek adventure and tranquillity.

Whether you are a beginner or an expert, increasing numbers of operators are offering day, weekend and even weeklong trips off the coast. Indeed, at weekends between April and October it's not unusual to see cars with kayaks on the roof driving out of the cities.

Some argue that the Uists of the Outer Hebrides, complete with turquoise waters and white sands offer some of Europe's best sea kayaking, though both The Shetland Islands and the Argyll coast could also make such a claim.

Skiing

Despite erratic snowfall, Scotland's five ski centres (Cairngorm, The Lecht, Glenshee, Glencoe and Nevis Range) continue to survive, albeit with at least three now also diversifying into activities such as hiking, mountain biking and even go-karting to balance the books. However, when the snow does fall (the main season is between January and April), groomed pistes and miles of challenging off-piste terrain become the playground for skiers, boarders and ski-mountaineers (www.ski-scotland.com).

Mountain biking

If one sport has emphatically captured the imagination of the Scottish public and activity-minded visitors to Scotland alike, it is mountain biking. While in the early 1990s, keen mountain bikers were forced to seek out their own trails through glens and forests, today there are dozens of purpose-built mountain bike centres offering mile upon mile of graded track (green for easy, black for experts) through forests, open countryside, and even down mountain sides. Worth consulting is Forestry and Land Scotland (formerly the Forestry Commission), which has extensive information on the country's extensive network of trails (tel: 0300 067 6000; www.forestryandland.gov.scot/visit/activities-mountain-biking).

Diving

Scuba divers won't be disappointed when they visit Scotland. Fish and plants abound in the clear waters that bathe the Scottish coast. Outstanding sub-aqua areas with good facilities and experienced locals are the waters around Oban, the Summer Isles near Ullapool, Scapa Flow in Orkney and St Abb's Head on the southern part of the east coast.

Football

Rangers and Celtic are the two rival football teams that dominate the top of the Scottish Premier League, although the former has only recently returned to the top flight having been demoted to the bottom tier of the football league pyramid several years ago for financial irregularities.

Shinty

Many Scots are fiercely proud of the heritage of this ancient Celtic sport of the *camanachd* or 'curved stick'. It demands stamina, speed and courage from the 11 players in two opposing teams who defend their goal on a football-like pitch. Fort William and Kingussie are among the most famous teams, which compete in the annual shinty league and vie for the honour of contesting the greatest shinty prize of all, the Camanachd Cup. See www.shinty.com for more information.

Curling

It's an indigenous sport almost as old as the hills themselves and, like shinty, firmly embedded in the Scottish sporting culture. Played by teams on ice rinks across the land, between September and March thousands of men and women of all ages descend on rinks to 'throw' and 'sweep' their weighty granite-fashioned curling stones from the 'hack' (foothold). Two teams vie with each other to place their 'stones' inside the 'house' of concentric rings. Over the years, Scottish curlers have won European, World and Olympic medals in the sport. See www.scottishcurling.org for more information.

T

Telephones

When dialling from abroad, the international access code for the UK is 44, followed by the area code without the initial 0 (Edinburgh 131, Glasgow 141, Aberdeen 1224, etc.).

To reach other countries from Scotland, first dial the **international access code 00**, then the country code (eg Australia 61, Canada 1, France 33, Germany 49, Ireland 353, Japan 81, the Netherlands 31, New Zealand 64, Spain 34, South Africa 27, US 1).

Mobile phone coverage in Scotland is generally good, with extensive 3G

Brass door plate at the Glasgow School of Art.

coverage in place and also 4G, though there are some blind spots in more rugged mountain areas and remote islands. Cheap ways to use your mobile phone include buying an international call top-up from your network before leaving home, or buying a UK SIM card from any of the numerous mobile service providers you will find competing shops in all town centres. You may even wish to leave your own mobile device at home and buy a cheap pre-paid disposable phone on arrival; these cost as little as £5. Devices that can handle Skype calls work in Scotland as they would anywhere. Calls from hotel room phones are usually much more expensive than any other option.

Time zones

Scotland, like the rest of the UK, follows Greenwich Mean Time (GMT). In spring the clock is moved forward one hour for British Summer Time (BST), and in autumn moved back to GMT. Especially in the far north, this means that it is light until at least 10pm in midsummer.

When it is noon GMT, it is:
4am in Los Angeles
7am in New York and Toronto
noon in London and Dublin
2pm in Cape Town
10pm in Melbourne and Sydney

Tourist information

In Scotland

General postal enquiries should be made to VisitScotland, OceanPoint One, 94 Ocean Drive, Leith, Edinburgh EH6 6JH. Tel: 0845-225 5121.

VisitScotland has an Edinburgh iCentre at 3 Princes Street in the centre of Edinburgh (tel: 0131-473 3868). Other tourist information is provided by 15 areas throughout Scotland. Their main information centres, with the areas covered, are:
Aberdeen City and Shire: 23 Union Street, Aberdeen AB11 5BP. Tel: 01224-269 180; email: Aberdeen@visitscotland.com; www.visitabdn.com
Angus and City of Dundee: 16 City Square, Dundee, Angus DD1 3BG. Tel: 01382-527 527; email: dundee@visitscotland.com; www.dundee.com, www.visitangus.com
Argyll and the Isles: North Pier, Oban PA34 5QD. Tel: 01631-563 122; email oban@visitscotland.com; www.wildaboutargyll.co.uk (Argyll and Bute, Mull, Islay)
Ayrshire and Arran: The Pier, Brodick, Arran KA27 8AU. Tel: 01770-303 774; email brodick@visitscotland.com; www.visitarran.com.
Dumfries and Galloway: 64 Whitesands, Dumfries DG1 2RS. Tel: 01387-253 862; email: dumfries@visitscotland.com; www.dumfriesandgalloway.co.uk.
Edinburgh and the Lothians: 3 Princes Street (Waverley Market), Edinburgh EH2 2QP. Tel: 0131-473 3868; email: info@visitscotland.com; (City of Edinburgh, East Lothian, Midlothian, West Lothian).
Glasgow and the Clyde Valley: 156/158 Buchanan Street, Glasgow G1 2LL; email: glasgow@visitscotland.com; www.peoplemakeglasgow.com (City of Glasgow, East Dunbartonshire, Inverclyde, South and North Lanarkshire, Renfrewshire).
The Highlands and Moray: 36 High Street, Inverness IV1 1JQ. Tel: 01463-252 401; email: inverness@visitscotland.com; www.visitinvernesslochness.com; (Moray, Aviemore Inverness, Fort William, Northern Highlands and the Isle of Skye).
Kingdom of Fife: 70 Market Street, St Andrews KY16 9NU. Tel: 01334-472 021; email: standrews@visitscotland; www.welcometofife.com.
Loch Lomond, Stirling and Trossachs: Old Town Jail, St John Street, FK8 1EA; tel: 01786-475 019; email: stirling@visitscotland.com; www.yourstirling.com. (Clackmananshire, West Dumbarton and Clydebank, Falkirk and Stirling).
Orkney: West Castle Street, Kirkwall KW15 1GU. Tel: 01856-872 856; email: kirkwall@visitscotland.com; www.orkney.com.
The Outer Hebrides: 26 Cromwell Street, Stornoway, Isle of Lewis HS1 2DD. Tel: 01851-703 088; email: stornoway@visitscotland.com; (Lewis, Harris, North Uist, Benbecula, South Uist, Barra and St Kilda).
Perthshire: 45 High Street, Perth PH1 5TJ. Tel: 01738-450 600; email: perth@visitscotland.com; www.perthcity.co.uk.
Scottish Borders: Murray's Green, Jedburgh, Roxburghshire, TD8 6BE. Tel: 01835-863 170; email: jedburgh@visitscotland.com.
Shetland: Market Cross, Lerwick ZE1 0LU. Tel: 01595-693 434; email: lerwick.information@visitscotland.com; www.shetland.org
In addition, many towns have **iCentres**; not all are open in the winter months. See www.visitscotland.com for locations and opening times.

Outside Scotland

There are no official tourist offices representing Scotland or the UK in London or overseas. However comprehensive information to help you plan your trip can be found at the official sites of VisitBritain (www.visitbritain.com) and VisitScotland (www.visitscotland.com), or on the websites of the Scottish regional tourist offices.

Tours

From literary tours of Edinburgh's New and Old Town and wildlife tours on Mull to specialist adventure breaks by bike, foot and kayaking in the rugged Highlands, visitors are spoilt for choice with specialist tours.

The following are just a few of dozens to be found through local tourist information centres.
Haggis Adventures
60 High Street, Edinburgh
Tel: 0131-557 9393
www.haggisadventures.com
Especially designed for travellers on a budget. Visitors are taken into the furthest reaches of the Highlands aboard their distinctive yellow 'haggis' buses.

Hiking the West Highland Way.

Islay Birding
Port Charlotte, Isle of Islay
Tel: 01496-850 010
www.islaybirding.co.uk
Award-winning operator who also runs bushcraft courses involving night navigation and sleeping in caves.

Mercat Tours
28 Blair Street, Edinburgh
Tel: 0131-225 5445
www.mercattours.com
Literary and ghost tours promise delight and fright.

Wilderness Scotland
Dalfaber Drive, Aviemore
Tel: 01479-898 729
www.wildernessscotland.com
Another award-winning operator who promises adventure and wildlife in abundance, as small groups explore the remotest corners of Scotland's Highlands and islands by sea kayak, mountain bike, skis or on their own two feet.

Visas and passports

Your best starting point for a visa-related enquiry concerning entry to the UK is to contact the UK Foreign and Commonwealth Offices visa website (www.visa4uk.fco.gov.uk).

Citizens of EU countries, and of the US, New Zealand, Australia and some other Commonwealth and European countries don't require a visa (just a passport) to visit Scotland on holiday. For all other nationalities, it's best to check with the British consulate in your own country before travelling to access the latest advice on the documentation required to holiday/study/work in the UK.

W

Websites

The following website addresses could prove useful on your travels throughout Scotland:

Accommodation
www.hostellingscotland.org.uk Hostelling Scotland.
www.assc.co.uk the Association of Scotland's self-caterers.

Eating and drinking
www.smws.co.uk Scotch Malt Whisky Society.
www.5pm.co.uk For last-minute deals on restaurant and bar food.
www.taste-of-scotland.com Guide to some of Scotland's most acclaimed places to eat and stay.
www.visitscotland.com/see-do/food-drink Comprehensive guide to restaurants, cafés, pubs, delis and distilleries countrywide.

Entertainment
www.list.co.uk The List magazine highlights the latest and best entertainment venues and gigs across the Central Belt.
www.eventscotland.org A handy reference for key forthcoming festivals

and sports events to be staged in Scotland.
www.theskinny.co.uk Independent cultural journalism aimed mainly at the student community in Scotland's main cities.

Outdoors
www.visitscotland.com/see-do/active/walking For everything from walking guides and operators to more than 800 suggested walking routes.
www.forestryandland.gov.scot Forest and Land Scotland (formerly Forestry Commission Scotland).
www.nature.scot Scottish Natural Heritage works with various conservation agencies to protect sensitive areas of fauna and flora throughout the country.
www.mountaineering.scot Mountaineering Council of Scotland's site for walkers and climbers.
www.visitscotland.com/see-do/active/sailing VisitScotland's site for sailing and boating on offshore and inland waters.
www.metoffice.gov.uk Find out the latest weather reports around the country, including sea and mountain conditions.

Travel
www.visitscotland.com Scotland's national tourism agency, which is also accessed through www.visitbritain.com.
www.visitbritain.com The UK's tourism agency that links through to www.visitscotland.com.
www.undiscoveredscotland.co.uk A very informative online guide to Scotland.
www.edinburgh.org The official tourist information site for Edinburgh.
www.eif.co.uk All you need to know about Edinburgh's famous Festival.
www.edintattoo.co.uk Find out about Edinburgh's Royal Military Tattoo.

Weights and measures

Like the rest of Britain, Scotland grudgingly accepts the metric system; draft beer comes in 500ml and 250ml measures, but is still ordered by the pint or half-pint; similarly, cheese, butter, meat and fish are officially sold in grams and kilos, but most people still order 'a pound' even though they will be served the close metric equivalent (500g). Road signs give distances in miles, not kilometres, but fuel is sold by the litre, not the gallon.

FURTHER READING

The Scottish Enlightenment – The Scots Invention of the Modern World by A. Herman. Profile of the scientists, philosophers and engineers who made Edinburgh the 'Athens of the North'.

Mary Queen of Scots by Antonia Fraser. Readable biography of Scotland's tragic queen.

Bonnie Prince Charlie by Fitzroy MacLean. The inglorious life of the last Stuart pretender to the Scottish throne.

The Lion in the North, Glencoe, Culloden, and The Highland Clearances by John Prebble. Four definitive but easy-to-read accounts of Scotland's turbulent past.

A History of the Scottish People 1560–1830 by T.C. Smout. Christopher Smout's overview of Scotland's history from the industrial revolution to the mid-20th century now feels slightly dated but is still definitive.

Scotland's Story by Tom Steel. An accessible if necessarily superficial introduction to the history of Scotland from its early antecedents until recent times.

POETRY

Many editions are available of Robert Burns's poems.

100 Favourite Scottish Poems by Stewart Conn (ed.). Fine introduction to some of Scotland's greatest poets, past and present.

Fiere Jackie Kay's bold, plain style and outspoken courage make her one of 21st century Scotland's finest poets.

Outside the Narrative Tom Leonard writes using the vernacular of his native Glasgow.

Bagpipe Muzak Works by poet and dramatist Liz Lochead, Scotland's second Makar (national poet).

Love and a Life Collection of 50 poems by the late Edwin Morgan, who became the first Scots Makar in 2004.

Selected Poems by William Dunbar. Poetry by the greatest poet of pre-reformation, 16th century Scotland.

MISCELLANEOUS

Rebus's Scotland by Ian Rankin. A personal journey through the Scottish locations which inspired Ian Rankin's series of 'Scottish noir' crime novels.

Raw Spirit by Iain Banks. The late Iain Banks's celebration of malt whisky and the people who make it and drink it.

The Battle for the North by Charles McKean. The dramatic story of how the railways came to Scotland.

Calum's Road by Roger Hutchison. Account of how Raasay man Calum Macleod spent ten years single-handedly building a road to connect his home village with the outside world.

I Never Knew That About Scotland by Christopher Winn. This miscellany of little-known facts, legends and local apocrypha is an amusing companion on any journey through Scotland.

⊙ Send us your thoughts

We do our best to ensure the information in our books is as accurate and up-to-date as possible. The books are updated on a regular basis using local contacts, who painstakingly add, amend and correct as required. However, some details (such as telephone numbers and opening times) are liable to change, and we are ultimately reliant on our readers to put us in the picture.

We welcome your feedback, especially your experience of using the book "on the road". Maybe you came across a great bar or new attraction we missed.

We will acknowledge all contributions, and we'll offer an Insight Guide to the best letters received.

Please write to us at:
Insight Guides
PO Box 7910
London SE1 1WE

Or email us at:
hello@insightguides.com

FICTION

Kidnapped by Robert Louis Stevenson. Classic historical novel (by the author of *Treasure Island*) set in the aftermath of the Jacobite rebellion.

How Late It Was, How Late by James Kelman. An uncompromisingly harsh novel of working class Glasgow life, told as a meandering interior monologue in the urban vernacular.

The Prime of Miss Jean Brodie by Muriel Spark. An unconventional schoolteacher instructs her girl pupils on the ways of love and life.

The Thirty-Nine Steps by John Buchan. The best-known of Buchan's thrillers, set in Scotland.

Trainspotting by Irvine Welsh. A horrifying look at Edinburgh's drug scene.

Exit Music by Ian Rankin. Inspector Rebus's last case. Or is it?

Whisky Galore by Compton Mackenzie. A comic novel about a wreck of a cargo of whisky.

44 Scotland Street by Alexander McCall Smith. A series of light-hearted novels about the eccentric comings and goings in Edinburgh's New Town. Plus his Isabel Dalhousie series about an Edinburgh detective.

The Wasp Factory by Iain Banks. This off-beat, gruesome novel, Banks's first, is set on an un-named Scottish island was panned by critics but launched a glittering career which was cut short by the Fife-born author's early death.

OTHER INSIGHT GUIDES

More than 120 Insight Guides and Insight City Guides cover every continent, providing information on culture and all the top sights, as well as superb photography and detailed maps. Insight Guides' Great Breaks series, which includes *Edinburgh* and *Glasgow*, offer clearly laid-out walks and tours in these highlight cities.

CREDITS

PHOTO CREDITS

Abe Nowitz/Apa Publications 235
Alamy 52, 55, 66, 146, 151B, 168B, 207, 220/221T, 220BR, 260, 285T
AWL Images 154BL, 230, 232
Bigstock 269
Bill Wassman/Apa Publications 24, 147, 148T, 162, 168T, 176T, 210T, 210B, 227T, 248T, 261T, 265T, 268, 278T, 280T
Bridgeman Art Library 40, 46
Corbis 61, 289, 294/295, 296
Courtesy of Her Majesty the Queen 38/39
David Cruickshanks/Apa Publications 18, 60, 149, 151T, 253, 305
Douglas Macgilvray/Apa Publications 71, 87, 101, 118, 154/155T, 170/171
Dreamstime 98, 148B, 150, 156/157, 200/201, 202, 205, 214, 217T, 218T, 218B, 220BL, 222/223, 227B, 233, 237, 239, 242, 243, 245, 247, 248B, 250/251, 259, 262, 271, 276, 278B, 282, 284B, 286/287, 288, 290B, 291, 293, 297, 299T
Eric Ellington 263

FLPA 229
FLPA/Michael Durham 231
Fotolia 7MR, 68, 145, 153, 155, 212/213, 261B, 275, 280B, 290T
FotoLibra 159, 215, 216, 217B
Getty Images 1, 4, 10/11, 14/15, 16, 48/49, 59, 86
Glasgow Museums & Art Galleries 34, 50
Hulton Picture Library 29, 37, 41, 42, 43, 51, 53, 54, 73
Hunterian Museum and Art Gallery, University of Glasgow 84
iStock 6ML, 6MR, 7ML, 7BL, 7BR, 7TL, 9T, 17, 70, 113B, 154BR, 169, 173, 211T, 211B, 219B, 221BL, 225, 236, 238T, 238B, 264, 266, 270, 272/273, 284/285T, 285B, 292, 299B, 317
Library of Congress 22/23, 25
Mary Evans Picture Library 26, 30, 31, 32, 33, 35L, 36, 44, 45, 47, 67, 76, 78, 79, 221ML, 221BR
Mockford & Bonetti/Apa Publications 6BL, 6BR, 8T, 8B, 9B, 19, 20, 21, 58, 63,

77, 88, 106/107, 113T, 116, 117, 119, 120T, 120B, 121, 122T, 122B, 123B, 123T, 124, 125T, 125B, 126T, 126B, 127, 128T, 128B, 129T, 129B, 130T, 130B, 131T, 131B, 132, 133, 135, 136, 138/139T, 138BR, 138BL, 139ML, 139BR, 139BL, 139TR, 158, 160, 164, 166B, 166T, 167T, 167B, 172, 174T, 174B, 175, 176B, 177B, 177T, 178/179, 182, 183, 184T, 184B, 185, 186, 187B, 187T, 188, 189, 190, 191, 192T, 192B, 193, 194, 195T, 195B, 196, 197, 198, 199, 249T, 249B, 302, 303, 306/307, 308, 311, 315, 316
National Galleries of Scotland 72, 80/81, 82, 83
Pictures Colour Library 161, 219T, 224, 228, 265B
Press Association Images 74
Public domain 35R, 85
REX/Shutterstock 75
Scala Archives 27
Still Pictures 93

COVER CREDITS

Front cover: Mangersta beach, Isle of Lewis *Maurizio Rellini/4Corners Images*
Back cover: Loch Morlich *Dreamstime*
Front flap: (from top) Skye *Shutterstock*; Culzean Castle *iStock*; Highland dancing *Dreamstime*; Victoria Street, Edinburgh *iStock*
Back flap: Glen Coe *Shutterstock*

INSIGHT GUIDE CREDITS

Distribution
UK, Ireland and Europe
Apa Publications (UK) Ltd;
sales@insightguides.com
United States and Canada
Ingram Publisher Services;
ips@ingramcontent.com
Australia and New Zealand
Woodslane; info@woodslane.com.au
Southeast Asia
Apa Publications (SN) Pte;
singaporeoffice@insightguides.com
Worldwide
Apa Publications (UK) Ltd;
sales@insightguides.com
Special Sales, Content Licensing and CoPublishing
Insight Guides can be purchased in bulk quantities at discounted prices. We can create special editions, personalised jackets and corporate imprints tailored to your needs.
sales@insightguides.com
www.insightguides.biz

Printed in China by RR Donnelley

All Rights Reserved
© 2020 Apa Digital (CH) AG and
Apa Publications (UK) Ltd

First Edition 1984
Eighth Edition 2020

Every effort has been made to provide accurate information in this publication, but changes are inevitable. The publisher cannot be responsible for any resulting loss, inconvenience or injury. We would appreciate it if readers would call our attention to any errors or outdated information. We also welcome your suggestions; please contact us at:
hello@insightguides.com

www.insightguides.com

Editor: Tom Fleming
Author: Zoe Ross, Norm Longley
Head of DTP and Pre-Press: Rebeka Davies
Layout: Aga Bylica
Update Production: Apa Digital
Managing Editor: Carine Tracanelli
Picture Editor: Tom Smyth
Cartography: original cartography Colourmap Scanning Ltd, London, updated by Carte

CONTRIBUTORS

This new edition of *Insight Guide Scotland* was edited by **Tom Fleming** and updated by **Norm Longley**, building on work completed on the previous edition by **Zoe Ross**. Norm is an experienced travel writer, who has lived in Central and Eastern Europe for most of his life, but now specialises in the United Kingdom.

Zoe Ross is an experienced travel writer too, and specialises in Scotland. Based in Edinburgh, she has also written Insight Guides' *Great Breaks Glasgow*. Other former contributors to *Insight Guide Scotland* include **Jackie Staddon, Hilary Weston, Colin Hutchison, Brian Bell, George Rosie, Julie Davidson** and **Marcus Brooke**.

ABOUT INSIGHT GUIDES

Insight Guides have more than 45 years' experience of publishing high-quality, visual travel guides. We produce 400 full-colour titles, in both print and digital form, covering more than 200 destinations across the globe, in a variety of formats to meet your different needs.

Insight Guides are written by local authors, whose expertise is evident in the extensive historical and cultural background features. Each destination is carefully researched by regional experts to ensure our guides provide the very latest information. All the reviews in **Insight Guides** are independent; we strive to maintain an impartial view. Our reviews are carefully selected to guide you to the best places to eat, go out and shop, so you can be confident that when we say a place is special, we really mean it.

Legend

City maps

Freeway/Highway/Motorway
Divided Highway
Main Roads
Minor Roads
Pedestrian Roads
Steps
Footpath
Railway
Funicular Railway
Cable Car
Tunnel
City Wall
Important Building
Built Up Area
Other Land
Transport Hub
Park
Pedestrian Area
Bus Station
Tourist Information
Main Post Office
Cathedral/Church
Mosque
Synagogue
Statue/Monument
Beach
Airport

Regional maps

Freeway/Highway/Motorway (with junction)
Freeway/Highway/Motorway (under construction)
Divided Highway
Main Road
Secondary Road
Minor Road
Track
Footpath
International Boundary
State/Province Boundary
National Park/Reserve
Marine Park
Ferry Route
Marshland/Swamp
Glacier   Salt Lake
Airport/Airfield
Ancient Site
Border Control
Cable Car
Castle/Castle Ruins
Cave
Chateau/Stately Home
Church/Church Ruins
Crater
Lighthouse
Mountain Peak
Place of Interest
Viewpoint

INDEX

MAIN REFERENCES ARE IN BOLD TYPE

INSIGHT ⦿ GUIDES

OFF THE SHELF

Since 1970, INSIGHT GUIDES has provided a unique perspective on the world's best travel destinations by using specially commissioned photography and illuminating text written by local authors.

Whether you're planning a city break, a walking tour or the journey of a lifetime, our superb range of guidebooks and phrasebooks will inspire you to discover more about your chosen destination.

INSIGHT GUIDES

offer a unique combination of stunning photos, absorbing narrative and detailed maps, providing all the inspiration and information you need.

PHRASEBOOKS & DICTIONARIES

help users to feel at home, when away. Pocket-sized with a free app to download, they go where you do.

CITY GUIDES

pack hundreds of great photos into a smaller format with detailed practical information, so you can navigate the world's top cities with confidence.

EXPLORE GUIDES

feature easy-to-follow walks and itineraries in the world's most exciting destinations, with our choice of the best places to eat and drink along the way.

POCKET GUIDES

combine concise information on where to go and what to do in a handy compact format, ideal on the ground. Includes a full-colour, fold-out map.

EXPERIENCE GUIDES

feature offbeat perspectives and secret gems for experienced travellers, with a collection of over 100 ideas for a memorable stay in a city.

www.insightguides.com